Unbeaten

Mike Stanton is an associate professor of journalism at the University of Connecticut, having previously headed the investigative team at the *Providence Journal*, where he shared a Pulitzer Prize.

ALSO BY MIKE STANTON

The Prince of Providence:
The Rise and Fall of Buddy Cianci,
America's Most Notorious Mayor

'A satisfying biography of the iconic boxer, the only heavyweight champion to retire undefeated . . . [and] a sturdy contribution to the literature of the sweet science, reminding readers of a bygone era of fighting.'

Kirkus Reviews

'This is a story that has waited a long time to be told this well, by a gifted writer and reporter like Mike Stanton . . . Finally, at long last, the real Rocky has met his match.' Mike Lupica, *New York Daily News*

'Mike Stanton's book on Rocky Marciano teems with marvelous scenes and revealing insights into the chaotic boxing world of the unbeaten heavyweight champ.'

David Maraniss, author of *When Pride Still Mattered: A Life of Vince Lombardi*

'Plug into the excitement, the jostle, the sweat and the grind, the 1950s action when boxing was important and the heavyweight champion of the world was the king of all athletes . . . This book is wonderful.'

Leigh Montville, author of *Sting Like a Bee: Muhammad Ali vs. the United States of America, 1966–1971*

UNBEATEN

The Triumphs
and Tragedies of
Rocky Marciano

MIKE STANTON

PAN BOOKS

First published 2018 by Henry Holt, New York

First published in the UK 2018 by Macmillan

This paperback edition first published 2019 by Pan Books
an imprint of Pan Macmillan
20 New Wharf Road, London N1 9RR
Associated companies throughout the world
www.panmacmillan.com

ISBN 978-1-5098-2250-8

1 3 5 7 9 8 6 4 2

A CIP catalogue record for this book is available from the British Library.

Designed by Meryl Sussman Levavi
Printed and bound by CPI Group (UK) Ltd, Croydon, CR0 4YY

Visit **www.panmacmillan.com** to read more about all our books
and to buy them. You will also find features, author interviews and
news of any author events, and you can sign up for e-newsletters
so that you're always first to hear about our new releases.

To Susan, always

I woke up as the sun was reddening; and that was the one distinct time in my life, the strangest moment of all, when I didn't know who I was—I was far away from home, haunted and tired . . . I was halfway across America, at the dividing line between the East of my youth and the West of my future.

—JACK KEROUAC, *On the Road*

When I woke, I didn't know where I was or nothing, but I had a feeling something nice had happened.

—ROCKY MARCIANO, the morning after becoming heavyweight champion of the world

Contents

Prologue: Two Funerals

H E DIED WITH THE BLUNT FORCE HE HAD USED TO DISPATCH SO MANY opponents in the ring—suddenly and violently, in a cornfield in the middle of America, the month after man first walked on the moon.

Early in the Sunday evening of August 31, 1969, Rocco Francis Marchegiano, known the world over as Rocky Marciano, climbed into a single-engine Cessna airplane at Chicago's Midway Airport and took off for Des Moines, Iowa.

Joining him was the pilot, Glenn Belz, and a twenty-two-year-old insurance salesman, Frank Farrell, who had asked the champ to attend the opening of a Des Moines steakhouse that night. It would be an early celebration of Marciano's forty-sixth birthday, which was the next day, when he planned to fly home to Florida to celebrate with his family. This side trip, like much of Marciano's peripatetic life since his retirement from the ring thirteen years earlier, had been spontaneous, a last-minute favor to a friend and Chicago mobster who was Farrell's uncle.

The Rock felt good. He had several business deals cooking, including a health spa and a chain of spaghetti restaurants. He had recently dropped forty pounds, laying off the rich Italian food he had gorged himself on in retirement. America had transformed from the black-and-white 1950s of his prime to this kaleidoscopic summer of Woodstock and the Zodiac Killer. Boxing no longer rivaled baseball as the nation's top spectator sport. Muhammad Ali, the brash unbeaten heavyweight whom most sports writers still insisted on calling Cassius Clay, had been stripped of his title for refusing to be drafted into the army and fight in Vietnam; "I ain't got no quarrel with the Viet Cong," he famously declared.

If Marciano belonged to a faded era, a seemingly more innocent time, he was still a recognizable figure, the only undefeated heavyweight champion in history, with a record of 49-0, forty-three by knockout. During a 1965 recording session for their album *Rubber Soul*, Paul McCartney and John Lennon of the Beatles talked about a television interview of Rocky they had watched the night before.

"He was a great fighter," said Paul.

"'And what do you attribute it to, Rocky?'" said John, reenacting the interview. "'Training.'"

"I had a good condition," echoed Paul.

Rocky took pride in his conditioning and where it had taken him. "What can be better than walking down any street in any city and knowing that you are the champion?" he said. Two days before his plane left Chicago, a breathless reader of the *Chicago Tribune* called the city desk to say that he had seen Rocky jogging on the beach along Lake Michigan. Over breakfast at the Continental Hotel, Rocky told a reporter that he was in town to film a TV commercial and check on a young heavyweight. The conversation turned to two young fighters; they had talent, Rocky said, but he questioned whether they had the hunger.

"They both like girls," he said. "They don't realize you've got to make boxing a kind of religion. You believe in yourself and you believe in the things you got to do. You never forget them for a minute. Then you get there and you think of what you had to go through and you say to yourself, 'It was worth it; it was worth everything.'"

The little Cessna beat west into the dusk, directly into a gathering storm system over central Iowa. Belz was an inexperienced pilot who was not rated for instrument flying and had logged only thirty-five hours of nighttime flying. Low on fuel, he decided to divert to a small airfield in the farming town of Newton, thirty miles east of Des Moines. At 8:50 p.m., Belz contacted the Des Moines control tower to say that the plane was trapped in a layer of clouds and to request radar assistance to find the airport. Moments later, he reported that he had broken through the clouds and spotted the airport. He was preparing to land.

Banking north toward the landing strip, skimming the Cessna barely one hundred feet off the ground, Belz disappeared again into a cloud bank. A thirty-year-old farmer's wife, Colleen Swarts, heard the sputtering of a small plane and stepped outside to watch. The plane seemed to stall right over her house. She saw its lights as it shot out of the mist. The plane disappeared again, and then she heard an awful thud.

The plane struck a lone oak tree in the middle of a cornfield on Henry Eilander's farm, shearing off a wing. The twisted fuselage skidded another 250 feet, strewing wreckage and the bodies of Belz and Farrell, before coming to rest in a drainage ditch. Rocky's battered body was pinned beneath the mangled front of the plane. A shard of metal pierced his skull. All three men died instantly.

The death of Rocky Marciano, unbeaten in life, stunned the world.

"Start the count, he'll get up," wrote *Los Angeles Times* sports columnist Jim Murray. "A lot of us today are wishing there were an honest referee in a cornfield in Iowa."

The morning after the crash, a New York dockworker named Carmine Vingo woke in disbelief to the news. Vingo had been vanquished by Rocky back in 1949 in a particularly vicious fight in Madison Square Garden that left him in a coma, ending his promising boxing career and leaving him with a permanent limp.

"I don't remember a thing about that fight," said Vingo. "But I remember Rocky. He was a fine man."

The sports columnists wrote that he was the last of his kind and that his death marked the end of an era. Rocky Marciano embodied an optimistic postwar America of prosperity and conformity, when everyone dreamed of being a contender. Americans followed the fights closely, immigrants sought assimilation in the ring, and boxing was a prism that refracted the changes sweeping the nation. The son of Italian immigrants, whose father worked in a shoe factory in Brockton, Massachusetts, Rocky was born in the anti-immigrant 1920s, came of age during the Great Depression, boxed in the army during World War II, and fought his way to the top in the late 1940s and 1950s, when the Mafia seized control of professional boxing to cash in on the flood of television money.

When he took the title in 1952, Rocky also won acclaim that he had never sought, as the first white champion since 1937, when James Braddock, the "Cinderella Man," lost the title to Joe Louis. Although Rocky fought classic fights against the underrated black champions Jersey Joe Walcott, Ezzard Charles, and Archie Moore, they were, to white America, so many invisible men, to paraphrase the title of Ralph Ellison's novel published the same year Rocky became champ. Even as a contender, Rocky was reluctantly cast as the Great White Hope, a poster boy for the Greatest Generation and a symbol of American masculinity.

Politicians, celebrities, and movie stars went to his fights. Humphrey Bogart was ringside to research his last film, *The Harder They Fall*, about the fixed fight game. Bob Hope turned to shake hands with Tony Zale at one of Rocky's title defenses and missed a first-round knockout. President Dwight D. Eisenhower invited the Rock to the White House and beamed as he measured the champ's right fist. Rocky visited his pal Frank Sinatra on the set of *Guys and Dolls*, the movie based on Damon Runyon's accounts of a gritty, glamorous Manhattan populated by gamblers and hustlers, chorus girls and mobsters, racetrack touts and broken-down fighters. That was the world where Rocky fought, a city of docks and subways and a thriving working class that shouldered into the cheap seats of Yankee Stadium and smoke-filled Madison Square Garden for championship fights, then took the subway home while the sportswriters and celebrities, gangsters and swells mingled at Toots Shor's saloon. Popping flashbulbs etched Rocky in a square of white surrounded by a sea of darkness, his gloved fist distorting an opponent's jaw, droplets of sweat suspended in midair. Outside the ring, Rocky was an All-American postcard from a simpler, more innocent age: immigrant son, family man, strong but soft-spoken. He talked in the high-pitched voice of a choirboy, not a ring assassin.

Rocky was an unlikely champion. He didn't start boxing seriously until age twenty-four and was often overmatched in size and skill. He was five foot ten and weighed 185 pounds, with short, stubby arms, clumsy feet, and a bulldozer style that opened him up to fierce punishment. But he trained relentlessly, was in outstanding physical condition, and had an indomitable heart that enabled him to withstand savage beatings. And he had a punch—the Suzie Q—that was like a near-death experience. "Every time he hit you," said one foe, "you saw a flash of light." He trudged into the ring like a factory worker punching a time clock and started pounding on the wall in front of him with apparent futility until suddenly it crumbled.

"I got a guy who's short, stoop-shouldered, and balding with two left feet," his trainer, Charley Goldman, said. "They all look better than he does as far as the moves are concerned, but they don't look so good on the canvas."

Before an early amateur fight, Rocky ate a big dish of macaroni, then stumbled around the ring, winded and out of shape, until the referee disqualified him for kicking his opponent in the crotch. Five years later, after one of the greatest title fights of all time, he was the heavyweight champion of the world.

Rocky was guided to the top by an improbable trio—a childhood friend from Brockton who quit his job and withdrew his army savings to finance Rocky's training; a canny Jewish trainer who had fought illegal barge fights in New York in the early 1900s; and a domineering, cigar-chewing Broadway manager who started as a dancer and wound up as the Mafia's matchmaker. When Rocky walked away from the ring in 1956, still in his prime at age thirty-two, it was in part to spite his manager, who was stealing from him, and to repudiate the Mafia's control of boxing, which was so pervasive that people called it the Octopus. Rocky also quit because he feared becoming one of the broke, washed-up, brain-addled fighters he had encountered on the way up.

"Rocky Marciano stood out in boxing like a rose in a garbage dump," wrote New York sports columnist Jimmy Cannon.

But Rocky had his demons, which he managed to conceal in a more adulatory age of sports heroes.

When his army combat engineers unit was storming the beaches of Normandy on D-day, Rocky sat out the climactic battle of World War II in a military stockade in England, confronting a grim future. That, in turn, would lead him to his first serious boxing matches, and to a fateful meeting with a Japanese American army surgeon without whom Rocky might have become just another forgotten member of the Greatest Generation.

In retirement, cut off from the routine of training and boxing, Rocky lost his way. He drifted away from his family and his Brockton roots, moved to Florida, and traveled ceaselessly across a changing America. He parlayed his celebrity and unbeaten record into free hotels, free plane rides, free meals, and free clothes; the comedian Jimmy Durante called him "America's guest." He insisted on being paid cash for personal appearances, threatened people who owed him money like a leg breaker for a loan shark, and hid cash in toilet bowls and curtain rods. The breadwinner for his family, Rocky kept them in the dark about his finances; after his death, unable to find his money, they were nearly broke. He cheated on his wife and gorged his huge appetites for food and sex, which he had denied himself during his monastic years of training. (He once rejected the advances of Hollywood bombshell Jayne Mansfield when she came to his cabin at his training camp in the Catskills.)

Rocky could be generous to down-and-out ex-fighters, like Joe Louis, and he testified before Congress about the need to reform boxing from the corrupt influence of the mob. But he palled around with mobsters, fascinated by the tough-guy persona and seeking a substitute for the danger of the ring. He was offered a stake in mob-run casinos in Havana and Las Vegas, visited a dying Mafia don in prison, and went into business with other wiseguys, including a Cleveland loan shark who was gunned down on an Ohio golf course.

"I don't think he was real happy with himself for some of the things he did," says his youngest brother, Peter. "If Rocky was like they said he was, he never would have been heavyweight champion—he never would have hit anyone. At the end of his life, he was no longer the pure kid from Ward Two in Brockton."

Affable and modest, Rocky cultivated his image carefully and concealed his unsavory ties. Few had a bad thing to say about him, in life or in death.

His death triggered grief around the world. Outside London, British boxers filled a church for a requiem Mass. In the southern Italian coastal village of Ripa Teatina, where Rocky's father was born and Marchegianos still lived, townspeople milled about the village square in tears. In Washington, on the floor of Congress, several representatives paid tribute to the fallen champ, including a former University of Michigan football lineman and future president, Gerald Ford.

Two days after his death, the Brockton Blockbuster returned home one last time. Jubilant crowds had welcomed him with victory parades down Main Street when he knocked out Joe Louis, his boyhood hero, and again when he won the title, fifty thousand strong, more than had greeted presidents Franklin Roosevelt and Harry Truman when they had campaigned in Brockton. Now, thousands stood somberly in the rain outside Hickey's Funeral Home to pay their respects. The Marchegianos were dismayed that Rocky's wife had chosen the Irish funeral home instead of

Pica's, the Italian one next door. But that was Barbara, the daughter of an Irish policeman in Brockton. Joseph Pica, who had sat ringside with Sugar Ray Robinson when Rocky won the title, reassured the family that it was okay. He opened his parking lot to the overflow throng of mourners and then, for the only time in his life, went inside his Irish competitor's funeral parlor to say good-bye to the champ.

A cross section of mourners came: celebrities, politicians, members of the boxing world, former champions like Tony Zale and Willie Pep. Long before Pep and Rocky became close friends, when Rocky was hitching overnight truck rides to New York and living in dollar-a-night rooming houses, he had spied the stylishly dressed Pep strolling down Broadway, a showgirl on his arm, and followed the couple for blocks, dreaming of what it would be like to be champ.

Rocky's time had been Brockton's time, his triumphs theirs. He personified his rough, immigrant town's perseverance and endurance in pursuit of the American dream, the factories and hardscrabble neighborhoods. When Rocky fought, everything else stopped in Brockton. The people gathered around radios or the few television sets. They mobbed the Ward Two Memorial Club in Rocky's Italian neighborhood and milled outside the *Brockton Enterprise* for round-by-round updates. They bet their grocery money, their rent, their paychecks, their crumpled dollar bills stashed in kitchen coffee tins, on the Rock. They rolled over their winnings to the next fight, and the next, as the challenges grew steeper, until they could afford to buy a new refrigerator or a new car or even their own house. Rocky carried the financial fortunes of Brockton's working class into the ring, no small thing for a child of the Depression. "They couldn't afford to see me lose," he said. For them, "I always knew I would get up."

The day after his wake, two thousand people filled St. Colman's, an imposing fieldstone church where Rocky had been married and where his wife had had his boxing shoes blessed before each fight. Another thousand stood outside. An elderly woman watched the bronze coffin carried by, led by a funeral cortege that included eleven priests, and said quietly, "He was good to his family."

Rocky's mother, Pasqualena, clad in black, her face masked by a veil, marched near the front of the procession. A large, vivacious woman, Lena was the force of the family, the source of her son's strength, a traditional Italian matriarch who doted on her eldest son—"*Figlio mio, figlio mio,*

cuore della mia vita." (My son, my son, heart of my life.) She had implored
him not to box and refused to ever see him fight, going to church instead
to pray and to light candles for her son—and for his opponents. Shuffling
brokenly beside Lena was her husband, Pierino, a thin, frail, bespectacled
man who looked dazed. Pierino had been gassed fighting in the trenches
of France for America in World War I and had never been the same afterward. But he came home, married Lena, had six children, and labored for
decades in the shoe factory to support them.

Father Richard O'Donovan delivered the eulogy. He reminisced
about the hours Rocky had spent with parish youth, counseling them to
stay in school, and the proud moment when he had worn his St. Colman's
Catholic Youth Organization (CYO) jacket, a gift from the boys, into the
ring.

"Rocky was a warm, humble, friendly man," said Father O'Donovan.
"He was a good living man, a model for all, a friend to all who knew him.

"He was a hero to everybody everywhere."

That night, hundreds followed Rocky's body to Fort Lauderdale,
where unopened birthday presents had been packed away, for a second
funeral. The wattage of the assembled boxing royalty lent it the aura of a
heavyweight championship fight. Sonny Liston called Rocky one of the
greatest champions. Joe Frazier, the reigning New York State Athletic
Commission champion, stared down a sportswriter who asked if he could
have beaten the Rock. Jimmy Ellis, the current World Boxing Association
champ, comforted Rocky's family. Beau Jack was there, the popular former
lightweight champ whom Rocky had found shining shoes at the Fontainebleau Hotel in Miami Beach. Ex-champ Jersey Joe Walcott, Rocky's greatest
foe, also came.

Joe Louis and Muhammad Ali stood together in a back room, links in
a chain of greatness, bookends to Rocky's career. As a boy, Rocky had
listened on the radio as Louis knocked out Max Schmeling. Later, Rocky
cried after knocking his idol through the ropes in Madison Square Garden
to end his career and launch his own. Meanwhile, a teenage boy in Louisville, Kentucky, who had had his bicycle stolen, Cassius Clay, listened to
Rocky's fights on his transistor radio and savored the announcer's words,
"heavyweight champion of the world." When Ali heard the news that
Rocky had been killed in the plane crash, he cried. "I'd never seen Muhammad cry before," said his wife Belinda.

Rocky had turned down offers to come out of retirement and fight Ali. But in the months before his death, the two champions did meet in the ring. The pair secretly sparred for the movie cameras in a Miami gym, for a "computer fight" to be released in theaters that winter. Ali needed the money. He was 29-0 but hadn't fought in two years, stripped of his title and facing prison for his refusal to enter the military draft. Surprisingly, the brash, black, Muslim war protester bonded with this quiet, modest, white man of the fifties. Afterward, his arms sore from the forty-five-year-old Rocky's pounding, Ali came away with a new respect for the ex-champ.

"He was the onliest one that would've given me some trouble," Ali said in eulogy.

Louis leaned over and kissed the top of Rocky's coffin, looked skyward, and said, "God is getting himself a beautiful man." Peter Marchegiano turned teary-eyed to Louis and pleaded, "Tell me something about my brother."

"He was the greatest," Louis responded in his soft voice. "He was the greatest."

Rocky was boxing in heaven, said Ali.

Archie Moore, Rocky's last opponent, couldn't be there. But he wrote a poem that he read before a boxing match in the San Diego Coliseum:

> At the end of the trail
> When the master calls
> However we stand
> We surely must fall.
> Our memories will be measured
> By our good deeds
> We know that you have spread them
> Large and small
> Wish you Godspeed.

On September 6, six days after his plane went down in Iowa, Rocky was laid to rest after another funeral Mass, this one at St. Pius Catholic Church in his adopted home of Fort Lauderdale. Several hundred mourners, including his wife and his sixteen-year-old daughter, Mary Anne, filled the church; Rocky's parents were unable to make the journey. Curious onlookers in shorts and bathing suits stood outside in the muggy heat.

A military escort from the Palm Beach Military Academy, where Rocky served on the board and often spoke to the boys about health and good sportsmanship, accompanied his remains to Lauderdale Memorial Gardens. A thirteen-year-old cadet played taps on a silver bugle as Rocky's coffin was slid into a crypt surrounded by floral arrangements, including a three-foot-high set of boxing gloves filled with red roses.

A few weeks later, two old fight guys sat reminiscing in Toots Shor's famous New York saloon—Billy Conn, the dancing Irishman from Pittsburgh, and Toots himself, who had lost $100,000 betting on Conn to beat Louis at the Garden in 1941. Well ahead on points, Conn had tried to knock Louis out in the thirteenth round but found himself on the canvas instead. He could run, but he couldn't hide.

"There'll never be another guy quite like Rocky Marciano," Toots said. "He had that real soft, pipsqueak voice like a choirboy. Like one of them itty-bitty choirboys. Never raised that voice. Always spoke kindly.

"And I remember when I had this joint closed for more than a year. I'll never forget it. One night Marciano comes over to see me, and he's clutching $5,000 in his big fist, and in that choirboy voice he says, 'This is all I can spare right now, Toots, but maybe it'll come in handy as some walking around money.' How about that? A guy hears your crummy saloon is closed and he figures you're in a jam and he volunteers to help you. Well, that was Rocky Marciano."

And this was Rocky Marciano: the fighter who knew a secret of life discovered in the ring. Behind their bravado, boxers live with fear. For Rocky, it was fear of losing and the consequences. No money, no fame, no future—a life in the factory with its stink of shoe leather, or as a used-up ex-pug, slurring his words and shuffling his feet as he relived dimly remembered battles.

"When it's all over, it would be nice to be one of the two or three men that people remember in the boxing book," he said on the eve of his first title fight. "Now it's Jack Dempsey and Joe Louis. I hope some day it's Jack Dempsey, Joe Louis, and Rocky Marchegiano—Marciano."

To do that, he needed to conquer his fear.

"You're not in the ring to demonstrate your courage. You're in there to win the fight," he wrote, shortly before he died. "So you handle the fear, maybe even use it. It's out of sight, somewhere behind you, but if you're not completely prepared, it pops out in front of you and then you're finished."

This is Rocky Marciano's story, the tale of an immigrant son and his battles inside and out of the ring—how he fought for his identity in a brutal and corrupt sport that defined a changing America in the middle of the twentieth century.

"I was a nobody," he said. "In the ring, I became a somebody."

The Terrific Three

ROCKY MARCIANO WORE OUT A PAIR OF SHOES THE WAY HE WORE OUT his opponents in the ring.

Running tirelessly through the streets of his childhood in Brockton, Massachusetts, he chased a dream while fleeing the tedium of a life in the shoe factories. Rocco was a familiar sight around town, his feet pounding through the Italian second ward with its triple-deckers and grape arbors, past the sandlots where he played baseball and the woods where a one-legged gambler ran a Sunday dice game, through the bustling downtown with its impressive architecture, church spires, and movie palaces where a boy could sit in the balcony and daydream. Some days he ran through the West Side, where the factory managers and Brockton's well-to-do lived, past their fieldstone mansions and elegant white colonials where he delivered the *Brockton Enterprise* and occasionally filched a bottle of milk left by the dairyman. On workdays, when the factory whistles blew, he ran by the sprawling brick shoe plants to bring his father his lunch. His father, Pierino Marchegiano, an Italian immigrant, worked at one of the city's several dozen shoe factories, laboring over a backbreaking machine that formed the heels and toes, helping produce the twelve million pairs of shoes that Brockton sent the world every year.

When Rocky became a famous boxer, the Doyle Shoe Company started giving him ten pairs of black Vici kid road shoes a year. He returned one pair after running seven hundred miles in them, worn through on both soles. He thought nothing of walking twenty miles to see a Brockton

High School football road game, or thirty-five miles to Providence, Rhode Island, after he started boxing there.

The shoes Rocky wore when he trained fared little better. He wore a hole in the left front sole, illustrating the force with which he pivoted on the ball of his foot to launch his wrecking ball of a right hand. In 1951, when he beat Joe Louis to establish himself as the top heavyweight contender, Webster's dictionary marked the first use of the expression "shoe leather," for "basic, direct or old-fashioned methods." Rocky's shoes were the size of an ordinary man's, 10½, but the width hinted at his broader stature—EE.

Two other local shoe factories made the shoes that Rocky wore when he stepped into the ring, carrying the hopes of Brockton on his squat shoulders. For each fight, the Howard & Foster Shoe Company made him two pairs of some of the lightest boxing shoes ever produced, attaching black yellow-back kangaroo uppers to a lightweight sole manufactured by the Potvin Shoe Company. After Rocky became champion, the women in the stitching room asked if they could sign their names in his shoes. They were allowed to sign one pair. It was a perfect marriage of form and function, Rocky wearing out Brockton's shoes with the industry that made him and his city great. Brockton made shoes, shoes made Brockton, and Brockton made Rocky Marciano, who would become its most famous export.

"The important thing," said the vice president of Howard & Foster, "is that our employees feel as though they're helping Rocky in the ring."

□ □ □

IN THE EARLY 1920s, Rocky's grandfather Luigi Picciuto bought a simple white-shingled cottage at 80 Brook Street in Brockton's Ward Two. His daughter and new son-in-law moved in upstairs. He planted grapevines in the side yard and strung lights in the backyard so that the men in the neighborhood could come over on Saturday nights to play bocce and drink his homemade wine.

Luigi was a muscular, broad-shouldered man, six foot two and 220 pounds, with a flowing black mustache and dark, sensitive eyes. He was a commanding presence, a natural-born leader back in his native Italy and in Brockton, where everyone in the neighborhood called him *mastro*, master artisan.

"Everything about him was big," Rocky recalled. "He played big, he worked big, he gambled big, he drank big, he ate big, he talked in a big voice."

Luigi was a blacksmith from the Italian hill town of San Bartolomeo in Galdo ("in the clouds"), a tiny village perched on a mountainside near Naples with houses clinging to the steep slopes. He was a respected man in his community, a local *cavour*, or leader, who mediated disputes in the absence of any formal government. But Italy was racked by corruption and poverty, and in 1914 Luigi joined the tide of four and a half million Italians who immigrated to America between 1880 and 1920.

Luigi's blacksmith skills made it easy for him to get a job with a railroad in New Jersey, and he soon brought over his two oldest daughters, Carmella and Pasqualena. The women went to work in a garment factory in Newark. Within a year, Luigi was able to bring over his wife and their four younger children. The family settled in Bridgeport, Connecticut. There, tragedy struck. Luigi's nine-year-old son Nicholas was run over and killed by a truck while riding a wagon that Luigi had built him for Christmas. Heartbroken, Luigi said that he couldn't bear to stay in Bridgeport. He took his family to Brockton, where Carmella had moved after getting married.

Luigi's second-oldest daughter Pasqualena, or Lena, born in 1902, was a bright, vivacious, dark-haired young woman who had inherited Luigi's exuberance, determination, and strength. As a girl in San Bartolomeo, she walked down one hundred steps every day to fetch water from the village well, balancing the jugs on her sturdy shoulders as she climbed back up. The curious and quick-witted Lena was not content to fulfill the traditional role of a woman of her times. She wanted an education so that she could become a schoolteacher. That put her in conflict with Luigi, who saw no reason to waste money on schoolbooks for a girl. When he caught her sneaking off to a school in a neighboring village, he grabbed a wooden chair in his blacksmithing shop and broke it over Lena's head. The chair shattered into pieces as a sobbing but unhurt Lena protested her father's stubbornness.

In Brockton, Lena got a job in a corset factory. When she was eighteen, she began to notice a quiet young man whom she had first seen at a friend's house. He was not loud and boisterous like the other boys in the neighborhood. His name was Pierino Marchegiano, and he worked in a shoe factory. He was seven years older and had emigrated from Italy to America a few years before Luigi.

Pierino was born in 1894 in Ripa Teatina, a village on the Alento River in Italy's Abruzzi region near the Adriatic coast. Despite its placid beauty, the region had a history of association with great fighters. Warriors who fought with Achilles in the Trojan War were said to have founded the nearby city of Teate. For centuries, the region resisted conquest by the Roman Empire. As a boy, Pierino played in the shadow of two medieval watchtowers, monuments to a lawless age when mercenaries had protected the village. Pierino liked to use a phrase coined by a nineteenth-century diplomat to describe the region's beauty and people—*forte e gentile*, strong and gentle.

Pierino was a strong boy with large hands who spoke little of what must have been a painful childhood. He never knew his own father, Rocco, who died when the boy was young. His mother died when he was twelve, and his grandmother raised him. When he was seventeen, Pierino set sail for America alone. An uncle knew the owner of a construction company outside Boston, who agreed to offer Pierino a job. Eventually he settled in Brockton and found work in a shoe factory.

Pierino was proud of his adoptive country, and when America entered World War I, he was one of the first Italians in Brockton to enlist in the U.S. armed forces. He joined the U.S. Marines, and fought on the Marne and in the Argonne during some of the war's bloodiest battles. In the spring of 1918, his brigade repelled the last great German offensive of the war at Château-Thierry, fifty miles from Paris. When shrapnel from a grenade pierced his left cheek, Pierino spit out three teeth and kept fighting. Later, when a tank exploded near his trench, more shrapnel pierced his right leg; subsequent surgeries left that leg shorter, forcing him to wear a platform shoe on his right foot and walk with a limp.

But the worst injury Pierino suffered was from being gassed, one of the horrors of modern chemical warfare introduced during World War I. The mustard gas poisoned his lungs and left him weak and frail and gasping for breath for the rest of his life. He sucked on Life Savers to mask the bitter taste in his mouth. A photograph of Pierino when he entered the U.S. Marines shows the squat, muscular physique of his firstborn son, the future heavyweight champion. But when he returned to Brockton in 1919, he had lost his youthful strength and vigor. Had it been worth it? For the rest of his life, he would remember the parting words of his commanding officer: "Pierino, you can be proud to call yourself an American."

The war may have shattered Pierino's constitution but not his toughness. He went to work at the E. E. Taylor shoe factory in Brockton, in one of the plant's most physically demanding jobs, operating a No. 5 bed laster. Pushing the pedals of the clattering machine with his feet, tacks in his mouth, Pierino shaped the shoe leather around a mold, or last, to form the toes and heels of the shoe, then used a hammer to tack the pieces of leather together for stitching. The smell of leather was overpowering, especially in the summer, when the factory became a sweatbox.

One night at a church social, Pierino met Lena. They embarked on a traditional Italian courtship, the ever-vigilant Luigi chaperoning them everywhere. Once, at an amusement park, Luigi panicked when he briefly lost track of the couple in the Tunnel of Love. Pierino stole a first kiss on the Ferris wheel, when Luigi couldn't see, and proposed at a concert.

They were a study in contrasts, the thin, serious Pierino and the plump, vivacious Lena. They married on August 7, 1921, at St. Patrick's Church in Brockton. She was nineteen and he was twenty-six. At their wedding reception, Luigi raised a glass of wine in a toast to his new son-in-law and pronounced, "May you and my beautiful daughter live to be a hundred—and may your firstborn be very famous."

❑ ❑ ❑

ROCCO FRANCIS MARCHEGIANO entered the ring for the first time shortly after one a.m. on September 1, 1923. At twelve pounds, ten ounces, he was a natural heavyweight. Dr. Josephat Phaneuf, who delivered the baby on the second floor of Luigi's cottage on Brook Street, recalled that it was a difficult delivery because of the size of the head. Years later, Dr. Phaneuf would tell patients, "I was the first one ever to hit him."

Someone sent a card that Pierino would cherish always, with a drawing of tiny boxing gloves, inscribed, "Hail to the Champ."

His parents were elated. It was Lena's second pregnancy; her first had ended the year before, with the birth of a thirteen-pound son who died the same day. Worried that her job at the corset factory had contributed to the loss of the baby, a distraught Pierino insisted that Lena quit and stay home when she became pregnant again.

It was a rare victory for Pierino in a household dominated by his forceful wife. Pierino wanted to stop at two children, so they could afford to give them everything and send them to college. But Lena insisted on six, telling Pierino that the children could share. In the years that followed, Lena gave birth to Alice in 1925, Concetta in 1927, Betty in 1931, Louis (or Sonny) in 1933, and Peter in 1940. She also suffered two more miscarriages.

Not long after Rocco was born, the fates seemed to be conspiring to take him away. During the cold, rainy March of 1925, when he was eighteen months old, Rocco came down with pneumonia. He was sick for more than a week. His parents took turns sleeping on the floor beside his bed, listening for the raspy sound of his breathing. His fever climbed to 105. Dr. Phaneuf came and went, doing what he could, but there were no antibiotics and not much that could be done for pneumonia, which killed many babies in the 1920s. Ultimately, the doctor told Pierino and Lena that it was up to the baby's spirit to fight the sickness. If he survived, Dr. Phaneuf said, he would probably grow up to be a very strong man.

Leaning over her son, watching the life drain from his still, pale body, Lena repeated, "*Figlio mio, figlio mio. Cuore della mia vita.*" While other women consoled her, male relatives and friends stood vigil in the kitchen with a disconsolate Pierino and Luigi.

One woman dipped her finger into a teaspoon of olive oil and dropped it into a bowl of water, chanting an incantation to remove the *malocchio*, or evil eye, that seemed to hover over the child. Frantic, Lena took off her most valuable possession—a diamond solitaire ring from Pierino—and hung it on a statue of Saint Anthony as an offering to cure her son.

The next day, the baby's great-aunt Paolina Mangifesti, a gnarled woman in her nineties, came to pay her respects. She found Lena and the other women gathered around the listless baby, clutching their rosary beads. But she had seen pneumonia in babies before, back in Italy. She took one look at the listless Rocco and called for some warm water and a teaspoon. Parting the baby's lips, she dribbled the liquid into the baby's mouth. Almost immediately, Rocco made a big noise in his chest, his eyes fluttered open, and his lips moved.

He was dehydrated, Paolina explained. Give him some chicken broth. If he doesn't want it, force it down. Lena followed her instructions, and the fever subsided. Before long, the baby had regained what would become a prodigious appetite.

In the joy of Rocco's recovery, and the bustle of taking care of him and cooking and cleaning, several days passed before Lena remembered her offering to Saint Anthony. She checked the statue. Her diamond ring was gone. She refused to believe that one of the friends or relatives who had been in and out of the house during Rocco's illness would have stolen it. Saint Anthony had taken it, in answer to her prayers.

■ ■ ■

THEY CALLED THEMSELVES the Terrific Three: Eugene Sylvester, Izzy Gold, and Rocco Marchegiano. They were three Depression-era boys running through the streets of Brockton—playing baseball at James Edgar Playground, fighting for their honor behind Petti's garage, sneaking under the fence at the Brockton Fair, bumming day-old doughnuts from the friendly baker at Bob's Lunch on Crescent Street, washed down with quarts of fresh milk swiped from the doorsteps of Brockton's affluent West Side.

The three friends modeled themselves after a trio of street urchins in the popular 1930s comic strip *Red Barry*. The syndicated strip chronicled the adventures of a square-jawed, hard-punching detective who fought crime with the help of three boys—the Terrific Three. Red Barry was inspired by Sherlock Holmes and Dick Tracy, but he fought crime with his fists, not his brains or fancy gadgets.

Eugene, Izzy, and Rocky banded together when they were around twelve. Izzy, a tough, wiry Jewish kid who liked to gamble and take risks, had just moved into the neighborhood from the East Side, Brockton's poorest neighborhood. Eugene and Rocky had grown up near each other. Eugene, tall and thin, with dark black hair and a handsome face that he highlighted by pushing back the brim of his baseball cap, was an impish wiseacre always stirring up trouble. Rocky was the strong, silent one, good-natured and shy but a fierce competitor and sore loser. Often, he was the one called on to bail his fast-talking friends out of a scrape.

Summers and after school, the boys lived outside, in the parks, on the streets, banging through their kitchen doors to eat and sleep, then hurrying back out to play ball or chase some mischief until their parents sent a brother or sister to fetch them home. There was little extra money for entertainment. But despite the Great Depression, it was in many ways an idyllic childhood. Families scraped by and looked out for one another. Despite layoffs and cutbacks, the shoe factories remained open; Pierino kept working. Mothers saw to it that there was enough food on the table, supplemented by fruit and vegetable gardens, wild mushrooms and dande-lion greens, and public assistance provided through the "bean line," the daily dole of baked beans, a slab of pork, and brown bread. Lena cooked generous Italian meals that her eldest son gorged on, and always made sure that her children had a dollar for the Brockton Fair.

The Brockton of Rocky's youth was a melting pot of Italians, Irish, Lithuanians, Swedes, Poles, Germans, and French Canadians. The immi-grants had helped build a thriving manufacturing city defined by the name of its leading newspaper—the *Brockton Enterprise*. Wrote one local nineteenth-century historian, "You could always tell a Brockton man by his smile. He was just about the most thoroughly alert and modernized commodity that New England has to show." In 1883, Thomas Edison chose Brockton for a historic breakthrough, throwing a switch that illu-minated downtown through the world's first three-wire underground electrical system. The city also boasted the nation's first electric fire station and trolley system. The stately downtown, walking distance from Rocky's house, had impressive brick blocks of department stores, elegant bank buildings, a modern train station, and a graceful stone city hall and pub-lic library. Rocky lived across the street from James Edgar Playground, named for the Scottish immigrant who had founded one of the city's biggest department stores. In the 1890s, Edgar had started dressing up as Santa Claus to entertain shoppers at Christmastime, creating a phe-nomenon that drew visitors from Boston and inspired department stores in larger cities to follow suit.

The shoe factories spread out from downtown, and the men and women who worked there moved into neighborhoods built nearby so they could walk to work. When he was little, Rocky stood on the street corner and waited for Pierino to trudge home from the factory.

If Pierino didn't enjoy his grueling work, or felt put upon by the Irish foremen, he and his co-workers took pride in their craft. Shoemaking had been respected in Massachusetts since colonial times, when Puritan judges spared the life of a cobbler who had been sentenced to hang for stealing his neighbor's corn. Colonial cobblers shod George Washington's bedraggled troops during the Revolutionary War. After the war, returning soldiers set up cottage industries making shoes by hand in several towns on Boston's South Shore. With the Industrial Revolution, nearly a dozen factories sprang up in Brockton, then called North Bridgewater, twenty miles south of Boston, and the immigrants flowed in. The city, known for its tolerance, became a major stop on the Underground Railroad; down the street from Rocky's school was a white buttonwood tree known as the Liberty Tree, a rendezvous spot for fleeing slaves where the abolitionist leader William Lloyd Garrison had spoken. During the Civil War, the city churned out boots for the Union army. As the city prospered and immigrants flowed in, the leading citizens decided that their city needed a new name. They rejected a proposal to call it Standish, after Myles Standish, the Pilgrim leader from nearby Plymouth, who had bought the land from the Wampanoag Indians in 1649. Instead, a local businessman suggested Brockton, after a town he had visited in Canada. It was modern, strong, forceful.

Brockton had grown to about sixty thousand people when Rocky was born. The city's different ethnic groups clustered in different neighborhoods, fostering turf rivalries, but for the most part got along. Brockton was small enough that children traveled easily from one neighborhood to another, playing pickup baseball or sledding in winter near the reservoir in D. W. Field Municipal Park, named for a local shoe baron who had donated the land. When they got older, they came together at Brockton High School. The city's only high school forged a working-class immigrant identity manifested in its powerhouse sports teams, particularly football. The entire community proudly supported the Shoe Men.

"It didn't make any difference if a kid was Italian or Irish or Jewish or Negro—we all worked with our hands or our folks worked with theirs," recalled Rocky.

Still, cultural differences existed. Leo Ball, one of the few Jewish kids in Rocky's neighborhood, remembers being taunted by the Italian boys as a "Christ killer." After they got to know him, he was "okay for a Jew" and became one of the gang. Leo lived around the corner from Rocky, who was four years older. One day, Rocky and Eugene Sylvester approached him about his new bicycle, the first in the neighborhood. Rocky persuaded Leo to let him borrow the bike; for every minute he rode it, Leo could give him one kick in the pants. But then Rocky disappeared down the street, Eugene running alongside, and never returned. That night, Leo's furious mother walked over to the Marchegianos and retrieved the bicycle. Leo overheard her tell his father that Rocky's house reeked of garlic and olive oil. And so Leo learned the source of "that strange, exotic smell my friends constantly carried with them."

Despite their relative comfort in Brockton, opportunities for Rocky, his friends, and their families were limited by hostile outside forces. In Massachusetts, where foreign-born workers outnumbered the native-born in factory towns like Brockton, Lowell, and Fall River, the prosperous surrounding communities put up signs saying NO ITALIANS OR IRISH NEED APPLY. Three Harvard University graduates whipped up nativist sentiment when they founded the Immigration Restriction League, which successfully lobbied Congress to slam the doors on immigrants from southern and eastern Europe in the early 1920s. Prominent authors and government officials described Italians as "a race of pickpockets," an "indiscriminate horde of unfit foreigners," and a group that should be "catalogued, photographed [and] finger-printed." Federal agents were rounding up suspected Italian anarchists and deporting many with little or no proof. The harshest reminder of anti-Italian prejudice struck close to home, when two Italian laborers and anarchists, Nicola Sacco and Bartolomeo Vanzetti, were arrested on the Brockton trolley not far from Luigi's house. Despite a lack of evidence, the pair was convicted of participating in the robbery of a shoe-factory payroll in a neighboring town in which a guard and paymaster were shot dead. Their case became an international cause célèbre, but after a trial marred by conflicting evidence, recanted testimony, and blatant prejudice, they were convicted. The week before Rocky's fourth birthday, in 1927, they were executed in the electric chair. Luigi, outspoken as ever, lamented that there was no justice for Sacco and Vanzetti; he even spoke of moving back to Italy. As Rocky's friend Izzy Gold put it, "America's a cruel place if you don't know your way around."

□ □ □

LUIGI PICCIUTO WAS the patriarch of Rocky's family. He and his wife lived on the first floor of his cottage on Brook Street, with the growing Marchegiano family crowded into four rooms upstairs. Lena and Pierino had one bedroom, and the girls shared the other. Sonny slept downstairs with his grandparents, and Rocky slept in the living room on a folding cot. He liked to sleep beneath an open window, even in winter, because he loved the fresh air. (When Peter arrived in 1940, he would sleep in his parents' room.)

The house had no central heat, hot water, or bathtub. Two coal stoves on the first floor provided heat. Every Saturday night, Lena heated water on the kitchen stove and washed the children in a large tin washtub in the kitchen, the girls one week, boys the next.

Lena's outsize personality filled the tiny rooms. She was a short, stout woman with a vivacious smile and sparkling eyes, who spoke broken English with a heavy Italian accent. She was loud like Luigi, strict but indulgent, intelligent but superstitious. She feared the *malocchio*—the evil eye—and lit candles in church to ask the saints to watch over her family. Although she never realized her dream of becoming a schoolteacher, she loved to read and had a wide-ranging curiosity about the world. She was also the neighborhood letter writer for the illiterate. Fiercely proud of her Italian heritage, she insisted that her children attend twice-a-week lessons in Italian language and grammar at the Novelli Club, a neighborhood social club. Rocky learned to speak Italian fluently, though he could not write it.

Lena loved opera. She liked to sing and dance to her favorite Italian songs on the radio while she did housework, sometimes grabbing a child or relative and whirling them around gaily. She was up early, cooking simmering Italian dishes that took all day, like her chicken dumpling soup and *pasta fagioli*. She was a terrific cook and could improvise with dandelion greens, wild mushrooms, and other odds and ends to stretch the thin family budget.

Lena wanted Rocky to become a singer or dancer; she signed him up for accordion lessons, but he quit after a couple of sessions when his parents found out how much an accordion cost. Rocky played the bugle and marched in the American Legion children's band. He wasn't good enough to play solo but liked to join in.

Lena spoiled her children, sparing them many of the chores that other children had to do. During the Depression, she never let them know how precarious the family's finances were, quietly borrowing money so that she could give each child a dollar for the Brockton Fair. But she was strict if they misbehaved. She hated when they got into fights and punished them by grounding them. But if Rocky broke someone's window playing baseball, she just shrugged and said, "That's nothing. When you have children, you know you're going to have to pay for windows."

Rocky didn't fear anybody, his brother Peter said, "except maybe Mom." Rocky may have inherited his father's toughness and large hands, but he drew his strength and determination from his mother.

"She was a very dominating personality, and I think a lot of the things that Rocky did in his life had to do with the strength that Mom had," said Peter.

The house was always filled with family, friends, and neighbors. Luigi's Saturday night gatherings to play bocce and drink wine could get quite boisterous. This was during Prohibition, when wine was difficult to get, so he made his own. (An exception for homemade wine had been written into the federal law establishing Prohibition.) He carried on a spirited competition with his neighbor Luigi Colombo to see who made the best wine.

The bocce game in the backyard was noisy enough, but the nights grew rowdier after the men moved into the basement to drink and play an Italian card game called *scopa*. The winner was called the boss, and he chose a second boss, sometimes by playing a finger-pointing game called *morra*. The two bosses decided who could drink and who couldn't. They made one guy the goat, meaning he couldn't drink. As the night wore on, the other men grew drunker and drunker, and the goat got madder and madder. Soon, they were all hollering at one another, then pushing and shoving and fighting. Rocky witnessed some "terrible, terrible fights" that he had to help break up. When these old Italian men got really mad, he said, they didn't fight with their fists—they butted heads like goats, lowering their heads and taking a running start at one another across the dirt floor.

"You'd think they'd kill each other, but I never saw anyone laid out on the floor with a busted head," said Rocky.

Luigi was semiretired and spent much of his time tending his small vineyard. Given the large quantity of wine he made—a dozen or so barrels—he also bought an annual consignment of 175 crates of grapes from a local vendor. Sometimes, Rocky and his friends would steal a crate or two from the back of the truck as it drove slowly through the neighborhood, and carry it into the woods to feast.

Then Rocky and his friends hurried back to Luigi's to help lug the heavy crates down to the basement, where a large wooden winepress stood in a corner. Rocky was thirteen and fanatical about physical fitness. He raced to carry more crates than his friends. They dumped a crateful of grapes at a time into the vat, then Rocky took turns with the other boys pulling the heavy handle to force the press down onto the grapes and squeeze out the juice. It was hard work, and most of the boys had to rest after two or three crates. Rocky, switching between his right and left arm, prided himself on doing twenty crates without a break, muscles rippling beneath his T-shirt.

Luigi belonged to a club with about twenty other men who gathered every month at someone's house for impressive eating contests. Before the eating began, the men placed bets. Luigi Colombo's son Mike was always the favorite. One night, Rocky watched him eat forty-two meatballs. Another time, he put away sixteen pounds of spaghetti. But the occasion that stood out was the time that Mike and his rival du jour each devoured twenty-one chickens. "When [Mike] started eating the bones," said Rocky, "the other guy quit."

Inspired by his elders, and spoiled by Lena's cooking, Rocky also was a prodigious eater. When his mother cooked a big pot of spaghetti for supper, everyone in the family filled their plate, then Rocky got everything left in the pot. For breakfast, he ate a large bowl of cereal with a quart of milk and six bananas cut up on top. He loved fruit cocktail and could eat two cans at a sitting. One time, after he polished off two large cans, Lena scolded him that he had brothers and sisters who also needed to eat. "Aw Ma, I had a good feed," he replied. "Next time they can have it all."

One Sunday, Lena roasted a large chicken for company that night. When she went to the icebox later to take it out, Rocky had eaten it down to the bones. Another time, she brought home six large pies from the bakery. Rocky devoured four. But the boy was health-conscious, avoiding fried foods and constantly asking if something was good for him. He avoided meat on Friday; if Lena slipped and cooked spaghetti with meat gravy on a Friday, he'd scold her and say, "What kind of Catholic are you?"

Not surprisingly, Rocky was a stout boy.

"When I go to buy him pants," Lena recalled, "I would say, 'You better give me double-seat pants.'"

When he was little, Rocky would follow his mother around the house as she did her chores, promising that someday he was going to make her rich. As the oldest son, he helped as best he could, getting a paper route when he was seven years old and giving his earnings to his mother. If one of his siblings got into trouble at school, Rocky accompanied his parents, who were self-conscious of their broken English, to the meeting with the teacher.

His generosity set an example for his brothers and sisters, especially in the depths of the Depression. When his teachers asked for donations of food for the less fortunate, Lena would give Rocky a paper bag with four potatoes, but he usually managed to sneak in something extra. When he was thirteen he took his nine-year-old sister Concetta, or Conge, downtown to go Christmas shopping. Lena had given Conge fifty cents to buy something, but when they passed the Salvation Army bucket on Main Street, Rocky told her to put the money in. She protested. He insisted, squeezing her hand until she dropped the coins in.

He was a protective big brother. Once at Edgar Park, an older boy threatened to beat up Sonny if Sonny didn't give him his baseball bat and let the older boy hit. Rocky, who was nearby, saw this, ran into the park, and grabbed the boy. "For the next hour, you're going to pitch to him," Rocky said. "And if you open your mouth, you've got problems." The boy obeyed and pitched to Sonny without a word. Another time, when a boy hit Sonny, Rocky confronted him on the street and "whacked me on the arm," the boy said. "I felt it for a week."

Rocky hated being teased by the other boys when his mother made him take his sister Alice with him at night to fetch something from the market, because she didn't want the children walking alone. One night, his parents went to the movies and left Rocky to babysit his sister. He wanted to practice football instead, so he took Alice to Edgar Park, sat her on a crate under a streetlight, and told her not to move. Alice obeyed, but when her brother and the other boys moved off into the darkness at the other end of the field, she began to cry. Annoyed, Rocky came over and slapped her. Later that night, after Alice had gone to bed, her big brother woke her up and apologized.

◻ ◻ ◻

ROCKY'S FIRST LOVE was baseball.

He and Eugene Sylvester, of the Terrific Three, were good ballplayers. They played for the Ward Two team, and also for their St. Patrick's CYO team. Eugene was a good pitcher, and Rocky could mash the ball. In one pickup game, he drove the ball out of the park into the street, where it bounced once and smacked into the side of a house five hundred feet away.

When it rained, snowed, or sleeted, and the other boys' parents wouldn't let them outside, they could look out their windows and see Rocky, alone in the park, hitting a baseball. If he had a baseball game, the customers on his afternoon paper route would have to wait. His uncle Johnny, Luigi's son, would pitch to him for hours, paying Rocky's sister Alice and brother Sonny a nickel to chase the balls. It was hard to dislodge Rocky from the batter's box, where he could seemingly hit forever. When the priest who coached his CYO team chastised him for monopolizing batting practice, he replied, "Gee, Father, I got to get my whacks."

With his short, squat frame, Rocky was a prototypical catcher. Errant pitches didn't get by him, and neither did runners trying to score when he blocked the plate. But he couldn't run. When he played for Brockton High School, he hit a four-hundred-foot drive to the fence against New Bedford that another player would have easily turned into an inside-the-park home run; Rocky lumbered into second base with a double. His style resembled one of his favorite major leaguers, the all-star catcher Ernie Lombardi of the Cincinnati Reds. A fellow Italian American, Lombardi was a powerful hitter and superb defender who ran so slowly that an opposing manager joked he looked like he was carrying a piano—and the man tuning it.

Rocky had big-league dreams and trained fanatically. He borrowed his uncle Johnny's exerciser, with straps and springs, repeatedly stretching it across his chest and over his arms. Self-conscious about his friends knowing that he used the exerciser, he swore his sisters to secrecy. To strengthen his wrists and forearms, Rocky did chin-ups every morning and evening from the limb of a cherry tree in the backyard. At night, his sisters in bed in the next room could hear him "bouncing around" as he worked out. When he got older and he and Sonny shared a bedroom, Sonny would wake in the night to see Rocky squatting on the floor in the catcher's position, lifting a heavy wooden chair over his head one hundred times with each arm.

His uncle Johnny, a bachelor who lived downstairs, encouraged Rocky's interest in sports. With Pierino too tired after work and enfeebled by his war injuries, Johnny took on a father's role of participating in sports activities with Rocky. He took him swimming at the YMCA and brought him to Red Sox and Braves baseball games in Boston. Johnny had a crippled left arm and was a shy man who kept to himself, more comfortable around his nieces and nephews than other adults. He was generous, buying the children secondhand skates and bicycles, paying for tap-dancing lessons for one niece, and buying a new Flexible Flyer sled that was big enough for all the children to ride together.

Though Rocky was slow to anger, it was inevitable that he would be involved in neighborhood fights. Fistfights were part of the code of the streets of his youth, a way of settling differences, proving yourself, defending your honor. But they passed quickly, like summer storms. There were no grudges, no knives, no guns.

When Leo Ball, the Jewish boy whose bicycle Rocky had "borrowed," and his best friend Mike developed a crush on the same girl, Rocky found out and arranged for them to fight for her affections. A crowd of boys gathered around the combatants as they fought. When Leo won, Rocky took him over to the girl's house to announce the results. The girl tossed a note from her window, which Rocky picked up and read: "I love you both very much, but I love Mike more." Rocky put his hand gently on Leo's shoulder, said, "Sorry, Leo," and sauntered away with his friends. Later, Rocky arranged for Leo to fight another Italian boy, a fight that Leo saw as having racial overtones. The half-Jewish boxer Max Baer, wearing trunks with the Star of David, had recently beaten the Italian champion Primo Carnera for the heavyweight title, which "cast quite a pall over our neighborhood," said Leo. With Rocky serving as his corner man, the Italian boy ended the fight quickly, recalled Leo, "preserving the integrity of Italy, and sending me back up Brook Street, lip bloodied."

When Rocky was ten years old, he was walking home from school with his friend and neighbor Vinnie Colombo, the two boys taking turns bouncing a small rubber ball. Soon they started arguing over whose ball it was. Exchanges of "It's mine" and "No, it's mine" escalated to pushing and shoving. The boys started rolling around on the cobblestones in the middle of Brook Street, wrestling and throwing wild punches. Finally, bloody and dirty and crying, they separated and staggered home. The ball lay forgotten in the gutter. A few hours later, Rocky was outside Vinnie's house, calling up to the window for him to come out and play as if nothing had happened.

But when a horrified Lena saw Rocky's torn school clothes, bloody lip, and tear-streaked face, she demanded to know what had happened. He said Vinnie had punched him and taken his ball. Rocky frequently ran to his mother after getting into fights, and he had a reputation as a crybaby. On this day, his uncle Johnny stood quietly behind Lena, listening to his nephew's latest plea for sympathy.

"Rocky, don't come home crying and bother your mother," Johnny said. "Fight your own battles." Rocky slunk into the house, too embarrassed to answer.

The next day, Uncle Johnny took some canvas he had scrounged from the fairgrounds and had it stitched together into a bag. He took the bag to a lumberyard and filled it with sawdust, then hung it in the basement, near Luigi's grape press. He instructed Rocky to hit the bag for a half hour every day, drilling him to use his left hand as well as his right. Johnny also gave the boy his first pair of boxing gloves. Rocky went to the cellar faithfully every day and attacked the bag. Because the basement ceiling was low, he had to crouch down to hit the bag solidly with an uppercut chop—an unconventional style that would serve him well years later.

The family also hung a punching bag in the backyard for Rocky to use. Even the family dog, Prince, liked jumping up to scratch at the swaying canvas bag.

Rocky's first "official" boxing match took place when he was around eleven, in a makeshift canvas ring in a nearby backyard. His friend Allie Colombo matched him against a bigger, older boy from the neighborhood. They wore oversize gloves, so nobody could get seriously hurt. The fight was set for three rounds, but neither boy was tired so they kept going for ten, aggressively trading blows. There were no knockdowns, and the fight ended in a draw.

Recalling his childhood, Rocky said, "You really had to get me mad to fight." But he hung around with smart alecks like Eugene Sylvester, who ran his mouth and would get into fights, "then he'd holler for me and I'd just back him up. I got in a lot of fights that way."

That's how Rocky wound up in an epic fight when he was fourteen with a black boy named Julie Durham, who had a reputation as one of the toughest fighters in the neighborhood. Julie, who was a few years older, was tough and strong, and served as ball boy for a semipro baseball team that played at Edgar Playground. Since baseballs were precious, Julie's job was to chase down any foul balls before one of the boys lurking behind the backstop could grab it.

One day, when Izzy, Eugene, and Rocky were hanging around watching the game, the batter fouled back a pitch into the woods. The boys ran after the ball. Izzy got there first and stuffed it under his shirt. Julie ran into the woods and demanded the ball. Izzy denied having it. Eugene said they would help Julie look. But Julie wasn't buying it. The argument escalated.

Julie threatened the smaller Izzy. Rocky told Julie to pick on someone his own size. The two boys started shoving, then swinging. Julie jabbed Rocky in the nose with a hard punch. Startled, Rocky stumbled and fell down in the leaves. When he got up, his nose was bloody. The two boys circled each other, Rocky holding his arms up clumsily, unable to block the quicker Julie's accurate punches.

News of the fight spread quickly. The people who had been watching the baseball game abandoned the bleachers and formed a circle around the two boys. Julie kept tagging Rocky, who was too slow and awkward to land a good punch. Leo Ball, who was there, recalled Julie "hitting, dancing, taunting, until Rocky was frustrated to tears." Then Julie took his eyes off Rocky for an instant to say something to a friend. Like a bolt of lightning from a blue sky, Rocky swung hard with an overhead right that caught Julie on the jaw and sent him toppling to the ground. He stood over Julie, his right fist cocked. The small crowd, which by then included some of the players from the baseball game, cheered. Rocky seemed almost as surprised as Julie. But it had felt good. The fight cemented Rocky's reputation as the toughest kid in the neighborhood. But he respected his adversary; he and Julie became friends and later played football together at Brockton High School.

◻ ◻ ◻

NEIGHBORHOOD FISTFIGHTS REFLECTED the fight culture dominant in America in the 1930s. Boxing was second only to baseball in popularity, and its appeal filtered down from big-city arenas to small-town fight clubs. In an age of machines and skyscrapers, the boxing ring was a place where the individual could still shine by displaying courage and heart, cunning and toughness, skill and determination. The ring was a showcase for ethnic rivalries and provided an escape for immigrants struggling to find their place in a harsh new world. Immigrants sought acceptance and assimilation in the ring—there were many Jewish, Irish, and Italian fighters, and African Americans soon followed. The great John L. Sullivan, America's first heavyweight champion, who had dragged the sport from the bare-knuckle era into the mainstream, had retired to a farm in West Abington, a few miles up the road from Brockton.

It was enough to make a boy dream. On the night of June 29, 1933, when Rocky was nine, Ward Two erupted in shouting and singing after

Primo Carnera knocked out Jack Sharkey in New York to win the world heavyweight title. As Rocky watched the glow of the celebratory bonfires in Edgar Playground, he thought, "If I could win the title, I'd come back to Brockton and throw a party for the whole town."

Shortly thereafter, Carnera came to Brockton to referee the boxing matches at the Brockton Arena. Uncle Johnny took Rocky to see the man who was known as the Ambling Alp. After the show, as the six-foot-six, 260-pound Carnera walked past them, Rocky reached up and touched the champ on the elbow. He gushed about it later to his father.

"I saw Carnera and I touched him. I really did," he said. Pierino asked how big Carnera was. "Bigger than this ceiling," answered Rocky. "And you should see how big his hands are!"

Rocky was too young and innocent to see the darker side of boxing. He didn't realize that his boyhood hero was actually a Mafia stooge, a clumsy, lumbering ex–circus strongman plucked from obscurity in Italy and fattened up with a string of fixed fights against dubious opponents. Four months before Carnera won the title, he had knocked out Ernie Schaaf in a dull, controversial fight that had the crowd booing and shouting "fake." Then Schaaf collapsed and died a few days later. Investigators concluded that he had suffered brain damage in previous fights and never should have been allowed in the ring. Prior to Carnera's title fight against Sharkey, mobsters hung out openly at both fighters' training camps. Sharkey was knocked out without putting up much of a fight. Carnera's undistinguished reign lasted one year, until the lords of boxing had squeezed every last dollar out of him and sent him into the ring to be destroyed by Max Baer—the fight that upset Rocky and his Ward Two friends.

On those occasions when Uncle Johnny didn't have money for tickets, he and Rocky climbed onto the roof of the shabby, cavernous Brockton Arena and watched the fights through the skylight. When Rocky and Izzy were in junior high, they started getting into the fights for free by working. One of their jobs was to help the fighters get their gloves on and off. The fight promoter only had two pairs of gloves, so the entire fight card had to share. Rocky and Izzy would cut the laces off the gloves of one boxer as he left the ring, take the gloves to the next boxer, and lace them up for him before he stepped into the ring.

One night when the boys were working, another champ, Joe Louis, made an appearance at the Brockton Arena as a guest referee. Louis, the first black heavyweight champion in twenty years, had beaten Carnera en route to the title and then became an American hero by knocking out Hitler's strongman, Max Schmeling, in the epic 1938 fight that reflected the growing tensions between Nazi Germany and the United States. Rocky and Izzy were starstruck; they loved Louis, and they especially loved how hard he punched. They followed the Brown Bomber everywhere he went that night, even the bathroom. When the champ went into a stall, Izzy later recalled, he boosted Rocky up for a better look. Louis was good-natured about it and gave each boy fifty cents when he left the bathroom. The boys stammered their thanks.

◻ ◻ ◻

THE TERRIFIC THREE were always hustling. Izzy and Rocky shined shoes downtown. Izzy helped Rocky with his paper route. Their clubhouse was the dirt cellar of the triple-decker where Izzy's family lived, outfitted with a punching bag, a dartboard, and pictures of baseball heroes like Babe Ruth and Lou Gehrig hanging on rusty nails.

One day, in their basement clubhouse, Eugene said, "We're blood brothers."

"Yeah," Izzy responded. "But we haven't crossed blood."

They got a razor, made small cuts in their wrists, and rubbed the cuts together. The initiation to be in their club, Izzy said, was to jump from the rooftop of one downtown building to another—a distance of about ten feet, four or five stories above Brockton. "If you fell, if you didn't jump far enough, you were gone," said Izzy. "That was the deal. You had to jump them roofs to make it in our gang, which we did."

Most of their downtown treks were less hair-raising. When their mothers gave them twenty-five cents for a haircut, they spent it at the movies instead. When they could, they saved their quarters by persuading a friendly usher to let them slip into the Modern Theater for free, or wedging open the back door atop the fire escape behind the Rialto. Rocky would wolf down a quart of ice cream filched from McCann's market next door. The boys also gobbled peanuts, which they paid less for by sneaking a finger underneath the scale to hide the true weight.

Money was often on their minds. "We had a thing in our head, we were going to make it big time, you know, we're going to get rich," recalled Izzy.

Gambling was the way. Like boxing, games of chance were part of the culture that Rocky grew up with. It was a world, said Izzy, where kids "grew up fast." Rocky and his friends played blackjack on the bleachers in the park for pennies. Once, Rocky remembered, his friend Angie picked up a penny under a tree in Edgar Playground and ran it up to forty bucks in a blackjack game under another tree.

But the Terrific Three's big score involved a small-time hood from Providence, Rhode Island.

Every Sunday morning after church, about thirty men gathered in a clearing in the woods off Dover Street, behind Edgar Playground, to shoot craps. The game was run by a heavyset one-legged bookie from Providence called Peg-Leg Pete. Every Sunday morning, Pete would show up in the Gamblers Woods, as the spot was called, open a folding chair, sit down heavily, and spread out a chart on the grass that had the odds printed on it. He pulled a pistol out of his pocket and laid it on the ground. He was open for business.

The stakes were small, quarters and dollars, but could add up fast. Rocky's uncle Mike—another of Lena's brothers—came home once with $200. Another time, a player lost all his money and walked out. He returned a half hour later wearing a mask and pointing a gun and held up the crap game.

The Terrific Three plotted how to profit from Peg-Leg Pete's game. Izzy hatched the idea of hiding in the woods and throwing stones until the gamblers, who didn't want to draw attention and the police, gave them a few bucks to stop. The plan worked the first few times, but there were some tough men in the group, and they threatened to come after the boys if they didn't stop.

Now Eugene had an idea. They would call the cops, and when the gamblers fled, the boys would swoop in and grab the money in the pot, maybe fifty or sixty bucks. The plan worked, sort of. When the gamblers heard the police, they scrambled into the woods, leaving their money on the ground. But the boys could only scoop up a few dollars before the police were on them, and they had to flee, too.

When they got older, Izzy started rolling the dice himself. His stake was a few bucks earned from his paper route or selling empty bottles or his bleacher blackjack winnings. The men liked to see him coming. He was usually no threat and invariably lost his money. After he lost, they teased him about the evils of gambling, then tossed him a quarter to buy himself an ice cream.

When the boys starting missing Sunday Mass at St. Patrick's, their CYO baseball coach, Father Jeremiah Minnihan, stormed down to the Gamblers Woods as Rocky was shooting the dice. The priest called Rocky a heathen and threatened to toss him and his friends from the baseball team. Rocky apologized. He and his friends started showing up at church more regularly. But they didn't stop gambling.

Then, one steamy summer Sunday, Lady Luck shone on Izzy Gold. As Eugene and Rocky watched, transfixed, he started rolling sevens and made five straight passes. The gamblers grumbled about wise-ass luck. Izzy cleaned out the crap game, and the boys found themselves stuffing a few hundred dollars under their shirts in crumpled bills. They didn't want their parents to know they'd been gambling, so Rocky said they should hide the money. They retreated to their clubhouse in Izzy's basement, where Rocky dug a hole in the dirt floor with a coal shovel and buried the loot in cigar boxes.

The boys decided to spend their windfall at the Brockton Fair in September, more than a month away. Worried that something would happen to the money, Rocky checked it frequently, sometimes reburying it in a different spot.

When the fair opened, Rocky, Izzy, and Eugene dug up the cigar boxes and went on a weeklong spree. They rode the rides; attended the sideshows; gorged themselves on hot dogs, cotton candy, and candied apples; and lost money at the roulette games and on the horse races. Rocky loved not only the excitement but also the thrill of seeing the vagabond lifestyle of the wandering carnival folk. One day, one of the performers, the famous burlesque dancer Sally Rand, was rehearsing her balloon bubble dance when the wind blew away one of her balloons. Rocky chased it down and returned it to her, receiving a warm smile of thanks.

By the end, the boys were broke but happy. For one week, the Terrific Three had known what it felt like to be rich, to have the world at their feet.

* * *

WHEN ROCKY REACHED Brockton High School, he was more interested in sports than books. Even in class or while talking to a teacher, it wasn't unusual for him to be tossing a baseball idly in his hands. He wasn't stupid, but he didn't care. All he wanted to do was play professional baseball.

As a sophomore, Rocky tried out for the Brockton High School football team. On the first day of practice, the coach looked him over and saw a boy who was stocky and rugged, with a thick torso, heavy legs, and a wide, flat nose that looked as if it had been pushed in by a lineman.

"What position do you play?" the coach asked.

"I'm a back," Rocky replied. "I can pass pretty good."

"Well," said the coach, "you'll do your passing between your legs. From now on you're a center."

Rocky became one of the only sophomores to start for the varsity team in 1940. He was strong, a terrific athlete, and, not surprisingly, he hit hard. But he couldn't run fast. That was evident in the play that proved the highlight of his high school career, when he intercepted a pass in the Columbus Day game against New Bedford. He lumbered sixty yards down the sideline and barely made it into the end zone as a would-be tackler came from way back to catch him at the one. Rocky stumbled across the goal line with the player hanging on his leg. He played nearly sixty minutes a game for the Shoe Men his sophomore year, a bright spot on a team that saw its twenty-two-game unbeaten streak snapped and finished a disappointing 5-4-1.

After football season, a decision loomed. The Brockton High School baseball coach had a rule that his players couldn't play for other teams in town. That was a quandary for Rocky and his friends, who played for St. Patrick's and for other sandlot teams around town. Without baseball, he saw little reason to stay in school. He was discouraged by his low grades, his football coach said, and was not enthusiastic about the effort it would take to raise them. "I just didn't care for the books," Rocky said.

As the oldest son, Rocky also felt a duty to drop out and go to work to help support the family. He had seen how the shoe factory seemed to drain the life out of his father, and so he told his parents at dinner one night that he was quitting school. Uncle Johnny could get him a job on a coal truck, he said—and he would still have time to pursue a major-league baseball career.

Both his parents worried. Lena had dreamed of being a teacher and saw education as the path for her children to a better life. Pierino fretted that Rocky would wind up like him, in the shoe factory.

"No, no, *figlio mio*," Lena said. "You got to finish school. We want you to graduate."

As Rocky later recalled, he told his mother, "Look, I ain't a good student and I don't like school. I can make twenty dollars a week and play so much baseball that I can be in the big leagues in a few years."

"Hah," Lena shot back. "Who's done good in baseball around here? Everybody plays, but nobody makes any money at it."

Just then, Uncle Johnny walked in. Lena started in on him for encouraging her son to quit school. The two of them argued back and forth until finally Rocky cut in, striking a conciliatory tone.

"Mom, let me go to work," he pleaded. "I want to help out. Maybe things will pick up later, and I promise you I'll go to night school and maybe even graduate."

Reluctantly, Lena relented.

Rocky went to work on a coal truck, for fifty cents an hour, delivering coal to the basements of Brockton houses. He liked the work, the sense of freedom riding around town, being outdoors, and using his muscles. But he grew to dislike climbing down into the dank coal bins, inhaling the chalky black dust that coated his skin and his clothes. After four months, he quit and found a better-paying job in a candy factory. But now he felt trapped in a room with windows that didn't open, inhaling the sicky-sweet smell of the candy eight hours a day. He told Izzy it felt like being in jail.

He quit the candy factory and drifted through a series of dead-end jobs. He worked in a beverage plant and a shoe factory, neither for long. He felt cooped up. He complained to Izzy about the noise and smell of the shoe factory; even his food tasted like leather. The bosses were always yelling at him to work harder. He wondered how their fathers could stand it for so many years. Next was a job as a short-order cook at a diner. But the owner let him go because of his monstrous appetite, saying, "I'd rather clothe you than feed you."

Rocky gravitated to outdoor work. He dug holes for the Brockton Gas Company and worked as a laborer for the city, building and repairing sidewalks. He loved the backbreaking work, developing his strength, being outside. When he wasn't working, he practiced baseball and played on a series of local semipro teams. He played with such intensity, Vinnie Colombo recalled, that the crowd used to ride him for being so serious, which he hated.

In December 1941, the Japanese bombed Pearl Harbor, and America went to war. As it was for millions of Americans, Rocky Marchegiano's fortunes would be changed by the global conflict. At first, it meant better defense jobs close to home. He cleared land for a factory in South Weymouth, hacking away underbrush with a sickle. He worked on the construction of a blimp hangar. From his first job, which had paid fifty cents an hour, he was now earning $1.25 an hour, with plenty of overtime. One week he brought home his sealed pay envelope and handed it to Lena. She counted out $150, a small fortune.

"I felt sorry for Pop that day," Rocky recalled. "He sort of hung his head when he saw me, a seventeen-year-old kid, come home with all that money. The most he ever made in a week was about forty bucks."

With money in his pocket, Rocky continued to gamble, betting on the dog races, shooting dice, and finding local card games with Izzy. But they were no match for the experienced players and invariably lost their money. When they were working a construction job, Rocky and Izzy would get paid on Fridays, then shoot dice that night and wind up broke and have to borrow money from Rocky's uncle. After a few weeks, they discovered that the man who ran the game was using loaded dice. "Rocky went up and broke his jaw," recalled Izzy. "Tipped him upside down and took whatever he had."

The war intensified, and life moved on. In March 1942, Rocky's grandfather Luigi died. That spring, Rocky found work helping to build Camp Myles Standish, a nearby army embarkation center. He worked there for a year, hurrying home at night to throw on his baseball uniform, then wolfing down a large Italian sub as he headed to the game. He also played football for a semipro team sponsored by the Young Men's Lithuanian Association. In one game, his friend Vinnie Colombo was running with the ball for the other team when Rocky hit him. The next thing Vinnie knew, he was lying on the ground and regaining consciousness to see a concerned Rocky standing over him, asking in his soft voice, "You all right, Vinnie?"

Life was good. Then, in the winter of 1943, at the age of nineteen, Rocky was drafted. He would soon face his own private battles, as the fortunes that carried him away from Brockton set him on a new path.

2

Brawler in the Brig

PRIVATE ROCCO MARCHEGIANO WAS INDUCTED INTO THE ARMY ON March 3, 1943, and assigned to a combat engineers unit.

Before leaving for basic training, Rocky and the other Brockton boys who had been drafted gathered outside city hall for a group photo, which was printed in the *Brockton Enterprise*. Rocky was then sent to the embarkation center at Camp Myles Standish, which he had helped build the year before as a civilian, and then to Fort Devens in northern Massachusetts. As a member of a combat engineers unit, he found himself doing the same kind of hard manual labor he had done since dropping out of high school: digging ditches, hauling equipment, practicing building bridges for when his unit would have to build bridges across rivers to allow combat troops to advance.

The only difference was that now Rocky was under military discipline, earning $1.60 a day in soldier's pay, isolated in the woods far from home and unable to come and go as he pleased. He chafed under the rules. Even so, two months after his enlistment, Rocky was promoted to private first class. But he didn't like the new job he was assigned and went absent without leave for seven days. Another soldier in his outfit had seen him in Boston with a woman and reported him to their commander, leading to Rocky's demotion back to private. Rocky asked his lieutenant if the two men could be allowed to settle their grudge by boxing, and Rocky gave his accuser a furious beating.

Still, Rocky didn't have it too bad at Fort Devens. In a letter home, he said that he had gotten friendly with the sergeants, so he didn't have to help clean the barracks. It was reminiscent of his childhood, when he had also gotten out of doing chores. His parents, he told an army doctor, had been "very easy on me." The doctor wrote that Rocky was easygoing, well spoken, and "a trifle spoiled."

Rocky was also able to get away from Fort Devens and continue to see women. He had been interested in girls since the age of fifteen, he told the army doctor, losing his virginity after he turned seventeen, in 1940, and having intercourse about once a month since then, with different girls. In a letter home to his sister Conge, he asked if anyone had called the house looking for him in the past week because he was expecting someone.

"I broke up with Marie she was a jerk but I know a better girl," he wrote. In subsequent letters, he confessed how much he loved a girl named Jo, and asked his sister if Jo had feelings for him.

In another letter to Conge, Rocky voiced his frustration at how hard it was to get passes, noting, "Nothing happens around here but when it does I'll let you know." He apologized for not being able to get home more often and took the tone of a playful but solicitous big brother.

"Watch Peter," he wrote of their youngest brother, "he's always hooking on the backs of cars I saw him last week myself. The lights are about to go out so until I hear from you god bless the Marchegiano family and keep working so you can help Pa and [their sister] Alice turn in some dough." The family was about to move into a new house, on the other side of the Edgar Playground, and Rocky teased Conge to let him know when, "so I can go home to the right house."

He signed his letter, "big brother Rock."

In September, Rocky was transferred to Camp Pickett in Virginia as a member of Company A of the 348th Engineer Combat Battalion. Shortly thereafter, he wrote home that he was already getting used to the South, despite the absence of any town within twenty miles. But he didn't have it as easy as at Fort Devens, where he had befriended the sergeants to get out of menial duties. "Boy am I tired," he wrote home, "we just had to clean the whole barracks because some big shots are coming around tomorrow to see how we're doing and there isn't supposed to be a spec ask Pa he'll tell ya. I guess I'm in the Army now . . . I guess I earned my $1.60 today allright."

On maneuvers in Chesapeake Bay, the men of the 348th practiced loading and unloading Liberty ships and became familiar with the large, flat-bottom landing craft that American troops would use to ferry soldiers and supplies ashore. Navy and army planes flew overhead, laying down a short barrage of gunfire and spreading a screen of tear gas along the beach to simulate what to expect from German defenders.

Early in October, the men boarded trains for the two-day trip back north to Camp Myles Standish, where they spent much of their time doing calisthenics, running obstacle courses, and taking long hikes through the piney woods. But Rocky's homecoming to Massachusetts was short-lived. At the end of October, as big band swing music played over the public-address system, he and the rest of his company climbed aboard another train that took them north to Canada. As the train pulled into Halifax, Nova Scotia, the next day, Rocky could see the funnels and bridge of a massive ship rising above the warehouses that lined the docks of the bustling port.

The men were marched up the long gangplank onto the RMS *Mauretania*, a former luxury liner that had been converted into a troopship that could hold more than seven thousand soldiers. They were crammed belowdecks on bunks, hammocks, the deck, and mess tables—a floating city of soldiers and nurses from the United States, Canada, Australia, New Zealand, Norway, Scotland, and Poland. On November 2, the *Mauretania* steamed into the Atlantic. Hundreds of soldiers clung to the railings to watch the last hilltops of North America slip from sight.

The ship sailed without an escort, zigzagging frequently to evade prowling German U-boats. Rocky's transatlantic voyage was marked with regular abandon-ship drills and nightly admonishments not to smoke on deck after dark, to maintain a blackout. The seven-day crossing was uneventful—except for the rolling seas halfway across that sent the bow dipping into the waves and stomachs lurching.

Still, for Rocky, the voyage marked another run of good luck with the dice. Broke, he borrowed a quarter and got into a blackjack game, won $8, and moved on to a poker game, where he won $50, and then joined a high-stakes crap game, where he got hot and ran his winnings up to $1,300. He lent much of his bankroll to other soldiers, never to see it again. Looking back years later, he wrote: "That taught me a lesson. Ever since then, I've been very careful with my money."

The *Mauretania* arrived in Liverpool on November 9. Disembarking after dark, Rocky and the other men of the 348th took in their first view of the war as they marched silently through the blacked-out, moonlit streets, past gutted buildings that had been ravaged by Luftwaffe bombers. At the Liverpool railway station, they boarded trains that carried them south through the English countryside. At three a.m., they reached Swansea, in South Wales, and transferred to double-decker buses for the short ride to their new home, a small seaside resort called Mumbles.

At first, Rocky was billeted on the Mumbles pier, sleeping on a straw mattress. The British weather was damp and cold, and when the men weren't working, they were training, including long marches with full packs and M1 rifles. In December, Rocky and his company moved to Camp Manselton, on the outskirts of Swansea.

While he didn't love the army life, he enjoyed the camaraderie, the occasional softball games, and the football games on the beach of Caswell Bay. On Thanksgiving, the men of Rocky's Company A played a football game against Company C. "Making the best of it Conge," he wrote his sister. "I am with a good bunch of fellows so the days go by quick we play a lot of sports and you no [sic] how much I like that."

Rocky missed the comforts of home. In one letter, he asked his sister to send him a carton of Hershey almond candy bars. In another, he dreamed of Lena's spaghetti: "Don't ever mention spags to me again until I get home. I'd give $10,000 for a plate but when I get to Rome I'll go to Cheiti (I see it on the map) and look up Pa's brother Steve."

"Gee Conge, you don't realize how lucky all of you are back there," he wrote on January 5, 1944. "The poor kids over here haven't heard of ice cream, bananas and oranges and for a piece of candy or gum they beg." He went on to describe the lifestyle: "There [sic] homes are cheap, there [sic] life is simple, if they ever visited the States I swear you couldn't get them back here."

Still, Rocky developed an affection for the place, including a taste for fish and chips and such local specialties as hot laverbread that the Welsh cooked from seaweed.

At night, Rocky and the other soldiers got passes into Swansea and flocked to the roaring, brawling pubs of Wind Street. The air was charged with testosterone and the anticipation of battle. One night at the Adelphi Hotel, a popular pub packed with overseas servicemen, Rocky and a few of his mates got into an argument with a loud, obnoxious Australian soldier. The row may have started after a man in Rocky's unit, Roland Regan, started playing the Irish folk song "The Wild Colonial Boy" on the piano. Rocky and his mates started singing along to the song, about an Irish rebel who immigrates to Australia, where he is shot dead by the police. Some British and Australian soldiers in the pub objected. Tempers flared, and an altercation ensued, with Rocky in the middle.

As Rocky recalled years later, the Australian soldier he tangled with was six foot six, 240 pounds, and "all muscle." They started to fight, but Rocky ended it with a single punch to the jaw, sending the Aussie to the floor in a puddle of his warm beer.

"By rights, he should of tore me in two," Rocky wrote a Brockton friend. "But I got the first one in and that's all she was."

Rocky recalled another time when he got into a brawl in a local pub, swapping blows with a miner who was "as big as Tommy Farr," the bruising Welsh heavyweight who had lost a controversial decision to Joe Louis six years earlier. Rocky didn't say how that one turned out, but he noted that the military police intervened. Still, Rocky for the most part managed to stay a step ahead of the "Snow Drops," the white-helmeted MPs who had their hands full with unruly American GIs.

Whether to avoid being disciplined, escape camp duty, or develop his punching prowess, Rocky apparently began his formal education as a boxer in Swansea. "It all started for me down there in Wales," he later told a British writer, noting the great prizefighting tradition there. Rocky started taking the Mumbles train into Swansea and going to a gym next to the railway station that was run by a Welsh heavyweight named Jim Wilde.

There are scant details of his army bouts. He fought to a three-round draw against Dr. Jack "Iron Man" Matthews, who would become one of Wales's greatest rugby players and chief medical officer of the Wales Boxing Association. Their bout took place at a local air force base, where Matthews was serving in the Royal Army Medical Corps.

There was a boxing ring in a tent at the base, where Rocky and the other men in his unit sparred for fun and exercise. One day, Roland Regan put on the gloves and started boxing with Rocky. Regan, who was thirty pounds lighter, was able to land some punches while Rocky, heavier and slower, didn't connect as frequently. But when Rocky did finally land a punch on Regan's left arm, the arm went numb.

◼ ◼ ◼

ROCKY'S BUDDING PUGILISTIC career was interrupted in late January 1944. His company was on maneuvers, building a bridge at night, when he accidentally smashed his right thumb with a hammer, fracturing it. Early in March, he and other men in his company got three days of leave in London, sleeping in British Army barracks and touring the sights. Rocky wrote home that London reminded him of New York, which he had visited as a boy for a family wedding. He enjoyed seeing the famous sights—Big Ben, London Bridge, and the Tower of London—but was more excited to run into an old friend from Brockton who was also in the army.

During this time, the men of the 348th learned that they would be part of an amphibious assault on the Continent but weren't told when or where it would take place. They trained on the beaches around Mumbles—getting on and off boats, loading and unloading supplies, clearing the beach of land mines and debris, and building pontoon and Bailey bridges. A soldier in Rocky's battalion later wrote: "Preparing for the invasion that was to come, we were told our job was to go through wire fences, build roads and to build bridges over water. We were to engage in combat action, if necessary." Soldiers writing home had to watch their words, as did the military censors looking over their shoulder. As Rocky explained to Conge in March, "Can't write too much sis nothing new happens except in the line of duty and that's forbidden."

As the invasion neared, anticipation grew. The 348th moved down the coast to Weymouth, on the English Channel, awaiting deployment. Security was ratcheted up. Fewer passes into town were granted. On May 30, and over the next four days, the men began loading the ships.

Rocky was not among the first wave who steamed out of Weymouth on D-day, and he later downplayed his military service; he called himself "just a fellow in the land mines over there." He told reporters that he helped ferry supplies to Normandy after the beaches had been taken and the Germans pushed back. In the long months to come, the 348th Combat Engineers would join the bloody march across Europe, taking fire and withstanding the Battle of the Bulge, the Germans' last great counterpunch.

Rocky did not join the Allied march to victory. In June 1944, as his unit was about to deploy to France, Rocky was fighting his own war. Ten days after D-day, he was in a military stockade, facing court-martial for robbery and assault.

■ ■ ■

THE NIGHT OF June 15, 1944, was supposed to be a quiet night for Rocky. His lieutenant told him and the other men in the unit that they were not allowed to leave camp, as they were about to be sent to France. But Rocky and a fellow private, James Murphy, decided to sneak out for one last night on the town.

They went to the bar at the Anchor Hotel in the town of Filton, and started drinking beer. Around nine thirty, an Englishman named Frederick Neath came over and said hello to Murphy, whom he had met the week before at a dance. Neath was the general secretary of the Bristol Aeroplane Company, and he had brought several women who worked at his firm to the dance.

Murphy introduced Neath to Rocky, and the three started talking. Murphy complained about life in the army. He said he was "fed up"—he hadn't been able to send any money home to his wife, and he was about to be sent into combat in France. Neath felt sorry for Murphy and invited him and Rocky to his apartment for more drinks. He drove the two American GIs to his rooms at the Sports Pavilion, a bar and recreation club for the Bristol Aeroplane Company's employees, and served them drinks in his sitting room.

The accounts of what happened next diverge.

Neath said that Murphy asked him for a loan. Neath said he couldn't lend him money but would try to help if Murphy accompanied him to a local welfare agency the following night. They talked for a while, and Murphy asked again about the loan. When Neath again refused, Murphy propositioned him, saying, "Well, if you want to have a bit of fun, what's it worth to you?" Neath said he wasn't interested but gave Murphy ten shillings. Neath, Murphy, and Rocky were then joined by Neath's roommate, Eric Ashford, who also worked for Bristol. It was now past eleven o'clock, and Neath said it was time for his guests to leave. A belligerent Murphy refused, shoved Neath onto the couch, then fiddled with the radio, searching for music. Ashford went downstairs to get his briefcase, and when he returned Rocky barred the door and warned him not to go any farther.

When the door opened, the five-foot-nine, 140-pound Neath walked out, his eye blackened, his face bleeding, followed by the six-foot, 185-pound Murphy. Neath said that Murphy had punched him in the face half a dozen times and had then taken his wallet.

Neath stumbled out of the room, Murphy trailing behind, and went to the bathroom to wash his face. Rocky followed, apologizing; he explained that Murphy had had too much to drink and offered to get Neath's wallet back. But he didn't. Instead, Rocky and Murphy decided it was time to go. Ashford took them downstairs to get their coats and hats out of Neath's car. But when Ashford leaned into the car, he said, the two Americans grabbed him and punched him several times in the face. Then Rocky held Ashford while Murphy went through his pockets, taking his wallet, a fountain pen, and £22 in savings certificates. The two GIs then fled into the night and caught a ride back to their base, hustling into their tents before bed check.

The next day, Rocky and Murphy acted as if nothing had happened, but that afternoon they were summoned to meet with their commanding officers and Inspector William Hart of the Gloucestershire constabulary. Hart told them that he was investigating a complaint from Neath and Ashford that they had been assaulted and robbed by two American GIs. Rocky and Murphy denied it. Rocky said they had been playing cards and had never left camp, and could produce witnesses to prove it. "We know nothing about it," he said.

But Hart and a U.S. Army captain quickly disproved their lie, searching around Murphy's tent and finding Ashford's fountain pen and Neath's wallet, the money still inside. Now, with their commanding officers present, Murphy and Rocky were informed of their rights and questioned again. This time, they gave a story that was also hard to believe. They admitted sneaking off the base and going to the Englishmen's apartment for drinks. But they claimed that Neath and Ashford were "queers" who had sexually propositioned them; Rocky and Murphy had taken their wallets to get their IDs so they could report them to the authorities. But then they contradicted themselves, saying that they didn't want to make a police report because they didn't want to be punished for sneaking off base.

Rocky said that Ashford had followed him into the bathroom at the apartment, grabbed his penis, and "acted very strange." He then pushed Ashford away and went back to the other room, where he said he saw Neath grabbing Murphy in the same way.

Rocky said he told Murphy it was time to leave and went downstairs to Neath's car. As he leaned into the car to get his things, he said, Ashford came up behind him and grabbed him. Rocky said he pushed him away and tried again to retrieve his things from the car. When Ashford came back, Rocky struck him.

By then, Rocky said, Murphy had come outside and told him to get Ashford's ID. Rocky said he searched the man's pockets and took his wallet. Then they left the scene.

Rocky said that when he returned to base, he couldn't find Ashford's wallet and concluded it had fallen out of his pocket when he clambered over a hedgerow during his escape. He agreed to go with Inspector Hart, and they drove to the hedgerow and found the wallet.

Rocky and Murphy were taken into custody and placed in a U.S. military stockade. They were fingerprinted and photographed. In his mug shot, Rocky stares almost defiantly at the camera, trying to look tough. But there is an undercurrent of uncertainty. In his profile photo, the right collar of his coat is turned up, and he wears a slight smirk as if to say this is nothing to worry about.

Five days later, their commanding officer, Major Richard L. Powell, gave statements leaving no doubt what he thought of their stories or their abilities as soldiers.

Powell described Murphy as a bright, physically imposing man who had the makings of an A-1 soldier but unfortunately had channeled his leadership abilities into getting men to follow him into drunken brawls and other disciplinary infractions. On the voyage to England, Murphy had punched a soldier as he lay in his bunk, sending him to the ship's sick bay with head injuries. Other men in his company were afraid to report him for additional assaults because they feared him. He was, in Powell's words, "a dominating bully."

Powell described Private Marchegiano as "an unreliable and unsatisfactory soldier," known to his officers as "untrustworthy." He had been punished in the past for going AWOL. "His derelictions have always been minor enough to avoid trial by court martial, but they have been consistent and numerous. . . . I believe this man to be of no value to the Army."

Their stories about "immoral advances" sounded like a "fabrication," said Powell, who recommended that both men face a trial by general court-martial. Should they be acquitted and returned to the 348th Engineers, he concluded, it would be a detriment to discipline and morale.

On July 17, 1944, having been pronounced fit to stand trial by an army psychiatrist, Rocky and Murphy faced court-martial before nine military judges at the U.S. Western Base section in Newport, South Wales.

Neath and Ashford testified first, recounting the night's events and their injuries. Neath suffered a black eye, a cut on the nose, and bruises to his ear and neck. Ashford also had a black eye, along with damage to his dental plate. The prosecution highlighted the tale of the tape—the difference in size between the victims and their alleged assailants. Rocky said he was five foot ten and a half and 190 pounds, and that Ashford was "much smaller."

When Rocky took the stand, he repeated his story about how Ashford had "started to get fresh with me" in the apartment's bathroom. "That's why I pushed him in the latrine," he said. "I probably would have hurt him if I hit him up there." Later, when he went downstairs to the car to get his things, Rocky testified that Ashford "put his hand again on my leg and he said he liked me."

"I struck him just once and he was unconscious I guess. He didn't move and when Murphy told me to take his identification card I took it as I went through his pockets."

The prosecutor asked Rocky why he took the whole wallet if he just wanted Ashford's ID.

"I was so mad I didn't realize" was his reply.

Rocky and Murphy presented statements from four soldiers in their unit—who couldn't be there in person because they had deployed to Europe—saying that Neath and Ashford were "queer" and had made "improper advances" on them on at army dances. But those men were the defendants' friends and not considered credible. No other evidence was introduced to suggest that the Englishmen were gay.

The court-martial was over by midafternoon. Privates Marchegiano and Murphy were convicted of felony assault and robbery. Rocky was acquitted of a second count in the robbery and assault of Neath, since he hadn't been in the room.

Private Murphy, who was convicted on both counts, was sentenced to serve ten years of hard labor.

Private Marchegiano was sentenced to seven years of hard labor.

One month later, a colonel at base headquarters approved the convictions and assigned the men to be confined at the federal reformatory in Chilli-cothe, Ohio. That same week, Allied troops liberated Paris.

For Rocky, the war was over.

◻ ◻ ◻

IN THE PUBLIC story of Rocky Marciano's life, he served with the 348th Engineers in Europe in 1944, then came home and was stationed at Fort Lewis in Washington State, where he formally took up boxing. The narrative skips over a nearly two-year gap, in which he was a military prisoner. His army service file, for years marked confidential, helps fill in some of that blank canvas.

Following his court-martial, an army staff judge advocate reviewed Rocky's conviction and reduced his sentence from seven years to three. Rocky received a dishonorable discharge, and his classification was changed from private to general prisoner. On November 13, he was put on a ship back to the States, arriving on November 26. On December 7, the third anniversary of the Japanese bombing of Pearl Harbor, Rocky received a physical at Fort Jay in upstate New York.

On May 25, 1945, two and a half weeks after Germany's surrender, the judge advocate general in Washington received a packet of cases to con-sider for clemency, including Rocky's. The one-paragraph ruling came back six days later: "In view of the serious nature of the offenses commit-ted by General Prisoner Rocco Marchegiano, formerly Private, Company A, 348th Engineer Combat Battalion, his poor military record, and the comparatively short period he has been in confinement, clemency is not recommended at this time."

The following spring, Rocky was a prisoner at Fort Benjamin Harri-son in Indiana. During the war, Fort Harrison had been a camp for Ger-man prisoners, and it was now a barracks for U.S. servicemen convicted of crimes in military courts. The most notable event during Rocky's time there was that on March 16, 1946, he was admitted to the prison hospital with a 102-degree fever and hospitalized for twelve days with pneumonia.

Not long after, Rocky left Fort Benjamin Harrison a free man—well, semi-free. He remained in the army, was reinstated from prisoner to private, and assigned to Fort Lewis, a sprawling army base outside Tacoma, Washington. He served there for the rest of 1946.

It wasn't uncommon for soldiers convicted of crimes to extend their army service in order to win an honorable discharge. When Rocky finally did receive an honorable discharge, his separation papers said that he had lost 663 days of active service in the three and a half years since his enlistment—about one year and ten months. He wasn't paid for that time. That must have stung the conscientious eldest son and big brother who had sent money home during the war.

Rocky never spoke publicly of his time at Fort Benjamin Harrison, except to indicate, while testifying in a trial years later, that he was in the army in Indianapolis, not Fort Lewis, when he came home to Brockton in April 1946 for a one-month furlough.

◻ ◻ ◻

BROCKTON NEVER LOOKED so good to Private Rocky Marchegiano as it did when he returned home in April 1946 from his own private war. Army duffel bag slung over his shoulder, he walked home from the train station through the teeming streets of downtown, past the shoe factories and into Ward Two. The baseball diamond at Edgar Playground beckoned like Opening Day in the first warming days of spring.

After all the hugs and kisses and tearful greetings from Lena and Pierino and his brothers and sisters, one of the first things Rocky did when he returned to the Marchegianos' new house on Dover Street was tuck into a plate of his mother's spaghetti.

He caught up with old friends, including Allie Colombo, who, like Rocky, was on leave from the army. Allie was four years older than Rocky, and while he had also been a fixture on the sandlots growing up, he was more of an organizer, the one who put teams together. It was Allie who had arranged the backyard boxing match for Rocky when he was eleven. He was also, as Rocky would learn, a big dreamer. The two friends started talking about boxing. Allie said he could use his connections in western Massachusetts, where he was stationed at Westover Field, to try to arrange some fights for Rocky when he got out of the army.

Rocky had no aspirations to be a boxer. He wanted to finish his army service, and he still dreamed of being a big-league baseball player. But he also said he could use the money. The subject came up again when Rocky visited with his uncle Mike Picciuto, who took him downtown to meet Gene Caggiano, an ex-fighter who ran weekly amateur boxing shows.

Generoso Caggiano was a pug-nosed, thirty-five-year-old former featherweight who worked as a mechanic for the Eastern Massachusetts Street Railway. He was originally from Boston but was raised in a state home after the early deaths of his parents. He had a history of larceny in Boston before moving to Brockton. Caggiano's ring record was undistinguished, but in 1933, fighting in Ventura, California, he went the distance in a six-round loss to Henry Armstrong, the lightning-quick puncher who would become the first man to simultaneously hold titles in three weight classes (featherweight, welterweight, and lightweight).

Uncle Mike told Caggiano that his nephew was home from the army and looking for a fight. Caggiano looked Rocky over skeptically and asked him to suit up. After a minute of shadowboxing around the ring, Rocky sat down, winded. Caggiano told him to get up, that he needed to go three minutes, the length of a round. He got up, went another minute or so, and sat down again, panting. Caggiano eyed Rocky's flabby belly, big butt, trunk-like legs, and stubby arms and told him he was too out of shape to fight. But Rocky and his uncle Mike persisted. Rocky needed the money and was confident of his athletic ability. Hadn't he always been the biggest, toughest kid in Ward Two? And being a Brockton boy, Rocky would help fill the seats.

Caggiano, who had trouble drawing people to his Tuesday night shows, said he would like to see Rocky win his first few fights, to start bringing in bigger crowds. He promised Rocky that he wouldn't have to work that hard, that he would find him a soft touch. He agreed to pay him $30 for "expenses," since this was an amateur bout. Fighters who got paid were considered professional and were ineligible to compete in the Golden Gloves, Amateur Athletic Union (AAU), and other amateur showcases so crucial to young fighters. The rule was winked at all the time, with fighters competing under false names and promoters slipping them money under the table. Rocky jokingly called it "bootleg boxing."

Rocky's first fight was set for the following Tuesday, April 16, 1946. Rocky weighed 215 pounds, thirty pounds over the weight he would normally fight at as a pro. The news that week carried stories about the postwar meat shortage, with President Truman saying that most Americans ate too much and that the "hunger diet" was good. But no shortage curbed Rocky's appetite. He spent his furlough loafing around, gorging himself on Lena's rich Italian food, drinking with his friends, and smoking cigars. The night of the fight, he was supposed to be at the hall at eight o'clock. But when he stopped by his uncle Mike's, he couldn't resist helping himself to a big dish of macaroni.

They arrived at the Ancient Order of Hibernians Hall to discover that the easy opponent Caggiano had promised, a novice from Lynn, Massachusetts, couldn't make it. As a last-minute replacement, Caggiano had gotten Henry "Ted" Lester, a tough, experienced heavyweight who had been runner-up in the New England amateur championship the year before. Uncle Mike protested to Caggiano. Rocky, unconcerned, went to the dressing room to change and have his hands taped and gloves laced on, as he had once helped other fighters to do as a boy.

The dim, smoky hall was filled, mustachioed older Italians jostling for position with the Irish, factory workers with supervisors, policemen with politicians, shopkeepers with short-order cooks, young laborers with retirees. In the most anticipated fight of the evening, the scrappy local bantamweight Joe Feroli would face New England bantam champ George Cote of Lawrence, Massachusetts, a factory town north of Boston. Feroli, who was managed by a Brockton fireman, came into the ring wearing a robe given to him by the Brockton Fire Department with his name and the city's name emblazoned on the back.

Two other Brockton fighters were on the card: featherweight George McKinley and heavyweight Rocco Marchegiano, a former outstanding football and baseball player at Brockton High who was "enjoying a furlough from army duties," according to the *Brockton Enterprise*. "Rock," the story noted, had taken an interest in boxing while in the service and would be making his ring debut "outside of an Army camp." The newspaper said that Rocky was unbeaten in six fights in the army, which was either an embellishment by Rocky to convince Caggiano to let him fight or by the promoter to hype the gate.

Ethnic pride and local pride were often at stake in the ring, and this night was no exception. The hall was loud and boisterous, filled with many of Rocky's friends and family—with the notable exception of Lena, who disapproved of his fighting. Rocky's opponent, Henry Lester, was thirty-two years old, a veteran of gritty arenas around New England. A black fighter, Lester had to endure racial epithets and abuse from small-town whites cheering on their hometown heroes. Lester's real name was Hendrik Van Leesten; his father was the mixed-race son of parents from the Dutch colony of Surinam in South America and had met Van Leesten's mother, a Providence native, at the Tuskegee Institute in Alabama. Van Leesten was more educated than most fighters, black or white, having been the first black to graduate from La Salle Academy, a Catholic high school in Providence, in 1932, then studying at Providence College. When he faced Rocky in Brockton, he was near the end of his amateur career, having decided that while he had talent, he lacked the killer instinct to continue and had a brighter future as an engineer.

At six foot two and a rock-solid 187 pounds, Lester towered over the stumpy Rocky as they touched gloves at the start of their four-round match. The raucous crowd cheered Rocky's name. They were happy to see the unbeaten Feroli win a split decision over Cote, but most had come to see Rocky. And at first, they weren't disappointed.

At the opening bell, Rocky charged across the ring at Lester like a man in an alley fight. He swung wildly, high, arcing overhand rights and dangerous-looking uppercuts from down near his ankles. But while his punches looked powerful, most connected with nothing but air. Lester slipped his awkward advances easily and countered with stiff counterpunches that scored points but didn't seem to hurt Rocky or slow him down. He kept coming, like a windmill, throwing punches from all angles, off balance and grunting from his exertions. The crowd cheered "Get him" and "Kill him Rock," and groaned with Rocky when he missed. Lester was smart enough and experienced enough to fight a more tactical fight and conserve his strength, but even he was forced to fight at a faster pace to withstand Rocky's relentless onslaught.

By the end of the first round, both men were tired. In the second round, perspiring freely, Rocky had trouble lifting his arms and moving his feet, but he still stumbled after Lester, trying to land a knockout punch that would send his friends and family home happy. By this point, Lester knew he was in control. Rocky, who had always hated to lose, going back to his days at Edgar Playground, knew he couldn't win. Worse, he was embarrassing himself in front of his hometown fans.

Midway through the second round, Lester had Rocky crowded against the ropes and was pummeling his midsection. Rocky fell back against the ropes. As Lester moved in to deliver a right uppercut, Rocky scissored his knee up into Lester's groin. A loud groan erupted from the crowd. The referee disqualified Rocky and awarded the fight to Lester. There were no protests from the fans, just jeers and shouts of dismay.

The *Brockton Enterprise* described it politely the next day: "Marchegiano, with only six Army bouts behind him, showed his inexperience in the second round when he got excited and fouled his opponent, at which time Referee MacDonald stepped in and awarded the bout to Lester. At the time of the foul, neither of the two were able to gather enough strength to throw a lethal punch, as they had nearly exhausted themselves in the first round."

One of the fight judges that night, Joe Monte, put it more bluntly: "He lost his head, kicked his opponent, got disqualified." Immediately afterward, Monte said, Rocky apologized. Lester was confident that he was dominating the fight and would have won if it had continued. His manager, John Powers, agreed. "Lester was giving him a licking and Marchegiano got excited, made a kick at Lester, and got disqualified," he said. Sned MacDonald, the referee who stopped the fight, put it more succinctly: "The kid just plain kneed him in the balls."

Rocky was humiliated. Years later, he would try to pass it off as an accident; he was so tired that he had slipped, and his foot accidentally came up and caught Lester in the groin. Some of his friends tried to explain it that way, too, but others just smiled as if he had been a naughty boy. Later, Rocky admitted to his brother Sonny that he had kicked Lester on purpose. What was he supposed to do, lose? He was disqualified, he said, but he hadn't lost. He had shown some impressive punching power that awed his old Edgar Playground pals. And Lester hadn't seriously hurt him. He'd simply run out of gas. But as he later acknowledged, "That was my first home-town fight and I lost it."

Lester never fought again and went on to become a nuclear engineer. Rocky, meanwhile, learned an important lesson that night that would drive him for the rest of his career. He would never embarrass himself like that again, or disappoint his family, his friends, or the city of Brockton. He would never be out of shape for another fight. His youngest brother, Peter, called it a turning point.

□ □ □

WHEN ROCKY ARRIVED at Fort Lewis in May 1946, he dedicated himself to boxing. The base sported a strong boxing team, led by four fighters who had won Golden Gloves championships in their home states, including featherweight Sammy Butera, who had won 103 of 105 amateur fights, 100 by knockout.

Rocky was friendly and popular, and he also played first base on the Fort Lewis baseball team. But he took boxing more seriously. He trained hard, lost weight, watched what he ate, and gave up drinking and smoking. He fought five times in the spring and early summer, winning four, three by knockout. He recalled his first fight in front of an army audience. Before the fight, as he and his opponent dressed in the same room, his foe tried to psych him out.

"He was talking in a loud voice about how he was a pro and what he was going to do to me," Rocky later recalled. "He didn't scare me, because I knew I was in good enough condition so he couldn't hurt me. But I knew I could lose, and I wondered what it would feel like to lose a fight in front of all those people."

When they got into the ring, Rocky's opponent was warming up in his corner, shadowboxing, showing his experience. The trainer turned to Rocky and asked, "How many fights have you had, kid?" Rocky told him this was his first. "Well, you look like a good strong boy," the trainer replied. "You got nothing to worry about." Rocky won the three-round fight, by a decision, and was thrilled afterward to see his name in the base newspaper.

Broke and looking to earn a few dollars, Rocky answered an ad looking for sparring partners at a gym in Tacoma. He walked into the gym one afternoon and found himself staring up at Big Bill Little, a towering logging truck driver and promising young heavyweight. Big Bill was six foot five, 225 pounds, and looked like a blond Superman; his nephew had once seen him lift a car with his bare hands to fix a flat tire. Little's manager, a local lumber dealer named Harold Bird, was struck by the contrast between the giant lumberjack and the stocky GI.

"When he gets his tights on and with those short arms, hairy chest and waddling style, he makes me think of a bear," Bird said of Rocky.

They sparred for a few rounds, the bear and the redwood. Rocky couldn't come close to hitting Big Bill, who was in good shape and fast for his size. But he wasn't intimidated and kept attacking.

"Here was a man half my size," said Little, "who showed absolutely no fear and gallons of guts. It was easy to see he came to fight."

In August, Rocky was invited to join the Fort Lewis boxing team that was going to Portland, Oregon, for the 1946 national junior AAU boxing championships. The camp's baseball team was also in a tournament that weekend, but Rocky, for the first time in his life, chose boxing over base-ball.

In a letter home to Conge on August 7, Rocky mentioned his boxing and added, "I'm having the time of my life. I never had so much respect all the officers whether it's in town or camp want to take me someplace." The previous night, he had met "Two Ton" Tony Galento, the brawling ex-heavyweight famous for bruising fights with Joe Louis and Max Baer, and for training on beer. Galento visited Fort Lewis to referee boxing matches held to fill out the team that would represent the base in Portland.

"He told me I should make a living by boxing," wrote Rocky. "But I know better."

The tournament was held in Portland's outdoor Multnomah civic stadium, where the University of Oregon played its big football games. More than one hundred boxers from across the country competed the first night, "an evening filled with flying leather and twinkling stars," as the *Portland Oregonian* described it. The writer was impressed with the well-balanced team from Fort Lewis, which won seven of the first night's bouts.

That was a prelude to the second night, when Rocky knocked out Frederic Ross of nearby Klamath Falls shortly after the opening bell with "an overhand right that would make a Mack truck stop and think again." According to the *Portland Oregonian*, Rocky "came out quickly, measured his opponent, and it was all over." The front page of the sports section featured a photo of Rocky walking back to a neutral corner and Ross lying sideways, stunned, on the canvas. "CRASH!!!" said the caption.

The next day, two opponents stood between Rocky and the national junior AAU heavyweight title. In his first three-round bout, he knocked out his opponent, Robert Jarvis, again in the fight's first minute, again with an overhand right. But in the flurry of punches leading to the knock-out, Rocky landed an awkward left on Jarvis's head and felt a sharp pain stab from his left forefinger into his wrist. He had shattered the metacarpal bone in his left knuckle, driving it up into his hand. His fist was swollen and throbbing. There was no way he could fight in the final, his lieutenant told him. Rocky pleaded with him to fight. A trainer came over and sprayed "something that looked like Freezone on my hand," recalled Rocky. "It turned all the hairs white and then the hand was frozen." His lieutenant told Rocky to go ahead and fight if he wanted it that badly.

In the championship, Rocky faced another fighter from Massachusetts, Joe DeAngelis of Charlestown. DeAngelis had won the New England heavyweight title two years earlier and represented New England in Portland.

The two men had met the first night of the tournament. DeAngelis was eating supper in the cafeteria of an old navy shipyard where the fighters were being fed when the army group came in and Rocky came over and introduced himself, asking if Joe and his group were from Boston. Joe said yes. Rocky looked up at him and said: "You must be Joe DeAngelis. I've been reading about you. You're good. You'll make the finals here, and when you do, I'm going to stiffen you." DeAngelis was startled by the affable GI's bluntness.

Two nights later, as the referee gave the fighters their instructions for the three-round finale, DeAngelis stood in the center of the ring and sized up Rocky. He was five inches shorter than the six-foot-three DeAngelis, and his arms were seven inches shorter. But he was "the most solid, hard, muscular man I had ever seen."

When the bell rang, Rocky charged out of his corner at DeAngelis, like a bull with head lowered. Rocky's hands were like lightning as he bored in with relentless looping rights and lefts. But DeAngelis quickly realized that he was the better boxer. He held Rocky off with lefts, saw an opening for his right, and belted him square on the jaw as hard as he'd ever hit anyone. Rocky didn't even shake his head. Later in the first round, DeAngelis tagged him with a few more solid shots. Rocky ignored those as well and kept moving in, swinging wildly but missing as DeAngelis kept his left arm extended and bobbed and weaved from side to side and backed away. He started to time Rocky's rush, stepping inside his punches and throwing hooks into his body. It was, he said, like "hitting the side of a rhino."

"I've knocked out a lot of men in my day, but never hit anyone so hard or so often as Rocky, but with no result," said DeAngelis. "I was afraid I would break a hand."

Rocky, meanwhile, had never faced a boxer as skilled as DeAngelis, who kept slipping his ferocious punches. And Rocky was struggling to fight with only one good hand. Despite the furious pace that had the crowd roaring, DeAngelis's trainer shouted at him after the first round, "Joe, this guy didn't even hit you once."

Things got worse for Rocky in the second round. After several more wild misses, a fan at ringside started razzing him. Enraged, he walked over to the ropes and shouted at the fans, "If you can do any better, come up here! The kid won't stand still." The crowd was in a frenzy as the round ended. The fans, who had been cheering Rocky, were now pulling for DeAngelis.

Rocky's frustration and wildness grew in the third and final round. DeAngelis, well ahead on points, was cautious, focusing on avoiding Rocky's thunderous punches.

"Fifteen seconds," he heard his trainer yell from the corner. "You won!"

DeAngelis glanced down at his trainer. And that's when it happened. BOOM! BOOM! Rocky smashed him on the top of the head with a left, then a right. Stunned, DeAngelis ducked to one side as the bell rang.

The referee raised DeAngelis's hand in victory. The decision was unanimous. Not for the last time in a fight involving Rocky Marciano, the *Portland Oregonian* described it as a contest between a slugger and a boxer. The boxer won this time, but the slugger had flashed his potential—a relentless style, toughness, imperviousness to pain, and, most important, dazzling power in his fists.

▫ ▫ ▣

THE SLUGGER'S CAREER nearly ended before it could get started. The day after the fight with DeAngelis, Rocky was admitted to Madigan Hospital at Fort Lewis, his left hand throbbing in pain. He needed an operation to repair the damage, but the hand was too swollen. Doctors iced it and placed it in a splint, and put him in traction for a week.

His doctor was Captain Tom Taketa, a Japanese American surgeon who had earned his medical degree at Western Reserve University in Cleveland. Even before World War II, prejudice against Japanese Americans was strong; when Taketa was a medical student, he had to agree to abide by a "non-Caucasian" policy that would require him to leave school if patient objections to being treated by a non-white doctor interfered with his clinical training. Fortunately, this didn't happen. After Japan bombed Pearl Harbor, his immigrant parents were among more than one hundred thousand Japanese Americans and Japanese nationals forced into internment camps by the U.S. government. Taketa escaped their fate by joining the army but was not allowed to serve overseas. Instead, he cared for sick and wounded soldiers at U.S. military hospitals. Early in 1946, not long before Rocky arrived at Fort Lewis, Taketa had his picture taken at the base hospital with a patient and a visiting General Dwight D. Eisenhower. Fatefully for Rocky, Dr. Taketa was on duty when he suffered the injury that could have prematurely ended his boxing career.

Given the severity of the fracture, Dr. Taketa was concerned whether Rocky would be able to fully use the hand again. So the doctor attempted an unusual operation: he drilled into Rocky's left forefinger and inserted a stainless steel pin to anchor the bone fragments together. Then he used a splint to apply traction and gradually move the broken knuckle back into place. Rocky spent the next three weeks in a hospital bed, his left arm in a heavy cast. In late September, X-rays revealed that the knuckle was back in place and showed "almost complete bony union," according to a doctor's notes.

Years later, after retiring from the ring, Rocky credited the doctor with saving his boxing career. "He did a wonderful job," recalled Rocky. "If he hadn't, I'd never have been able to fight again. I wish I could think of his name, so I could thank him."

For Rocky, his boxing days in the army were over, and he spent the fall marking time until the end of his enlistment. In December, Private Rocco Marchegiano received his discharge papers. His dishonorable discharge had been suspended, and he now received an honorable discharge. He was returning to a postwar America that brimmed with optimism but presented uncertain prospects for a twenty-three-year-old high school dropout with a weak left grip and slightly enlarged knuckle, who only knew how to work with his hands but was desperate to avoid a tedious life of manual labor.

On his way home to Brockton, he stopped in Chicago to see an army buddy whose uncle trained boxers. The man, who worked in a small grocery store, had Rocky strip down to his shorts in the stockroom, looked him over, and told him to forget about becoming a boxer. His arms were too short, his legs were too thick, and he was too old. Don't turn pro, the man advised. "You'd get killed."

3

Rocky Mack

IT WAS A COLD NIGHT IN HOLYOKE, MASSACHUSETTS, ON MARCH 17, 1947, as fight fans streamed into the Valley Arena, an old brick gasworks tucked among the canals and long brick factories hard by the Connecticut River.

They came from the paper mills and corner bars and tenement houses, men in rough shirts and work boots, Irish and French Canadians and Poles, eager to cut loose at the weekly Monday night fights put on by the penny-pinching owner, Auriel Renault. They hooted and hollered and stomped their feet, shaking the balconies that looked down on the boxers in the pit below, close enough to almost reach out and touch the tops of their bobbing heads. Cigarette and cigar smoke curled to the sooty rafters.

Irish eyes were smiling, for it was St. Patrick's Day in the Paper City. Merriment rippled through the steepled factory town, from the "Big St. Patrick's Dance" advertised at O'Brien's Ballroom to a performance by Joe O'Leary and his Irish Minstrels sponsored by the Ancient Order of Hibernians.

At the Valley Arena, the featured bout promised a spirited battle between the middleweights Saint Paul, from nearby Springfield, and Tommy "Tee" Hubert of Washington, D.C. The pair had fought to a bloody draw four weeks earlier in a fight that the sportswriters and fans felt Saint Paul had won. Renault had moved quickly to book a ten-round rematch just a few days before, after the lightweight contender George LaRover, a veteran of thirteen fights in Holyoke, had for the second week in a row pulled out of the featured match with Cleo Shans of Los Angeles. LaRover wasn't the first boxer to come down with a fever—the "yellow fever," Holyoke fight fans called it—but a furious Renault filed a complaint with the Massachusetts Boxing Commission, which promptly suspended LaRover. Meanwhile, Renault added another last-minute bout to the card, an opening four-rounder between two young heavyweights making their professional debuts.

The local favorite was Les Epperson, a tough, rangy army veteran from Tennessee who had served in the South Pacific and settled in Holyoke to work in the mills. Epperson and his fans were anticipating the start of a successful professional career. His opponent was an unknown serviceman from Brockton who, according to the *Holyoke Transcript-Telegram*, was stationed at nearby Westover Field.

In an apparent nod to the city's dominant Irish and French Canadian population, Renault gave the Brockton fighter's name as Rocky Mackjeanne and pumped up his résumé. This Mackjeanne was said to have won sixteen of seventeen amateur fights, including a victory over Bob Fuller, the well-known New England heavyweight and son of the former governor of Massachusetts. This fight, however, had occurred only in the promoter's imagination.

A few days later, when the Brockton fighter climbed into the ring, he had shortened his name to Rocky Mack.

Rocky Marchegiano's reasons for fighting incognito were twofold. Most important, he wanted to protect his amateur status. And even though he was fighting in western Massachusetts, two hours from Brockton, he didn't want his mother, who hated the idea of him fighting, to find out.

So in his first professional fight, history's greatest Italian American heavyweight snuck away from home on St. Patrick's Day to a heavily Irish city to fight as an Irishman.

□ □ □

ROCKY CAME TO Holyoke because of his boyhood friend Allie Colombo. One year earlier, when Rocky had come home for his furlough and fought Ted Lester in Brockton, he had reunited with Allie and talked about boxing. Allie had also served in the army and was now a master sergeant at Westover Field. He told Rocky he could help arrange some boxing matches when Rocky got his discharge from the army.

When Rocky returned home from Fort Lewis at the end of 1946, the holidays held the joy of homecoming and family but also an uncertain future. He collected $20 a week in veteran's unemployment benefits and went to the nearby Veteran's Hospital to continue treatment on his hand. Otherwise, he loafed around Brockton with his boyhood friends, trying to figure out what to do.

Enter Alisay Colombo. Because Allie was a little older and more like a coach—the kid who would organize the teams and set up the games—he saw something in Rocky that others didn't. Allie had spent enough hours pitching batting practice to him, watching his drive to improve, his toughness, his heart, and his ability to beat the toughest boys of Brockton in a street fight. If the uncle of Rocky's army buddy in Chicago had seen a loser who would get killed in the ring, Allie knew better. He looked beyond the rough edges and saw a diamond that simply needed polishing.

Allie was still at Westover when Rocky got out of the army. Home on leave, he sat with Rocky on the bleachers in the wintry Edgar Playground and said that he was friendly with a man in Holyoke who knew the local boxing promoter. He would see about getting him a fight. Allie, who had no experience as a boxing trainer or manager, was already dreaming of guiding Rocky to the world heavyweight championship. Unbeknownst to Rocky, Allie would go to the Brockton Public Library and read everything he could find on boxing.

Meanwhile, Rocky talked to Gene Caggiano, the ex-boxer and local promoter who had put him in his Brockton boxing show against Ted Lester. They started working out at the Brockton YMCA. It was "like you teach a baby to walk," said Caggiano. On top of his inexperience, Rocky was limited because he was still recovering from his hand surgery and didn't know if he even could fight again.

By January, he had mended enough to try. He entered a Massachusetts AAU tournament at Mechanics Hall in Boston and fought three times in two weeks, with Caggiano in his corner. He beat Lon Thrasher on January 4 and Jim Connolly on January 11 and then lost a three-round decision on January 17 to Bob Girard, a hulking tannery worker from Lynn. In a replay of his experience with the Fort Lewis boxing team in Portland, Rocky aggravated his left hand in the fight against Connolly but insisted on fighting Girard for the championship six days later. Rocky was raw and off balance, wading in on his opponent, swinging wildly, content to absorb blows while waiting for a chance to land one of his looping over-hand rights. Many of his off-balance punches missed, but enough connected that Girard came away with an appreciation of Rocky's lethal power. Girard said later that he was lucky to have survived.

"There were a hundred guys who might have stayed three rounds with him," said Girard. "But no man in the world was going to beat Rocky in fifteen rounds. Every time he hit you, you saw a flash of light. You either grabbed him or you moved back. Because if he hit you twice, you were gone."

In March, Rocky received a call from Allie at Westover. Allie had a friend in Holyoke, Dick O'Connell, who was involved in the local boxing scene. Allie had talked to O'Connell, who then talked Rocky up to Auriel Renault, the owner of the Valley Arena. A week later, Allie called back to say that Renault had booked Rocky on the St. Patrick's Day card against a local heavyweight, Les Epperson. It was a four-round fight and would pay $50. Rocky had just been hired by the Brockton Gas Company to dig trenches for a dollar an hour, so fifty bucks was good money. Moreover, he hadn't been able to fight since re-aggravating his hand in January; although those fights were amateur bouts, Rocky had been paid $20 for "expenses." The Holyoke fight would be a professional fight, one that Rock viewed as a payday, not a debut. Since he wanted to keep fighting as an amateur, he decided not to use his real name and told few people in Brockton.

On Monday, March 17, Rocky got the day off from the gas company and took the train to Springfield. He had been training for the past few weeks—going to the Y more frequently, running in the park twice a day, and watching what he ate—and he felt confident. Allie picked him up at the train station and drove him to O'Connell's house in Holyoke, where he wolfed down a steak that O'Connell's wife had cooked—rare—and a large green salad. Then, pushing aside Allie's nervous questions about his hand, how hard he had trained, and his strategy for his first professional fight, Rocky excused himself and took a nap.

Early that evening, Rocky and Allie walked into the Valley Arena, a squat brick building on South Bridge Street. At the weigh-in, Les Epperson's manager looked over Rocky in his baggy work clothes and Allie in his army uniform and then looked confidently at his own fighter. Epperson was considered a good pro prospect, with strength, skill, and speed.

Allie whispered to Rocky that his opponent seemed to think he had an easy mark. Rocky smiled but said nothing.

A few minutes before the fight, while a local trainer was taping Rocky's hands, Allie went to Renault to confirm the $50 purse. Renault blew up. The pay for a four-rounder was $35, he said. Who did Rocky think he was, trying to stick him up at the last minute? O'Connell was mistaken if he'd said fifty. Allie complained that Rocky had been promised $50, had given up a day's pay, and had come all the way from Brockton. With the $15 he would have to pay for the required state boxing license, the fight would wind up costing him money. Allie told Rocky to get dressed, that they were leaving. It was too late for Renault to find a replacement, so the two sides went back and forth, the noise from the restless crowd filtering upstairs into the shabby second-floor dressing room. Finally, Allie agreed to accept thirty-five—if Renault paid for the $15 license. Grudgingly, Renault agreed.

Because it was a professional fight, they had to fill out an application for the Massachusetts license. Allie signed as Rocky's sponsor. Not wanting to use his real name, they agreed to put down "Rocky Mack." It might win him a few fans on St. Patrick's Day in a hostile arena.

Holyoke was part of a circuit of gritty New England cities where many of the boxers also punched a clock in a factory. They fought in obscurity for a paycheck, not glory. The New England boxing circuit ran from Portland, Maine, and Nashua, New Hampshire, through Haverhill and Worcester, Massachusetts, and on to Providence, Rhode Island, and Hartford and New Haven, Connecticut. Monday night was Fight Night in Holyoke, no matter if it was Christmas or St. Patrick's Day.

Renault sometimes brought in famous fighters like Beau Jack, Lou Ambers, Willie Pep, and Sandy Saddler. Jersey Joe Walcott fought an exhibition there. Jack Dempsey brought his vaudeville act to the arena several times, afterward playing gin rummy for high stakes with the locals. Joe Louis once refereed a Wednesday night wrestling match. (Wrestling was at least as popular as boxing—perhaps more so—with fans flocking to see such popular characters as the Masked Marvel and the diabolical Russian Count Zaroff.)

Renault filled out his fight cards with local favorites like Bobby Courchesne, Meyer Cohen, Sal Canata, and Danny Buckley. Another popular local fighter was Charles Della Penna, a lightweight who had fought as

Chick West from 1911 to 1921, then went blind from too many blows to the head but retained his wits and ran Chickie's, a bar near city hall. When his son became a fighter—Chick West II—his father tossed him his old boxing trunks and told him not to get them dirty. His grandson, also named Charles, had a brief amateur career and became friendly with Les Epperson, Marciano's opponent that night in 1947. Charles remembered his dad taking him to the Valley Arena, the riotous atmosphere, the locker room with hooks on the walls and the brothers who circled the ring between fights, taking bets. He remembered eying a tough-looking blond boxer from Canada with a pug nose who was going to fight Bobby Courchesne and saying to his father, "Oooh, he looks tough. He's gonna win."

"Nah," his father replied. "He looks that way because he's taken a lot of beatings. When a fighter looks like that, he ain't good. He's a bum."

Sure enough, the Canadian lost.

The crowd of twelve hundred was just settling into its seats when Les Epperson and Rocky Mack were introduced for the evening's first bout. Epperson, the local hero, received a rousing ovation. When Rocky climbed between the ropes, there was a smattering of applause from Dick O'Connell and his friends.

The bell clanged, and the fighters rushed from their corners swinging wildly, to the crowd's delight. Epperson was the more skillful boxer, with a crisp left jab that he repeatedly popped Rocky in the face with, countering his opponent's wild haymakers. Rocky was missing often, exposing himself to Epperson's punches. But his opponent wasn't hurting him. Then Rocky started connecting with rights to Epperson's body and head. Late in the second round, the momentum shifted as Rocky worked successfully on Epperson's body and then hit him with a few solid rights to the jaw. The crowd roared its approval.

Forty-two seconds into the third round, as Epperson tried to force Rocky against the ropes, his shorter opponent unleashed a right uppercut that seemed to explode from his shoe tops. He struck Epperson square on the jaw, sending him crashing to the canvas. The crowd now cheered for Rocky as the referee counted Epperson out. As Epperson later told Charlie Della Penna, Chickie West's grandson, "I remember the first two rounds, but not the third. I never, ever been hit so hard."

"No one knew this Rocky guy," Charlie later recalled. "Les thought it was a sure thing. He was already looking ahead. He told me, 'Yeah, I thought about being champion.' The crowd was excited for Les. Then the bell rang."

Epperson would later say that he would have had a chance had he fought Rocky again. He had, after all, held the advantage through the first two rounds. But there was no rematch. Epperson never fought professionally again.

Grinning through his sore and puffy face, Rocky had the tape cut off his hands as Allie praised his performance. His joy was short-lived. While Rocky changed into his street clothes, Allie went downstairs to the box office to collect the $35 purse. The cashier handed him a twenty-dollar bill. Protesting, Allie shoved the bill back and said it wasn't right. The cashier told him that the pay was thirty-five, but he was taking out fifteen for the license.

Allie stormed back to the locker room and told Rocky, who also got mad. When Renault saw how upset they were, he excused himself and returned with two Holyoke police officers. The police told Allie and Rocky they'd better leave. Allie protested that he had given the twenty back. They told him to get it and get out. Allie returned to the box office and told the cashier that Renault had approved the thirty-five. Without checking, the cashier gave Allie the money.

Allie hurried back to the locker room, where he had to coax Rocky, still arguing with the police, to leave quickly. Outside, Rocky's grin returned as Allie told him he had gotten their money.

They celebrated that night at a local bar with O'Connell and his friends. Flush with victory, Rocky bought drinks for the fight crowd. With all the money Rocky had shelled out, he had barely broken even. In the future, as the stakes grew larger, he would not throw his money away so freely.

Allie spoke excitedly about what Rocky could accomplish in the ring, but Rocky was noncommittal. Boxing was a brutal business. His hand hurt. The promoter had tried to screw him. And his first love beckoned. In a few weeks, he would head off to spring training for a baseball tryout with the Chicago Cubs.

◻ ◻ ◻

IT WAS ONE of those raw New England days at the end of March, when spring still seems like a dream, when Rocky Marciano headed for North Carolina and his shot at becoming a major-league baseball player.

Joining him were three childhood friends from the sandlots of Brockton: Allie's cousin Vinnie Colombo; Eugene Sylvester of the Terrific Three; and Red Gormley, another pal from the Ward Two sandlots. They drove down in Vinnie's battered gray 1939 Buick. After an overnight stop in New Jersey, the four drove nonstop to Fayetteville, North Carolina, where the Chicago Cubs had their minor-league camp. Babe Ruth had launched his first professional home run there in spring training with the Baltimore Orioles in 1914.

Ralph Wheeler, the schoolboy sports editor for the *Boston Herald* and an unofficial scout for the Cubs, had arranged the tryout. Wheeler, a huge Cubs fan, had steered other New England boys to Chicago, including the Cubs' starting shortstop, Lennie Merullo, who had played in the 1945 World Series, and their talented first baseman, Eddie Waitkus, dubbed "the Natural," whose shooting by an obsessive female fan would inspire the famous book and film.

Rocky's bat lived up to expectations in the camp, but his defense was another story. His squat legs and powerful torso made him a natural catcher. But in one of the enduring ironies of his life, the man who would go on to pack the most powerful punch in heavyweight history had a weak throwing arm.

Rocky said later that he threw his arm out and couldn't make a strong throw to second base to catch would-be base stealers. The Cubs had thirteen catchers in camp, including future all-star Smoky Burgess, and only planned on keeping four. Rocky was hitting the ball well; Vinnie Colombo recalled a shot to deep center field that drew the coaches' attention. But he was painfully slow running the bases.

The Cubs tried Rocky at first base, but his defense was poor there, too. One miscue, however, did lead to a memorable hit. One day, Red Gormley recalled, a southern player who was competing for a spot at first base hit a grounder that Rocky bobbled. The player safely reached first, and as the ball skipped away from Rocky, yelled, "Pick it up, you nigger-loving Yankee."

Rocky turned and punched the player in the nose, sending blood spurting everywhere. The manager didn't say a word as the player was helped off the field.

The stress was wearing on Rocky. He didn't smoke, but after a bad practice Gormley would see him puffing anxiously on a cigarette. In the room they shared at a local boarding house, where family-style meals cost fifty cents, Rocky did exercises in bed at night so fiercely that the bed collapsed.

Vinnie Colombo was the first of the Brockton friends to leave, moving on to try out for another minor-league team. Eugene Sylvester, who was pitching well, stuck with the Cubs in the minors. But after the third week, Red and Rocky were cut. As Rocky would later recall, "The coach called me over and said, 'Rocky, you're a good kid and you hustle real good, but a catcher without an arm?' He told me to go home and if the arm got better to come back."

Despondent, Rocky didn't want to go home. He and Red drifted over to Goldsboro, North Carolina, where Tully Colombo—another Colombo cousin—was playing for the minor-league Goldsboro Goldbugs in the Class D Coastal Plain League. They got a tryout, and Rocky got into a few games, but he still couldn't throw. Again he and Red were cut. Desperate, they moved farther south to Macon, Georgia, where they tried out for a team that gave the players day jobs so they could play at night. After a few days, the coach told them to go home.

Still, Rocky didn't want to return to Brockton and face his failure. His thoughts turned to boxing. He asked Red to be his manager and line up some fights down South. Rocky would win, and they would both make some dough. But Red didn't know anything about the fight game. It was time to go home, he said.

Rocky and Red hitchhiked back to Fayetteville, where the Cubs paid for their train tickets home. They rode the rails north, broke and dejected, staring out the window at a bleak future. For Rocky, it felt like the end of his last best shot to escape a life of manual labor and drudgery. He saw himself as the strong kid with little going for him other than his muscles. Now all his strength seemed good for was a succession of dead-end jobs. He wasn't sure what he'd do next.

□ □ □

BACK IN BROCKTON, Rocky discovered that Gene Caggiano had plans for him.

In May, Rocky and his uncle Mike went to see the Brockton promoter, who asked Rocky to participate in an amateur boxing show that he was organizing in Buzzards Bay, near Cape Cod, on May 30. Rocky told him about his first professional fight in Holyoke a few months earlier, but Caggiano said he didn't want to know about it. If anyone asked, Rocky should say he had never told the promoter. Caggiano saw Rocky as a good local drawing card for his amateur shows and promised to pay him as much as he could in "expenses" for the Buzzards Bay fight. Even though the Holyoke fight disqualified Rocky from fighting again as an amateur, including competing in the Golden Gloves, Caggiano told him not to worry; he hadn't fought under his real name in Holyoke. A lot of boxers skirted the rules that way.

By the end of 1947, Rocky was starting to take boxing more seriously. He played on a Brockton all-star baseball team and gave football a try, playing on a semipro team in Boston on Sundays. But once again, he was too slow, and professional football too insignificant, for it to be a viable option.

He continued digging ditches for the gas company, but now he spent more time after work training at the Brockton YMCA. He also worked out at the fire station on Pleasant Street, which had a room on the third floor with a heavy bag and a speed bag. Along with Gene Caggiano, he had an informal circle of advisers that included his uncle Mike; a firefighter named Arthur Bergman, who had been a good amateur heavyweight in Boston; another Brockton boxer named Harry Allen; and the former heavyweight Joe Monte, a Brockton beer salesman and friend of Rocky's father who knew his way around the ring. Monte had fought Max Schmeling in 1928 in Madison Square Garden, losing on an eighthround knockout, and two years later he fought James Braddock in Boston. Now he worked with local fighters and had been the judge in Rocky's fight with Ted Lester in 1946.

Later, another man started coming down to the gym to watch, to offer advice, and to time Rocky on the heavy bag. Lester Cousins was a Brockton police officer, but it was his daughter whom Rocky had noticed first.

Barbara Cousins was a tall, athletic blonde who had swum on the swim team at Brockton High School and worked as a lifeguard at the town pool. Vivacious and quick-witted, she was an only child, a tomboy who grew up accompanying her father to the Saturday night wrestling matches. She was nineteen, five years younger than Rocky, and worked as a telephone operator while living at home with her parents. She and Rocky had seen each other around Brockton but hadn't met.

One night in December 1947, Rocky went downtown to buy a newspaper and ran into some of his friends, who were going to a dance at the Brookville Grange. Rocky was clumsy and avoided dances, but his friends convinced him to go, and there he met Barbara. He was bashful at first; Barbara joked later about how he kept stepping on her feet when they tried to dance. But there was an instant connection. Rocky had had a serious Italian girlfriend before the war, but she had apparently broken it off after he joined the army and went overseas. Rocky was drawn not only to Barbara's beauty but also to her confidence, poise, and athletic grace. He asked her if he could see her the next day, and even though she had come to the dance with another boy, she said yes. That Christmas Eve, he took her to Midnight Mass. They started going steady. Rocky took her to the movies and wrestling matches. She went to his baseball games and fights. Often, he ended his training runs at her family's house.

After the May 30 amateur fight in Buzzards Bay, which Rocky won, he didn't box again in 1947. But as the holidays approached, he decided to enter the New England Golden Gloves amateur tournament, to be held in February. Allie Colombo, who had been discharged from the army, joined his circle of advisers and supporters.

The increased focus on boxing made sense for Rocky, but it didn't make for peace at home. His mother still hated boxing. It wasn't a respectable calling for a boy from a nice family to beat up another boy or risk serious injury himself.

Sonny recalled sneaking out of the house with Rocky to do roadwork or go to the Y, telling a suspicious Lena that they were training for baseball or football. As Sonny recalled, "We really had to lie to my mother for the longest time. And, of course, she suspected that something was up, because she would open up his bag and see hand wrap and boxing gloves. And she said, 'Rocky, are you lying to me?' And Rocky would say, 'Mama, boxing is a good sport to work out in for the other sports. And I'm very strong and it's good for my, my overall reflexes.'"

But as Rocky became more involved, Lena would hear the stories from friends or see a mention in the *Brockton Enterprise*. When she discovered he was training to be a fighter, says Sonny, "all hell broke out when Rocky came home."

Lena confronted Rocky, saying, "You promised me that you wouldn't become a fighter. That's a brutal sport. . . . I don't want you hurt and I don't want you to hurt some other mother's son." She wanted him to be a doctor or a lawyer. He told her he hated school and wasn't cut out for that. Then she would list her favorite Italian entertainers—Perry Como, Frank Sinatra, Dean Martin—and ask, "Well, why don't you become a singer or a dancer?"

Rocky would laugh and reply, "Ma, I can't sing and I can't dance. So sports is what I do best."

With Pierino's quiet support, Rocky continued to pursue boxing. His father went to his fights. But even after it was no longer a secret, Lena refused to watch. Throughout his career, she would never see him fight in person. Later, as he became more famous and his fights were on the radio or television, she never listened or watched. Early on, she made him promise to quit if he ever got hurt. When he came home after a fight, she made him lift up his shirt to show her that there were no marks. It was partly for that reason that he fought in the stand-up style that left him so exposed to body punches, so fearful was he of having his face marked up and upsetting Lena.

Rocky played along but also would question what Lena meant by "hurt." Every time he sparred, he told her, he was going to get some bruises. Or he might get some rope burns on his body. But it was no big deal. If he was ever knocked out, or seriously hurt, he promised to quit. Lena relented. She told Rocky she would hold him to his promise and see how things went.

Barbara, an athlete herself, was more supportive. Rocky confided to her, "If I get into the ring, I might amount to something. If I don't, what will I do the rest of my life? Dig ditches?"

◻ ◻ ◻

THE LOWELL SUN Charities Golden Gloves was a winter happening in Lowell, Massachusetts, the textile mill city on the Merrimack River north of Boston.

The dignified exterior of the Lowell Memorial Auditorium, with its Greek columns and friezes of battles from the American Revolution, gave way to a cauldron of noise inside. The ringside seats were filled with a Who's Who of local society—women in fur coats, businessmen and politicians in expensive suits, uniformed generals and admirals. The Harvard University band would come to play; one regular ringside spectator, Boston Pops conductor Arthur Fiedler, would leap up and lead them. Servicemen from the bustling navy yard in Charlestown, from Fort Devens, and from Hanscom Field in Bedford filled the cheaper seats, along with local factory workers and college students from Boston and Cambridge.

Rich and poor alike screamed for blood once the fights began, giving the place the feel of a large saloon. There were many eager fighters from the ranks of returning servicemen; the tournament organizers ran two buses from Boston's North Station filled with all the boys who wanted to box.

On the night of February 9, 1948, Rocky Marchegiano stood in the center of the ring before four thousand howling fans, touched gloves with a movie-star-handsome ex-marine named Charles Mortimer, and came out brawling. The two slugged it out pretty evenly for the first two rounds. Midway through the third, Rocky fired a straight left hand into Mortimer's gut, then crossed it with a vicious right uppercut to the jaw that sent Mortimer crashing to the canvas, where he remained for the count of ten.

The victory gave Rocky the Massachusetts–Rhode Island heavyweight Golden Gloves championship and propelled him into the New England semifinals the following week. He was presented with a golden glove with a ruby, which he gave to Barbara, as well as a gold medal and a gold-colored bathrobe.

The following week, a large contingent of Brockton fans made the fifty-mile trek to Lowell to see Rocky face George McInnis, the New Hampshire champion, for the New England heavyweight crown. Rocky had won his semifinal match the night before without throwing a punch; his opponent, the Maine champion, didn't show up, apparently because his wife was giving birth. Meanwhile, McInnis had knocked out the six-foot-three Vermont champion in the first round of his semifinal, his eighth straight knockout.

The fight started just past midnight, the Lowell crowd thunderous as the two fighters rushed each other from the opening bell. With McInnis coming in fast, Rocky met him with a solid left jab to the forehead, opening a horseshoe-shaped cut over his right eye. Rocky followed up quickly with five more left jabs at the bleeding cut, forcing a slightly groggy McInnis into the ropes. Then Rocky hit him with a right cross to the head. The referee stepped in to check the cut, now bleeding freely, and stopped the fight after two minutes and eleven seconds.

"Rocco did very well, smart in following up and taking advantage of that first important blow," said Caggiano, who had been in Rocky's corner and was identified in the *Brockton Enterprise* as his manager. "His opponent didn't have a chance for a comeback, not laying a glove on our Brockton champion."

Overnight, Rocky had gone from obscurity to national heavyweight contender in the Golden Gloves championship. He and the seven other weight-class winners in Lowell would compete as the New England team in the Eastern Golden Gloves tournament in New York in March. The *Brockton Enterprise* noted that his success in Lowell also made him a contender for the national AAU championships. A national title would earn Rocky a spot on the U.S. Olympic team in London that summer. Noting his unimpressive debut against Ted Lester a year before in Brockton, the newspaper said that even Rocky's staunch supporters were "stunned by his marked improvement."

"Rocco plans to continue his hard work, and chances are good the Ward Two athlete will make great headway," the *Brockton Enterprise* concluded.

After Lowell, Rocky began thinking more about turning pro. He talked it over with Caggiano.

"I told him I wasn't making any money, and that I would like to turn pro," said Rocky. They talked about Rocky turning pro after the national AAU championships that spring. The timing seemed right, given Rocky's recent success and the sorry state of the professional heavyweight ranks. On the night that Rocky beat Mortimer in Lowell, the reigning champ, thirty-three-year-old Joe Louis, looked listless in a four-round exhibition in Baltimore.

Rocky was due to leave for New York on Monday, March 1. The Friday before, Caggiano brought a contract by his house in Brockton, and Rocky signed it after showing it to his parents, who were grateful to Caggiano for their son's triumph in Lowell. The contract said that if Rocky turned pro within the next five years, Caggiano would be his manager and would receive the standard one-third cut of Rocky's earnings.

The two men later disagreed on the circumstances. Caggiano said that Rocky was insistent, so Caggiano had his lawyer draw up the contract. Rocky said that it was Caggiano's idea. The Golden Gloves tournament in New York would be swarming with professional managers looking for clients, and having a contract would shield Rocky from the more unscrupulous ones and allow him to focus on boxing. As Lena recalled, Caggiano told them that Rocky had a future and the contract was "to protect him; it is going to be a lot of managers after him. He doesn't want to be bothered, he is busy, you know."

It was no secret that Rocky was seriously considering turning pro. One day, a friend of Caggiano's recalled, Rocky talked about turning pro, predicting, "From here on we will be wearing diamonds." But given the timing, it makes more sense that Caggiano, fearing that the New York managers would swoop in, pushed for Rocky to sign with him first. In any event, it marked the beginning of the once-obscure fighter being viewed as a commodity.

Rocky and the rest of the New England Golden Gloves team traveled to New York in style. After a send-off dinner at Boston's Parker House, the team rode the Yankee Clipper train from Boston with their managers and an entourage of sponsors and sportswriters. In New York, they stayed at Brooklyn's Park Central Hotel. Early the next morning, Tuesday, March 2, the team went to the nearby St. Francis of Assisi church to pray.

That afternoon, at the Ridgewood Grove Arena on the Brooklyn-Queens line, Rocky drew as his first opponent Coley Wallace, a light-skinned black heavyweight who was being touted as "the next Joe Louis," both for his physical resemblance to the champ and a string of knockouts. Wallace was the heavy favorite, Rocky the unknown quantity. But Rocky soon had the crowd on its feet with his aggressive style, pummeling Wallace all over his body. Wallace, though only twenty years old, was the more polished boxer, and he adjusted to fend off Rocky's attacks. But while Wallace could outbox Rocky, he couldn't hurt him. The fast-paced, three-round fight ended with Rocky bludgeoning Wallace against the ropes.

When the judges announced a split decision for Wallace, the crowd booed and threw bottles into the ring. According to the *Lowell Sun's* account, "The fans from Brooklyn, Manhattan, Bronx and Queens, who up to the bell time didn't know Marchegiano from a hole in the wall, milled their way from the arena down to the very ropes. . . . They raged for fully 15 minutes in fruitless protest, button holing anybody who looked like an official and at times even threatening violence."

Colonel Eddie Eagan, the New York boxing commissioner, saw the fight and told Rocky that he thought he had earned the decision. Pete Mello, who worked Rocky's corner, said, "It wasn't even close."

Wallace would go on to win the national Golden Gloves heavyweight championship in Madison Square Garden, then turn pro. But his promise never panned out. He only became the next Joe Louis after becoming an actor and portraying Louis in two Hollywood films.

Rocky went home.

On March 13, Caggiano had Rocky back in the ring in Brockton, headlining one of his amateur boxing shows in Canton Hall, a dance hall. Caggiano wanted to cash in on Rocky's Golden Gloves success. Rocky and Allie Colombo hustled to sell nearly six hundred tickets at $1.25 apiece, for which Caggiano had promised them a 10 percent commission. They even helped set up the chairs the day of the show, squeezing nine hundred seats into the tiny hall while the fire marshal blinked.

Rocky gave the sellout hometown crowd what it wanted, a thunderous first-round knockout. As the crowd roared, the fallen fighter's manager said, "That boy Rocky hits like a mule."

After the show, Caggiano gave Rocky a check for $40. Rocky was expecting one hundred, for all the tickets he sold, and was furious. When he complained, he said later, Caggiano shot back that he was lucky to get forty, that he was supposed to be an amateur, after all, and "I was getting too big for my breeches." Rocky handed the check back and said he didn't want anything more to do with him. Later, Caggiano delivered an envelope with $25 to Rocky's mother.

A week later, on March 22, when Rocky fought in the New England AAU championships in Boston, Caggiano was back, asking to work his corner, and Rocky agreed. Rocky won the New England heavyweight championship, but it was a costly triumph. In his semifinal victory at the Boston Arena, he knocked out an evasive Fred Fischera in the second round, but he looked unimpressive and injured his left hand again with an awkward blow to Fischera's head. In the locker room, Rocky flinched when his left glove was removed, Allie Colombo recalled. Even so, Rocky insisted on fighting in the finals later that night and won a unanimous decision over George McInnis, the same fighter he'd beaten in February in Lowell. Using only his right hand, Rocky battered McInnis in the third round, knocking him down twice. Afterward, he smiled at the prospect of a rematch with Coley Wallace and a shot at the national AAU title in April and the Olympics that summer.

But when the gloves came off, Rocky's left thumb was swollen to twice its normal size. A doctor said it was broken and put Rocky's hand in a cast.

He wouldn't be able to use it for four to six weeks and had to withdraw from the nationals, thus missing his shot at the Olympics. Worse, when he reported to work the next morning at the Brockton Gas Company, his boss took one look at the cast and said, "I can't use you like this," and let him go. He was in and out of Brockton Hospital so often with injuries to his hands that one nurse, the wife of his old high school football coach, said, "Oh, Rocky, what do you want to be a fighter for?"

Unable to work and unable to fight, a frustrated Rocky was sitting with some friends late one night at the Waldorf, an all-night restaurant in Brockton. Leo Ball, the boy whose bicycle Rocky had "borrowed" when they were growing up in Ward Two, was in the group; he and some friends had become musicians, and were wearing tuxedos and had their instruments with them after playing a gig. Two large marines at the next table, who had had too much to drink, took note and called them "faggots." Rocky, his left hand still in a cast, walked over to their table and punched one of the marines in the face with his right, bloodying him and knocking him down. The second marine fled up Main Street, Rocky and his friends in hot pursuit. After about five blocks, the out-of-breath marine stopped and took a futile swing at Rocky, who knocked him down with another right. Rocky and his friends returned to the Waldorf and resumed their evening, "with Rocky obviously in much better spirits," Leo recalled.

Still, it was a discouraging time. Rocky was unable to make a living, and he was getting serious with Barbara. In a few months he would turn twenty-five, which was old for a fighter.

But what seemed like the end was actually a beginning. Rocky had fought his last amateur fight. Years later, after he became champ, his old boss at the gas company who had fired him asked if Rocky could get him tickets to see him fight.

"I'll get you ringside," replied Rocky. "You did me the biggest favor of my life!"

4

Suzie Q's Broadway Debut

ROCKY MARCHEGIANO AND ALLIE COLOMBO WERE IN THE MIDST OF A baseball game for their Ward Two team at Edgar Playground when the phone call came from New York.

It was June 1948. Rocky's hand had healed, but he still wasn't working. After he was injured in March and lost his job at the gas company, his relatives and friends in Ward Two organized a fund-raiser to pay his medical bills. While planning the testimonial, the Marchegianos held a family conference in their parlor that included Rocky and Allie, Rocky's father Pierino, his uncle Mike, his future father-in-law Lester Cousins, and Pierino's friend Joe Monte, the respected former heavyweight who had fought Max Schmeling. The topic: mapping a strategy for Rocky to turn pro.

Monte explained that the fight game was as much about connections as talent, and he urged Rocky to go to New York. He needed a big-time manager, with the contacts to get him big fights and protect him from being exploited in a treacherous world of chicanery, double-dealing, and outright stealing that left many boxers penniless and broken down. To survive in the cutthroat heavyweight ranks, Rocky would also need an experienced trainer who could sand away the rough edges. New York was the center of the boxing universe, so that's where he had to go.

At Rocky's Boston AAU fight in March, Allie had met a local trainer named Eddie Boland, who also recommended New York and gave him the names of some managers there. One stood out: Al Weill, the former matchmaker for Madison Square Garden. Weill had managed one of Rocky's boyhood heroes, Lou Ambers (born Luigi d'Ambrosio), to the lightweight title in 1936. Boxing's bible, *Ring* magazine, had named Weill manager of the year in 1940, for getting another one of his fighters, the Chilean heavyweight Arturo Godoy, two title fights against Joe Louis.

In May, Allie got Weill's address out of *The Ring Record Book and Boxing Encyclopedia* and wrote him a letter. Subtracting a year from Rocky's real age, Allie wrote Weill that Boland had recommended the twenty-three-year-old heavyweight prospect. Rocky had just finished competing in the Golden Gloves, wrote Allie, and had been robbed in a fight with Coley Wallace, a fighter he was sure Weill had heard of. Allie said that he had known Rocky his whole life and praised him as a former high school football star and good all-around athlete who was strong, durable, and determined. With the proper handling, Allie wrote, Rocky could win the heavyweight championship. Boland, who was part of Weill's vast network of contacts, had also offered to write the manager.

One afternoon in June, while Rocky and Allie were in the middle of their baseball game at Edgar Playground, Allie's sister ran over to say that he had a long-distance call from an Al Weill. Allie, who was catching that day, ran home in his shin guards to take the call. Weill asked him if he could bring his fighter to New York for a tryout.

❑ ❑ ❑

ONE WAS A ballroom dancer. The other was a barroom brawler. Together, Al Weill and Charley Goldman went on to form one of the most successful partnerships in boxing history.

Weill was the manager, Goldman the trainer. They came of age in boxing's bootleg era, early in the twentieth century, when prizefighting was illegal but still flourished in the back rooms of saloons and private clubs.

After New York legalized boxing in 1920, the pair rented an office in the Gaiety Theatre Building on Broadway and put their names on the door: WEILL AND GOLDMAN, BOXING MANAGERS. Weill was the consummate matchmaker, a shrewd evaluator of talent, and a ruthless negotiator. Goldman was the consummate trainer, a man who had learned to fight in the streets of South Brooklyn and carried the knowledge of more than four hundred fights as a bantamweight etched in the scar tissue around his eyes, his cauliflower ears, his gnarled fingers, and his knobby hands.

Weill was a born showman, a short, jowly, portly, fast-talking, English-language-butchering man with thick, horn-rimmed glasses. He relished the limelight, accepting with equanimity the barbs of the New York sports columnists who delighted in caricaturing him. One favorite sobriquet was "the Vest" or "Weskit King," for his exaggerated tendency to spill soup on the vests he favored to accentuate his sartorial splendor. Envious rivals joked that while the coats and pants did all the work, the Vest got all the gravy. The Vest would simply chomp down on his cigar and tell another story, like the one about his first job in New York, as third assistant to a shipping clerk in a wholesale hosiery factory. "And that's where I foist loined about boxing—boxing hosiery for shipment. I knew every kind of a sock there wuz."

Weill inspired many nicknames, including Avaricious Alphonse, Mitt Machiavelli, and the Most Despised Man in Boxing. Some of that was jealousy. And some was Weill doing what he had to do to survive, and thrive, in this cutthroat business. As one columnist observed, "Boxing will never be the spiritual leader of sports. And Al Weill will never be the spiritual leader of boxing." A profile in *Boxing & Wrestling Annual* said, "He is Hitler, Mussolini, Stalin and Simon Legree rolled into one person"—and this was a favorable piece.

Weill considered himself a father to his extended family of fighters, but whether doting or domineering depended on your point of view. Weill treated his fighters like overgrown children, telling them how to act, dress, eat, and behave. "Never ask a fighter for advice or he'll lose respect for you," he advised.

Alphonse Étienne Weill was born in 1893 to a poor Jewish family in the Alsace-Lorraine region straddling France and Germany and sailed to New York with his father at the age of thirteen. "We came storage," he later recalled, "because the old gent didn't have any sugar."

Weill's homesick father returned to Germany a year later, leaving his son in New York. Weill left school as soon as he could and went to work in the hosiery factory, where he thrived as a salesman until a disagreement with his boss prompted him to quit. Hungry and hustling odd jobs, he wandered one night into a Yorkville dance hall where a ten-dollar prize was being offered for a waltz contest. Weill grabbed a blond woman with a squint as his partner, won the contest, then slipped out the side door with the prize money and rushed to a restaurant to gorge himself. *The Vest gets all the gravy.* The next day, Weill rented a tuxedo for $2 and competed in three dance contests at three different theaters, winning two first prizes and $20. Ballroom-dancing contests were all the rage in the early 1900s, and the roly-poly Weill danced the circuit, excelling at the waltz and the Texas Tommy. He thrived in a competitive field that included a handsome ex-boxer from Hell's Kitchen named George Raft, the future Hollywood movie star.

Weill shared a cheap furnished room in Yorkville with a young boxer named Andy Brown. One night Brown asked Weill to come to one of his fights, at the Olympic Club in Harlem, and handle him in a bout. Weill knew nothing about boxing, but he served in Brown's corner as Brown won. He immediately fell in love with the sport, and started hanging around the fight crowd. Weill met Jack Dempsey when the future champion first came to New York in 1916, and was associated with his camp when Dempsey, who was so broke that he slept in Central Park the night before, broke three ribs in a savage ten-round draw with John Lester Johnson at the Harlem Sporting Club. Dempsey's manager, John "the Barber" Reisler, later made Weill the preliminary card matchmaker at the Harlem club, and Weill discovered his true talent. "It was my destination calling me," he later said.

Still, Weill didn't immediately leap toward his destiny. He kept dancing and hustling odd jobs. In the summer, he worked at the Golden City Amusement Park in Canarsie, on the Brooklyn waterfront, a poor man's Coney Island that offered boxing, performances by a young Mae West, and such attractions as King Pharaoh the Wonder Horse. Standing on a midway paved with clam and oyster shells, the carnival barker Weill cajoled, insulted, and challenged young men to prove their strength to their girlfriends by taking their chance at the "high striker." Pay a dime, ring the bell, win a cigar.

Weill got to know one carny in particular, a small, gnarled, gentle exboxer who ran the wheel of fortune. In the winter, they saw each other again, working a penny arcade in Brooklyn. A few years later, in 1920, the New York legislature legalized boxing. Weill saw an opportunity and secured the second boxing manager's license issued by the state of New York. Not long after, the wheel of fortune spun Weill back into the company of his old pal from Canarsie, Charley Goldman.

◻ ◻ ◻

THE FIGHT WAS a clandestine affair, held in a dance hall behind a tavern in South Brooklyn when beer sold for a nickel. Spectators were brought in two at a time, to avoid attracting attention to a spectacle that was illegal in New York in 1904.

This was how Charley Goldman made his professional debut. He was a scrawny kid of sixteen, five foot one, 105 pounds. His opponent, Eddie "Young" Gardner, was ten years older and a ring veteran. The saloon's dusky, low-ceilinged back room was packed. The bout was scheduled "to the finish," or until one fighter was knocked out. For nearly three hours, Goldman held his own against his more experienced foe. Both men were still standing in the forty-second round when the police raided the joint.

"Cheese it, the cops!" someone yelled. The fighters dropped their gloves and scattered into the night, along with the patrons and, unfortunately, the promoter holding their money. Goldman wondered later whether it was the promoter who had tipped off the cops.

Early boxers in New York had been "shoulder hitters"—members of mostly Irish criminal gangs who worked for Tammany Hall to make sure voters chose the right candidate. After prizefighting was outlawed, corrupt Tammany bosses allowed boxing matches at private clubs. Politicians and the public debated whether to legalize boxing. Critics said it was a barbaric and corrupt spectacle that served no useful purpose in a civilized society. Supporters promoted it as a scientific exhibition of skill well suited to the Industrial Age and Darwin's "survival of the fittest." The glamorous champion John L. Sullivan popularized the sport in the 1880s, winning the heavyweight crown and defending it against Jake Kilrain in 1889 at a secret location in the backwoods of Mississippi that nevertheless attracted tremendous national interest. The *New York Times*, which condemned prizefighting, acknowledged that the fight had aroused more enthusiasm than any presidential election. Eager spectators from all levels of society found boxing matches wherever they could—in backwoods clearings, floating barges, warehouses, and other furtive settings. Gambling and fixed fights were rampant.

Charley Goldman knew none of that history growing up—only that the rough environs of Red Hook, Brooklyn, with its docks, alleys, lumberyards, and tenements, provided a natural outlet for his fists. Born Israel Goldman in Warsaw in 1887, he emigrated to America with his parents as an infant. He was one of the only Jewish kids in the neighborhood, and the other boys would holler epithets and chase him and beat him up. He learned to fight back and "got to love it," fighting often in a lumberyard across the street from his tenement. "Every time my mother saw a kid come out of the yard with a bloody nose she would say, 'Charley's been fighting again,'" he recalled. His classroom education ended in the fourth grade, when a teacher hit him and Charley hit the teacher back. He ran out of the class and never went back. Instead, he left home every morning pretending to go to school, then went to the back of a saloon and fought for loose change.

Goldman found a new classroom, a gym where a new champion, "Terrible" Terry McGovern, trained. McGovern was one of boxing's first heavy hitters, a ferocious puncher who electrified crowds with his early knockouts in an era when matches were long tests of endurance. McGovern's swarming style carried him to the bantamweight and featherweight titles, and in 1900, during a brief window when boxing was legal in New York, he knocked out the lightweight champ in a non–title fight before thirteen thousand people at Madison Square Garden.

McGovern, the son of Irish immigrants, took the twelve-year-old Goldman under his wing, bringing in neighborhood kids to challenge him in the ring. Goldman not only adopted McGovern's ferocious style but also started parting his hair down the middle, like McGovern, and wearing a black derby, like McGovern's, that would become his trademark fifty years later. Goldman watched McGovern bathe his face in brine, to toughen his skin.

After his 1904 debut in the back of the South Brooklyn saloon, Goldman went on to fight more than four hundred times as a bantamweight over the next decade. He fought up and down the East Coast, in New Orleans, in Midwest towns, and up in Canada. Goldman fought one opponent, Georgie Kitson, sixty times. "We fought three fifteen-round draws in Savannah, Georgia, and three in Charleston, South Carolina," Goldman said. "Then we fought again in Charleston and I won and we came north and boxed two ten-round, no-decision contests, one in New York and one in Brooklyn." There was one punch of Goldman's that Kitson never could block, a left hook that followed a jab. After every fight he'd shake his head and say, "I always see the jab but I never see the hook." It was, Goldman reminisced, "a beautiful combination. All combinations are beautiful, but this one is the best." Years later, Goldman would teach it to the boxers he trained.

Goldman became a durable fighter in New York, appearing at the network of private clubs that provided a fig leaf to boxing's legitimacy. Boxing, though illegal, flourished nightly in the two dozen or so "members-only" clubs where Goldman fought, like the Fairmont Athletic Club in the Bronx, which enjoyed political protection from Tammany Hall; the Olympic in Harlem; and Sharkey's, a Manhattan saloon owned by tattooed heavyweight Sailor Tom Sharkey.

A typical review of a Goldman fight, from the summer of 1910, said, "Charley Goldman, the New York bantam, defeated Kid Black in a rattling fast bout at Walden, N.Y., recently. Black put up a good argument. Goldman's cleverness carried off the honors." In a crowd-pleasing slugfest in Savannah in 1909, Young Britt of Baltimore was losing so badly to Goldman that he started head-butting him, whereupon, one newspaper account said, "Goldman dropped his head, covered himself in great style and bored into his man. The crowd roared lustily when the great little scrapper began to rough it." In 1911, Goldman's photo appeared on a boxing card—like a baseball card—issued by Mecca Cigarettes.

In 1912, Goldman fought for the bantamweight title in Brooklyn against Johnny Coulon, putting up a good fight but failing to win. "I stayed ten rounds with Johnny, but I was fighting in a trance," he said. "Any time a fighter meets his first champion, it's bound to have an effect on him."

Two years later, Goldman retired and became a trainer. He was twenty-six years old but had the experience and scars of an older man. His hands were like gnarled knots of wood. His cauliflower ears were a badge of honor in an era when fighters never trained with headgear and went into fights with bruised ears that, after a few punches, sprouted out. Clever fighters like Goldman were more susceptible, because when they ducked a punch, their opponent's glove would brush against their ear, or they'd get caught in a headlock and their ears would get mashed.

Goldman quickly found success as a trainer. In 1914, he steered Al

McCoy, an Orthodox Jew fighting under an Irish name, to an upset victory over middleweight champion George Chip. Following Goldman's instructions to lead with his right and then hit Chip in the belly with his left, McCoy knocked out the champion.

□ □ □

YUSSELL PEARLSTEIN WASN'T much of a fighter. But he deserves a place in the annals of boxing, because he helped bring Al Weill and Charley Goldman together.

By the early 1920s, Goldman had opened a gym on West 34th Street and had begun training fighters. A doctor friend from Boston came by with a big, good-looking kid who had fought in Boston as a light heavyweight under the name Joe Stone. The doctor suggested that maybe Goldman could do something with him. Goldman was intrigued. "Battling" Levinsky, the light heavyweight champ, was about washed up, and, Goldman thought, "You can always make money with a good Jewish fighter."

Goldman sent Stone to the state boxing commission to get his license. Stone came back and said they wouldn't give him one because there were too many Stones. Goldman suggested he try "Joe Bernstein," after one of the first great Jewish fighters, known as the "Pride of the Ghetto" during Goldman's fighting days. But there were too many Bernsteins, too. The commission told Stone he would have to fight under his real name. Goldman asked what his real name was. It was Joe Pearlstein. A name he could work with. Goldman renamed him Yussell Pearlstein—"Yussell is Joe in Jewish"—and concocted a backstory: he was the champion of Palestine, come to America to fight to raise money for his homeland. Goldman dressed Pearlstein in a rented Turkish costume, had his picture taken, and sent the photo to the newspapers, along with a challenge to the reigning light heavyweight champion, Gene Tunney. The challenge was ignored, as Goldman knew it would be, but the national publicity generated offers from around the country. A promoter in Denver offered $750, ending his letter to Goldman, "Can the bum fight?"

Al Weill, who by now had abandoned the dance floor for the boxing ring, wanted in on the Yussell Pearlstein gold rush. He suggested that he and Goldman become partners. Goldman agreed, he said later, because Weill was "a nice fellow and a hustler" and "very smart." They rented the office in the Gaiety Theatre Building and put their names on the door.

Yussell Pearlstein never amounted to much—the *Brooklyn Daily Eagle* reported him taking a "bad beating" in 1923—but Weill and Goldman worked well together. Goldman took a hiatus in 1925 to run a roadhouse in Newburgh, New York, but he found he missed boxing. Weill continued to send him fighters who needed fine-tuning for an important match, and in 1928 Goldman helped heavyweight Johnny Risko stun the future champion Jack Sharkey in Madison Square Garden. Eventually, Goldman moved back to New York and resumed training full-time.

Weill, meanwhile, had become one of boxing's top managers and promoters. He went to work as matchmaker for Mike Jacobs's Twentieth Century Sporting Club, the colossus that controlled Joe Louis and ran championship fights in all the major arenas. Since matchmakers weren't also supposed to manage fighters, Weill leaned more heavily on Goldman. The pair began a run of champions: lightweight Lou Ambers, featherweight Joey Archibald, and welterweight Marty Servo. When Ambers suffered a broken jaw in a crucial fight against Fritzie Zivic, he came to his corner, blood gushing from his mouth, and pleaded with Weill and Goldman not to stop the fight. They didn't, and Ambers went on to win en route to the title. But later, when Ambers was past his prime and wanted to keep fighting, Weill refused to book him another fight, forcing him into retirement, and saw to it that he was financially comfortable.

Jacobs became furious with Weill after the Artful Alsatian convinced him to guarantee Ambers $82,500 for a boxing extravaganza that was a financial flop. Weill, in turn, resented Jacobs for not giving him his fair share of all the successful fights he promoted. The two men parted ways, but Weill and Goldman continued to thrive. In 1940, *Ring* magazine named Weill its manager of the year. "Fighters drop in and drop out," the story concluded. "But the managers—they go on forever!"

Weill didn't care where a fighter came from or the color of his skin, so long as he could fight, possessed courage, and could sell tickets. "Let him be white, black, green, red or any other shade except yellow. That, by the way, does not bar the Chinese."

Pairing fighters to produce an exciting fight and a box-office bonanza was as much art as sweet science, and Weill was good at it. "How do I do it? I jest study the styles," he said. "And after you've studied them long enough, you know which style will beat which and why." He had a shrewd sense of timing, knowing when an up-and-coming fighter was ready for a tougher opponent or when an aging champion was ripe for the picking.

"Nobody, nobody—I know what I'm saying—moves like Al Weill," Goldman said.

Although he eschewed the limelight, Charley Goldman also was highly acclaimed. A *Life* magazine profile described him as "the gnome-like master of boxing skills . . . teacher, disciplinarian, mascot, friend." To call Goldman merely a trainer, wrote the sportswriter Jimmy Cannon, would be "like calling Rodin a stone mason." The morning after a championship fight invariably found Goldman in the CYO gym on West 17th Street, working with young fighters. "The part I like best is starting from the beginning with a green kid and watching him develop," he said. It was "like putting a quarter in one pocket and taking a dollar out of the other."

Endlessly patient, Goldman never raised his voice. He jotted down a fighter's flaws in a tiny notebook, then worked, through constant repetition, to correct them. He became a mentor to a generation of younger trainers, like Angelo Dundee, who would train Muhammad Ali.

While Weill lived with his wife in a nice apartment building on Riverside Drive, Goldman was content in a boardinghouse on West 92nd Street run by a crusty older woman named Ma Brown. Several of Weill's fighters also lived at Ma Brown's, where Goldman could watch over them like a mother hen. His room was decorated with old boxing pictures, including one of him from a 1909 *National Police Gazette*. The room doubled as his workshop, where he mixed his own liniment from egg whites, turpentine, and vinegar. He carried the tools of his trade—liniment, Vaseline, smelling salts, tape, scissors, swabs, tongue depressors, and so on—in a battered black satchel that a grateful fighter had given him, engraved DR. C.G. During a fight, he preferred to have his implements strapped around his waist, for quicker access. The only jewelry he wore was a simple gold ring from his father. "People who wear jewelry get stuck up," he said.

Goldman was an avid reader and gifted conversationalist, and said his secret to staying young was to hang around young people and avoid people his age, who complained about their health and read the obituaries. He dated younger women, whom he referred to as "nieces." "I usually take them to the fights," he said. "I get free passes." Asked if he ever thought of getting married, he replied, "I prefer my life à la carte."

Goldman was sixty years old in the spring of 1948 when a young man in Brockton read a wire-service story in the *Brockton Enterprise* about him and Al Weill and their great success with fighters. One prize had eluded them, though, the most illustrious in sports—the heavyweight crown. That June, a few days after receiving Weill's phone call, Allie and Rocky headed to Broadway, to see if the great manager would help them.

◻ ◻ ◻

AL WEILL'S OFFICE was controlled chaos that June day in 1948 when Rocco Marchegiano walked in.

Weill sat at a cluttered desk by a grimy window that looked out on Broadway through peeling black letters that said AL WEILL PROMOTIONS. The office was dismal and dilapidated. The phone rang constantly. The hangers-on included a *Guys and Dolls* cast of characters ready to do Weill's bidding: Chick Wergeles. Musky Magee. An ex-pug named Young Leroy. It wasn't unusual to walk in as Weill was berating one of his subordinates. "Dumb sucker, how could you put that four-round kid in without asking me?"

Weill was typically blunt when Rocky sat down across from him, flanked by Allie and his uncle Mike, who had driven them to New York. As Rocky later recalled, Allie and Mike did most of the talking, and the conversation went like this:

"Who told you you could fight?" asked Weill, looking Rocky in the eye.

"He won all the fights he's been in," replied Allie.

"How many amateur fights you had?"

"About twelve," said Allie.

"Can you punch?"

"Oh, ho," said Allie.

"Yah, with just the right hand?"

"No, with both hands," said Allie. "He can punch with both hands."

On the drive down from Brockton, Uncle Mike had warned Rocky not to take his eyes off Weill, but he also said that Weill had the connections to take Rocky places, if his nephew played his cards right. In Weill's office, when Uncle Mike started to ask what the manager could do for his nephew, Weill gruffly cut him off. He picked up the phone and called Goldman.

"Charley, I'm bringing down a new kid, a heavyweight," Weill said. "Get somebody ready for him. I want to see him work a couple of rounds. . . . What, you got nobody there? Is Godoy around? . . . Well tell Godoy to wait a few minutes. I want to see the kid work."

Rocky's mind was racing as they caught a cab to the CYO gymnasium on West 17th Street. He was going to get in the ring with Arturo Godoy, who had fought Joe Louis for the heavyweight championship. Twice. They arrived and went up to a large room on the second floor that was a whirl of activity: fighters jumping rope, shadowboxing, hitting the heavy bag, working on the speed bag, and sparring in the ring as hard-eyed older men watched. In the center of it all, Rocky noticed "this little tiny guy."

Charley Goldman had seen a lot of green fighters in his day, but "I'll eat my derby hat if I ever saw anyone cruder than Rocky." That first day, Goldman just had Rocky work out on the heavy bag. He didn't even know how to face the bag. His feet were wide apart, his head too high, and his arms wide apart. "He didn't punch the bag, he swooped down on it," said Goldman. "But he had something, a strong right arm, I could see." Goldman told him to come back the next day.

Rocky, Allie, and Uncle Mike stayed at the Forrest Hotel on West 49th Street, one block south of Madison Square Garden, one block north of Weill's office, and down the street from Jack Dempsey's Broadway Restaurant. Across the street was the famed Jacobs Beach, the sidewalk in front of Mike Jacobs's ticket office that was the geographic and spiritual center of the boxing world, where managers and trainers, promoters and sportswriters, gamblers and wiseguys congregated with has-been, never-were, and would-be fighters. The boxing chatter and deal making often spilled into the lobby of the Forrest, where Damon Runyon, one of Jacobs's original partners, had lived in the penthouse and Bob Hope joked that the maids changed the rats once a day. In the lobby, where prostitutes and other questionable characters lurked, the sportswriter Westbrook Pegler wrote: "There was always some hungry heavyweight sitting in the big fat chair in the corner, squinting down the street at the clock to see if it was time to eat yet. Sometimes it would be an old, gnarly heavyweight with a dried apple ear and a husky voice from getting punched in the neck.

Sometimes it would be a young pink one with the dumb, polite expression that young heavyweights have."

The next day, Rocky returned to the CYO gym, this time for a live workout. Godoy was there, but Goldman put Rocky in the ring instead with one of Godoy's sparring partners, Wade Chancey, a beefy young heavyweight from Florida and a fair prospect who had had about a dozen professional fights. Chancey had fought on the undercard at Yankee Stadium the year before, when Joe Louis beat Jersey Joe Walcott. Before that, Chancey had been a sparring partner for Billy Conn when Conn trained for his second fight against Louis.

Rocky came out swinging clumsily against Chancey, who easily avoided his wind-milling punches and jabbed him repeatedly. Chancey had no trouble hitting Rocky, but he soon discovered that the kid from Brockton could take a punch. Goldman, meanwhile, was busy cataloging all of Rocky's deficiencies. His arms were too slow. His footwork was a mess. He jabbed with the palm of his left glove facing up. He couldn't block a punch. And he was too old; a fighter should be in his prime when he was Rocky's age, not just starting out. (Since Allie had subtracted a year from Rocky's age, Goldman thought he was twenty-three instead of twenty-four.)

When Chancey peppered Rocky's head with punches, Goldman noticed that Rocky put his arms up in front of his face, allowing Chancey to batter his midsection with hard punches. Goldman stopped the workout and asked Rocky what he was doing. Rocky looked surprised. He said that's what people had always told him to do—let the other fellow hit him in the belly until he got tired. It wasn't until later that the incredulous Goldman learned that Rocky had developed the habit to keep his face from being marked up so that his mother wouldn't see any cuts or bruises and make him quit.

"He was so awkward that we just stood there and laughed," Goldman recalled.

Then, in the second round, Chancey let his guard down and Rocky smashed him on the chin with a looping overhand right that staggered him against the ropes. Weill started yelling, "Kill him! Kill him! Let's see you kill him!" Nobody else said a word. Goldman called time; if he hadn't, he said, Rocky might have seriously hurt Chancey.

Afterward, Goldman told Rocky, "Kid, if you done anything right, I ain't seen it." Goldman walked over to another trainer and asked, "Does he look like anything?"

"Any truck driver can knock a guy out if he gets in a lucky shot," the trainer replied.

Goldman didn't answer. He was thinking about that punch. Rocky had done everything wrong, Goldman said later, and "then, all of a sudden, he hit Chancey with a roundhouse right and the big guy went out like a mackerel." Goldman could teach technique, but he couldn't teach that. He had sent many a wannabe kid home for failing his punch test, advising them to give up fighting. A punch, he said, was like a lightning bolt—"the shortcut to the money." Later, Goldman would give the punch he'd seen that afternoon a name: the Suzie Q.

□ □ □

WEILL AND GOLDMAN talked it over. Neither was enthusiastic. They had seen enough to work with Rocky, but not enough to sign him to a contract. They agreed to take him on, Goldman explained, because "he didn't cost us anything."

When Rocky asked Goldman if he thought he should turn professional, Goldman offered him sound advice: "It isn't easy. It's rough. It takes a lot of work, a lot of sacrificing, a lot of bats in the nose. But I think you might be able to do okay. You're a strong kid. That's about all I can say for you right now. You're strong and you're willing. And I can tell that you like it. You've gotta like it, otherwise you just don't belong in it."

Back at Weill's office, Weill told Rocky that he could move into Ma Brown's boardinghouse and train with Goldman. "You'll do everything Charley tells you," he said, "and then we'll get you a couple of fourrounders."

Rocky asked about expenses and told Weill that he wanted Allie to get 10 percent of his earnings. The manager erupted.

"What? Ten percent? Who do you think you're talking to?" shouted Weill. "Nobody has ten percent of my fighters."

As for expenses, Weill said, Rocky hadn't done anything yet to deserve it. Allie responded that Rocky didn't have a job and couldn't afford to live in New York. Weill said he was sorry. He thought for a minute, then asked if Providence, Rhode Island, was near Brockton. It was. Weill told Rocky to go home and train, then let him know when he was ready and Weill would get him some fights in Providence. The promoter there, Manny Almeida, was a friend of Weill's—part of the network he'd built up over the years to prospect for promising young fighters.

Rocky was on his way down in the elevator when Weill hollered, "Hey kid, come back here!" The elevator operator took him back up, and Weill handed him a twenty-dollar bill. Rocky thanked him, and he and Allie went to lunch at the Garden Café. While they were eating they struck up a conversation with another fight manager, Jack Martin, who handled Pete Fuller, the heavyweight boxer who was the son of the former governor of Massachusetts. They told him about their meeting with Weill, and their anger at how he had treated them. Martin asked if they'd signed a contract, and when they said they hadn't, he asked how much they wanted to sign with him. Allie said $1,000. Martin agreed and went to call Fuller. When he returned, he said he couldn't reach Fuller and asked if he could call them the next day. But he never did.

Rocky had been mad enough to slug Weill, if he hadn't needed him so much. For now, he headed back to Brockton with a new sense of purpose. He was going to turn pro. And it looked like he would have Al Weill and Charley Goldman in his corner.

5

Timmmberrr!

PROVIDENCE WAS A GOOD PLACE TO BE AN APPRENTICE.

From the bustling shipyards that built Liberty ships for World War II to the old factories teeming with immigrants, the capital of Rhode Island curled like a fist around the head of Narragansett Bay. Providence was a city of extremes. Old moneyed Yankee descendants of slave traders and mill owners lived in mansions near Brown University while immigrants from Ireland, Italy, Portugal, and France populated the tenement neighborhoods and powered the factories that had driven the Industrial Revolution in New England. In the postwar years, as the middle class left for the suburbs, the shipyards wound down and the factories began moving south for cheaper nonunion labor, Providence became a wide-open town of vice that lived up to its colonial reputation of "Rogue's Isle," a city of hustlers, gangsters, and ward heelers, bookie parlors and brassy nightclubs—Sodom by the Bay. As a boy, Rocky knew Providence as the hometown of Peg-Leg Pete, the one-legged gambler who had come to Brockton every Sunday to run the illegal dice game in the Gamblers Woods behind Edgar Playground.

The great *New Yorker* magazine writer A. J. Liebling had gotten his start as a cub reporter in Providence in the 1920s, and he recalled crowded weekly amateur boxing tournaments at the Arcadia Ballroom, a downtown dance hall. Still, the town had never produced a world champion—not for a lack of aspirants, wrote Liebling, or "for lack of scheming—there were more old fighters around than you could shake a towel at, all saturated with good counsel and looking for a likely young ear to pour it into."

Some of those fighters became strong-arms for the mob, which was entrenched in the Providence fight scene. In 1948, when Rocky launched his professional career in Providence, the local promoter was Manny Almeida, Al Weill's friend and associate. Almeida was also friendly with the ruthless Providence crime boss, Raymond L. S. Patriarca, who was climbing quickly through the underworld's ranks to seize control of the New England rackets. Patriarca's predecessor as New England mob boss, Boston's Phil Buccola, managed local fighters and had a rivalry with a Jewish bootlegger named Charles "King" Solomon, who maintained his own stable of boxers until he was shot dead in a Boston speakeasy. Patriarca was a regular presence at the Monday night fights in Providence, loitering in the back with the bookies and gamblers.

By the late 1940s, Providence was arguably New England's premier fight town. Crowds came out to see local heroes like Ralph Zanelli, who lived with his wife and children in Mount Pleasant and could be spotted working in his yard like a suburban dad, albeit one who had gone the distance with Sugar Ray Robinson and Henry Armstrong. The fans also saw famous out-of-town fighters like Willie Pep, Sandy Saddler, Kid Gavilan, Ezzard Charles, and Jersey Joe Walcott. Sugar Ray Robinson once popped out of the Biltmore Hotel with an entourage that included a midget, a barber, and a tailor and asked a teenage Clark Sammartino for directions to the Celebrity Club, one of the country's first mixed-race jazz clubs and a regular stop for Duke Ellington and Louis Armstrong. Robinson, who was tap-dancing at the Celebrity Club, got into his chartreuse Cadillac and followed Sammartino there, then autographed a picture of himself and invited the boy and his friends to his show. Sammartino, who later became a world-renowned boxing judge, said that Providence had a reputation among visiting fighters. One ex-boxer who fought on the same cards as Rocky told Sammartino that he had been frightened when he came to Providence, because of the rumors of fixed fights.

"You heard that fights were fixed," recalled Sammartino. "In the old days, they used to have erasers on those pencils they used for scoring. There was a different feeling in Providence than somewhere else, because the bad guys were here."

■ ■ ■

FOLLOWING HIS AUDITION in New York with Al Weill and Charley Goldman, Rocky returned to Brockton and started training in earnest. He and Allie became a familiar sight, running through the streets early in the morning. Rocky had gotten engaged to Barbara, who was working as a telephone operator. He saw her one night a week; he'd take her to a show, or just hang out at her parents' house. He always left at 10:00 p.m., so he could be home and in bed by 10:30. He was in a hurry to start making money and to establish himself as a fighter. "Now I was twenty-four years old—although I said I was twenty-three—and I'd never been anything more than an ordinary laborer," he said later. "I guess I realized the fight game was my last chance to better myself."

Within a few weeks, Rocky was ready. Weill arranged with Manny Almeida to get him his first professional fight under his own name in Providence on July 12, 1948.

On the night before the fight, Lena Marchegiano renewed her objections to her son becoming a boxer. Rocky told her gently that he was not going to quit and promised once again that he wouldn't get hurt. Unhappy, she directed her anger at Pierino and her brother Mike for encouraging her son. She reminded Rocky that she would be checking him for marks and bruises.

The featured attraction of the five fights that Monday night at the Rhode Island Auditorium was the Cuban featherweight champion Miguel Acevedo, ranked third in the world, facing Teddy "Red Top" Davis of Brooklyn in a ten-round bout. In the first fight, a four-rounder, Rocky was matched against Harry Bilazarian of Worcester, Massachusetts, the twenty-one-year-old U.S. Army light heavyweight champion in Japan in 1947. Bilazarian had been a sparring partner and army teammate of the highly regarded heavyweight Rex Layne, and his manager had assured him that Rocky was a raw, crude opponent he should have no trouble with.

Rocky was typically unfazed. He arrived in Providence midafternoon with Allie and his Ward Two pal and sparring partner, Tony "Snap" Tartaglia. Snap's sister lived in Providence, so they went to her house after the weigh-in, where Rocky took a nap while she cooked him a steak dinner.

It was a hot, muggy night. A desultory crowd of 993 people paid $1.25 for general admission or $3.50 for a ringside seat. Many had not even arrived when Rocky made his way to the ring for the first bout at 8:30 p.m., the strains of the national anthem from the Hammond organ used for hockey games echoing off the empty chairs. Rocky's seconds were Allie and Snap. Because they had little ring experience, Almeida grabbed a local manager to tape Rocky's hands and be in his corner.

Bilazarian bolted out of his corner at the opening bell and swarmed Rocky, who easily avoided his punches and countered with some fierce shots to his midsection. Less than a minute into the fight, Rocky used a right cross to send Bilazarian crashing to the canvas. He stumbled to his feet at the count of nine but was an easy target for a barrage of hooks and jabs to the body before Rocky leveled him again with another smashing right to the head. Bilazarian landed on his back and rolled over on his face. The referee didn't even bother to count; he called the fight after one minute and thirty-two seconds.

As Bilazarian later recalled: "The first time he knocked me down, he broke my tooth. When I got up, I was afraid I'd swallow it. Then he knocked me down again. Then I don't remember anything."

Rocky earned $40. When he went home, he was able to show his mother that he didn't have a scratch on him. He was eager to keep fighting, and Almeida obliged. One week later, Rocky beat another journeyman, John Edwards of Hartford, knocking him out with an overhand right just one minute and nineteen seconds after the opening bell.

People still weren't paying him that much attention. The big excitement the night he beat Edwards was the professional debut of the lightweight Georgie Araujo, a Cape Verdean fighter from Providence's Portuguese Fox Point neighborhood, who had built a large following during a successful amateur career. The *Providence Journal* noted that Rocky was "regarded as a good prospect" managed by Al Weill. But neither Weill nor Goldman had seen Rocky fight an actual match.

That fact irritated the Boston promoter Sam Silverman, who worked closely with Almeida on his Providence fight cards but, like many rival promoters, intensely disliked Weill. Silverman had seen Rocky's first two fights in Providence and was unimpressed. When Rocky had his third fight, on August 9, Silverman tried to do a favor for a friend in Boston who was grooming a rising young fighter named Bobby Quinn. Quinn had fifteen victories in sixteen fights, fourteen by knockout. Silverman matched him against Rocky, figuring to help advance Quinn and also stick it to Weill and his overhyped new heavyweight.

The first round was uneventful, as Rocky came out warily against the hard-hitting Quinn. In the second round, the more seasoned Quinn dominated with a series of sharp left hooks and powerful rights to Rocky's body that had the crowd of 1,321 cheering. When the bell opened the third round, Quinn rushed in for the kill—and directly into a powerful right that Rocky launched from his knees and connected with a crunch on the side of Quinn's head. He went down twenty-two seconds into the round, and Rocky had his third straight knockout. The crowd was stunned, then electrified. That punch had been a revelation. That night, a star was born.

Silverman was furious. Quinn hadn't been in shape, he reasoned, and had still dominated his clumsy opponent until Rocky caught him with a lucky punch. Silverman sought to correct things when Rocky fought again two weeks later. This time, he sent Almeida an unbeaten young heavyweight from Montreal named Eddie Ross, who had twenty-five straight wins—twenty-three by knockout. Ross, who had been fighting for Silverman in New Bedford, Massachusetts, was the man to take down this oafish fighter from Brockton.

The fight lasted just one minute and three seconds. That's when Rocky caught Ross with a murderous right high to his head that sent his mouthpiece flying out of the ring and sliced open his skull, a cut that required two stitches to close. Ross was out cold before he hit the canvas.

"He is unquestionably one of the hardest hitters to show here in many a year and his punching power really has awed local audiences," the *Providence Journal* said. "He still is crude and awkward and frequently he gets caught with sucker punches, but when he lands brother, that's all there is!" The newspaper went on to say that promoters were "clamoring for his services" and predicted that Weill would bring him along carefully.

What the sportswriters didn't realize was that Weill had barely noticed. Almeida tried to reassure Rocky and Allie that he had spoken to Weill on the phone and that the manager was enthusiastic. But they had heard nothing directly, and nobody from New York had come up to see him fight. They were living off Allie's savings from the army and Rocky's forty-dollar purses, and they were itching to get bigger, more lucrative fights. Rocky's naïveté was evident when he enthusiastically approached Silverman after the Ross win and said he could sell a lot of extra tickets to his fans in Brockton, just as he had for Gene Caggiano's amateur shows. "How about letting me try and cutting me in for half of everything I sell?" he proposed. Joe Dow, a fight manager and ex-bantamweight who was standing with Silverman, looked at Rocky and said, "Hey, this guy is a lawyer." Silverman hid his surprise and responded, "Just keep fighting, kid, and don't worry about money." He didn't report Rocky's offer to Weill.

Rocky didn't know where his young career was headed, but Allie later said he had only one goal from the very start, as improbable as it seemed: the world heavyweight championship. With Joe Louis's impending retirement, the *Providence Journal* observed, the New York promoter Mike Jacobs had "failed miserably" in his efforts to develop new fighters. "The lack of talent is viewed with alarm by matchmakers throughout the nation," the *Providence Journal* said. "There isn't a promising young heavyweight in sight."

On the day Rocky knocked out Ross, his old amateur manager, Gene Caggiano, sued Rocky for breach of contract in Plymouth County Superior Court. Rocky had lost faith in Caggiano after their dispute in the spring, when Rocky and Allie felt the promoter had shortchanged them on his amateur show in Brockton. When Caggiano discovered that Rocky had turned pro, he said in his complaint, he called Rocky to remind him of their contract, which Rocky had signed before competing in the Golden Gloves in New York. But Rocky allegedly told him: "Wipe your arse with it. I've got a big wheel for a manager now, Al Weill of New York, and when I see you on the street, I'll bounce one off your jaw."

Rocky denied threatening Caggiano. He said that Caggiano had told him he wouldn't hold him to the agreement and that he had only asked him to sign it so that other managers would leave him alone when he fought at the Golden Gloves in New York. Caggiano asked for a restraining order to stop Rocky from fighting again until the matter was resolved. The judge denied Caggiano's request but allowed the lawsuit to continue, which meant it would continue to hang over Rocky's head.

Others took notice after the Ross fight. Barbara's father, Lester Cousins, knew a wealthy local businessman named Russ Murray, who owned the Raynham Park dog track and had a big estate with a gym and a swimming pool near Brockton. Murray liked fighters; he had built the gym for the Boston boxer Johnny Shkor, whom Rocky would fight a few years later. Murray invited Rocky to train there. Rocky and Allie drove out in the evenings, sometimes bringing Snap Tartaglia or Rocky's younger brother Sonny to serve as a sparring partner.

They finally had their own training camp. But they still needed a trainer. Allie and Rocky figured out training methods as they went along, with ad hoc tips from friends in Brockton. To strengthen his arms and build his endurance, Rocky would get into the pool at the Brockton Y and throw punches underwater for a ten-round simulated fight. Visitors to the Y saw the water sloshing over the sides of the pool. A body builder Rocky met at the Y advised him not to lift weights because it would ruin his flexibility and make him too muscle-bound. It helped that Rocky was a fitness nut—he ate healthy, including lots of greens, and avoided fried foods. He stopped drinking milk and switched to tea after Allie read that milk could sour in the stomach. Tea was easier on the digestion.

Rocky's injury-prone hands could be troublesome. He was frequently hurting them because he hit so hard and didn't know how to punch correctly. Art Bergman, a Brockton firefighter and part-time boxer who punched hard, had a solution. He gave Rocky a heavy bag that weighed 180 pounds—a typical heavy bag weighed 40 or 50 pounds—and told him to hit it with his bare fists to toughen his hands. To strengthen his left arm and break up the monotony of his training runs, Rocky started throwing a football left-handed with Allie. One time, Rocky and his friend Nicky Sylvester walked the thirty-five miles to Providence to visit Manny Almeida. Only when Nicky protested did Rocky agree to hitchhike back to Brockton.

Rocky continued to play baseball for local Brockton semipro teams. He'd play first base for an Italian club team on Sundays, then fight in Providence on Monday nights. One day his friend Vinnie Colombo was pitching when Rocky complained about their third baseman, Snookey Smyth, who liked to fire the ball across the diamond so hard that it stung Rocky's sensitive hands. "So Rocky walks over and says, 'You throw the ball that hard again I'm gonna push it into your face,'" recalled Colombo. "The next time the ball comes to Snookey he picks it up, runs it across the diamond and throws it to Rocky underhand."

Another time, Colombo recalled, Rocky got into a heated argument with a big, burly umpire over balls and strikes after grounding out to end a game. The umpire, who had told Rocky he couldn't hit, tore off his chest protector and challenged Rocky to fight, snarling, "Who's afraid of you?" Someone informed him that this was Rocky Marchegiano the fighter, who had several knockouts. The ump ran to his car and sped away, not even waiting to close the car door.

Rocky was laying a strong foundation in Providence, but he needed someone with more ring savvy to build the house. Fortunately, word of his early success had finally gotten back to Weill, who realized it was time to start protecting his investment—an investment that up to that point had consisted of some halfhearted promises and a twenty-dollar bill for lunch but no written contract or expenses.

After the Ross fight, Manny Almeida told Allie that Rocky was the hardest puncher he had ever seen, including Joe Louis and Jack Dempsey. Almeida then called Weill and told him he might have another Dempsey on his hands and had better get someone up to Providence before another manager stole him away. On August 30, when Rocky next fought, Charley Goldman took the train from New York to see him for the first time.

Allie and Rocky were excited when Goldman stepped off the train in Providence the afternoon of the fight. But Goldman was uncharacteristically gruff and cranky. He had plenty of other fighters to train back home, and he must have questioned if this trip was a waste of time.

Weill arranged for Rocky to face Jimmy Meeks, a large, powerfully built black fighter from New York who reminded Allie of Joe Louis, with whom Meeks had sparred in the army. Meeks, whose last name was incorrectly listed as "Weeks" on the Providence fight card, trained at Stillman's Gym, where he worked out with Sugar Ray Robinson. Weill wanted Goldman to see Rocky against a fighter he knew could move around and handle himself. But Rocky didn't give Goldman much time to study his new fighter. Toward the end of the first round, Rocky nailed Meeks on the chin with a long, looping right that started below his knees, dropping him heavily to the canvas. Starry-eyed, Meeks staggered to his feet at the count of nine, only to be felled again by another crushing right. The referee stopped the fight.

The Rhode Island Auditorium crowd of 1,516 "hailed Marchegiano as the multitudes used to hail Jack Dempsey," gushed the *Providence Journal*'s Michael Thomas.

"If punching power will do it," Thomas began his story for the next day's paper, "Rocky Marchegiano may one day become the world heavyweight champion."

Meeks was also impressed. "He sure can punch and he has the heart. I tagged him with two solid rights. He took them gamely." For the first time, Rocky's picture appeared in the *Providence Journal*, his body taut, gloves down, lunging forward as his vanquished foe toppled into the ropes before him. The headline blared, "MARCHEGIANO STEALS SHOW."

Goldman was less effusive. The fight had ended too quickly for him to judge. Rocky sure could punch, the little trainer said, but he was crude and needed work. Still, he liked Rocky's temperament; he reminded Goldman of his former champion Lou Ambers.

Goldman told Rocky that Weill wanted him to come to New York to train. He could keep fighting in Providence, where he was becoming a crowd favorite, and a strong Brockton rooting section always turned out. But it was time for Goldman to get Rocky into the gym and see what he could teach him. He had a lot to learn, Goldman said bluntly, and he wasn't getting any younger. Goldman rejected Rocky's invitation to get something to eat. He had another kid coming to the gym in the morning, so he hopped on the train back to New York.

◘ ◘ ◘

THE EDUCATION OF Rocky Marchegiano began on a produce truck in Brockton and wound up, after the truck arrived in the predawn hours in Manhattan, at Charley Goldman's workshop in the grimy CYO gym on West 17th Street.

In the fall of 1948, when Rocky and Allie started going to New York, they met two truck drivers from Brockton, one a frustrated boxer named Bill O'Malley, who informed them that the trucks left Brockton every other night at eight for New York and returned to Brockton on the same schedule. He and Allie were welcome to hitch a ride anytime.

Rocky and Allie would arrive at the trucking terminal on West 34th Street at 3:00 a.m., then walk around as the sky over Manhattan lightened. After one trip, Goldman looked them over and cracked, "I hope the cabbages on that truck don't look as bad." Pressured by the controlling Weill, they stayed with Goldman at Ma Brown's boardinghouse, where many other boxers lived, including several from Latin America. Some were on the way up, others on the way down. One hot day, they walked into the CYO gym to find Goldman waiting impatiently. He was amazed to learn that they had walked all the way from Ma Brown's on 92nd Street to the gym on 17th Street. Goldman always rode the bus. Later, the truckers recommended even cheaper lodgings at the YMCA on 34th Street, which was closer to the CYO and also had its own gym. With Weill's permission, they moved there.

Rocky liked it better in midtown, because the streets were livelier. Without much money in their pockets, he and Allie spent hours walking up and down Broadway between 34th and 55th Streets, taking in the bright lights, dreaming of the big time, and watching for celebrities. They often saw the middleweight champion Rocky Graziano hanging out in front of the Forrest Hotel on West 49th Street. They never spoke to him but watched as different guys came up to him and he slapped them on the back. They also liked to walk over to the stage door of the Winter Garden Theatre, where the hit musical *As the Girls Go* was playing, and watch the actresses go in for the show. The women began to recognize them and say hello, which was a big thing for the boys from Brockton.

They were walking up Broadway one day when Allie grabbed Rocky's arm and pointed out Willie Pep, the world featherweight champion. Pep was smartly dressed and had a beautiful young woman on his arm. Rocky and Allie fell in behind, about twenty yards back, and followed as the couple strolled along Broadway, "just to see what happened to these important guys in New York," as Rocky later described. Pep stopped to buy the woman a flower, pinned it to her coat, and kissed her forehead. Then he took her into a theater. Another night, when Rocky and Allie had a little money in their pockets, Rocky wanted to eat at the famous Italian restaurant Mamma Leone's. But they were turned away because they weren't wearing ties. To hell with Mamma Leone's, Rocky said. Someday they would come back, without ties.

At the CYO gym, Charley Goldman began the painstaking process of transforming Rocky from street fighter to rudimentary boxer. Goldman was patient but demanding, soft-spoken but hard-driving, gentle yet intimidating. "I teach him slow, because I want him to feel natural," he said. The former bantamweight thought nothing of putting the gloves on and jumping in the ring to demonstrate the finer points of boxing, his derby perched on his head, his eyes peering owlishly through his horn-rimmed glasses.

"You wouldn't believe that this little man could be so rough in the gymnasium," Rocky reflected years later. "He certainly demanded discipline. He certainly had the patience of a saint."

Rocky preferred brawling during sparring sessions to mastering the subtleties of the sweet science. Once, Goldman ordered him not to spar for five days. He could only work on the heavy bag, shadowbox, and skip rope. When Rocky protested, Goldman said, "You got so much to learn, it ain't funny."

Goldman's challenge, and genius, was to break Rocky of his bad habits without robbing him of his strengths. He didn't believe in a one-style-fits-all approach. Rocky's looping overhand right was so unorthodox that other trainers laughed when they saw it. From its starting point to end point, the punch took so long to develop that, when thrown by most fighters, it would lose its force by the time it connected. More often it missed, leaving the fighter off balance and vulnerable to a counterpunch. Most trainers would have given up or told the fighter to shorten the punch. But Goldman recognized that it was a uniquely lethal weapon in Rocky's arsenal. "Nature gives you them things," Goldman explained. His job was to improve on nature, not mess with it.

Goldman worked to improve Rocky's balance and footwork, giving him the leverage to maximize the Suzie Q's lethal force. He taught Rocky to fight from a crouch instead of standing straight up, to leave him less exposed, and he taught Rocky to attack his opponent's body. Rocky developed a style of weaving in, head low, hands up, which allowed him to get inside a fighter's longer arms, slip under jabs, and crowd his opponent like Goldman's boyhood idol, Terrible Terry McGovern. In an effort to teach Rocky not to spread his legs so far apart, which robbed him of leverage and balance, Goldman tied his shoelaces together. When Rocky forgot, he would trip and fall down.

Utilizing Rocky's thick legs and baseball experience, Goldman showed him how to punch coming up out of a catcher's crouch. It was reminiscent of the instructions Goldman had given the clumsy Arturo Godoy during his 1940 fight with Joe Louis: "Put your nose down like you was smellin' the floor and punch up at the fella." Godoy obeyed and went the distance, losing a split decision.

Goldman spent many hours refining Rocky's punches and expanding his repertoire. He slid a folded newspaper under Rocky's arm to force him to keep his elbow close to his body and straighten his punches; if the elbow came too far away from his body, the newspaper would fall to the floor. Goldman looped a rolled-up towel around Rocky's neck and had him hold each end in one hand as he shadowboxed, teaching him to throw shorter punches. Goldman tied Rocky's right hand behind his back to force him to develop a left hook and a left jab. He taught him to feint, to jab with his left fist palm down instead of palm up, and to keep his wrist stiff when he punched. He showed him how to throw combinations instead of single punches and how to put his knee, hip, and shoulder behind a punch. Goldman preached the value of shadow boxing as the best way to learn, to think, to anticipate. "The punch you throw will take care of itself," Goldman said. "It's the next one you gotta have ready."

Still, Rocky couldn't get enough of sparring. He had some wild, brawling sessions with sparring partners like Cesar Brion and Gene Cooney, a big slugger Goldman had brought in to test his pupil. One day, Jack Dempsey came into the gym with a young heavyweight from Vienna named Joe Weidin, and Goldman introduced Rocky to the famous ex-champ. Dempsey wanted to see if Weidin could take a punch. "Kid, I want you to hit this guy right on the chin if you can," said Dempsey. "And watch out for yourself, because he is a pretty good puncher himself." The pair boxed for a few minutes, and then Rocky hit Weidin on the chin with a terrific left hook that opened up a big cut. Dempsey had to stop the fight and take Weidin to the hospital to get stitched up.

Rocky developed slowly. He remained clumsy and awkward and wasn't going to win any style points. Still, Goldman could see the progress, even if others couldn't, though he wasn't ready to admit that to his student. Rocky soaked up everything and trained with a dedication that Goldman grew to respect. Goldman and Weill deliberately trained Rocky away from the limelight of Stillman's Gym in midtown, where the fight crowd congregated and there were no secrets. Instead, the trainer kept to the relative privacy of the CYO to polish this rough-cut diamond. But in those early days, even at the CYO, "I got kidded plenty for sticking by 'that clumsy, too-green muscle man from Brockton,'" Goldman recalled. "I always said, 'Someday, he's going to surprise you fellows.'"

◼ ◻ ◻

THE RHODE ISLAND Auditorium, an old barn of a building with a leaky roof and, some nights, more rats than people, billed itself as the House of Action.

That was never truer than in the fall of 1948, when fans started flocking to the arena on North Main Street to see the new knockout artist. After Rocky knocked out Meeks, people started paying attention. He scored two more first-round knockouts a week apart in September, then went to Washington, D.C., to fight Gilbert Cardione.

This was the first time that Al Weill was going to see Rocky fight, and Allie Colombo was nervous, wanting his friend to make a good impression. The fight, scheduled for an outdoor arena, had been postponed twice because of rain before it was finally moved indoors. Rocky usually didn't get to know his opponents outside of the ring; and at the pace he was punching, he didn't spend too much time with them in the ring, either. But now, waiting around Washington for the fight, he became friendly with Cardione, a Puerto Rican fighter who was down on his luck. Cardione told Rocky that he only fought because he needed the money, that his father was ill and he had four brothers and sisters to support. When Rocky told Allie that he felt sorry for Cardione, Allie chastised him.

"Rock, you can't feel sorry for anyone like that," said Allie. "He's an opponent, a guy in your way. You got to get by him. He's out there to hurt you."

Allie had no need to worry. Rocky knocked out Cardione just thirty-six seconds into the fight. With Weill screaming excitedly at ringside, Rocky surprised Cardione with a left uppercut that snapped his jaw back and sent him crashing to the canvas, unconscious. Shaken, Rocky refused to leave the ring until Cardione had fully regained consciousness, about ten minutes later.

"I still felt sorry for him," Rocky said later. "After that, I tried not to get too friendly with the other fighters."

Afterward, Weill signed Rocky to a formal contract. Four days later, the young heavyweight was back in Providence, where he scored his ninth straight knockout, stopping Bob Jefferson in the second round. But in the process he hurt his hand—this time his right hand. When he woke up the next morning, the middle knuckle was swollen. It would be two months before he fought again. The layoff was frustrating; Rocky was hungry to fight every week, for the money, and he was in a hurry to advance to bigger-money fights. He was making $40 a fight in Providence, and the $200 he had earned against Cardione in Washington had made him hungry for more. He went back to Brockton to work out and get treatment on his hand from the trainer at the Brockton Y. Wishing he had a whirlpool so his hand would heal faster, Rocky was standing at home one day, watching Lena put laundry in the washing machine, when an idea struck him. He dumped Epsom salts in the washer and stuck his hand in the hot, bubbling water, which helped him heal faster.

Rocky showed no rust when he returned to action in Providence on November 29, 1948. He floored six-foot-five Pat "Red" Connolly of Boston just fifty-seven seconds into the fight. The *Providence Journal*'s Michael Thomas described the knockout punch as "a rapier-like hook to the head." Connolly dropped to the canvas with a thud, wobbled to his feet at the count of ten, and "rocked forward, like a ship in a storm." The referee stopped the fight. Connolly sat down on his stool, the skin under his right eye swelling. The impression of Rocky's glove was pressed into the right side of Connolly's face.

Unbeknownst to his growing legion of fans, Rocky had experienced more action on the way to Providence that afternoon. It was snowing when Snap Tartaglia drove Rocky and Allie, along with Snap's brother and another friend, to the weigh-in. Outside Providence, he lost control of his new 1948 DeSoto on an icy road. The car skidded into the side of an oncoming truck, the front doors flew open, and Snap and his brother George, who was riding up front, fell out. Rocky, Allie, and their friend, sitting in the back, were slammed against the seat. The Tartaglias were not badly hurt, though George had a bleeding cut on his head. Rocky said he was unhurt and insisted on fighting that night, making short work of Connolly for his tenth straight knockout. The crowd of 2,960 gave him a tremendous ovation.

By now, the fans knew him as Rocky Marciano. Previously, his name had been butchered in various ways. The *Providence Journal* had actually listed him as "Rocky Marciano" in his first fight against Harry Bilazarian, then called him "Marcegino" in his third fight. It was back to

"Marchegiano" for his fourth fight. The ring announcer in Providence was having trouble pronouncing "Marchegiano." The referee Sharkey Buonanno joked that the announcer couldn't get the whole name out before Rocky knocked out his opponent. Manny Almeida suggested to Al Weill that they take out the middle three letters and shorten it to Marciano. Rocky, satisfied that the name still reflected his Italian heritage, agreed.

Being an Italian in Providence certainly didn't hurt at the box office. But his punching prowess appealed to all ethnicities. It was electrifying. As Rocky's knockout streak grew, the fans flocked to the Auditorium.

Rocky Marciano soon became the biggest show in town. Thanks to him and Georgie Araujo, the other local hero, Almeida's fight cards started drawing more spectators. Tom McDonough, a teenager who worked various jobs at the Auditorium, including stick boy for the Providence Reds hockey team, recalled boxers slip-sliding onto the ice between periods of the Sunday night hockey games to promote their Monday night fights. After the hockey game, a gang of firefighters would install a wooden floor and boxing ring over the ice, and McDonough would help set up the wooden folding chairs around the ring. When the fights began, McDonough usually managed to grab an open seat near ringside, where he had a prime vantage point to observe Rocky.

"The crowd was always anticipating a knockout—they liked that aggression," says McDonough. "I was enamored. He knocked everybody out."

When Rocky walked by him, McDonough remembers being amazed at how short he was. "I expected him to be bigger than life, but he wasn't. But he was rugged."

McDonough was sitting in the third or fourth row for one fight when Rocky hit his opponent so hard that his head rocked back and his mouthpiece flew out of his mouth—and landed in McDonough's lap. The referee briefly stopped the fight while a corner man hurried over and retrieved the mouthpiece from the gaping boy's lap, dipped it in the water bucket, and returned it to the fighter—who only needed it briefly before Rocky delivered the knockout blow.

Sharkey Buonanno, a tough ex-fighter from Providence who refereed many of Rocky's fights, remembered going in to break up a clinch and accidentally catching one of Rocky's punches on his arm. The arm was sore for weeks. Every time Rocky threw a punch, Sharkey noticed, he stuck his tongue out, like a snake.

Sharkey's thirteen-year-old son, Anthony, went to the fights and sat near the ring with his mother, who each week had to soak Sharkey's shirts to get the blood out. They sat with the other wives of the boxers or managers. Manny Almeida's wife and the Boston promoter Sam Silverman's wife were regulars. Sometimes, Rocky's fiancée Barbara came.

"Mom and I always prayed for a knockout, to avoid the controversy that could come with a close decision that Dad might be criticized for," recalled Anthony. "Often with Rocky, our prayers were answered."

Rocky was becoming as big an attraction as the Ice Capades or the cowboy Roy Rogers and his horse Trigger, advertised on posters that hung behind him at his prefight weigh-ins. Attendance at the Monday fights grew from under one thousand to thirty-five hundred or four thousand. Rocky may have been from Brockton, but the Providence fans quickly adopted him as one of their own. "When he fought, everybody in that building was excited," said George Patrick Duffy, the arena's publicity man. "On occasion, if someone slipped in a right hand and got it through to him, the fans became a little bit concerned. But that didn't last too long. Most of the time, that person was on the ground."

As Rocky's streak of knockouts grew, the crowd learned to anticipate the ending of a Rocky Marciano fight. Rocky would hit a guy, Anthony Buonanno said, and then there would be a delayed reaction—like a tree poised in midair, after a lumberjack's ax has severed its trunk from its roots. Then, gravity would exert itself, and the fighter would slowly topple over. And the fans yelled, "Timmmberrr!"

◻ ◻ ◻

AL WEILL WAS excited about his new heavyweight. In December 1948, he brought Rocky to Philadelphia to show him off.

Joe Louis was about to retire, and he was fighting an exhibition against his old adversary Arturo Godoy. The fight drew seven thousand fans to Convention Hall, including many prominent fight people and sportswriters. Weill got Rocky a spot on the undercard against Gilley Ferron, a huge but undistinguished fighter and Louis sparring partner who, at six foot two, towered over Rocky and outweighed him by twenty pounds. The night before the fight, Weill bragged to Jimmy Cannon, the influential New York columnist, that Rocky was a future champion.

At the weigh-in, Weill introduced Rocky to Louis. The two shook hands. It was a long way from when the teenage Rocky had snuck into the bathroom at the Brockton Arena with Izzy Gold to spy on Louis and the champ had given them fifty cents. Rocky was impressed by how massive Louis was, and by his stylish, expensive clothes. "He looked like a mountain, and he had on a big, beautiful overcoat and a mohair hat, light brown with a nice feather in it," Rocky recalled years later. "I figured that hat alone must have cost $50."

Weill was more agitated than usual that day and interrupted Rocky's regular prefight nap. When the fight began, Weill was in Rocky's corner, a disruptive presence overshadowing Goldman's calm. Rocky, wound up by his manager and the large crowd, forgot Goldman's lessons. He attacked Ferron, swinging wildly at his head and staggering when he missed. After one lunge, he stumbled to his knee. Weill screamed at him to attack Ferron's body, but Rocky ignored him. In the second round, Rocky bludgeoned Ferron into submission, knocking him down three times and ending the fight after slashing open his left eyebrow. But he broke a knuckle on his right hand after landing an awkward punch to the top of Ferron's head.

Weill was furious. He was a laughingstock among his peers and sportswriters, who joked about Weill's new "champeen." Weill told Rocky that he had looked like an amateur. Rocky iced his swollen hand as he watched Louis fight, admiring the champion's style in the ring. As he headed home to Brockton, his hand in a cast, there were now doubts over how far he could go, despite his promising start in Providence.

When he got home, his mother pointed to his cast and pressed him again to quit. Why did he want to hurt people, she asked again. He promised that he would quit if he were ever beaten decisively. Boxing was his life now, he told Lena, and he was going to become famous and take care of the family. Then he gave her the $500 he had earned from the Ferron fight and told her, "I'm your bankroll."

Rocky was unable to fight for three months while his hand healed. When he returned to the ring in Providence in March 1949, he was the headliner for the first time, and a crowd of 3,595 came to the Rhode Island Auditorium to see him face a Boston journeyman named Johnny

Pretzie. Pretzie was never a serious threat, but Rocky once again showed no boxing skill, just brute strength, as he knocked Pretzie down once in the third round and three times in the fourth before the referee stopped the fight in the fifth. Some attributed his lackluster performance to rust. Allie Colombo blamed Weill, who was once again in Rocky's corner; every time Pretzie seemed to be fading, Weill shouted some abusive remarks that would reinvigorate him.

Rocky had become a hometown favorite in Providence, but the fans began to question how good he really was. The debate spilled over into the city's barrooms, and one night led to a memorable tangle between Rocky and a prominent local college student.

Bill Wirtz was a barrel-chested football end at Brown University and the son of Arthur Wirtz, a wealthy Chicago businessman who owned several sports arenas, including Chicago Stadium, Detroit's Olympia Stadium, and part of Madison Square Garden. Besides football, Bill Wirtz also knew boxing. He had trained as a boxer, even sparring with the future middleweight champ Rocky Graziano. In the late 1940s, when Bill was at Brown and watching Rocky box at the Auditorium, his father and a partner, James Norris, were teaming up with Joe Louis to form the International Boxing Club. The IBC would monopolize professional boxing over the next decade, with the help of organized crime, and would hire Rocky's manager, Al Weill, as its matchmaker.

Now, here was the son of one of the men who would control Rocky's fortunes, sitting in the Imperial Café in Providence when Rocky walked in one night with some friends from Brockton. Wirtz, there with some of his Brown football buddies, recognized Rocky from his fights at the Auditorium and started loudly disparaging his boxing abilities. It takes more than a punch to succeed, said Wirtz, and besides, he didn't think Rocky punched that hard. One thing led to another, and Rocky wound up dumping a beer on Wirtz. Undeterred, Wirtz poured a pitcher of beer over Rocky's head. A barroom brawl ensued, as the men's friends jumped in. As Wirtz recalled, "I was hit in the back with a barstool and as I was going down, Rocky hit me with a left hook and I had a contusion for at least six weeks."

Wirtz also recalled that Rocky hit him so hard that he blacked out. When he woke up, he had a bump the size of a grapefruit on his head, and he and Rocky were in adjoining jail cells at the Providence police station.

The two men made their peace. Wirtz told Rocky he respected him and was just trying to make the point that he lacked polish. Rocky had no hard feelings. Wirtz was afraid to call his father for bail, so he had to spend two days in jail before he reached his father's partner, James Norris, and asked him to come from New York and get him out. Wirtz advised Norris to keep an eye on Rocky, telling him, "God, this guy can hit!"

(In time, Bill Wirtz and Rocky would develop a friendly relationship. Two weeks after Rocky won the world championship, in 1952, Wirtz had a son and named him Rocky; Rockwell was a family name, but Rocky Marciano, the new champ, was another inspiration. Rocky Wirtz, the current owner of the National Hockey League's Chicago Blackhawks, said that Rocky sent his mother flowers, with tiny boxing gloves.)

Following his disappointing performance against Pretzie in March 1949, Rocky erased some of the doubts in his next three fights. One week later, he knocked out Artie Donato with one punch, a right to the jaw that landed the fighter on the seat of his pants just thirty-three seconds after the opening bell. On April 11, Rocky stopped Jimmy Walls in the third round, this time with a hard left to the body.

He faced a stiffer test on May 2 in the tough, talented Jimmy Evans, "far and away the best fighter that Marciano yet has faced," wrote the *Providence Journal*'s Michael Thomas. Showing that he could be more than a brawler, Rocky used short, crisp rights and a new left hook to dominate Evans in a fast-paced fight, stopping him in the third round. It was his sixteenth straight knockout.

His progress would be further tested in his next fight, which would be against Don Mogard, a strong, clever fighter from New Jersey who had never been knocked out. Mogard had gone the distance with the young heavyweight contender Roland LaStarza and had fought at Yankee Stadium the previous summer, on the undercard to the Joe Louis–Jersey Joe Walcott title fight. Mogard was a protégé of another heavyweight contender, Lee Savold, who was scheduled to work in Mogard's corner in Providence before heading to London for a match. Savold, no doubt, would be watching Rocky with interest, wrote Thomas, as "it could be that the two will clash one day."

"We sure will step him up if he beats this boy," vowed Al Weill.

Another good crowd of 3,489 turned out to see Rocky fight Mogard on May 23, 1949. But for the first time, the bookies in the back of the Auditorium laying odds on which round Rocky would score a knockout were wrong. Rocky came out as the aggressor, as usual, and continued to look good landing his left hook, which was becoming an important new weapon. But Mogard skillfully evaded Rocky's deadly right hand. And when Rocky's punches did land, they lacked their usual explosive power. "Some of the old dynamite was missing," wrote Thomas.

Mogard frustrated Rocky by frequently backpedaling out of range. And when Rocky cornered him, he seemed to be pressing too hard for the knockout. His feet weren't set and his timing was off. Mogard won the second round, bloodied Rocky's nose in the third, and opened a bruise under his left eye with two sharp rights in the eighth. Still, Mogard never hurt Rocky badly enough to seriously threaten, as Rocky won a unanimous ten-round decision. It was the first time that a professional fighter had taken Rocky the distance. The crowd was not pleased with his performance. Making the night even more disappointing, Savold couldn't make it to Providence to watch Rocky in person.

Rocky was dejected afterward. Instead of chalking it up as a valuable lesson against an experienced fighter, he felt that he should have knocked out Mogard. Allie tried to cheer him up, saying it was a good experience to go ten rounds.

He didn't fight for another two months. That spring, Rocky had begun waking up with a stiff back. Allie first noticed it in the mornings in their room at the YMCA in New York, when Rocky had trouble bending over to put on his socks or tie his shoes. Usually, his back would loosen up after he got moving. It was worrisome enough that Weill sent him to a doctor in New York, who recommended additional stretching. Not long after, a friend in Rhode Island recommended he see another doctor there, who diagnosed a pinched nerve. The second doctor said the condition could take two years to correct but that Rocky should keep fighting because inactivity could cause it to worsen.

That August, while driving to a fight in New Bedford, Massachusetts, Rocky's back was so sore that he asked Allie to stop the car several times so he could get out and walk around. At the arena, as Allie was taping his hands, Rocky had to go outside and walk some more. He was in so much pain that Allie had to hold the ropes apart for him to climb into the ring. Fighting from a crouch because he couldn't straighten up, Rocky knocked out his opponent, Peter Louthis, in the third round with a vicious left hook. Afterward, they went to see another doctor in Massachusetts, who took X-rays and told Rocky he had a ruptured disk and might require surgery. But Rocky couldn't afford to interrupt his career. As Allie remembered, "Rocky simply pivoted on his heel when the doctor told him about possible surgery and walked out, determined to keep fighting regardless of how much it hurt him." They never told Weill or Goldman.

Rocky's back was not an issue in his other fight that summer, against the journeyman Harry Haft in Providence. But there was some behind-the-scenes drama that reflected Providence's unsavory reputation.

Haft, a twenty-four-year-old Jewish fighter from Poland, was even cruder than Rocky, but he had a compelling life story. Boxing had enabled him to survive the horrors of the Nazi concentration camps during World War II, and he pursued a professional career in America, hoping that fame would help him find the girl he had loved and lost during the war.

At Auschwitz, Haft had been rescued from a job throwing gassed Jews into the ovens by a German officer who recognized his strength and turned him into a boxer for the entertainment of the guards. At a slave-labor camp, the Nazis called him the "Jew Animal" of Jaworzno and forced Haft to beat up emaciated Jewish prisoners in a makeshift ring for the Germans' entertainment. As his reward, he was well fed and given sips of whiskey. Once, however, some generals from Berlin who had heard about Haft brought their own prisoner, an experienced, well-conditioned boxer, for him to fight. Facing threats from his own handlers who had bet heavily on him, Haft overcame an early beating and pounded his opponent, a French Jew, unconscious.

After the war, Haft came to New Jersey to live with an aunt and uncle and started boxing professionally. He hoped to become famous, so that his lost girlfriend in Poland would find him if she were still alive. But his career was in a downward spiral when he met Rocky. Haft fought with rage but not much skill. Three weeks earlier, he had been knocked out by the promising young heavyweight Roland LaStarza, his former sparring partner. Haft viewed the Marciano fight as a last chance to revive his career, and he trained hard at Greenwood Lake, in the mountains outside New York. There, he crossed paths with Charley Goldman, who was at the camp training another fighter.

During a conversation one day, Goldman confided to Haft that the Nazis had killed some of his Jewish relatives in Warsaw. Haft, in a striking breach of etiquette, then asked Goldman if he could give him some pointers for fighting Rocky. Goldman looked thoughtfully at the green numbers tattooed on Haft's forearm and repeated them aloud. Then he offered Haft some advice, including how to handle Rocky's punishing body punches, before heading to Providence to prepare Rocky for their match.

It may be that Goldman, sympathetic to a fellow Polish Jew, had offered some commonsense advice, knowing that Haft still would be no match for Rocky. In any event, after Haft arrived in Providence, he let it slip to Maxie Rosenbloom, a former light heavyweight champion who had made a name for himself as the comedian Slapsie Maxie, that Goldman had given him some help. That night, prior to the fight, an upset Goldman came into Haft's dressing room and chastised him for talking. He said that Weill was furious and had called him a traitor.

Later, while Haft sat on the massage table, going over strategy with his manager, three men in suits walked in uninvited. The preliminary fights had started, and Haft had about an hour before the main event with Rocky. According to Haft, the men did not introduce themselves. One told his manager to take a walk, but the manager refused. Then one of the men said they were there "to protect Rocky" and that Haft must go down in the first round. Sitting there in his purple trunks decorated with a Star of David, Haft swore at them. They persisted, threatening him. Finally, they left. Haft asked his manager what he should do. His manager shrugged and asked if he wanted to call a cop. Haft didn't, worrying about his safety if he did. *Not here in America*, Haft thought. *Not over a prizefight.* A short time later, he headed to the ring. As the introductions were made, he searched the small crowd of 1,655 for the three men but didn't see them. For the first time in the ring, he felt fear.

Uncharacteristically, both fighters came out cautiously. In the first round, Haft landed a hard right to the stomach, which Rocky countered with a long right to the jaw. In the second round, the men stood toe to toe and traded punches before Rocky sent Haft reeling to the ropes with another long right to the jaw, then hit him with two lefts to the head that had him groggy at the bell. Rocky came out aggressively in the third, hitting Haft in the head with a left and a right. Haft rallied midway through the round but went down after Rocky hit him with a hard left to the midsection and a short right.

The Providence crowd applauded Haft as he left the ring, appreciative of his valiant effort. In his dressing room, Haft told reporters that Rocky had not hurt him that badly. Angry and disgusted, he never fought again.

Haft's story is impossible to confirm. There are no living witnesses. His account raises several questions. Why would anyone feel it necessary to pressure him to take a dive? Rocky was heavily favored and, as it turned out, dominated Haft. If Haft was threatened, the three men could have been acting on their own, playing their own angle or hedging their own bets. Given the likelihood of a Rocky knockout, the betting action would likely have centered on which round. There is no evidence that Rocky or anyone in his camp was aware.

The culture of Providence invited such speculation and made such a scenario plausible. The bookies and gamblers were thick at the Auditorium. George Patrick Duffy, the venue's public relations man, said that gamblers were always accosting him in the lobby, begging for scraps of inside information. The bookies who operated there worked for the mob boss Raymond Patriarca, who would stand in the back with them during the fights, chewing on a cigar.

"These guys controlled everything—they were respected," recalled Lou Marciano, a Rhode Island man who was no relation to Rocky, and whose uncle was a bookie for Patriarca. "No one knew if someone was taking a fall."

As the knockouts continued to pile up for Rocky, some questioned the quality of his opponents. The nation was hungry for a successor to Joe Louis, and as Al Weill sought to position Rocky as a contender, critics like Jimmy Cannon sniffed that the manager was padding Rocky's record. It was smart not to rush a promising young fighter by matching him against someone too good too soon. But it was also not uncommon for an unscrupulous manager to build up a weak boxer by having him fight a string of stiffs. In cases like Primo Carnera, it was done with the connivance of mobsters, who greased his rise by fixing fights. Some boxers knew they were supposed to lose and that they had to play ball if they wanted to continue to get meaningful fights. After his retirement, the middleweight champion Jake LaMotta admitted what many had long suspected happened frequently—that he had thrown a 1947 fight against Billy Fox in Madison Square Garden in a deal with the mob to assure himself of a title shot a few years later.

Cynical fans reacted with anger and suspicion if a match didn't live up to expectations, if it wasn't competitive, if it appeared that a fighter wasn't really trying, or if a decision went against someone they felt had clearly won. So the forces that ruled boxing had to at least make a show of protecting the integrity of the sport.

In the spring of 1949, the Rhode Island state boxing commission began questioning Rocky's competition and required that it approve his opponents. The commissioners said they wanted to make sure that Rocky didn't face any "soft touches." There's no doubt that Rocky fought some journeymen and club fighters, even some who met the Rhode Island commission's seal of approval. As Rocky kept winning, it was in Weill's interest to see that the streak continued. But now he was starting to face more experienced opponents who could have beaten him.

◻ ◻ ◻

TIGER TED LOWRY would go down in boxing history as the only man to go the distance twice with Rocky Marciano. But it was their first fight, on October 10, 1949, that many felt he won.

Lowry was a crafty, battle-tested road warrior with fifty-six wins and forty-five losses. He was seldom knocked out and had fought draws with two ranked heavyweights, Lee Oma and Lee Savold, and he had gone the distance with another top-rated fighter, Archie Moore. His boxing career was interrupted by World War II, when he became a member of the army's first black paratrooper unit, which served in the Pacific Northwest as "smoke jumpers," fighting forest fires and searching for balloons with explosive devices released by the Japanese. During his army training in Louisiana, Lowry sparred with Joe Louis when the champ visited his base. He refused to let Louis knock him down, thanks to advice from an unexpected corner man, Sugar Ray Robinson, who accompanied Louis on the tour. Louis complimented Lowry and said he had a good future in boxing.

But as a black fighter from New Haven, Connecticut, who fought defensively and lacked a powerful punch or connections, Lowry was destined to the life of a journeyman—a victim of "hometown decisions" that favored opponents being groomed for the bright lights. "I fought all the 'white hopes,'" he said. He once lost a decision in Havana to a Cuban fighter in a fight in which the referee, seeing that Lowry was winning, started hitting him when he moved in to break up clinches. Another time, Lowry appeared to have beaten the light heavyweight champion

Joey Maxim in a non–title fight in Saint Paul, Minnesota. But one of Maxim's managers came to him and said that a loss would hurt the gate for Maxim's upcoming title fight at Yankee Stadium against Sugar Ray Robinson. If Lowry let them change the decision, the manager promised, they would give him another shot for bigger money, maybe at Madison Square Garden. He agreed, but they reneged.

Lowry described being threatened before a fight in Buffalo, New York, against Billy Fox on November 23, 1948, one year after LaMotta had taken a dive for the mob against Fox. The afternoon of the fight, Lowry was told he had to lose the fight and that he had better do as he was told if he didn't want anything to happen to his wife and children. Upset, Lowry left and went across the street to his black-owned hotel, where he confided his dilemma to the bartender. The bartender said that several local black fans had bet on Lowry and that he needed to make a phone call. As he did, a white man with a wide-brimmed hat came into the bar, a sawed-off shotgun under his coat. The bartender sent Lowry to his room; a short time later, a black man who had bet on Lowry showed up with a gun. He summoned three more friends, who served as his bodyguards through the fight. After Lowry won a split decision, they accompanied him to the airport and put him safely on the plane.

Lowry was twenty-nine years old when he faced Rocky in Providence—on his way down, but still dangerous. Michael Thomas described the fight in the *Providence Journal* as the "sternest test" of Rocky's career. Sam Silverman, the Boston promoter who had made the match, still had revenge against Weill on his mind. "I thought Lowry was gonna lick Rocky," said Silverman. "I was disgusted with Al Weill, and wouldn't have minded getting rid of him. Weill wanted too much money. He was getting twenty-five percent of the gate, but the greedy guy wanted thirty. And Weill was looking to get Rocky soft fights now that he thought he had found something in Marciano. But I had to protect my club. . . . A lot of people were talking about how he was being fed setups."

A large crowd of 3,696 anticipated a fast-paced battle as they settled into their seats for the main event. The Auditorium was filled with cigar and cigarette smoke, leaving a haze around the ring pricked by the flaring of hundreds of matches and the glare of the floodlights trained on the white canvas square. The smells of boiled peanuts and steamed hot dogs mingled with leather and sweat.

Rocky was on the attack from the opening bell, but Lowry refused to face him straight on, presenting only his right side and making himself a difficult target. Rocky, fighting from his crouch, kept swinging and missing. Lowry hammered him with uppercuts, but Rocky's superb conditioning enabled him to keep up the attack. Still, Lowry's early blitz seemed to take some of the steam out of Rocky; at times Rocky merely "pawed at his opponent," Thomas wrote. After the second round, Rocky wore a worried expression. To Lowry, he seemed "befuddled and surprised." He had no defense and was struggling with Lowry's style and constant punishment. He stung Rocky with two terrific rights in the first and rocked him with two vicious uppercuts in the second, "either of which would have finished a less durable boxer," wrote Thomas. In the fourth, it seemed only a matter of time before Lowry "would complete the kill." As the round ended, Rocky was on the ropes. Lowry thought that only the bell saved him.

But in the fifth, the fight strangely shifted. Lowry stopped attacking and retreated into a defensive shell. Rocky threw more punches than Lowry the rest of the way but had trouble connecting. The crowd grew restive. Referee Ben Maculan warned Lowry three times to start fighting. "Open up, or I'll toss you!" he yelled in the fifth.

It may have been that Lowry had tired from his exertions in the first four rounds. Or that he was worn down from Rocky's body blows; when he put up his right hand to block a left hook, Rocky hit him so hard on the arm that he almost broke it. Rocky also changed his style and slowed his attack.

Just before the finish of the ten-round bout, Lowry showed some life and slugged Rocky with a right hook that nearly knocked him down. Rocky rocked backward, then regained his balance. As the fight ended, Rocky threw a punch after the final bell and Lowry, aroused, seemed to want to continue.

Even with Lowry's baffling retreat, Michael Thomas and many of the spectators thought Lowry had earned the decision. Thomas had him winning the first four rounds, plus two of the final six. But the three officials awarded a unanimous decision to Rocky. Thomas wrote that Rocky's aggressiveness and constant punching had probably convinced the officials, "but his thrusts lacked sting to be effective. Many should have been discounted altogether."

Surprisingly, many in the largely white, heavily Italian crowd booed the decision. Clark Sammartino, who was there, thought that Lowry had won. Asked what turned the tide, he said, "The judges." George Patrick Duffy, the Auditorium publicist, said, "There were a lot of people questioning whether or not Marciano was the winner." Tom McDonough, the kid who set up chairs and scored good seats near ringside, thought Rocky had lost as well. In his story the next day, Thomas wondered whether Lowry "deliberately had bogged down in his attack." He concluded, "It didn't look good to the crowd, nor to this observer."

Lowry showed no reaction as the crowd lustily booed the decision. He simply stepped through the ropes and walked quietly back to his dressing room, ignoring the pats on the back from people who shouted that he'd been robbed and that the fight had been fixed. He was sitting in his dressing room, a towel draped over his bowed head, still dripping sweat, when a Providence firefighter, Richard Craven, walked in. Craven worked a coveted detail at the Auditorium, checking attendance and monitoring fire safety. A fight fan, Craven was disgusted at how Lowry had stopped fighting.

"Why did you do that?" he asked. "Why did you go down?"

Lowry looked up slowly and told Craven that he had children, and they all liked to eat.

Later in life, Lowry insisted that he had won the fight and that he had been robbed by a "hometown decision" because of Rocky's popularity and Al Weill's influence. He said, however, that there was more to the story. Asked in an interview years later why he had stopped fighting, Lowry said: "I can't answer that question. Some people said I was taking it easy after the fourth round. . . . I can't really say what happened. I never will. Rocky's not here to protect himself. It's not right for me to say what happened. . . . No, it's not right at all." The article also quoted an unnamed boxing official who was at the fight saying that Lowry met shortly before the fight in his dressing room with a representative of Al Weill, who was not in Providence. In the brief discussion, it was made clear that Rocky would win that night.

"Lowry couldn't have won it that night—no matter what happened," the official said. "He was told he couldn't win it. . . . In those days, if you didn't do what you were told you were all through in boxing. Lowry would have never gotten another fight if he didn't follow the instructions."

He made $2,500 that night. In later years, Lowry would not dismiss speculation that he had agreed to lose in return for a guaranteed rematch when Rocky was a bigger contender and the payday would be larger. And in fact, one year later, on November 13, 1950, he would fight Rocky again at the Rhode Island Auditorium, once again going the distance but losing a unanimous decision. This time, he said, Rocky won fair and square. But Lowry's payday wasn't any larger; once again he got $2,500.

Lowry died in 2010, at the age of ninety. He took his secret to the grave.

"I feel as if I was cheated out of my little piece of history," he said a few years before he died.

6

A Good Dream and a Hard Fall

THERE ARE RITUALS IN BOXING TO WARD OFF THE UNIMAGINABLE. Before each of Rocky Marciano's fights, his fiancée would bring his boxing shoes to a priest in Brockton to bless, and his mother would go to church to light a candle and pray, alone with the silence and far removed from the smoky violence and bloodthirsty shouts of the crowd.

Other mothers and sweethearts practiced their own rituals, for the specter of death, unspoken, always hovered behind the hum of the crowd and the bludgeoning of fists into skulls. As Rocky prepared for his first feature fight in New York on Friday, December 30, 1949, eighteen boxers had died that year from injuries suffered in the ring. A festive holiday crowd of more than nine thousand, preparing to ring in the 1950s, piled into Madison Square Garden to see an action-packed card featuring a match between two promising young Italian sluggers, Rocky Marciano and Carmine Vingo. A few miles away, in the poor South Bronx neighborhood where Vingo had grown up, his pretty, dark-haired fiancée, Kitty Rea, waited at the kitchen table in her apartment with a cake she had baked for his birthday. The day before, Vingo had turned twenty, old enough to fight in ten-rounders. Not that his fights lasted that long. He had won sixteen of seventeen, twelve in a row, seven by knockout, and he attracted the same sort of rabid Italian following in the Bronx that Rocky enjoyed in Brockton. Vingo, a happy-go-lucky kid nicknamed Bingo, didn't care about any of that. His eye was on the $1,500 purse, the most money he'd ever seen. He and Kitty had recently set their wedding date for February. He was looking forward to using the money to buy a house in the suburbs, and maybe a nice car like the ones he used to steal and take for joyrides until the police caught up to him and put him in jail. Boxing had been his way out.

There was a code among boxers. As savagely as they tried to beat each other, it wasn't personal. "Boxing was my business," Rocky said, "and no fighter gets pleasure out of hitting anybody else." Although he hid it, Rocky said, fear was always there, "out of sight, somewhere behind you, but if you're not prepared, it pops up in front of you and then you're finished." The bond between fighters didn't eliminate the "competitive animal" that stalked his prey in the ring. Even Rocky's brother Sonny could recall sparring with him, and in a moment of cockiness tagging him with a good shot, only to see Rocky's face change—his eyes flare, his tongue stick out—and the killer emerge until somebody shouted and Rocky snapped out of it before he mauled his younger brother.

Vingo confessed that he sometimes felt sick being in a business "where you were a person one minute and a killer the next." He remembered his reluctance to fight a friend, back when he was an amateur. His manager told him that if he wasn't willing to fight anyone, he might as well give up. The fight began, and Vingo still felt strange about it, but then he hit his friend and trapped him against the ropes, and the crowd sensed his vulnerability and started yelling, "Kill him, Bingo! Kill him!"

"Suddenly I went crazy," said Vingo. "The guy in front of me wasn't my buddy anymore. He was just something I wanted to bring down." Vingo hit him over and over, but he wouldn't fall, pinned against the ropes. Finally, he slid sideways to the canvas. He pulled himself up by the ropes, and Vingo went after him again. This time, he fell hard, like a board, legs stiff, arms by his sides. "He was on the canvas five minutes before he came out of it, and all that time I was thinking I killed him—I killed my buddy. He was my buddy again, see, and I was a human being once more."

To be a good fighter required having "a little of the killer in you," said Vingo. "You can't be afraid of what's going to happen to you or the other guy." Despite the punishment he took in the ring—broken knuckles, a head butt that opened a gash over his eye, an assortment of cuts and bruises that made his face look different in the mirror every day—Vingo was fearless. "Queer Street or blindness or death happened only to guys you didn't know," he said.

◻ ◻ ◻

ONE OF THE few times Rocky was genuinely angry in the ring came in a fight against Joe Dominic, a journeyman out of Holyoke, whom he faced in Providence on November 7, 1949, four weeks after his controversial decision over Tiger Ted Lowry. Dominic was ridiculing Rocky, calling him an amateur. Rocky floored him in the second round with a thunderous right that sent his mouthpiece spinning into the crowd, a punch that Dominic did not remember after he awoke.

That earned Rocky his first fight in Madison Square Garden, boxing's mecca, against Pat Richards on December 2. The main event pitted the young darling of the heavyweight division, Roland LaStarza, against the hard-punching South American Cesar Brion, a member of Al Weill's stable and one of Rocky's sparring partners.

With Louis's retirement, the heavyweight division was unsettled. The twenty-eight-year-old Ezzard Charles had assumed Louis's open title, but he lacked charisma and, as a black fighter, didn't generate much enthusiasm among white fans. Assessing the drop in attendance that year and the undistinguished caliber of the competition, *Ring* magazine observed that "boxing took it on the chin" in 1949. Promoters turned their eyes to a young crop of "white hopes," most prominently LaStarza, a college-educated boxer from the Bronx who was 37-0.

People were also starting to take notice of Rocky's string of knockouts. He fretted that he was on the undercard to LaStarza and Brion, fighters he felt he could have beaten. Rocky took out his frustration on the unimpressive Richards, dubbed "Poor Richards" by his Philadelphia handler, the mobster Blinky Palermo, in a backhanded reference to that other famous Philadelphian, Ben Franklin. Palermo had arranged to get Richards out of jail for the fight, going to court and pleading, "Look, judge, he's getting $2,500 and he ain't gonna get hurt." Richards survived one knockdown in the first round but spent most of the fight trying desperately to clinch with Rocky. Thirty-nine seconds into the second round, Rocky hit Richards with a right to the jaw that dropped him to a sitting position on the bottom rope. The referee ended the fight as the crowd heckled Poor Richards. It was such a lackluster matchup that Jimmy Cannon noted acerbically, "Mr. Marciano's reputation was damaged by the victory." Rocky's win merited just one sentence at the bottom of the *New York Times* story about LaStarza's victory over Brion in a sloppy decision that actually dropped LaStarza's standing among heavyweight contenders.

Back in Providence, fighting before a standing-room crowd of 6,775, Rocky redeemed himself on December 19 with an impressive knockout of Phil Muscato, a respected and experienced heavyweight who had beaten the contenders Lee Savold and Lee Oma and the future light heavyweight champ Joey Maxim. Rocky pounded Muscato relentlessly with overhand rights and left hooks, knocking him down nine times before the referee stopped the fight in the fifth round. The crowd gave Muscato a standing ovation for his valiant effort. The *Providence Journal*'s Michael Thomas was convinced that Rocky was ready for a shot at the title. "The boxing world, at long last, appears to have the smashing, power-punching heavyweight it has sought," he wrote. The ever-cautious Charley Goldman told the Providence writers, "He still needs seasoning, but he sure has come a long way since his first five fights here."

That set up Rocky's final test of 1949, the December 30 match with Carmine Vingo at the Garden. This time his fight would be one of three featured ten-rounders on a card showcasing promising young sluggers. The *New York Times* questioned why it wasn't the main event, given Rocky's 25-0 record, twenty-three by knockout; still, he was one of the biggest "magnets" on the Friday night card. Although Rocky was favored, Vingo, "the durable gladiator from the Bronx . . . has the punch to put the first dent into Rocky's flawless record," the *New York Times* reported.

To hype the card, the International Boxing Club summoned all six featured fighters to appear together on Tuesday, December 27, at the New York State Athletic Commission to be physically examined by the commission's physician, Dr. Vincent A. Nardiello. A newspaper photo showed the fighters (absent one whose flight was delayed) in their trunks lined up before Nardiello, who checked their heartbeats with a stethoscope. The six-foot-four Vingo towered over Rocky. Nardiello pronounced all of the fighters in satisfactory condition.

Vingo had never trained harder for a fight. Boxing, which he had taken up during a twelve-day stay in jail for stealing a car, came easily to him, and as the wins piled up, he became a neighborhood big shot. He bought sports jackets and fancy slacks. He had never owned more than one pair of shoes at a time; now, he owned three. He dreamed of buying a long convertible and watching everyone from the neighborhood swarm around it, stroking it and asking how much it cost.

Vingo met Kitty around the time he signed with a big-time manager, Jackie Levine, and went to his first training camp. She didn't like fighters, but after they started going steady he discovered that it was the fight game she disliked. She begged him to quit. He said he would after he made enough money to start a business. But he was on the way up. How could he quit now? In November, he and Kitty made plans to get married. Vingo asked his manager to get him a big-money fight so they could set a date. Levine arranged for him to fight Rocky at the Garden, the day after his twentieth birthday, in what would be his first ten-rounder. People said that Vingo was being pushed along too fast, that he wasn't ready to meet the more experienced Rocky. But he wanted the fight; he needed the money. He saw Kitty on Thursday afternoon, his birthday, the day before the fight. They made plans to celebrate his birthday, and his victory, the next night. Kitty said she wanted to come to the fight, for luck, but Vingo said no. He had never let her come to any of his bouts, afraid she might see him lose or get cut.

The night before the fight, in his hotel room in Manhattan where his manager had put him to make sure he trained seriously, Vingo had trouble sleeping. Not because he was worried; he knew little about Rocky and cared even less. He lay in bed, already thinking past the fight, daydreaming how he was going to spend his money and the purses to follow. Over at Lindy's deli on Broadway, the sports columnist Jimmy Cannon sat with Jackie Levine. Cannon, who wrote eloquently about boxing but mistrusted it, famously calling it "the red light district of sports," questioned if Vingo was ready for Rocky.

"I had to take the shot," said Levine. "This isn't a kid you can bring along nice and easy. You got to take the shots when they come. I never know when I'm going to see him again.

"Carmine's not a bad kid. He's one of them kids who just wants to hang around someplace. He'd stay up all night just eating peanuts in a bar, one of them kind of kids. I tell him you can't get any place without training. . . . He's a good kid, but he never listened to me before I made the Marciano match. He's going with a nice girl now, and he does what she tells him." Still, on Christmas Eve, Vingo had skipped out on his trainer, and Levine tracked him down watching a card game.

Cannon, in his column two days before the fight, had cynically noted Al Weill's dual role as Rocky's manager and Garden matchmaker; earlier that year, Weill had been hired as the International Boxing Club's matchmaker, giving him more power to boost Rocky's career. Cannon wrote that Weill wasn't going to sanction a contest "which would harm the future of his prize. Movie stars don't get killed in the early reels of movies. Young fighters, who have a connection with matchmakers, aren't belted out the first time they come into the Garden."

"I know all about Marciano," Levine told Cannon. "It'll be a war. But if Carmine nails him, he's going to hurt him."

◘ ◘ ◘

AL WEILL WARNED Rocky that Carmine Vingo was no pushover.

"This guy is no sucker," Weill said. "I'm afraid of it. It's a tough match. But stand up for me this time, and we'll do all right."

At the CYO gym on West 17th Street, Charley Goldman offered his own scouting report: "Vingo's young and tough, and the kid can punch. But he fights flat-footed, and stands up straight. If he don't make no changes, he'll be all right."

At Stillman's Gym in midtown, Vingo's trainer, Whitey Bimstein, warned him about the power that Rocky packed in either fist but said he was susceptible to a good boxer who moved in and out quickly.

Unconcerned, Rocky took his customary prefight nap on the training table in the dressing room at the Garden. Allie Colombo woke him forty-five minutes before the fight.

Down the hall, Vingo was excited but not nervous. The roar of the crowd echoed in the corridor outside as Bimstein taped his hands and put on his gloves. Vingo shot a few punches and danced up and down. "Show him who's boss right away," Levine told him. Outside, a loud roar signaled that the previous fight had ended. Whitey tied the cord to Vingo's robe. Vingo blessed himself twice, then walked out with his manager and his trainer and his other corner man behind him, down the hall, to the six big steps that led up to the floor of the Garden and the crowd beyond.

He climbed the steps and saw the blur of anticipatory faces in the crowd, and that's the last thing he would remember of that night.

The fight was everything the fans could have hoped for. At the opening bell, the two fighters rushed together like two waves crashing into each other. They traded blows at a furious pace, like a pair of lightweights. Rocky unleashed a barrage of punches, capped by a left hook to the jaw, that sent Vingo crashing to the canvas for a count of nine. Vingo popped back up and came right back at Rocky with a fierce desperation, rocking him with a right to the jaw that the crowd sensed had turned the tide. But Rocky answered with another fusillade that had the crowd on its feet, shouting wildly.

The frenzied pace continued in the second round. They stood toe to toe, trading wicked shots to the body, the head, and the jaw, neither man backing away as they moved savagely around the ring. Again, Rocky smashed a left into Vingo's jaw that sent him down for another nine-count. Again, Vingo leaped up, signaled he was all right, and staggered Rocky with a vicious right to the jaw. The crowd went crazy.

Back and forth they raged, the pace never slackening through the third round, the fourth, the fifth, "until it seemed human endurance could stand no more," wrote James Dawson in the *New York Times*. "One or the other must drop from the combination of punch and exhaustion." It was, he wrote, "the best heavyweight action seen here since the rise of Joe Louis."

In the third, Rocky would remember, "Vingo hit me with a right hand and I blacked out but didn't go down. Just fell into a clinch." Later, Vingo stunned Rocky with the best left hook he ever felt. "I didn't see it coming," said Rocky. "It just exploded and I staggered." Later, as Rocky tried to describe what it felt like, he said it wasn't pain—"It's more like a daze. A sort of blackout." Charley Goldman interjected: "You're in a room and the lights are on and then somebody pulls the switch. That's what a real punch is like. But for Rocky, the lights always come on again."

Both men were bleeding, Vingo from a cut over his eye and from his nose. His face was a bloody mask. Through the first five rounds, the fight could have gone either way. Both fighters were weakening from the torrid pace. Rocky was pressing the action, but Vingo fought back fearlessly and ferociously. He staggered Rocky again in the fifth with a punch that sent him stumbling several steps backward. But Vingo just stood there, flat-footed, too winded to capitalize. The moment passed, and Rocky was on him again.

Between the fifth and sixth rounds, referee Harry Ebbets went to Vingo's corner and asked him and his handlers if he wanted to continue. As Jimmy Cannon, sitting ringside, wrote afterward, "The fighter could have admitted his inadequacy and his torment would have ended there." But boxing's machismo code would not allow it. "Men suffer unnecessarily and endure pain because they are too proud to quit. They accept suffering because to avoid it deliberately would be a renunciation of what a fighter is supposed to be. It will touch you when it happens because even point-less courage has a splendor which demeans the spectator who realizes this occurs because he has paid to see it."

And so Vingo went out for the sixth round. By this point he was punched out. Bleeding profusely, he only managed a couple of strong shots. Rocky was also tired, but now he was clearly the aggressor. Vingo couldn't lift his arms to protect himself. His manager said later that he would have thrown in the towel, but this wasn't allowed under New York boxing rules because of the fear of fixed fights. The referee could have stopped the fight but didn't. Rocky moved in for the kill. Midway through the round, he hit Vingo with a short left hook that sent him tumbling onto his back. As he crashed down, his head thumped on the hard canvas. He tried to lift himself up on his elbows but fell backward helplessly. The referee counted to three and then stopped. He removed Vingo's mouth-piece while the timekeeper finished the count. Vingo tried again to get up, then collapsed, unconscious.

By now, the victorious Rocky had left the ring and headed back to his dressing room to nurse his own wounds. Dr. Nardiello rushed into the ring and worked to revive Vingo. He jabbed a syringe with a stimulant, caffeine sodium benzoate, into his chest, but he didn't wake up. Garden security guards carried Vingo on a stretcher to his dressing room, where the doctor worked on him unsuccessfully for another twenty-five min-utes, still unable to revive him. He lay on the table, his snarling breath the only sound in the room. Two other fighters waiting for their matches watched nervously, then moved to benches against the wall on the oppo-site side of the room.

Father Paul Galvin, a Catholic priest from Barbara Cousins's church in Brockton, had come to New York to see the fight. He was headed to the dressing room to congratulate Rocky, but Garden staff intercepted him and rushed him into Vingo's dressing room to administer absolution.

Someone called an ambulance. The minutes ticked by, but it didn't come. Vingo's condition was worsening. Desperate, Dr. Nardiello had blankets and overcoats piled on top of Vingo's body and directed ten men to carry him by stretcher through the freezing streets to Saint Clare's Hospital, a few blocks away.

Shortly after midnight, X-rays revealed that Vingo had a contusion of the brain—much more serious than a concussion, Dr. Nardiello explained, "as if the brain had been torn." He also had a blood clot, and his left side was paralyzed. Vingo had briefly regained consciousness but lapsed in and out as the night wore on. He recognized his mother but not other people.

Dr. Nardiello gave Vingo a fifty-fifty chance to live. The hospital's chaplain came in and, for the second time that night, Vingo received the last rites.

Back at the Garden, Rocky was talking excitedly with reporters in his dressing room. It had been his toughest fight, but he had emerged unhurt, with another knockout, his perfect record intact. A reporter came in and said: "That Vingo boy is in bad shape. Rocky, they think you better go to the hospital." Stunned, Rocky threw his clothes on and hurried over to Saint Clare's with Allie Colombo and Charley Goldman.

Other reporters had gathered at the hospital. They speculated whether Vingo would be the first boxer killed at the Garden since Primo Carnera had delivered a fatal punch to Ernie Schaaf in 1938.

Vingo's parents, brother, and sister came to the hospital, along with Kitty. While Allie paced nervously, an ashen Rocky approached Vingo's mother, who sat sobbing in a chair in the waiting room, biting on a handkerchief. Rocky stood in front of her and said, "I'm sorry." She didn't answer. He spoke to Vingo's brother, who had also boxed, and who told Rocky that they didn't blame him for what had happened. Rocky stood there, not knowing what to do. A nun came over and touched his arm and said, "We're praying—all praying for this boy. I know you're praying, too, Rocky."

Charley Goldman stood off to the side, puffing on his cigar and clutching his derby. He went over to try to reassure Rocky, saying that Vingo had probably been hurt when his head struck the canvas. It was a fluke. Goldman watched Rocky warily; he had seen men die in the ring, and trained some who had killed them; his fighter Lou Ambers had killed Tony Scarpati in the ring six months before winning the lightweight title. Some fighters never recovered after killing an opponent; others ventured back into the ring, but tentatively, their killer instinct gone.

It was past midnight when Dr. Nardiello came out to update them. Rocky pleaded with him to save Vingo's life. The doctor reassured him that they were doing everything they could. By now, Rocky's father and uncles and Barbara, who had all been at the fight, had joined him at Saint Clare's. "I heard all about it," Barbara said softly, and then neither of them spoke. They looked at each other with tears in their eyes.

The night and the vigil wore on. Around three a.m., the doctor told Rocky to go back to his hotel. Rocky did, but he couldn't sleep. At dawn, he and Allie went for a walk; Allie stopped at a newsstand and bought the papers, which carried huge banner headlines about the fight and Vingo's struggle for life. At the hospital, Dr. Nardiello greeted them with a small smile and said, "We've got hope—good hope now, Rocky."

Rocky and Allie maintained their vigil through New Year's Eve, oblivious to the revelry in Times Square as New Yorkers rang in 1950. Rocky said that if Vingo died, he would never fight again. Others told him that Ezzard Charles had returned to the ring after threatening to quit when he killed Sam Baroudi in a fight the year before. Six months before Baroudi died, he had, in turn, knocked out Newton Smith, who died of a massive brain trauma.

On New Year's Day, Dr. Nardiello told Rocky to go home to Brockton. Vingo was still in and out of consciousness but stable. The doctor promised to keep Rocky updated. When Rocky arrived in Brockton later that day, he went to St. Patrick's on Main Street and prayed for Vingo's recovery. He continued to go there and pray over the next few weeks, as Vingo continued his fight for survival in the hospital.

Vingo recovered, but slowly, and never completely. He would never fight again. For the rest of his life, his savage and epic battle with Rocky Marciano would be erased from his memory. The last thing he remembered was climbing the six steps from the hallway out of his dressing room to the floor of Madison Square Garden. In a first-person story for the *Saturday Evening Post* two years later, Vingo recalled the gap in his memory and what came next: "The steps, and then suddenly I'm looking up at a white ceiling and a face—it becomes my mother's face—is over me, and I try to reach up and touch her, but I can't move my left arm. I'm on a bed, and I fight to get up, but my left leg is dead too. I'm scared and I hear my own voice moaning, 'What's the matter with me? What's the matter with me?' Then another face appears—a man's. The man says, 'Do you know my name, Carmine?'"

The man was Dr. Nardiello, but for several days, Vingo struggled to remember his name, even though he looked familiar.

Two weeks after the fight, Jimmy Cannon was the first reporter to talk to Vingo, who still had trouble remembering people and moving his arms and legs. When Cannon asked him about his fight with Rocky, Vingo said he couldn't remember—but he wanted to fight Rocky again, and would beat him next time. An awkward silence filled the room. Vingo's career was finished, but nobody said anything. Vingo rolled over on his side facing the wall, an ice bag on his head, and asked the doctor to cover him with the blanket.

Vingo started physical therapy to try to learn to walk again. He scared the nurses by thrashing about in his sleep, screaming and throwing punches with his one good arm. One day, he was lying awake in his bed, thinking he was alone, when he heard a noise and looked over to see Kitty sitting by the bed. That's how he discovered he was blind in his left eye and could only see out of his right eye when he looked straight ahead.

Six weeks after fighting Rocky, Vingo was able to walk out of the hospital with the aid of a cane. He married Kitty in March, although he couldn't bend his left leg to kneel in church. When he was in the hospital, boxing people had visited him and promised to throw him a big benefit to raise enough money to set him up in a small business. When he protested that he didn't want to live off charity, one man said, "This isn't charity, kid. It's what the game owes you." He started thinking of opening a cigar store or a candy store. But time passed, and Vingo heard nothing more. The couple moved in with Kitty's parents, and Kitty went to work in a garment factory. More time passed. Ashamed to have his wife and in-laws supporting him, Vingo looked for work. He had no skills and no education, and not even his former strength for manual labor. He got a job at a slaughterhouse, sawing bones and hanging sides of beef on metal hooks, but he couldn't handle the work and got laid off.

One day, Vingo asked his cousin to find out how he could collect his $1,500 purse from his fight with Rocky. His cousin looked away awkwardly and said that the money had all gone to pay his medical bills. Vingo sat stunned, unable to speak. He learned that his medical bills had totaled $4,000. He collected $500 from a Garden insurance policy, and his manager gave him another $200.

Rocky donated part of his purse from his next few fights to Vingo, paying $2,000 to the hospital and giving Vingo $500. The money went quickly. Vingo never went back to the hospital for therapy treatments because he couldn't afford them, though he did have some damaged teeth removed.

One day he wandered into his old gym in the Bronx but hardly anyone knew him. Kitty tried to snap him out of his gloom by convincing him to take her to a fight, even though she hated boxing. They were sitting ringside before the main event when the announcer began introducing several fighters in the crowd. Rocky was there, and climbed into the ring and waved to the cheering crowd. His win over Vingo had put him on the map, and now he was a bona fide contender. People wanted to see the fighter with the tremendous knockout punch that had nearly killed a man. Vingo listened in vain, his palms sweating, but he wasn't introduced.

Ten days after Vingo left Saint Clare's, another boxer, the middleweight Lavern Roach, was admitted there after being knocked unconscious by George Small at St. Nicholas Arena. Roach, a handsome ex-marine and devout Christian from Texas, was making a comeback after a savage beating from Marcel Cerdan the year before. He was leading in the tenth and final round when Small tagged him with a series of hard punches with about one minute left. "My luck is running out," he said, just before he fell unconscious. Roach died the day after his twenty-fourth birthday, attended by Dr. Nardiello. He left a wife and two young children.

The one-two punch of Vingo and Roach created an outcry among sportswriters about boxing's mounting death toll. Investigations were launched. Reforms were discussed, including tougher medical screening, greater awareness of damage from previous fights, and a softer material for the canvas. The larger philosophical question of boxing was also addressed.

"Boxing is a brutal business, appealing as it does to man's lowest instincts," wrote Arthur Daley in the *New York Times*. "The game is faced with a situation where it must do something or die itself."

"If we can't have boxing without deaths, let's do without boxing," argued the *New York Post*'s Bert Gumpert.

But nothing happened. The fans kept coming, looking for blood.

□ □ □

LIFE CONTINUED TO be a struggle for Carmine Vingo. He grew bitter toward boxing but bore no ill will toward Rocky, calling him "one of the nicest guys you'd ever want to talk to." Rocky, for his part, said that it would have been difficult to continue boxing without Vingo's blessing.

"Carmine's my friend," said Rocky. "He's forgiven me. If he hadn't, I wouldn't have been able to go on."

Carmine and Kitty attended Rocky and Barbara's wedding in Brockton a year later. Rocky invited Vingo to his training camp at Grossinger's, in the Catskills, and gave him tickets to his fights; he also sent plane tickets for Vingo to fly to Chicago to see him defend his title against Jersey Joe Walcott in 1953. As the years passed, though, Kitty grew bitter toward Rocky. Despite repeated promises to help Vingo financially, or set him up in a business, nothing ever materialized.

"The only thing we ever got from Rocky were promises," said Kitty. "He'd tell Carmine that he'd have something going for him soon, to put him in some business, that he had some property for him in Florida, that he'd have some benefit for him. Nothing. Each man is for himself in the fight game."

"Maybe if I'da pushed," reflected Vingo. "But I'm not the type."

With Vingo's release from the hospital, a weight was lifted from Rocky's shoulders. He was also much more famous. The Vingo fight would be his last preliminary fight. From now on, it would be all main events. But Rocky was edgy, knowing that Vingo's fate was something he would carry with him into his next fight.

"Everybody kept asking me, would I keep on fighting, would I stay with it," Rocky told a reporter a few years later, after he was champion. "It got under my skin. I wasn't a nice guy to live with after that. It was a part of the business I had to get used to."

Vingo never got used to it. He did recover most of the use of his left side, but he never moved easily. He couldn't drive a car, couldn't dance, was half-blind, and had to lean against a wall to pull his pants on. He worked for years as a security porter at a Manhattan office building and died in 2015, at the age of eighty-five, in the Bronx.

Two years after his near-fatal encounter with Rocky, Vingo heard that a lesser-known boxer, Georgie Flores, was in a coma after a fight at the Garden. Vingo didn't know Flores but felt a kindred spirit. Flores was also twenty years old, fighting his first big fight at the Garden for his first $1,500 purse, and dreamed of using the money to buy a house for himself and his wife. Vingo sent Flores a telegram: KEEP PUNCHING. MY PRAYERS ARE WITH YOU. He wanted to go to the hospital and talk to him about what it was like, cheer him up, offer encouragement. But Flores died the day Vingo planned to visit. Instead, Vingo went to his wake. He stood a long time in front of the coffin, then told Flores's sobbing widow how sorry he was. He also spoke to the boxer who had killed Flores, Roger Donoghue, who sat with his face pale and tight. Donoghue soon quit boxing and later could be seen shadowboxing in Manhattan bars, mumbling to himself.

Wandering through the streets of New York after the funeral, Vingo reflected on all the boxers who had died, along with their dreams. He thought back to his own aspirations he had carried into the ring with Rocky. It was, he said, "a good dream and a hard fall." But it could have been worse.

"I was supposed to have been dead, but I was walking. I was one of the lucky ones, wasn't I?"

The Terrific Three—Rocky Marchegiano (back right), Izzy Gold (front center) and Eugene Sylvester (front right)—ran the Depression-era streets of Brockton, Massachusetts, and dreamed of a brighter future. A childhood fight with Vinnie Colombo (next to Rocky) led Rocky's uncle to teach him to box.

While his fellow soldiers participated in the D-day invasion in June 1944, Rocky faced an army court-martial in England for assault and robbery.

Rocky's friend and Ward Two neighbor Allie Colombo was the first to envision him as heavyweight champion and was by his side every step.

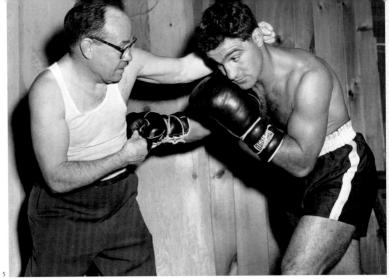

5

Charley Goldman, a veteran of New York's illicit boxing trade in the early 1900s, took Rocky into his classroom, sanding away his rough edges while preserving his dazzling punch, which he dubbed "Suzie Q."

6

Al Weill was the influential manager Rocky needed, but he was also abrasive, domineering, and mob-connected. One writer called him "Hitler, Mussolini, Stalin and Simon Legree rolled into one"—and that was a favorable piece. Soon after Rocky signed with Weill, he shortened his name to "Marciano."

Frankie Carbo was the "underworld commissioner of boxing," a Mafia heavyweight with a rap sheet that included suspicion in at least five murders. He secretly controlled Rocky's career.

7

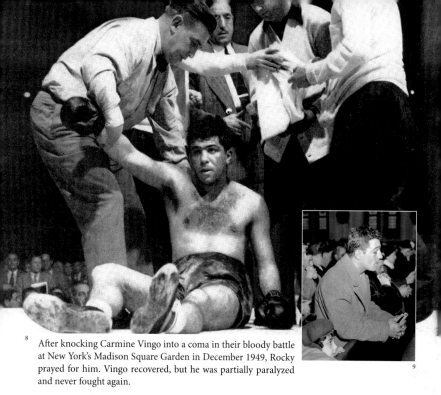

⁸ After knocking Carmine Vingo into a coma in their bloody battle at New York's Madison Square Garden in December 1949, Rocky prayed for him. Vingo recovered, but he was partially paralyzed and never fought again.

9

As a boy, Rocky once got to meet his hero, Joe Louis. On October 26, 1951, he knocked the aging Brown Bomber through the ropes in Madison Square Garden to end his storied career and establish himself as the leading contender for the heavyweight championship.

10

11

Trailing on points in the thirteenth round of an epic fight marked by blood and skulduggery, Rocky knocked out Jersey Joe Walcott to claim the heavyweight title on September 23, 1952. Afterward, he celebrated with Charley Goldman (holding his left arm) and, later, at a victory parade in his hometown, where people had bet heavily on the Brockton Blockbuster. It was, Rocky said, "like the best movie I ever saw."

13

At a White House event, President Dwight D. Eisenhower measures the champ's fist as a smiling Joe DiMaggio looks on. "You know," said Ike, "I thought you'd be bigger."

Rocky mugs with Frank Sinatra on the set of the film *Guys and Dolls*. Being the champ put him on a first-name basis with movie stars and made him a national icon. At Grossinger's resort in the Catskills, where he trained for his title fights, Rocky became good friends with Eddie Fisher and Debbie Reynolds, who confided in him about their engagement.

Rocky said that he drew his strength from his mother, Pasqualena, and his restraint from his father, Pierino. Lena's cooking fueled his prodigious appetite, and his ring earnings enabled Pierino, who had never recovered from being gassed by the Germans in World War I, to retire from the shoe factory.

Rocky was the eldest of six children in the tight-knit Marchegiano family. Back, left to right: Alice, Betty, Sonny, and Concetta. Front: Peter, Pierino, Rocky, and Lena.

Rocky and his wife, Barbara, celebrate their daughter Mary Anne's second birthday. Training kept Rocky away from home so often that he lamented his daughter "didn't even know me."

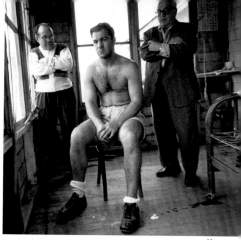

Former heavyweight champion Ezzard Charles won new respect by extending Rocky to fifteen rounds at Yankee Stadium in June 1954. Rocky got even with an eighth-round knockout three months later, but not before a badly split nose nearly cost him the title.

Tensions rose at Grossinger's before Rocky's fight against Archie Moore, which he hinted might be his last. Rocky suspected Weill (right) of stealing from him, while Goldman (left) fretted that Rocky was losing his edge.

The flamboyant Archie Moore knocked down Rocky for only the second time in his career, but Rocky KO'd him in the ninth round before a celebrity-studded crowd of sixty-one thousand at Yankee Stadium to run his record to a perfect 49-0.

In retirement, Rocky battled his waistline and his personal demons but resisted lucrative offers to return to the ring, living instead off his fame. His friend Jimmy Durante called him "America's Guest."

Rocky clowns around with Muhammad Ali outside the Florida studio where they filmed their computer fight in 1969. The two champions forged an unlikely bond and spoke of traveling together to America's riot-torn inner cities to preach racial harmony.

"Start the count, he'll get up," a sportswriter lamented after Rocky's fatal plane crash on August 31, 1969—the eve of Rocky's forty-sixth birthday. "A lot of us today are wishing there were an honest referee in a cornfield in Iowa."

7

The Octopus

ROCKY MARCIANO WAS COMING OUT OF STILLMAN'S GYM ON EIGHTH Avenue in New York one day with Allie Colombo and Chick Wergeles, who worked for Al Weill, when they encountered a couple of men who knew Wergeles.

Wergeles chatted with them, then turned and said, "Rocky, come over here. I want you to meet someone."

Wergeles gestured toward a well-dressed man in his forties, compact and muscular, and said, "This is Frankie."

Rocky introduced himself and shook hands.

"You're another Italian boy, aren't you?" said Frankie. "Kid, make me proud of you."

Rocky replied that he wanted to go out and win the heavyweight championship. Frankie wished him luck.

After they parted, Allie asked who the man was. Wergeles said it was Frankie Carbo.

No further introduction was necessary. Carbo was a notorious figure, known as the "underworld commissioner of boxing," a Mafia heavyweight with a rap sheet that included suspicion in at least five murders. He was acquitted in one case after a key witness fell to his death from the window of a Coney Island hotel, where he had been under heavy police guard. In 1947, underworld snitches said, Meyer Lansky had given Carbo the contract to kill his former partner, Bugsy Siegel.

When Carbo wasn't killing people, he was an inveterate gambler and sportsman who favored racehorses and boxers. In recent years, the New York district attorney had questioned Carbo about allegations that Rocky Graziano had been offered a bribe to throw a fight, and that Jake LaMotta had taken a dive at the Garden in return for a shot at the middleweight title. The allegations were true, but the fighters maintained the code of silence and Carbo walked. Still, prosecutors were under no illusions. An informant for the Federal Bureau of Investigation advised that Carbo was "the king fight fixer in the United States . . . the only way you can get top-notch boxers to perform for you is to cut in the mob."

Moreover, with the advent of lucrative televised fights following World War II, Carbo had seized tighter control of the sport. By the early 1950s, Carbo was "in full and complete control of boxing all through the country," in the assessment of the FBI. A promising fighter could not get a meaningful fight unless Carbo owned a piece of him.

Carbo was a flashy presence at ringside, in the gyms, at the nightclubs, and in the hotel suites where champions celebrated, flashing a fat roll of hundred-dollar bills. He dressed impeccably, favoring dark suits, white-on-white shirts, and silk ties. And yet he was never a manager of record, preferring to maneuver in the background, hence the nickname "Mr. Gray." Working through a number of front men—fight managers and other mobsters—Carbo manipulated fighters, building them up, then directing them to take a fall, and betting heavily through other subordinates on the fixed outcome.

Carbo needn't have wished Rocky luck when they met because the mobster made his own luck. And Carbo was secretly in the young fighter's corner because his most prominent front man was the man Carbo had installed as boxing's new matchmaker, a man who also happened to double as Rocky's manager—the Artful Alsatian, Alphonse Weill.

◻ ◻ ◻

IN THE SPRING of 1949, when Rocky was training at the CYO gym on West 17th Street, he received an urgent phone call from Weill.

"Come on right up to the office," Weill commanded. "Stop everything you're doing there and get up here. It's very important."

When Rocky arrived at Weill's office in the Strand Building, he saw three other fighters managed by Weill. The manager sent them out and called Rocky in privately.

"I'm the new IBC matchmaker," said Weill, referring to the newly formed International Boxing Club. "I just released those guys. I'm not managing them anymore."

Weill opened a desk drawer and pulled out a piece of paper and pushed it over to Rocky.

"Sign it."

Rocky didn't even read the paper, so dominant was Weill's control over his career. Obediently, he signed.

"That's a private agreement between you and me," explained Weill. "But if anyone asks you who your manager is, tell them Marty."

Marty Weill was Al's stepson, a salesman with a store in Dayton, Ohio, that sold jewelry, kitchenware, and television sets. Al Weill couldn't legally manage Rocky and simultaneously serve as the IBC's matchmaker, given the obvious conflict of interest. But Rocky was becoming too valuable a commodity to give up, so Weill installed his stepson as the fighter's new manager of record and continued to call the shots behind the scenes. Marty began showing up for Rocky's fights, but the ruse fooled no one and drew the scorn of New York's cynical sportswriters. Al Weill was unperturbed. "He's my own son, ain't he?" Weill told one writer. "Why shouldn't I keep it in the family?" Asked once when Rocky's next fight would be, Al Weill said, "Marty Weill, Rocky's manager, thinks that it is unlikely that Rocky will fight again this year."

But if the arrangement proved embarrassing to the IBC, Weill would remain its matchmaker because Frankie Carbo wanted him there. FBI files reveal that Weill was a close associate of Carbo's and that Carbo owned a piece of Weill's fighters, including Rocky Marciano.

In 1942, when Carbo was under law-enforcement scrutiny, he gave his occupation as self-employed booking agent for prizefighters since 1934 and listed Weill's office as his business address. Weill, interviewed by the FBI, confirmed that he had known Carbo for years. In 1947, Weill vouched that he would help find work for one of Carbo's mobster pals, Jimmy Plumeri, a Teamsters Union official, when Plumeri was released from prison after serving time for extorting truckers in New York's Garment District. Plumeri, also known as Jimmy Doyle, was intimately involved with Carbo in fixing fights and controlling fighters—including Marciano. One report, in the spring of 1949, said that Anthony "Tony Ducks" Corallo, a Mafia capo who controlled the New York Teamsters, had stated that

Plumeri "had a 'piece' of Rocky Marciano." New York State's top boxing regulator described the "Carbo combine" as "an army that rides in Cadillacs while the real foot soldiers of boxing, the fighters, do the roadwork."

Rocky was one of those foot soldiers. While he wasn't privy to all of the mob's machinations guiding his career, he also wasn't naive. His knowledge of the mob dated back to the dice games run by Peg-Leg Pete from Providence in the woods behind Edgar Playground. In Providence, mob boss Raymond Patriarca was a visible presence. The role of gangsters and gamblers in boxing was an open secret. As Rocky climbed the boxing ranks, he knew he had struck a deal with the devil in the ruthless Weill, but he had to live with it if he wanted to become champ. Moreover, when Weill was named the IBC's matchmaker, he and Allie didn't bemoan the conflict of interest but rather rejoiced. Allie believed that Weill's influence would help Rocky get big fights at the Garden. Rocky saw the big money finally coming their way.

Still, Rocky chafed under Weill's abrasive, dictatorial style. Early in 1950, after the Vingo fight, Rocky and Barbara had been engaged for nearly two years and were desperate to get married. But Weill kept saying no. "Fighters' wives hurt fighters," Weill told Rocky. "When I think you're ready to get married, I'll tell you."

That didn't make Barbara happy. One night she got so mad that she called Weill and confronted him. But he wouldn't budge. "Barbara, I've been a manager all my life and I know best," he told her. "You're a smart girl. You're doing the right thing. Rocky will be proud of you. You wait and see. . . . I'll make a lot of money for Rocky. As soon as the right time comes, I want you kids should get married."

Rocky was annoyed that Weill sent his stepson or his flunky Wergeles to collect his purses, not even trusting Charley Goldman. Still, he kept his mouth shut and accepted Weill's domination as the price he had to pay for a shot at the title. "You do your talking with your fist," Weill told him. "I do all the negotiating."

One time, Rocky made an offhand remark in front of Weill that he was glad he had gotten a match. Weill erupted. "You're glad *who* got this match?" he shouted at Rocky. "You think *you* got it? *I* got it. I made this match for you. You ought to pay me for making this match. What are you? You're just the fighter. Without me, you're nothing."

Rocky's childhood friend Nicky Sylvester recalled having breakfast at Jack Dempsey's restaurant in New York with Rocky, Allie, Weill, Goldman, and several other fight people. While they were eating, Weill said: "Oh, Rock, I forgot to tell you, today's my birthday. Take care of the bill." A flabbergasted Rocky said that he didn't have any money. Weill wound up paying, but he berated Rocky in front of the group.

Another Brockton pal, Izzy Gold, from the Terrific Three, said that it was uncomfortable to see Weill push Rocky around, but his friend had no choice. Weill was "a New York wiseguy," a "sharpy," and he had Frankie Carbo behind him. "You do as you got to do," said Gold. "You want the shot for the title, it's all rackets."

□ □ □

UNSAVORY CHARACTERS HAD gravitated to boxing since the heyday of John L. Sullivan in the 1880s.

Gambling was central to boxing's appeal during Charley Goldman's fighting days in the backrooms of saloons in the early 1900s, when the sport was illegal. The sport saw plenty of disreputable characters, like Abe Attell, the featherweight champ who regularly bet on his own fights and was later indicted as the bagman in gambling kingpin Arnold Rothstein's plot to fix the 1919 World Series. In the 1920s, after boxing was legalized, a new generation of mobsters and bootleggers flocked ringside; the scene, with its high rollers and violence, glamour and intrigue, perfectly suited the lifestyle of the Roaring Twenties. Al Capone was a big fan of Jack Dempsey's, betting $50,000 on him when he fought Gene Tunney in the famous Long Count Fight in Chicago in 1927. During the prefight hype, speculation ran rampant that Chicago gangsters were trying to fix the fight for Dempsey, while rival Philadelphia mobsters were trying to rig the outcome for Tunney. No fix was ever proven. But it was reflective of the era that the referee who presided over the Long Count—which enabled Tunney to escape a knockout and win the decision—ran a Chicago speakeasy controlled by Capone's rivals.

After Prohibition, boxing became a lucrative new frontier for mobsters. The biggest of the bootleggers in New York, Owney Madden, became a boxing promoter and celebrity nightclub owner, purchasing a Harlem club from the former heavyweight champ Jack Johnson and renaming it the Cotton Club. Madden controlled the heavyweight champions Primo Carnera and Max Baer, fixing a series of fights that led Carnera to the title and then deserting the oafish Italian strongman by arranging for him to lose the crown to Baer in 1934. In 1937, the ambitious promoter Mike Jacobs turned to Madden when he was trying to get Joe Louis a shot at the title held by James Braddock. Madden, who was widely suspected of owning a piece of Braddock, arranged a meeting with Braddock's manager, Joe Gould. Jacobs made a staggering offer: If Braddock broke his contract to defend his title against Max Schmeling and fought Louis instead, Jacobs would guarantee Braddock and Gould $500,000 plus 10 percent of Louis's earnings for the next decade. Gould agreed. When Louis knocked out Braddock to become champion, Jacobs became boxing's dominant promoter.

The popular Louis embodied an era when boxing's fortunes soared. His rise enabled Jacobs's Twentieth Century Sporting Club to monopolize boxing from the middle of the 1930s through the late 1940s. Then, with Jacobs's health failing and Louis's skills fading, Louis became a pawn in the creation of the International Boxing Club, which would control boxing well into the 1950s.

The institutional corruption of boxing began, fittingly, with stealing milk from babies. The operators of Madison Square Garden controlled the big fights and also promoted boxing shows to benefit Mrs. William Randolph Hearst's Free Milk Fund for Babies. When the Garden announced in 1933 that it was raising the milk fund's rent, Hearst's powerful newspapers retaliated by attacking the Garden's management for stealing milk from helpless infants. Secretly, a trio of Hearst journalists met with Jacobs at the Forrest Hotel and plotted to create the Twentieth Century Sporting Club to promote boxing shows. One of those Hearst journalists was the syndicated columnist Damon Runyon. Jacobs was not a big boxing guy but a savvy promoter who had risen from poverty on the Lower East Side by hustling tickets to Broadway shows and sporting events. His ticket agency was located across West 49th Street from the Forrest Hotel, and the sidewalk in front became a popular hangout for boxing managers, trainers, fighters, celebrities, gamblers, ex-pugs, and assorted hangers-on who looked like they had stepped out of the pages of one of Damon Runyon's stories. One day, Runyon saw several boxing managers sunning themselves in brightly colored chairs and christened the unassuming strip of midtown asphalt "Jacobs Beach." The name stuck.

Stock for the Twentieth Century Sporting Club was held in Jacobs's name. Meanwhile, his silent journalist partners shamelessly promoted the club's fights in the pages of the Hearst newspapers. Jacobs was already the most powerful sports promoter in America when he was tipped off to a promising young black fighter in Chicago. The fighter's managers, also black, had struck out in getting a fight at the Garden, after the arena's manager advised, "Well, you understand he's a nigger and he can't win every time he goes into the ring." Jacobs signed Joe Louis to fight exclusively for the Twentieth Century Sporting Club. Louis proved a box-office bonanza. On September 24, 1935, he knocked out Baer, the former champion, before eighty-eight thousand at Yankee Stadium, in a fight that brought boxing's first million-dollar gate since Jack Dempsey's heyday. Before long, the Garden capitulated, and the Twentieth Century Sporting Club took over the promotion of fights there. Jacobs, by this time having forced out his silent Hearst newspaper partners, was the undisputed king of boxing. From 1937 to 1947, he promoted sixty-one title fights and more than fifteen hundred boxing cards. Jacobs grossed more than $10 million from Louis alone and sold ten million tickets worth $30 million—not counting the money he grabbed under the table by scalping tickets reserved for the working press.

But Jacobs didn't do it alone. Lurking in the shadows, a growing presence, was Mr. Gray—Frankie Carbo.

◻ ◻ ◻

ELUSIVE SINCE CHILDHOOD, Frankie Carbo was a man of many aliases: John Carbo, Paul Carbo, Frank Fortunate, Frank Russo, Jimmy the Wop, Mr. Fury, and Mr. Gray. He was born Paolo Corbo on August 10, 1904, on New York's Lower East Side and grew up in the Bronx. At the age of twelve, he was sent to the Catholic Protectory for juvenile delinquents. At seventeen, he was arrested for assault, then grand larceny. In 1926, while exacting tribute from taxi drivers in the Bronx, Carbo argued with a cabbie who refused to pay, then shot to death a butcher who came to the driver's aid. Convicted, Carbo was sent to Sing Sing Prison for two years.

Paroled in 1930, Carbo became a triggerman in the Prohibition bootlegger wars and went to work for Bugsy Siegel's Murder, Inc., in Brooklyn, which operated out of the borough's City Democratic Club, planning mob hits all over the country. An FBI report later called Carbo one of the top killers for Frank Costello, the country's leading Mafia boss from the late 1930s to the late 1950s.

In 1931, Carbo was arrested, along with a nineteen-year-old showgirl, as a suspect in the murder of a Philadelphia racketeer slain at the Ambassador Hotel in Atlantic City. Carbo provided an alibi and was released. In 1936, he was arrested at a boxing match at Madison Square Garden and charged with murdering two bootleggers who worked for the Jewish gangster Waxey Gordon, at a hotel in Elizabeth, New Jersey. Those charges, too, were dropped.

Several witnesses fingered Carbo as the shooter in the notorious gangland slaying of the mobster Harry "Big Greenie" Greenberg in Los Angeles on Thanksgiving Eve, 1939. Greenberg had threatened to rat out his bosses after being indicted for labor racketeering in Brooklyn. The contract to kill Greenberg was assigned to Siegel, who tracked him down in California and drove the murder car; Carbo pumped five bullets into Greenberg as he sat behind the wheel of his car at an intersection in Hollywood at 11:00 p.m. But Carbo was acquitted after a key witness who was under heavy police protection, Abe "Kid Twist" Reles, flew out the window of the Half Moon Hotel in Coney Island and plunged five stories to his death.

Finally, in 1947, Meyer Lansky gave Carbo the contract to kill his old boss, Bugsy Siegel, after Siegel had welshed on his loans from the mob in the construction of the Flamingo Hotel in Las Vegas, according to Mafia snitch Jimmy Fratianno. Carbo was never charged with Siegel's murder. By then, he was firmly entrenched as the underworld commissioner of boxing.

Carbo's involvement with boxing began in 1934, when the mobster Gabe Genovese took him on as a partner in managing Babe Risko, an obscure middleweight from Syracuse. Risko won the title the following year, and Carbo was on his way. He controlled a succession of middleweight champs and other boxers, including Al Weill's welterweight champ Marty Servo, and he earned a reputation as a man who could "move" a fighter. Carbo liked to flash his money at Billy La Hiff's Tavern or the 18 Club, and he held court in the dining room of the Forrest Hotel, where he and other mobsters also had the entire fifteenth floor to themselves for more intimate gatherings. Carbo entertained a Who's Who of the underworld in Suite 1506, including Frank Costello and Lucky Luciano. Carbo also ran the Broadway gambling trade in midtown Manhattan and oversaw a floating dice game in New York.

Through his influence in boxing, an FBI informant advised, "Carbo can work gambling coups and make huge sums of money." One of the managers who placed Carbo's bets on fixed fights was a Manhattan furrier named Herman "Hymie the Mink" Wallman. Another subordinate nicknamed "Champ"—an accomplice in the Hollywood hit on Big Greenie Greenberg—would move around midtown, placing bets at various restaurants, including Dempsey's, to drive up the odds and guarantee Carbo a big score on a tanked fight. Carbo openly boasted to his ever-present circle of stooges about his ability to get his fighters into the Garden. Once, when one of his men spoke out of turn regarding a match Carbo was pushing on the Garden, Carbo knocked him to the ground. In a meeting with a New Orleans mobster to carve up control over boxing, Carbo pointed to a wall map of the United States and said, "You have the downstairs and I have the upstairs."

Not surprisingly, Carbo attracted the attention of law enforcement. Having been investigated for fixing fights from Detroit to San Antonio, he was also a target of the Manhattan district attorney, Frank Hogan. Early in 1947, Hogan heard that Rocky Graziano had been offered a bribe to throw a fight. Instead, Graziano feigned a back injury and the fight was canceled. Prosecutors pressured Graziano to talk, interrogating him for eighteen hours, but he didn't crack. In truth, Graziano belonged to Carbo. Graziano told prosecutors that some character he didn't know had approached him at Stillman's Gym and offered him $100,000 to take a dive. But he claimed it was a gag.

"There's more to the story than Graziano has told us," Hogan insisted to reporters. "He was apparently afraid of the characters—gangsters and gamblers—he's been associating with, so he does not tell us the truth."

Hogan forwarded the matter to the New York State Athletic Commission, which had done little to police boxing. The commission revoked Graziano's license to fight in New York "for acts detrimental to the best interests of boxing"—failing to report a bribe attempt. Undeterred, Graziano was granted a license in Illinois and beat Tony Zale in Chicago that summer for the middleweight title. Among the many important mobsters waiting to greet the new champion in his hotel suite in Chicago was Frankie Carbo, who had disappeared from Jacobs Beach during Hogan's inquisition.

Hogan pressed on. Seeking to rid boxing of managers with criminal records, he subpoenaed fifty witnesses to appear before a grand jury, including several of Carbo's associates and, briefly, Mr. Gray himself. Hogan was not able to bring criminal charges but handed over the grand jury testimony to the New York State Athletic Commission. The commission fined the Twentieth Century Sporting Club $2,500—a slap on the wrist—for dealing with people with criminal records in scheduling fights at the Garden. The meeting, in the commission's offices at the Garden, adjourned in time for everyone to make it to that night's fight card.

In November 1947, Carbo arranged one of the most famous fixes in boxing history: Jake LaMotta's dive against Billy Fox at the Garden. Three nights before the fight, LaMotta received a visit from Carbo and his lieutenant, Frank "Blinky" Palermo, a fight manager and the Philadelphia numbers king. The men struck a deal: LaMotta would lose in exchange for a future shot at the title. He got his shot two years later, beating Marcel Cerdan, but he would later tell a U.S. Senate rackets committee that he had to pay the mob, including Carbo, $20,000 to get the fight.

Mike Jacobs wasn't thrilled with his arrangement with Carbo. An informant told the FBI that Jacobs "would like to disassociate with Carbo, but must tolerate his presence and association because a man who controls the fight promotion racket must also control the managers of the best fighters."

◻ ◻ ◻

In 1948 the two public faces of boxing were in decline, setting the stage for a major power shift that would benefit Frankie Carbo—and Al Weill.

At age thirty-four, Joe Louis was contemplating retirement, and Mike Jacobs had suffered a stroke and was spending most of his time in semiretirement in Miami Beach. Time had robbed the Brown Bomber of his grace and power, and after he beat Jersey Joe Walcott in June 1948, he announced that he was finished. But he delayed a formal retirement announcement, embarking instead on a long exhibition tour.

Privately, Louis was anxious to retire, but he was also desperate for money to maintain his lavish lifestyle and pay off his considerable debts, including hundreds of thousands of dollars in back taxes. With the help of his lawyer, Truman Gibson, and his press agent, Harry Mendel, Louis hatched a plan that would allow him to walk away from the ring and secure his financial future. The men would form a promotional company to replace the Twentieth Century Sporting Club and control the heavyweight championship. As the reigning champion, Louis would sign the top four contenders to exclusive contracts, then sell those contracts to a promoter who would have the exclusive rights to promote world heavyweight championship fights. In return, Louis would retire and get stock in the new company and a steady salary.

But they had trouble finding a viable investor. They started talking to a slippery character named Harry Voiler, whose name had been in the papers a dozen years earlier for allegedly masterminding a Hollywood jewel heist from his friend, the actress Mae West. Voiler had fled to Chicago to escape prosecution and was running a hotel in Miami when Gibson started meeting with him late in 1948. They discussed forming a corporation and giving Louis 51 percent of the stock; Voiler would invest $100,000 and allow Louis to withdraw $60,000. But after several meetings, it became apparent that Voiler didn't have the money, so Gibson called off the deal.

In January 1949, Louis was in Miami for an exhibition and Gibson flew down to meet him and Mendel. When Gibson briefed them on the failed talks, Mendel spoke up.

"I've got a guy I know who'd be right for the deal," he said.

The man was Jim Norris. Mendel had gotten to know Norris years ago, when Mendel was promoting six-day bicycle races in Madison Square Garden. Norris, a Garden shareholder, was wealthy and had a palatial home in nearby Coral Gables. Mendel called Norris the next day and set up a meeting. There, he laid out what became known as the Mendel Plan, under which Louis would sign the top four heavyweight contenders, then retire and turn over their contracts to a newly formed entity in return for an ownership stake and steady salary. Norris liked it and suggested they speak to his partner in Chicago, Arthur Wirtz. When Wirtz signed on, the International Boxing Club was born. For Wirtz and Norris, the plan made sense. They controlled sports arenas in Chicago, Detroit, Saint Louis, Cincinnati, Indianapolis, and Omaha, and they owned stock in Madison Square Garden. Always on the lookout for events to put fans in the seats, their families had become the owners of the National Hockey League's Chicago Blackhawks and Detroit Red Wings, and were the creators of the popular Hollywood Ice Revue, starring Olympic gold medalist Sonja Henie.

For Wirtz, it was strictly business. Son of a Chicago cop, Wirtz had built a real estate fortune in Chicago, including a stake in the Chicago Furniture Mart. During the Great Depression, he capitalized on the depressed real estate market to snap up properties at a fraction of their value, including Chicago Stadium and Detroit's Olympia Stadium. Asked once if he wanted the seats at Chicago Stadium painted during a renovation, he replied, "I don't want paint on the seats, I want butts."

Norris, an avid sportsman, embraced the boxing deal as more than just business. So it was fitting that he would run the company and become the new public face of boxing.

James Dougan Norris was the son of a Chicago grain dealer whose empire encompassed Canadian wheat fields, West Indies sugar plantations, Arkansas rice fields, and a fleet of Great Lakes freighters. Tall, rugged, and handsome, genial and easygoing, Norris had played football in prep school but was an indifferent student, despite an army of tutors hired by his father. The son had apprenticed on his father's trading floor but preferred the *Daily Racing Form* and the company of bookies, gamblers, and underworld figures, including several associates of Al Capone. Norris called the jockeys, fighters, trainers, and managers by their first names and was quick with a loan, peeling off a hundred-dollar bill or two from a fat roll.

Norris bought a Kentucky horse-racing stable when he was nineteen, and later, when his father acquired the Red Wings hockey team, he helped run it. He traced his love of sports to an enduring childhood memory, when he was twelve and his father took him to see Jack Dempsey knock out Jess Willard on a sweltering Fourth of July in Toledo, Ohio, in 1919. Wyatt Earp and Bat Masterson collected guns and knives from the crowd entering the arena. Dempsey broke Willard's jaw and ruptured his eardrum. Norris was so thrilled that he couldn't sleep on the train ride home.

Drawn to boxing, Norris invested in a heavyweight fighter named Harry Thomas in the 1930s. Later, Thomas would accuse Norris of telling him that he would have to throw a fight against Max Schmeling in 1937, a tune-up for Schmeling's famous rematch with Joe Louis six months later. Thomas said he went on to lose and in return got a title shot against Louis, which he lost fair and square. But he said he never got the $30,000 or so he'd been promised for losing, receiving $5,000 instead. Norris angrily denied the story, but another ex-boxer said Norris had also told him about the fix.

Another one of Norris's racetrack pals was Frankie Carbo. They were so close that Norris named a racehorse after him—Mr. Gray.

When a friend asked Norris whether he, his father, or his grandfather had built the family fortune, Norris laughed and replied, "Hell, I hope you don't think it was me. I'm doing my best to dissipate it."

Despite Norris's cavalier attitude, he and Wirtz drove a hard bargain with Joe Louis. They rejected his demand for 51 percent of the new company and a payment of $250,000. Instead, they agreed to give him 20 percent and $150,000. Later, they would decide that even that was too much.

By the spring of 1949, Truman Gibson had secured the signatures of the top four contenders to Louis's throne—Jersey Joe Walcott, Ezzard Charles, Lee Savold, and Gus Lesnevich—and Louis announced his retirement. Mike Jacobs was bought out for $100,000. Wirtz and Norris announced the formation of the International Boxing Club, with Norris as president. Norris took over Jacobs's desk on the first floor of the Garden. He would also inherit a familiar arrangement with his old racetrack pal, Frankie Carbo, who controlled the boxing managers' guild. In a demonstration that Carbo could still move a fighter, the IBC appointed Al Weill as its matchmaker.

One day, after receiving a phone call from Providence, Norris would excuse himself from his IBC duties and take the train to Rhode Island to bail Wirtz's son Bill out of jail. Norris, who liked to drink and had gotten into his share of barroom scrapes, could appreciate the Brown University student's story about getting into a fight with a local boxer at a downtown saloon. He promised to keep an eye on the slugging young heavyweight, not realizing that, a year or so later, Rocky Marciano would headline the IBC's coming-out party at the Garden.

◻ ◻ ◻

OPPOSITES ATTRACT. THAT helped explain the excitement that rippled through Madison Square Garden on March 24, 1950, as Rocky Marciano squared off in a ten-round main event against Roland LaStarza before a crowd of 13,658.

It was billed as a matchup of brains against brawn, boxer versus brawler, college boy versus ditchdigger. It was also a fight between two young heavyweight contenders with unbeaten records. Rocky was 26-0, LaStarza 37-0.

LaStarza was Gene Tunney to Rocky's Jack Dempsey. His parents owned a grocery store and butcher shop in the Bronx, so he grew up without the hunger and poverty that drove many boys into the ring. An A student who didn't like street fighting, LaStarza graduated from high school at sixteen and spent two years at City College of New York. He began boxing because his older brother Jerry wanted to be a fighter, so their father set up a makeshift ring in the basement of the family store. Sparring with the more aggressive Jerry, LaStarza took a beating until he discovered that if he used a left jab, his big brother couldn't touch him. He went on to become a national Golden Gloves champion, turned pro, and became the darling of the New York sporting press. Still, some critics had trouble accepting the college boy; they thought he was too smart for his own good, too defensive and mechanical, that he lacked a killer instinct. LaStarza approached the ring like one of the crossword puzzles he liked to do in training camp. He preferred to win without hurting his opponent. In 1948, he had fought what he considered a perfect fight, winning a six-round decision over Benny Rusk at Yankee Stadium on the undercard to the Louis-Walcott title fight. Rusk never once hit LaStarza with a good punch, but the fans weren't excited. "That's the object of fighting, isn't it?" said LaStarza. "You're supposed to hit a fella and not get hit back, but they didn't like it. No blood, no deaths, nobody hurt."

LaStarza was favored over Rocky, partly because he was a hometown favorite, partly because he was seen as more battle-tested, and partly because little was known about the Brockton brawler, who had spent most of his young career in the hinterlands of Providence. Rocky's Garden slugfest against Vingo had gotten fans to take notice and built interest in this fight, but Rocky hadn't faced a boxer of LaStarza's caliber. LaStarza, who trained at Stillman's, the center of the boxing universe, was Broadway. Rocky, hidden away in the CYO gym on West 17th Street, was off-

Broadway. Rocky was a devastating "one-punch" man, with twenty-four knockouts, the *New York Times* noted. But LaStarza had recorded a not-so-shabby seventeen knockouts himself—not by attacking but by waiting for his opponents to attack and then methodically wearing them down with effective counterpunching. In LaStarza, the *New York Times* said, Rocky "will be facing a warrior who is one of the soundest boxers among the younger crop of heavyweights."

Al Weill was nervous. The winner would remain on an upward trajectory; the loser would drop back into the pack. The year before, Rocky had sat with Weill at a LaStarza fight, and Weill asked what he thought.

"That LaStarza is a good boxer, but I'd just as soon step in with him," said Rocky.

"LaStarza's better than he looks," cautioned Weill. "Sometime, you'll fight him, but you're not ready yet."

The reluctant Weill was trying to walk a tightrope between his dual roles as the International Boxing Club's matchmaker and Rocky's secret manager. After the match was made, an angry Sam Silverman, the New England promoter, called and complained that Weill had rejected his earlier attempts to have Rocky fight LaStarza in Providence. So why now? Weill replied that Norris had forced him and that he had to do it because it was his job as the IBC's matchmaker. Why, Silverman asked in disgust, would Weill risk what was best for Rocky for the sake of a $200-a-week job? Weill didn't answer.

Charley Goldman also was worried. "I was afraid of that fight," he said. "I didn't think Rocky could win it."

Rocky's uncle Mike had no such qualms. When he and his raucous pals from Ward Two in Brockton arrived in New York and learned that the odds favored LaStarza, they bet on Rocky. Uncle Mike said that that was the first time he bet on Rocky; he bet $500, and from that day on he would bet on every one of his nephew's fights.

Betting was heavier than it had been on any fight in years. Raising the stakes was a promise from the manager of the reigning champion, Ezzard Charles, to give the winner a title shot in June—*if* he won convincingly. By the night of the fight, the odds favoring LaStarza had shifted to about even.

This was Rocky's first big fight. Moreover, it was the first time he would fight on television. Maybe it was the bright lights, or the pressure, or his first time back in the ring after nearly killing Vingo. But when the opening bell rang, the hard-charging Brockton Blockbuster appeared to have vanished. He was nervous and tentative; perhaps he was also feeling the rust from not having fought in three months, or soreness in the left hand he had injured against Vingo. Later, Rocky admitted that Vingo was on his mind and that all the prefight hype, including questions about whether he would keep fighting, had gotten to him and made him uncharacteristically nervous and irritable. "I was really keyed up," he said. He also felt like a stranger in the Garden, where he had fought twice compared to LaStarza's seven times. "In Providence, I know everybody is on my side," he told a friend. "In New York I feel they don't care."

Through the first three rounds, the slugger tried to outbox the boxer and looked foolish. Rocky was swinging and missing wildly. He landed a right in the first that bloodied LaStarza's nose. But he wasn't punching with power, and Goldman feared that he might be subconsciously holding back because of Vingo. LaStarza dodged most of Rocky's punches easily, then stepped in and made him pay with effective, if mechanical, counterpunches. Some of Rocky's wilder misses drew derisive laughter from the crowd. In the corner, Goldman's worries grew; he had trained Cesar Brion when Brion lost to LaStarza and considered Brion the better boxer. Worse, during a clinch in the second round, Rocky wrenched his troublesome back.

In the fourth, ignoring the catcalls and boos, Rocky started to find his rhythm. He tagged LaStarza with a series of rights to the head, opening cuts over both of his eyes. Near the end of the round, Rocky shot a quick, looping right that LaStarza didn't see coming. He hit him square on the jaw, knocking LaStarza back against the ropes and then crashing to the canvas. He was dazed until the count of four. As the fans leaped from their seats and roared, LaStarza rose to his knees at the count of five and stayed there, one arm looped over the rope, until the count of eight, when the bell rang, ending the round. He stood alertly and walked to his corner without any apparent difficulty.

Rocky tried to swarm LaStarza in the fifth, but LaStarza kept him at bay and was content, when they got in close, to tie him up and let his head clear. LaStarza regained his form to win the sixth and seventh rounds with crisp counterpunching that exploited Rocky's aggressiveness. In the eighth, fearing he was going to lose the decision, Rocky was more dominant. He fired right after right at LaStarza, connecting on several. This was Rocky's best round since the fourth. LaStarza's knees were wobbly, but he remained standing. During one barrage, Rocky hit him below the belt. The referee awarded the round to LaStarza.

The relentless Rocky—"fighting the only way he knew how," the *New York Times* noted—kept up his attack in the ninth and tenth rounds, scoring several times with a left hook that he hadn't used much earlier in the fight because he had been favoring his achy back. In the ninth, Rocky staggered LaStarza several times with the resurgent left hook but couldn't put him away. LaStarza continued to outbox him, stinging Rocky with quick jabs. In the tenth, with the crowd on its feet and screaming, they fought with uncontained fury. LaStarza abandoned his counterpunching for a two-fisted assault. Rocky staggered him again with another hard left hook. The fight ended with the two men standing toe to toe, slugging away at each other. When the bell rang, the crowd gave them a standing ovation.

The roar continued as the fans awaited the decision. As ring announcer Johnny Addie stepped to the microphone, the crowd hushed.

The first judge, Arthur Schwartz, marked his card five rounds for Rocky, four for LaStarza, and one even.

The second judge, Arthur Aidala, scored it five rounds for LaStarza, four for Rocky, and one even.

So it came down to referee Jack Watson. He scored it five rounds for Rocky and five rounds for LaStarza.

There was a long pause. The fight had come down to New York's supplementary points system; in the case of a tie on rounds, the outcome was determined by points based on knockdowns and fouls.

The announcer read the rest of Watson's decision: "Points: six for LaStarza and nine for Marciano. The winner: Marciano!"

LaStarza had won the first three rounds and, due to Rocky's foul, the eighth. Rocky was clearly in control in the fourth, ninth, and tenth and could be argued to have narrowly won the fifth, when LaStarza was regrouping from his fourth-round knockdown. But many observers had LaStarza rallying to take the sixth and seventh, which would have given him six rounds. Rocky's knockdown of LaStarza, the only one of the fight, and his strong finish had apparently lifted him to the narrowest of victories—one that would have been clearer had he not fouled LaStarza in his dominant eighth round.

Others weren't convinced. As the crowd erupted in a mixture of cheers and boos, a bewildered LaStarza rushed over to the ring announcer and asked, "Did Marciano win?" The crowd moved slowly for the exits, having witnessed, as one writer put it, a popular fight but an unpopular decision. The consensus among the sportswriters was that LaStarza should have won. The *New York Times*' Joseph Nichols thought that LaStarza had won, six rounds to four. It was "a paper thin and exceedingly odd decision," wrote the *New York Herald Tribune*'s Jesse Abramson. "Marciano won, but it was a gift." Even writers from New England, Rocky's home turf, questioned the decision.

The close, exciting fight and controversial finish should have made a rematch inevitable. But Weill, showing his conflict of interest, made sure that it didn't happen anytime soon. LaStarza's fate may have been sealed when Weill, in his capacity as Garden matchmaker, went to LaStarza's dressing room to offer his congratulations on a fine fight. When Weill opened the door to enter, LaStarza's manager, Jimmy "Fats" DeAngelo, slammed it in his face. LaStarza's camp was furious, feeling that their fighter had been robbed because of Weill's influence.

Afterward, Weill refused Jim Norris's pleas for a rematch. Perhaps his pride was hurt, or perhaps Weill saw no profit in it, only risk. Rocky remained undefeated, while LaStarza, in the prime of his career, slid off the fast track into exile. He wouldn't fight another meaningful fight for three and a half years and was only booked once by Weill to fight in the Garden. After his loss to Marciano, LaStarza's next fight was in Holyoke's Valley Arena, where Rocky had started his professional career as Rocky Mack three years and a seeming lifetime ago.

Rocky tried to keep his head down through the controversy. He had been too busy fighting to keep score, he told the writers. It had been a good fight, and he was happy to have the decision.

Not long after the fight, Jim Norris wrote a letter to the president of Madison Square Garden assessing the IBC's first year of operations. After working tirelessly to return boxing to profitability, wrote Norris, the March results were "the first encouraging signs." Thanks to three "big-money bouts," including Marciano versus LaStarza, the IBC had made a profit of $52,000 that month. Norris went on to voice his concerns about increased squabbling with the Boxing Managers Guild over the division of television revenues. Norris noted that the IBC's contract with the guild was about to expire, jeopardizing his efforts to strike deals with Gillette and NBC to televise Friday night fights, and with Pabst and CBS for Tuesday or Wednesday night boxing shows.

"A strike of the boxing managers with its resultant disruption of our relations with major sponsors would be most unfortunate," wrote Norris.

Not long after, Norris received word that Rocky Graziano had claimed an injury while training and would have to call off his highly anticipated fight against Jake LaMotta. A strike seemed imminent. Norris called Frankie Carbo. The mobster controlled many of the managers who ran the guild, and, with his intervention, they struck a deal with Norris that ensured peace. The IBC now controlled the major arenas, the television contracts, the managers, and the fighters. A monopoly had emerged, one that would control boxing for much of the next decade, freezing out those who challenged the power structure and advancing those who fell in line.

Carbo emerged as a power broker and met frequently with Norris. Norris saw to it that Carbo's girlfriend was put on the payroll of an advertising agency that handled the IBC's growing television revenues. Carbo remained a visible presence at the fights—at times, too visible. Before one fight, IBC officials scrambled to move his seat away from the television cameras.

According to a secret FBI report, "the mobsters managed all the fighters, and assigned exclusive promotion rights to the International Boxing Club owned by multi-millionaire Jim Norris, who has all the major boxing arenas in the country sewed up." Furthermore, Norris had exclusive television contracts with CBS, NBC, and ABC, which broadcast fights "from mob-controlled arenas, where none but mob-owned fighters are featured. The only way you can get top-notch boxers to perform for you is to cut in the mob and the IBC."

The top mobster in the operation, the FBI report said, was Carbo, and Weill was one of his top men. The report went on to list several fighters as "mob promotions"—including Joe Louis, Jersey Joe Walcott, Joe Maxim, Kid Gavilan, Jimmy Carter, Sandy Saddler, and Willie Pep.

Topping the list was Rocky Marciano.

The sports editor of *Look* magazine, Tim Cohane, who was close to

Rocky, reported that Carbo "had a 10 percent cut of Marciano, an arrangement Rocky was helpless to prevent, but never allowed to influence his actions in the ring."

By now, Carbo was openly referred to as the underworld commissioner of boxing.

And there was a new nickname for the powers that controlled boxing: the Octopus.

8

Requiem for a Heavyweight

Little, wizened Charley Goldman may have been the most excited man outside of Brockton when Rocky beat Roland LaStarza.

While the sportswriters and New York fight crowd groused about the decision and harped on Rocky's lack of style, the wily trainer saw something they didn't—his painstaking lessons about footwork and counterpunching were beginning to sink in. Until Rocky fought LaStarza, he had never faced a really good boxer. Goldman knew that Rocky could punch, but the LaStarza fight convinced him that his pupil also could box. "When he stood up to LaStarza, trading him punch for punch and actually outboxing him, I was convinced that we had something," said Goldman.

Rocky came away from the fight believing, for the first time, that he had a chance to go all the way to the heavyweight championship. The money was great, too. His purse was $9,900, by far the largest of his career; he had earned $1,500 from the Vingo fight just three months earlier. Rocky may have had his differences with Al Weill, but his abrasive manager knew what made him tick.

"Rocky is a poor Italian boy from a poor Italian family and he appreciates the buck more than almost anybody," said Weill. Rocky hadn't earned many good purses yet, so when he did, "it was like a tiger tasting blood."

The week after he beat LaStarza, Rocky was back at the Garden to watch Rocky Graziano win a split decision over Tony Janiro in a middleweight fight. Before the fight, he was introduced to the large crowd as the hard-punching heavyweight from Brockton, and a contender for the heavyweight crown.

"This kid hits like the atomic bomb," boasted Weill. But the manager also worried about the fragility of this new weapon and was determined to bring Rocky along slowly. It was the father of the real atomic bomb, J. Robert Oppenheimer, who had expressed what Weill feared—that "the future, which has so many elements of high promise, is yet only a stone's throw from despair."

So Weill sent Rocky back to Providence.

□ □ □

IN MAY 1950, the week before his return to the Rhode Island Auditorium, Rocky took the witness stand in a Boston courtroom in the lawsuit against him by his Brockton manager, Gene Caggiano.

Rocky had had just four fights in Providence, for negligible purses, when Caggiano sued two years earlier, claiming they had a contract that entitled Caggiano to a cut of his earnings and control over his career. Now, with Rocky 26-0 and a heavyweight contender, the stakes were considerably higher.

Over two days, a parade of witnesses in Boston's Suffolk County court testified. Caggiano and his witnesses painted a portrait of betrayal, describing how Caggiano had spent hours working with Rocky in Brockton, only to have Rocky ditch him for Al Weill when he turned pro.

Rocky and his witnesses, including his parents, his uncle Mike, and Allie Colombo, countered that Caggiano had exaggerated his role in Rocky's development and had wanted no part of Rocky turning pro, preferring to keep him as an attraction for his amateur shows in Brockton. Rocky testified that Caggiano had told him he only wanted him to sign the contract so that unscrupulous managers wouldn't pester him at the Golden Gloves tournament in New York. Rocky claimed that Caggiano told him the contract wouldn't be binding, that he would tear it up anytime.

There were some comical moments, as Caggiano's lawyers pressed Rocky as to whether Weill was secretly managing him, something Weill wasn't allowed to do as the IBC's matchmaker.

"He did tell you he was going to put his stepson Marty in as a front for him?" asked Caggiano's lawyer.

"Yes," replied Rocky. Moments later, Rocky protested that he hadn't understood the term "front" and insisted that Marty Weill was his manager. Later, he admitted that he had asked Al Weill after his recent LaStarza fight when he would fight again. Even Rocky's own lawyer had trouble keeping things straight, at one point asking Rocky, "How much are you paying Al Weill? I mean, Marty Weill?"

Rocky's lawyers attacked Caggiano's character, forcing him to admit on the stand that he had served jail time in Boston in 1935 for larceny. Caggiano countered by telling reporters that he had received anonymous threatening phone calls warning him to drop his lawsuit. "One voice told me, either drop the case or find yourself in cement."

Allie Colombo was so nervous that he developed a nosebleed when he testified. "Talk up, nobody is going to hurt you," the judge encouraged. What came through in Colombo's testimony was his total devotion to Rocky—how he worked out with him, lived with him in New York, was with him every day he trained and in his corner for every fight, sacrificing any career of his own, and, so far, for very little financial reward. Weill's agreement with Rocky called for Colombo to receive 10 percent of his earnings. In the past two years, that had amounted to less than $500.

"I wasn't interested in money," he testified.

Caggiano's lawyer pressed him, though, trying to paint Allie as someone who had "sold" Rocky to Weill and sought to profit from his career even though he knew little about boxing.

"You were only bucket boy, weren't you, in all those fights?" asked Caggiano's lawyer, alluding to Colombo's work as a corner man.

"I had a second's license," he said.

"You were bucket boy; Charley Goldman did all the handling."

"I handled him also."

Colombo explained: "I am trying to learn everything I can about the boxing business. Someday I hope to be a manager. I hope to make boxing my business."

Goldman shuffled to the stand on the second day of the trial and provided some comic relief. To illustrate what an inept teacher Caggiano had been, Goldman asked the judge if he could demonstrate how raw Rocky was when they first met. He hopped off the witness stand and gave the judge a boxing tutorial on balance, defensive techniques, and the proper way to clinch.

"In a clinch, he would put his left hand on the shoulder (of his opponent) and he wouldn't take it off his shoulder, regardless of how many punches he got in the stomach. He said, 'I was taught to let the fellow punch me in the stomach so I could punch him in the face.'"

Caggiano's lawyer tried to get Goldman to admit that Rocky was still a crude fighter.

"If you had Rocky a hundred years, if we could stay around that long, you couldn't make a boxer out of him?"

"I never tried to make a boxer out of him."

As the lawyer sparred with Goldman over fighters and their styles, they sounded like two men arguing in a bar.

"Tom Gibbons was one overstuffed light . . ."

"He was one of the greatest fighters we had," interrupted Goldman.

"You will never make a Fancy Dan out of Rocky?"

"I never try," shot back Goldman.

Testimony from the Providence promoter Manny Almeida and others revealed that Rocky's total ring earnings to date were $29,624. Deducting training expenses and Weill's 50 percent, Rocky had received considerably less than half of that.

◻ ◻ ◻

MORE THAN FOUR thousand fans crowded into the Rhode Island Auditorium on June 5, 1950, to welcome back Rocky, who had not fought there in nearly six months.

Leaders of the International Boxing Club had traveled from New York, while Rocky's *paisanos* had come from Brockton to see him fight the journeyman Eldridge Eatman. It was not pretty. In the third round, Eatman fell to the canvas, apparently untouched by Rocky. When the referee stepped in and spread his arms, in the signal that the fight was over, handlers for the two fighters rushed into the ring as the crowd booed and started for the exits. But the referee, Dolly Searle, believing that Eatman had tripped, had spread his arms to stop the count. Amid the confusion, he ordered the ring cleared and the fight to resume. When it did, Rocky promptly floored Eatman with a right to the jaw for his twenty-fourth knockout in twenty-seven professional fights. Kneeling beside his prone fighter, Eatman's manager shouted at Searle, "What did you want?"

A month later, Rocky fought his first professional fight in Boston, meeting the former Italian heavyweight champion Gino Buonvino in a cramped and tilted outdoor ring on a drizzly night at Braves Field. ("I felt like I was fighting uphill all night," Rocky said.) Despite knocking Buonvino down in the first round with a left hook to the jaw for a count of eight, Rocky faced a slog in this one. Buonvino, who had lost to Roland LaStarza and Lee Savold, refused to go down until the tenth and final round, when Rocky cut his eye and the referee stopped the fight. One Boston sports writer called Rocky nothing more than "a good club fighter" and wrote that the heavyweight boxing division was "a stinker" if Rocky was considered a top contender.

Rocky returned to Providence in September to face Johnny Shkor, a bruising, six-foot-five, 225-pound giant known as the "Fighting Sailor" because he had served in the navy. In his prime, Shkor had fought two exhibitions against Joe Louis, including a ten-round decision that went to the champ. Boston promoter Sam Silverman had tried several times to match Shkor against Rocky, but a wary Al Weill had always refused. Finally, Silverman sent Weill a photograph of Shkor being knocked out by Jersey Joe Walcott in the first round of their fight in Philadelphia that spring. Shkor "looked like a big oak tree falling," a chuckling Silverman recalled. Shkor had been fighting professionally since 1939, and his manager, Johnny Buckley, told Weill that Shkor couldn't fight anymore and was just looking for a good payday before he retired.

But Buckley had a score to settle. A few years earlier, he told friends, he had passed up a chance to manage Rocky because he didn't think he would amount to anything. Now, contrary to what he had told Weill, Buckley put Shkor into serious training and boasted that his fighter was going to surprise Rocky.

The fight was a bloodbath. From the opening bell, Rocky battered Shkor around the ring. Buckley, who had bet $200 on the fight, was beside himself, screaming at his fighter, "Hit him inna balls." As Buckley jumped up and down excitedly, his false teeth flew out of his mouth. He crawled under the ring to retrieve them as Rocky continued to pound Shkor.

Still in the first round, as Rocky moved forward on the attack, Shkor lowered his head and charged like a bull. His skull crashed into Rocky's forehead with a sickening thud, opening a bloody gash over Rocky's left eye. Shkor reopened the cut in the third round. The cut worsened over the next few rounds, blood flowing freely down Rocky's face. The referee threatened to stop the fight but allowed Rocky to continue. Fighting furiously, Rocky knocked Shkor down at the end of the fifth. Then, after Goldman worked frantically to stem the bleeding, Rocky came out for the sixth and floored Shkor three more times to end the fight and escape a devastating upset. Although he was 29-0, it was a sobering win. After each of his first twenty-eight professional fights, Rocky had been able to go home to his mother without showing any serious damage to his face. Now, as a doctor stitched up his cut in the dressing room, he knew that the ridge of scar tissue over his eye would be a point of vulnerability in the future, one that a cunning opponent could attack and start the blood flowing and force the referee to stop the fight.

On November 3, 1950, Rocky received more bad news. Suffolk County judge Frank E. Smith ruled against him in the Caggiano lawsuit. Smith said that the contract Rocky had signed in 1948 was binding. Therefore, the judge ordered, Rocky could not fight for another manager and had to sign a contract with Caggiano. The ruling threatened to destroy Weill's arrangement with Rocky and, potentially, his path to the top. But Caggiano would not be able to cash in right away. Rocky's lawyers immediately appealed the case to the Massachusetts Supreme Judicial Court.

Ten days after the ruling, still ostensibly managed by Marty Weill, Rocky returned to the ring in Providence for a rematch with Tiger Ted Lowry, the pesky fighter he had failed to knock out a year earlier in the controversial bout that many fans suspected had been fixed.

Fighting in front of a record crowd of 7,155 at the Rhode Island Auditorium, Rocky was more in charge this time. He controlled the fight from the opening bell, scoring with a series of body punches. But Lowry's style still gave him trouble, and while he didn't hurt Rocky, he also refused to be knocked out. Once again, Rocky had to settle for a decision, though this one was not controversial.

"I think Lowry would have gone the distance if we had fought a hundred times," Rocky said later. "I could never get used to his style of fighting."

Afterward, Lowry endorsed Weill's decision to send Rocky back to the minors for more seasoning. Rocky was "a comer," Lowry told reporters, but he wasn't ready to face veteran heavyweights like Ezzard Charles or Jersey Joe Walcott. "If I was managing him, I'd wait awhile before firing at the title."

On another front, Rocky was tired of waiting—to get married. Weill had been putting him and Barbara off for nearly two years, saying that marriage would interfere with his career. After Rocky beat Lowry for the second time, Weill weakened. Maybe one more fight, he told Rocky. Weill matched him against another journeyman, Bill Wilson, in Providence on December 18, 1950.

"Boy was I happy," recalled Rocky. "I couldn't hardly wait. . . . When the bell rang, all I had in my mind was Al saying, 'If you look good against this guy I'll let you know.'"

Determined not to have any cuts or bruises on his face for his wedding, Rocky destroyed Wilson quickly. Midway through the first round, he hit Wilson with a savage right that opened a deep cut over his left eye and forced the referee to stop the fight. Wilson never laid a glove on him.

Two days after the fight, Rocky went to Weill's office in New York to pick up his purse and finally received his manager's blessing to marry. Rocky was so excited that he immediately called Barbara with the news. Weill quickly intruded, taking the phone from Rocky's hand.

"Congratulations, honey," Weill told Barbara. "I want you to be the first to know it's okay for you to get married. I promised you, didn't I?"

Weill told Barbara that they could have ten days for a honeymoon but made her promise not to "bother my fighter."

"Now, Barbara, no distractions, remember!"

Barbara Cousins married Rocco Marchegiano—still his legal name— on December 30, 1950, at St. Colman's Church in Brockton. There weren't enough seats to accommodate the eight hundred guests. Rocky's brother Sonny was the best man. Allie Colombo and Nicky Sylvester were ushers. The wedding fell on the first anniversary of Rocky's bloody fight with Carmine Vingo, who came up from New York with his wife, Kitty. Al Weill and Charley Goldman also attended.

Afterward, a parade of cars, horns blaring, wound through downtown Brockton to the reception at Cappy's, a nightclub outside the city. The reception was a cultural clash between Rocky's Italian guests and Barbara's Irish family. "The wops would dance, then sit down. Then the micks would dance, and sit down," Nicky Sylvester recalled. "The band didn't know whether to play 'Volare' or 'Danny Boy.'"

The festivities obscured some of the underlying tensions between the two families. Rocky's mother wasn't thrilled with Barbara, whom she saw as pampered and not a good homemaker, while Barbara's mother felt that Rocky was beneath her daughter.

But the tensest moment came during the wedding toasts.

Things began lightly enough. The guests laughed when Charley Goldman, uncomfortable with speaking in public, surveyed the large crowd and exclaimed, "Gawd, they told me this was going to be a quiet little affair." After receiving a kiss from the bride, the little trainer toasted the newlyweds. He told Barbara that she was getting a wonderful husband "who was easy to control, always listened, and was eager to do the right thing. And Rocky, you've got a sweet, understanding girl. So here's wishing the best to both of you."

When Al Weill rose to deliver his toast, the crowd hushed to hear the big-shot manager from New York. Holding his wineglass aloft, Weill told Barbara that Rocky's boxing future came first and that she would have to play "second fiddle, because he'll have to pay strict attention to me. Rocky's number one goal is to be the champion of the world. And you will not be able to call him and bother him when he's away at camp. And I don't think that you should be visiting the training camp. And I hope you understand that, Barbara, you look like a nice young lady. I just want us to have an understanding right up front."

The guests laughed and cheered, thinking that Weill was just kidding around. But Rocky, who knew he was serious, was angry and deeply embarrassed. He didn't react publicly, but he would never forget. Barbara, smiling politely, was also upset, wondering why Weill couldn't have said those things in private.

"It's getting so this guy wants to do all my thinking for me," Rocky confided to his brother Sonny. "I can't do anything on my own. He's got his nose stuck into my marriage, my personal friends, and everything else. . . . The guy's becoming a real pain in the ass."

◻ ◻ ◻

ROCKY AND BARBARA honeymooned in Florida, checking into the Dempsey-Vanderbilt Hotel in Miami Beach. But within a few days, Weill was on the phone, checking up on him. Meanwhile, Rocky began slipping out of their hotel room early in the morning to go running on a nearby golf course. Finally, Barbara told him he didn't have to sneak out, that she understood. The next time he went running, she followed along in a borrowed convertible.

After about a week, Weill cut the honeymoon short. He ordered Rocky back to New York to take a bow at the Garden before the January 12 title fight between Ezzard Charles and Lee Oma. Rocky and Barbara flew back to New York, and Rocky took his bow at the fight. The next morning, Rocky went to Weill's office, where Weill announced that he had booked Rocky to fight Keene Simmons in Providence in two weeks. Weill wanted Rocky to stay in New York and start training right away. Rocky pleaded for another week, so he could take Barbara home to Brockton first. Weill refused, saying that the match was already scheduled.

Weill asked Barbara if she'd had a nice time in Florida and reminded her that he'd kept his word about letting them get married. "Now remember, Barbara, you promised me you wouldn't interfere with me and Rocky."

So Barbara went home to Brockton alone, while Rocky moved back into his dingy room at the YMCA and began training. He wouldn't see Barbara again until after the Simmons fight, and then only for a few days, when Weill ordered him back to New York to start training for his next fight.

What followed was the worst slump of Rocky's career. Perhaps he was out of sorts about being separated from his new bride. Maybe it was the steady diet of mediocre opponents that Weill was feeding him. Rocky fought four times over the next three months, but he struggled and seemed to regress.

The *Providence Journal*'s Earl Lofquist criticized Weill for bringing Rocky along too slowly, writing that it had become monotonous watching Rocky "knock over slightly animated punching bags." The time for "nursing Marciano along like a precious piece of porcelain is now in the past," argued Lofquist. "The guy has either got it or he hasn't."

Before the Simmons fight, Goldman pleaded for patience. "Folks forget that Rocky has been boxing only a few years and has only had thirty-one fights. He isn't as experienced as some top-notchers folks ask him to meet. We don't dodge any of them. But we still need time. Rocky has things to learn."

The Simmons fight was nearly a disaster. Simmons was a big, hard-hitting heavyweight from Bayonne, New Jersey, who had knocked down

Cesar Brion a few months earlier, before losing the decision. But his record was 8-8, and he could be hit easily, making him an inviting knockout target.

Rocky weighed in at 192 pounds, the heaviest he had fought in two years. Before the fight, as Goldman taped his hands, Rocky was quiet and businesslike. "He goes in for a fight like I go in for a glass of beer," Goldman remarked to a reporter.

Both fighters came out slugging, but Rocky couldn't put Simmons down. In the second round, Simmons tagged Rocky with two hard rights to the forehead, slicing open the scar tissue over his left eye where Shkor had butted him five months earlier. Blood spurted from the ugly gash.

The next five rounds became a struggle for survival, as the fighters traded hard punches, Simmons working on the cut over Rocky's eye, Rocky fighting back ferociously but unable to find his Suzie Q. Desperation magnified his brawling style, and Rocky started hearing boos from the crowd for hitting below the belt and after the bell. Between rounds, Goldman worked feverishly to stem the bleeding. He told Rocky to slip away from Simmons's punches to avoid further trouble.

In the fifth round, Rocky delivered a straight right that seemed to cave in the side of Simmons's face. A *Providence Journal* photographer captured the moment on film, and when the photo ran in *Life* magazine the following week, readers protested that it was too gory. A *Providence Journal* editor defended the photo, writing to a *Life* editor that the newspaper had received no complaints, but "it may be that the humanitarians don't read the sports pages." Regardless of how vicious the punch looked, it failed to put Simmons down.

By the end of the seventh round, Rocky was bleeding profusely. Fans were shouting, "Stop it!" The referee, Sharkey Buonanno, warned Goldman that he would have to stop the fight soon. Buonanno called in the ringside doctor, who examined the cut. Rocky pleaded to continue. The doctor agreed, for now.

When the bell for the eighth round rang, Rocky ran across the ring and began bludgeoning Simmons. Sam Silverman remembered his wild desperation: "Marciano threw a thousand punches, missed five hundred and almost tore Simmons' head off with the other five hundred." His arms pumping like pistons, Rocky fought like a runner spending his last reserves in a sprint to the finish line. But still, Simmons refused to go down. Then, as the round was about to end, Rocky pinned Simmons against the ropes and delivered a smashing right to the jaw. Simmons swayed, glassy-eyed, his face spraying sweat and twisting slowly. Defying gravity, Simmons remained on his feet but seemed helpless as Rocky kept battering him. Said Simmons, "Whenever he hit you, wherever he hit you, he hurt you."

With just six seconds left, Buonanno stepped between them and stopped the fight. Buonanno later told his son that he could have stopped the fight anytime from the second round on because of Rocky's bleeding. But he didn't, because Rocky was undefeated and a local crowd favorite, and because he was winning on points.

"I wasn't worried," Goldman told reporters afterward. "Rocky's a bulldog."

Because of the cut, Rocky couldn't spar for several weeks, and he wouldn't fight again for two months. But that didn't mean more time with Barbara. They spent a few days together in Brockton after the Simmons fight, and then Rocky returned to New York and Goldman's laboratory in the dank CYO gym. Goldman used the time to work with him on defense and leverage, his combinations and his evolving left hook, which was becoming a powerful complement to his devastating right.

For his next opponent, Weill selected the hapless Harold "Kid" Mitchell, who had just four wins in twenty-one professional fights, including one over a fighter named King Kong. Rocky planned to use their March 20 fight in Hartford, Connecticut, to work on some of the things Goldman had taught him. Rocky told his uncle Mike he might take it easy and go eight or nine rounds to get in a good workout. In the first round, he uncharacteristically danced around Mitchell, practicing the crouching style that Goldman had taught him and testing his left hook. Mitchell offered no resistance. Then, in the second, a Mitchell jab grazed the scar tissue over Rocky's left eye. The punch did no damage, but an electric shock seemed to jolt Rocky. He attacked Mitchell, flooring him with a left hook for a count of nine, then knocking him down twice more in quick succession with hard rights before the referee stopped the fight.

Six days later, a sluggish Rocky knocked out Art Henri in the ninth round in Providence. Henri used an effective left hook to outbox Rocky in the first three rounds and pummeled him with four uppercuts in the third. Rocky staggered Henri in the fourth. After that, the fight became a plodding, tedious affair, with Rocky taking the offensive but looking clumsy and disinterested until he knocked Henri out in the ninth.

Goldman was disgusted. Rocky looked like he had stopped learning. "I felt like telling Weill to quit on Marciano," recalled Goldman. "Rocky beat me to the gun, saying, 'Charley, I know I didn't do anything right. Please, don't give up on me. I know I'll get out of this.'"

He failed to knock out his next opponent, Red Applegate, when they met in Providence on April 30. But at least this fight was more fast-paced and crowd-pleasing, as Rocky came out more aggressively and used his left hook. But for only the fifth time in thirty-five fights, he failed to score a knockout, and this against a little-known foe. While handily winning the decision, Rocky lost the third round because of a low punch and couldn't knock down the aggressive Applegate, who had fought only twice in the past two years.

One year after his big win over Roland LaStarza at Madison Square Garden, Rocky was 35-0, but his career appeared to be stagnating.

"Rocky is not going to be the next world champion," predicted the *Providence Journal*'s Earl Lofquist. "Many are beginning to believe that he has been overrated all along."

Lofquist blamed the overprotective Weill.

"You'd think the guy was a fragile egg to be kept under glass the way his opponents (LaStarza excepted) have been handpicked," wrote Lofquist. "Whether this has been for Marciano's good can be doubted. His improvement over the past year has been slight. But then he has not been fighting anybody from whom he could learn anything."

That was about to change. Three weeks after the Applegate fight, the matchmaker for the International Boxing Club, Al Weill, announced that Rocky Marciano would fight in New York that summer. His opponent would be the new darling of the heavyweight division.

◻ ◻ ◻

REX LAYNE WAS hailed as the second coming of Jack Dempsey, a big, raw-boned Westerner who came out of the Rocky Mountains packing dynamite in his right fist to shake up the heavyweight ranks back east.

Layne was twenty-three years old, a former beet farmer from Lewiston, Utah, who had started boxing while serving as an army paratrooper in Japan in the late 1940s. He was five years younger than Rocky, with an eight-inch reach advantage, and was 34-1-2, with twenty-four knockouts and impressive victories over Jersey Joe Walcott, Cesar Brion, and Bob Satterfield. Layne had won over the New York boxing writers by outpointing the wily Walcott, then getting off the canvas to knock out the hard-punching Satterfield after suffering the first knockdown of his career. Layne had also fought exhibitions against the current champion, Ezzard Charles, and ex-champ Joe Louis. He was the fresh face that boxing was searching for.

Weill was reluctant to make the match, prompting Jim Norris's ire. "What is this?" said Norris. "Are you the matchmaker here, or aren't you?"

The sports writers and oddsmakers were nearly unanimous in picking Layne, who was installed as a 9-to-5 favorite. Anticipation was high for this battle between two young sluggers. Norris anticipated a big gate and had sold the rights to movie theaters in eight cities, where fans would pay to watch live on an experimental new technology, closed-circuit television. To convince Weill to take the fight, Norris agreed to give Rocky 30 percent of the gate and television revenue; Layne's cut was 25 percent.

While much of the prefight coverage was about Layne, the stories about Rocky focused on the manipulative Weill and on Rocky's second-rate opponents. One writer said that Layne's victories over Walcott and Satterfield "outweigh anything Marciano has displayed in all his 35 pro bouts." Sportswriters sought for new ways to describe Rocky's opponents— stumblebums, ham-donnies, cigar store Indians.

Sitting down with Rocky before the Layne fight, the *New York Post*'s Jimmy Cannon raised the touchy subject, telling Rocky, "You know, they say you fight a lot of stiffs."

Rocky, normally polite and popular with sportswriters, was visibly irritated.

"I don't know anything about it," he snapped. "I just go out and fight. I don't remember any easy fights."

This was a make-or-break fight for Rocky. If he won, he would establish himself as a top contender. But if he lost, he risked falling into the ranks of journeymen fighters, appearing on undercards in increasingly obscure arenas, existing from paycheck to paycheck, serving as a foil for younger, rising stars until his body and, possibly, his mind were worn out. Then it would be back to Brockton and a life of drudgery, digging ditches or working in a shoe factory, coming home at night to Barbara and the kids, muttering over beers at the Ward Two Club about what might have been.

But for now, Rocky was living the life of a contender, with all the trappings. Signaling this fight's high stakes, Weill sent him to his first training camp, on bucolic Greenwood Lake in the Ramapo Mountains, fifty miles from New York. It had become a ritual for boxers to prepare for a big fight by retreating to a rustic training camp, where they could escape the temptations of the city and prepare body and mind for the struggle ahead. Accompanied by trainers and sparring partners, and a cook who prepared large, healthy meals, the fighter would get up early for road work in the clean country air, then train in a wood-paneled gym.

Rocky stayed at the Long Pond Inn, a ramshackle hotel on the edge of Greenwood Lake, a nine-mile finger of water straddling the New York–New Jersey border. Joe Louis, Sugar Ray Robinson, and Billy Conn had trained there. Rocky, who had always trained fanatically and slept with his window open in the winter as a boy in Brockton, took to the mountain air and the Spartan regimen. Allie Colombo and Charley Goldman were there. Close friends from Brockton, like Nicky Sylvester, who was quick with a joke to keep things relaxed, also stayed at the camp. They whiled away their free time by taking long walks on the winding country roads, listening to the radio, reading stacks of *Reader's Digest*s and *True Detectives* and clowning around. One photo shows Rocky outdoors in his boxing trunks, grinning as he hoisted a large rock over his head like a caveman.

Ten days before the fight, another cloud lifted. The Massachusetts Judicial Court threw out Gene Caggiano's lawsuit, ruling that the contract Rocky had signed in 1948 was too vague to be enforceable. The case had cost $15,000 in lawyers' fees and court costs, but Rocky was elated; he was free of Caggiano. "It gave me a big lift when I got the news," he said.

As Rocky settled into his routine and sharpened himself for the Layne fight, Goldman could see him coming out of his slump. He was determined and relaxed. While the so-called experts were picking Layne, Goldman was confident of Rocky's chances. He had detected some chinks in King Rex's armor. Layne was slow and fought standing straight up, with a soft belly that was ripe for Rocky's crouching style and hard body shots. Furthermore, Layne didn't have much of a left hand and fought backing up, which would make it harder for him to hurt Rocky. The night before the fight, Goldman told Rocky, "Layne is a big, slow farmer, sent to you from heaven. Just pound him in the body and, when he slows down, let him have some long raps on the chin. You can't miss knocking him out."

Rocky's laser-like focus was evident on the afternoon of the fight, at the official weigh-in at the Garden. The city editor of the *Brockton Enterprise* asked Rocky if he had ever met or talked to Layne. To his surprise, Rocky snapped, "No. I don't want to! I'll meet him in the ring tonight, and that will be soon enough!"

On the steamy night of July 12, 1951, a crowd of 12,565 fans streamed into Madison Square Garden. Some 3,000 partisans from Brockton and other parts of New England formed a boisterous cheering section for Rocky.

Unlike his first big Garden fight against LaStarza more than a year earlier, Rocky exhibited no stage fright. From the opening bell, he executed Goldman's plan to perfection, crowding Layne inside and pounding him with hard left hooks to the body and stiff right uppercuts to the head. Scuttling around the ring in his crab-like crouch, Rocky stayed inside Layne's long arms and never gave his opponent an opening. For the first two rounds, Rocky planted his head on Layne's chest and, in a contest of brute strength, refused to let Layne push him away. A fierce uppercut wobbled Layne in the second, and another opened a wicked cut over his left eye that would drip blood for the rest of the fight.

In the third, Rocky shifted course and moved outside, attacking Layne with long, looping rights. Layne's knees buckled when Rocky connected with a hard right to the jaw, driving him against the ropes, but then Rocky missed with a wild left. Layne fought back with a series of hard rights to Rocky's body and a smash to the jaw; later, Rocky said it was the only time that Layne ever really hurt him. Rocky answered with a powerful right to the jaw that staggered Layne.

Layne was clearly befuddled by Rocky's shifting style. Layne looked slow and flabby; his left was nonexistent. In the fourth, he tried moving away, but Rocky kept crowding him. At one point, Rocky curled a looping right over Layne's left shoulder, striking the side of his head, then shoved him to the canvas. Layne bounced right back up, but Rocky nailed him with a couple of solid body shots.

After the fourth round, Layne's handlers worked desperately on his left eye, now a red blotch. Layne had no attack in the fifth and fought flat-footed, his energy leaking away like air from a balloon. With a minute to go in the round, Layne looked plaintively at the clock. By the end, he was sagging against the ropes.

The end came with electrifying swiftness at the start of the sixth round. Rocky struck Layne with two quick left jabs, then fired a long right that caught Layne on the left temple. He stood for a moment, leaned forward like he was going to go into a clinch, then crumpled to the canvas in slow motion, his head between his knees.

As the referee counted Layne out, a remarkable scene unfolded in the Garden. Shrieking with joy, Rocky's partisans from Brockton surged forward, drowning out the ring announcer. The *Hartford Courant* called it "the most exciting demonstration of hero worshiping" at the Garden "since Joe Louis's halcyon days." Several police officers struggled mightily to prevent Rocky's screaming fans from swarming onto the platform and through the ropes. Rocky stood in the midst of the cacophony, looking slightly dazed as he raised his arms in triumph, then blew kisses and waved to family and friends.

Layne, lying on the canvas, never lost consciousness but couldn't will his body to move. "I wasn't out," he said later, after being helped from the ring. "I could hear every damn count, only my legs wouldn't move. You go down and you're paralyzed. It's the strangest feeling."

An hour later, after Rocky had adjourned to his dressing room, "his wild-eyed enthusiasts from up New England way were chasing after him with such whoops of joy, you would have thought he was a conquering Caesar," wrote Bill Corum of the *New York Journal-American*. They waited for him to get dressed and talk to the sportswriters, then carried him through the Garden's lobby on their shoulders and out onto Eighth Avenue.

Goldman and Layne's manager agreed that Rocky had fought the perfect fight. One of Rocky's punches had sheered Layne's front teeth off at the nubs. "He hits hard," said Layne. "Not as hard as Louis, but hard."

"Marciano established himself as just about the most dangerous challenger for the heavyweight title now in action," wrote James Dawson in the *New York Times*, "a fighter of the old Jack Dempsey school, boasting just about the deadliest left hook in the business." Dempsey's old manager, Jack Kearns, standing at ringside after the fight, put it more succinctly: "What a puncher!"

The day after the fight, Rocky stopped by the IBC's headquarters, where he revealed that he had sprained the knuckle on the middle finger of his right hand with the punch that KO'd Layne. The swollen knuckle didn't stop him from picking up his check for the fight, for $19,463, his biggest payday yet. Even better, Jim Norris told him that the IBC hoped to arrange for him to fight in October for the world heavyweight championship.

That Sunday night, Rocky was a guest on Ed Sullivan's *Toast of the Town* national television show, where the studio audience gave him a warm welcome. The next day, he and Barbara took the train to Providence, where they were met by a motorcade of more than twenty cars that drove them the thirty-five miles to Brockton. A rainstorm that whipped through Providence threatened to dampen the homecoming, but as the motorcade reached the Brockton city limits, the skies cleared and the sun shone brightly. Ten thousand cheering Brocktonians lined the streets to give Rocky a hero's welcome, complete with a marching band, dancing majorettes, and a police escort with sirens screaming. The procession, which had swelled to more than two hundred cars, made its way downtown, where the mayor presented Rocky with a key to the city and a little girl showered him with confetti. His parents were escorted to the grandstand, where Lena was presented with a bouquet of roses. Then the motorcade toured Ward Two and the familiar streets of Rocky's childhood. Rocky said that he would fight anyone his manager matched him against, and hopefully bring the championship home to Brockton.

"All I can say is thanks," Rocky told the crowd. "It's great to be from Brockton."

* * *

ROCKY WAS FOURTEEN years old, at a carnival in Brockton with his friend Izzy Gold, on the summer night during the Great Depression when the world stopped for Joe Louis versus Max Schmeling.

The fight, in a sold-out Yankee Stadium on June 22, 1938, was billed as a preview of the coming struggle between the United States and Nazi Germany, pitting the American heavyweight champion against Hitler's poster boy. Someone at the Brockton carnival had a radio, and young Rocky and Izzy joined seventy million people around the world listening to the highly anticipated broadcast.

When Louis knocked out Schmeling just two minutes and four seconds into the fight, Izzy recalled, "We had about fifty cents in our pockets. And we were thinking about all that money that Louis made."

Thirteen years later, after his breakthrough win over Rex Layne, Rocky was matched against Louis at Madison Square Garden. To get a shot at the title, Rocky would have to slay a personal hero and American icon.

The fact that Louis was still fighting in 1951 spoke to the sorry state of professional boxing in the years following World War II. The war had interrupted the development of a new generation of heavyweights, and then television came along to shutter hundreds of neighborhood boxing clubs where younger fighters had learned their craft. Americans stayed home to watch the fights on TV instead. As a result, aging fighters like Jersey Joe Walcott, who said he was thirty-seven but was really older, lingered atop the heavyweight division.

Joe Louis had worn the heavyweight crown from 1937 to 1949, longer than any other champion. When he first won it, the sportswriter Grantland Rice predicted a long reign, saying that the fighter who would end Louis's career was "some young fellow now playing marbles or spinning a top." Louis thought he would be set for life when he retired and struck the deal with Jim Norris and Arthur Wirtz to sell his title to the newly formed International Boxing Club. But Norris and Wirtz reduced Louis's stock in the IBC, then steered most of the company's revenues from its profitable boxing shows to their own arenas for rental payments. Consequently, the IBC itself showed little or no profit, and Louis never collected a penny in dividends from his stock. That left him with just his $15,000 IBC salary, not nearly enough when the Internal Revenue Service slapped him with a $246,000 tax lien in 1950, pushing his total obligations for back taxes to more than $500,000 (about $5 million in 2018 dollars). Desperate for money, Louis did the only thing he knew—he came out of retirement and fought.

Norris was delighted. Louis's successor, Ezzard Charles, was a dull fighter who failed to excite the public. He was also black but lacked Louis's appeal to the growing white middle-class television audience. Even past his prime, Louis was a major drawing card. Norris matched him against Charles at Yankee Stadium on September 27, 1950, and sold the television rights for $200,000. Ticket sales were triple the level of Charles's previous fight but were still disappointing. Even worse, Louis looked slow and ponderous. He was badly beaten and bloodied by Charles, who said he hadn't gone for the knockout because he had too much respect for "the old fellow who did so much for the Negro in boxing."

But over the next year, Louis continued to fight. Financially, he had no choice. Aesthetically, he and his fans hoped that he could shake off the rust and regain his timing. And he did, reeling off eight straight wins, though not against top-caliber opponents, or with the verve of the Joe Louis of old. By the summer of 1951, Louis had regained some of his old magic and was still considered dangerous. He had been promised a title shot that fall against the winner of the Ezzard Charles–Jersey Joe Walcott fight, with Rocky—by virtue of his win over Rex Layne—in line for his own title shot against the winner of what everyone anticipated would be a Louis-Charles bout.

But Walcott scrambled those plans on July 18, 1951, when he knocked out Charles, six days after Rocky beat Layne. Walcott, the new champion, announced that he would not defend his title until the following summer, and would do so in a rematch against Charles. That put Louis on a collision course with Rocky—a fight that neither side initially wanted, for different reasons. In both cases, the reason involved Al Weill. Louis hated Weill, and Weill feared Louis. On Valentine's Day that year, Weill, an inveterate gambler on fights, had sat in the press section openly rooting for Jake LaMotta to beat Louis's friend Sugar Ray Robinson in their welterweight championship bout. Robinson won by a knockout, but Louis hadn't forgotten. Meanwhile, with Rocky so close to a title shot, the ever-cautious Weill was reluctant to risk his crude prospect against a legend like Louis.

A few years earlier, when Rocky was fighting for small purses in Providence, the local promoter Manny Almeida had offered Weill $3,000 for Rocky to fight an exhibition against Louis at the Rhode Island Auditorium. Weill turned him down. Eager for the money, Rocky asked, "Why don't you take it? It's only an exhibition."

"Why don't you mind your own business?" Weill shot back. "When you go in with Louis, it won't be no exhibition. It will be a real fight."

Norris had pushed Weill for a Louis-Marciano fight early in 1951, viewing Rocky as a tune-up to help sharpen Louis for his title rematch with Charles. But Weill was adamantly opposed.

Even after Rocky beat Layne and Louis emerged as a logical opponent, Weill resisted Norris's entreaties. In August, Louis fought Jimmy Bivins in Baltimore but looked unimpressive in winning a ten-round decision. Weill remembered when Louis used to fire his deadly left jab with machine-gun rapidity—a dozen at a time. Against Bivins, Weill noticed, "he throws three and then he has to come up for air. His reflexes are gone." Weill called Goldman and told him to start training Rocky to meet Louis. Goldman protested that Rocky wasn't ready for Louis. Weill said that he'd never be readier.

"Old guys like Louis go all of a sudden," Weill said. "If we don't get him first, someone else will. I think Rocky can make it. We must take the gamble now."

Traditionally, fighters split 60 percent of the gate. If one fighter was more visible, or the champion, he could get the larger cut. But Louis, driven by his need for money and his hatred of Weill, demanded a lopsided cut—45 percent for him versus only 15 percent for Rocky. Despite repeated visits from Weill, Louis refused to budge. "No sir, I'll take forty-five," Louis told Weill. And, he added, "I'll knock your boy into your lap."

Now it was Rocky's turn to plead. When Norris called him into his office at the Garden and laid out the terms, Rocky protested that he should get at least 20 percent. Sighing, Norris said, "You better take a walk around the corner and think it over." Rocky did, and took fifteen.

It wasn't until after the fight was announced at the end of August that the magnitude began to sink in for Rocky and his supporters.

His mother, Lena, had only been to one professional fight in her life. After hearing Rocky talk so much about the great Louis, she had gotten her brother to take her to see the champ in an exhibition in Providence. She was horrified when she learned that Rocky was going to fight Louis. He was so big, she told him. How could he fight someone he idolized? Rocky told her that he loved Louis, but it was time—he was a stepping-stone to the championship.

Louis may have been nine years older than Rocky, his reflexes dulled, and a bald spot on his head, but he was still Joe Louis. Age was for other fighters; the Brown Bomber was immortal. It had taken a rare black fighter to succeed as heavyweight champion in the 1930s, a combination of skill and power, humility and self-control—someone who, in the words of his trainer, "had to be very good outside the ring and very bad inside." By the time Louis retired in 1949, he had defended his title an unprecedented twenty-six times. Coming into his fight with Rocky, his record was 66-2, including the eight straight wins since his comeback loss to Ezzard Charles. The sportswriters who adored him were divided into two camps—those with wistful hopes that the old Louis magic would prevail against the crude challenger from Brockton and those who feared that he would tarnish his reputation by losing to Rocky.

As the fight approached, there was genuine fear in Rocky's camp. Rocky could see it in his family, friends, and neighbors. One day, Rocky was walking through Ward Two in Brockton with a cousin when they encountered a neighbor who was washing his car. "Well, Rocky, are you going to knock him out?" the man asked.

"I don't know," replied Rocky. "It's up to the good Lord." As they walked away, Rocky said to his cousin, "That guy's an awful stupid dope. What does he want me to say—I'm going to knock him out, I'm going to lose? What could I say?"

Just before Rocky left for camp, he was doing roadwork in Brockton and ran into his boyhood friend Eugene Sylvester, from the Terrific Three. Eugene talked about how big and tough Louis was and sought reassurance, telling Rocky that he didn't have any money to bet on the fight so he was thinking of putting up his car. Rocky told him to do it. He said he'd buy Eugene a new car if he lost.

At his training camp in Greenwood Lake, Rocky was walking on a country road with his brother Sonny one day after his roadwork when Sonny nervously broached the subject of whether Rocky could beat the great Louis.

Rocky cut him off. "Don't you ever question my ability," he said, staring into Sonny's eyes. "I will beat Joe Louis and I will beat any fighter I ever fight. If I didn't have that attitude, I would quit fighting today."

Privately, though, Rocky was worried. The talk out of Louis's camp in Pompton Lakes, New Jersey, seventeen miles away, was that Louis was training harder than he had in years. He had gotten his rapid-fire combinations back and was knocking down sparring partners left and right. A. J. Liebling of the *New Yorker* noted that Louis's body looked good, "leaner, if anything, than it had in 1938—and the jab was as sweet as ever." Most boxing writers considered Louis too clever for Rocky. With his long arms and four-inch height advantage, he would be able to keep Rocky at bay, inflict punishment with his jab, and straighten him from his crouch with his right uppercut. Earlier Louis opponents with an onrushing style had learned the hard way; in their classic 1941 fight, Billy Conn was beating Louis on points in the thirteenth round when he became foolhardy and moved in close, trying for a knockout. Louis knocked him out instead.

"Anybody who COMES TO LOUIS is heading for disaster, so long as Joe can throw a punch, no matter how old he is," wrote Joe Bostic in the *New York Amsterdam News*. "That goes if they wheel him into the ring in a chair."

Rocky trained even harder than usual, sparring 109 rounds. Bull-necked and broad-shouldered, he exuded strength; Liebling wrote that he "looked like the understander in the nine-man pyramid of a troupe of Arab acrobats." Not even Nicky Sylvester, the camp's court jester, could make Rocky laugh as the fight approached. With eleven days to go, Rocky was jogging on a mountain trail with Allie Colombo when they startled a copperhead snake, which darted out of the bushes at them. Allie struck the snake in the head with a stick he was carrying. From that day on, two trainers flanked Rocky when he ran.

Three days before the fight, Rocky was aggressively working over a sparring partner while the ancient ex-featherweight champ Abe Attell watched from a chair at ringside.

"Take it easy, Rocky! He's only a sparring partner!"

As his trainers removed his gloves, Rocky held up three fingers and called to Attell, "Only three days."

Attell turned to a companion. "I had five hundred on him. And after what I seen today, I'm making it a thousand. Louis is all through. If they get a referee who don't let Louis hang on, the kid will knock him out."

At his camp, Louis was dismissive of Rocky and talked more about a rematch with Ezzard Charles. He walked out of a theater showing a film of Rocky's fight against Layne, sniffing, "He can't fight." Rocky took it in stride. "I don't blame Joe for walking out on the pictures," he said. "I didn't look good to myself when I saw them. I only hope that after I beat Louis, the people don't say that I beat a washed-up fighter."

A few days before the fight, an old retired fight manager, "Dumb"

Dan Morgan, who had seen every heavyweight champion since John L. Sullivan, was holding forth at Jacobs Beach.

"Wanna know what I think?" he asked the *Boston Globe*'s Hy Hurwitz. "I think Louis'll murder the kid. I don't talk to Al Weill. But I talk to Marciano. He's a nice kid. There have been few like him come to this town. He talks to me and I've told him, 'How do you expect to beat a guy like Louis getting down in a crouch like you do? You ain't got a chance unless you change your style.' And if the kid changes his style, he's still got no chance. Louis is the best inside fighter there ever was. That's where he knocks 'em all stiff. What's more, they tell me Joe don't like Weill and he's going to make Marciano pay for it."

◻ ◻ ◻

THE LOUIS-MARCIANO FIGHT was originally scheduled for outdoors at the Polo Grounds, home to baseball's New York Giants. But the Giants' miracle pennant run that fall, climaxed by Bobby Thomson's home run to shock the Brooklyn Dodgers—the Shot Heard Round the World—pushed the fight back to October 26, 1951, at Madison Square Garden.

At seven o'clock that night, in a nearby hotel suite, Al Weill told Charley Goldman that he had better go ahead and wake the sleeping man in the next room. Goldman looked at his watch, nodded, then went in and tousled the man's curly black hair and said, "Up, Rocky. There's work to do."

Rocky woke, oblivious to the electric atmosphere in the streets below. Three hours before the main event, a near-capacity crowd of 17,241 was already swarming into the Garden. The IBC had opened a ticket office in Brockton a few weeks earlier and had sold nearly four thousand tickets. At the weigh-in that day, two hometown fans had held up a large sign that said, WIN, LOSE OR DRAW, ROCKY, WE LOVE YOU . . . BROCKTONIANS. Millions more would tune in on television. For only the second time in boxing history (the first being the Charles-Walcott title fight that summer), seven television-set manufacturers had joined with the Gillette Company to buy the rights for NBC to televise the fight nationally. Louis was a 7-to-5 favorite, the shortest odds of his career.

Among the luminaries sitting ringside were Jersey Joe Walcott, Ezzard Charles, and Sugar Ray Robinson. Nearby was FBI chief J. Edgar

Hoover, former secretary of the air force Stuart Symington, and the actress Elizabeth Taylor.

A tall blond woman sitting near A. J. Liebling in the Garden's mezzanine watched Rocky bounce up and down in his corner and told her companion, "I hate him! I hate him! I think he's the most horrible thing I've ever seen." When the fighters were introduced shortly before 10:00 p.m., Liebling noted, Rocky's partisans from New England "were cheering him as if he were a high-school football team." But Louis received an even bigger welcome.

Standing face-to-face with Louis for the referee's instructions, Rocky couldn't stop thinking how big Louis was. At six foot two and 212 pounds, Louis dwarfed the five-foot-ten, 187-pound Marciano. "I had never remembered Louis being such a big guy," he said. "The top of my head seemed to just about reach the bottom of his chin."

Standing in his corner waiting for the opening bell, Rocky received a final piece of advice from Goldman: "Make it a short fight. At my age I can't be runnin' up and down them steps all night."

Rocky tried. He was on Louis from the opening bell, following Goldman's instructions to work inside, attack his belly, and not give the old fighter time to catch his breath. Louis was stronger, shoving Rocky around in the clinches. But neither fighter was doing much damage. Then, in the closing seconds of the first round, Louis dropped his left shoulder after firing a jab. Rocky stepped in and threw an overhand right that struck Louis behind the left ear. He sagged imperceptibly toward the ropes, but the bell prevented any further attack. "I think that punch was the one that made Joe feel old," observed Liebling. As Louis retreated to his stool, his trainer yelled in his ear, "Are you all right? Are you all right?" Then he pressed an ice bag against the back of Louis's neck. In Rocky's corner, Goldman was grinning.

Rocky renewed his attack in the second, trying to pin Louis against the ropes but missing wildly with several rights; one grazed the rope and set it quivering like a bowstring. Over the next three rounds, Louis started moving better and scoring with his long left jab, keeping Rocky at bay. He stung Rocky with a series of punches that bloodied his nose and opened cuts over both eyes. "It was like getting hit in the face with a hammer," said Rocky. In the third, Rocky missed with another right and stepped into a jolting left hook. Still, none of Louis's punches seemed to bother Rocky much. Louis's corner men saw how open Rocky was leaving himself and begged Louis to throw his right. But he didn't, or couldn't. And the Brown Bomber didn't throw many left hooks, considered his best punch now that the power in his right had faded. Wary of Rocky's Suzie Q, Louis was content to jab and drop his left forearm onto Rocky's bicep to keep him from countering. In the fifth, Louis cut Rocky under the right eye. But he was fighting more flat-footed, a telltale sign of fatigue. Rocky was missing with a lot of his wild rights, but Louis wasn't able to capitalize.

Louis's legs seemed to desert him in the sixth. Now it was Rocky who was pushing him around in the clinches. "It wasn't that Marciano grew better or stronger," wrote Liebling, "it was that Louis seemed to get slower and weaker." Things worsened in the seventh. The indefatigable Rocky increased the pace. A hard right buckled Louis's knees. A hook doubled him over. Then Rocky hit him on the chin with another right, and he wobbled. Toward the end of the round, there was a flash of hope for Louis. He threw a beautiful left hook that caught Rocky flush on the right side of his jaw. "But it didn't seem to faze him a bit," noted Liebling. "I knew then that Joe was beaten."

Rocky went in for the kill in the eighth. A hard left hook to Louis's jaw sent the former champ sprawling onto the canvas. Pawing at the rope, Louis pulled himself up on one knee, shaking his head slightly. He rose unsteadily to his feet at the count of seven, and the referee resumed the fight. Rocky quickly backed him up against the ropes with a barrage of punches. Louis was nearly defenseless as Rocky hit him with a left to the belly, then two tremendous left hooks to the face. Louis fell back against the ropes, arms by his sides. He hung there, momentarily suspended, arms dangling helplessly by his sides. Rocky hesitated, then hit him with a straight right to the face that drove Louis backward, through the ropes and onto the apron of the ring, only one leg still inside.

After the first knockdown, Sugar Ray Robinson had left his seat and started making his way to the ring. During Rocky's final barrage, Robinson stood by the ring shouting encouragement to Louis, one hand on the lower rope as if ready to jump in. As nearby sportswriters tried to keep Louis from rolling off the edge, referee Ruby Goldstein started the count, then stopped at four and waved his arms, signaling the fight was over. Robinson rushed to Louis's side and cradled his friend's head, fighting back tears and saying, "Joe, Joe, you'll be all right, Joe. You'll be all right, man."

Much of the Garden crowd was stunned. They had come to see an idol, and instead they witnessed the end of an era. The tall blond woman sitting near Liebling was sobbing. The man with her tried consoling her, saying, "Rocky didn't do anything wrong. He didn't foul him. Why are you booing?"

The blonde replied, "You're so cold. I hate you, too."

As Rocky stood in the ring, the referee holding his arm up in triumph, he felt the elation of victory suddenly mix with sorrow as he looked down on the pathetic figure of Louis, sprawled on the apron.

"I remember looking out at the crowd and how everyone just sat there in silence," said Rocky. "Only the guys from my hometown Brockton were making any noise. And I remember this girl, this blonde, coming down the aisle and how she was crying and how she was calling me every name she could think of . . . 'You beast. . . . You brute. . . . You animal.' And how she threw this bottle at me and it bounced onto the canvas and how I looked at it, spinning around and around. . . ."

After Louis was helped to his feet, Rocky came over to him.

"I'm sorry, Joe. I'm sorry it had to be me."

"You don't have to be sorry," said Louis. "You licked me fair and square."

Hardened sportswriters fought back tears as they banged out their stories on their typewriters.

Sitting ringside, Barbara Marciano, too, was overcome with emotion, happy for her husband but sad for Louis. "When I realized that Rocky had won, I blacked out," she said.

In his locker room, which was more subdued than usual after a victory, Rocky cried. A beaming Al Weill strutted about, pointing at Rocky and declaring, "There stands two million bucks in cold cash."

Down the hallway beneath the Garden, Louis lay on his stomach on a rubbing table, his left hand dipped into a bucket of ice on the floor. He still wore his old blue robe, with the red trim with his name in white letters on the back. But the colors were faded and the letters frayed. Louis's head was turned to one side, his face mashed against a folded towel so that it was hard to make out what he said to the semicircle of newspapermen who knelt like mourners at a wake. They asked if Rocky punched harder than Schmeling did in their first fight fifteen years earlier, the only other night that Louis had been stopped.

"This kid knocked me out with what? Two punches. Schmeling knocked me out with—musta been a hundred punches," said Louis. "But I was twenty-two years old. You can take more then than later on."

Before the fight, Grantland Rice had written that Louis could still dream of regaining his throne. Now, Red Smith wrote in the *New York Herald Tribune*, that dream had been transferred to Rocky. Inevitably, Youth had conquered Age. Louis would never fight again.

"An old man's dream ended. A young man's vision of the future opened wide," wrote Smith. "Young men have visions, old men have dreams. But the place for old men to dream is beside the fire."

9

Twelve Inches to Glory

Rocky Marciano's life changed the night he knocked out Joe Louis. He went from a promising heavyweight contender to the uncrowned champion, from well-known fighter to national celebrity.

Rocky fit the culture of the 1950s like a fist in a glove. He was humble and polite and devoted to his family. He was a patriot who had learned to box in the army while serving his country during the war. Sportswriters, unaware of his court-martial, wrote that he had helped ferry supplies to Normandy to assist the D-day invasion.

"To hero-hungry fans from Brockton and across the nation, Rocky is far more than a winner," *Time* magazine gushed. "He is Hercules, Ivanhoe, Paul Bunyan. He stands for the comforting notion not that might makes right, but that might and right are somehow synonymous."

The press couldn't get enough of the homespun immigrant Marchegiano family, and of Lena feeding her son his favorite Italian dishes. Rocky bought his mother a new refrigerator and paid for his brother Sonny to go to college. After he beat Louis and collected his biggest purse yet, $50,000, Rocky handed his mother two hundred-dollar bills and told her that from now on, he was the family's bankbook. Then he marched down to the shoe factory, where Pierino continued to toil at the bed laster machine, despite the celebrity he had earned among the Irish foremen because of his son's boxing success. Rocky told his father that it was time to retire. The family worried for his health. Now, Rocky would be the family's breadwinner. He told Pierino that he needed him by his side when he went to training camp for the big fights that lay ahead. Pierino quit and began accompanying Rocky to his camps, where he helped cook, watched over him, and basked in the glow of his son's success.

In the spring of 1952, Barbara learned that she was pregnant. The baby was due in November. The young couple was still living at Barbara's parents' house in Brockton, on the rare occasions that Rocky was home, or at the suburban estate of Russ Murray, the wealthy businessman who owned a local dog-racing track and had let Rocky train at the estate. But with a baby on the way, Rocky wanted to buy his own house. He also wanted to send his parents on a trip to Italy and to own a small business someday, after he retired from the ring. Sportswriters wrote of the former ditchdigger on the threshold of the title. Holding up his gnarled fists with their misshapen knuckles, Rocky proclaimed, "These are my college degrees." In a typical homage, the *New York Daily News* sports columnist Gene Ward wrote, "My money is riding on Rocco Marchegiano to be one of the finest heavyweight champions we've ever had."

Although it was not as overt as in the past, the public was also fascinated by the prospect of a white champion. There had not been a white heavyweight champ in fifteen years, since Joe Louis knocked out James Braddock in 1937. While Louis appealed to white fans, his black successors, Ezzard Charles and Jersey Joe Walcott, had not captured the public imagination. Many mourned Louis's passing from the boxing stage, but they were eager to embrace Rocky as the torchbearer for a new age, a Cold War hero who, as Al Weill had said, "punches like the atom bomb."

The week after Rocky beat Louis, Brockton welcomed him home with an even bigger celebration than the one following his victory over Rex Layne. A cheering crowd of fifty thousand lined the streets as Rocky's motorcade rolled past, led by a truck carrying a ten-foot-tall cake bearing his name. Many people broke through the police lines to shake the hand that had knocked out the great Joe Louis. A few days earlier, a local shoe company had presented Lena with five pairs of expensive shoes. But the same day, she received letters threatening to kill her son for knocking out Louis. The letters turned out to be pranks—one was traced to a local teenage girl who said she sent the threat because "things were dull." But that didn't mollify Lena, who flung one of her new shoes across her living room and cried, "I wish I was buying them for $1.98 again. No one wanted to hurt Rocky then."

Of course, Rocky hadn't won the championship yet. He had reinjured his right knuckle in the Louis fight and didn't box again for the rest of 1951. He worked out obsessively, running or walking almost every day. And he added special finger exercises—pressing the fingers of both hands together for an hour a day to strengthen the backs of his hands against future injuries. He squeezed a rubber ball incessantly, and had a small ball rigged to a string on his bedside lamp that he followed with his eyes to improve his eye-hand coordination.

Meanwhile, the tangled title picture provided further frustration. By early 1952, the public and the press were clamoring for Rocky to get a title shot against Jersey Joe Walcott. But Walcott wanted to savor the crown he had captured from Ezzard Charles the previous summer and was in no hurry to defend his title. Jim Norris and the IBC insisted that Walcott fight Charles again, even though they had already fought three times for the title. Walcott wanted to fight Rocky instead, because it would be a bigger payday, and delayed signing a contract to fight Charles. Rocky, too, was unhappy, feeling that the IBC and its matchmaker, Al Weill, were putting their own interests ahead of his.

Once Rocky's hand mended, Weill arranged for him to stay sharp with a fight in Philadelphia on February 13, 1952, against Lee Savold, a harmless journeyman who had been fighting for nineteen years. Savold was thirty-five years old and had fought only twice in the past three years, most recently getting knocked out by Joe Louis. Because Savold worked in a bar, he was nicknamed the Battling Bartender, and he was often his own best customer, ballooning at one point to 253 pounds. For the first time in Rocky's career, one writer said, he "will share top billing with a bottle of beer."

The matchup was so ridiculed that bookmakers refused to take bets. Pennsylvania's boxing commissioner, John "Ox" DaGrosa, told the two fighters that he expected them to show the public "why this fight?" Savold had been knocked out by Louis, who had been knocked out by Rocky, so DaGrosa said they needed to put on a good fight to quiet the skeptics. "If there's any loafing, I'll stop the bout and hold up both purses."

Rocky's popularity attracted a curious crowd of ninety-two hundred to Philadelphia's Convention Hall, as well as a national CBS television audience. In one of the worst fights of his career, Rocky came out swinging—and missing and lunging and stumbling. His timing clearly off, he missed more punches than he landed, often by feet instead of inches. Savold put up virtually no fight and showed no willingness or ability to capitalize on openings a more skilled boxer would have exploited. With the crowd jeering and the referee warning Savold to fight back, Rocky hit him enough to carve up his face like a piece of raw hamburger. Blood sprayed from Savold's face every time he was hit. His corpulent body flushed a bright pink. His blood covered Rocky's white trunks. But Rocky couldn't knock him down. Then, in the sixth, Rocky missed badly with a roundhouse right and fell flat on his face. Kneeling on the canvas with his hand on the top rope, Rocky grinned up at Savold, who stood over him in mock triumph as the crowd laughed and hooted. Embarrassed, Rocky got up and went after Savold, clubbing him with both fists. At the bell ending the round, Savold's manager leaped through the ropes and waved a towel to stop the fight. Savold, his face a gory mask, sat on his stool, nodding blankly. Rocky smiled as the referee raised his hand in victory, then looked puzzled as the crowd booed, his smile fading.

Savold had suffered the worst beating of his career, but the press gave Rocky an equally savage working over. The *New York Daily Mirror*'s Dan Parker described the fight as "one of the crudest brawls ever held outside a barroom" and said Rocky "looked as if he was using boxing gloves for the first time in his life." Arthur Daley of the *New York Times* observed: "If Marciano is the second Jack Dempsey, the first Jack Dempsey should sue him for libel."

"He never hurt me, but he sure made me look bad," said Rocky, who attributed his rusty performance to his four-month layoff since beating Louis. His handlers revealed that he had received a shot of penicillin the week before, for a cold, but had kept it a secret for fear of the fight—and his $25,000 payday—being canceled. The fight was a setback. Clearly, Rocky wasn't ready for a title shot. A few days later, Walcott gave in to the IBC and agreed to defend his title against Ezzard Charles

It was back to New England for Rocky. Weill lined up two more tune-ups for the spring in Providence. Before that, Rocky embarked on an exhibition tour in Maine in March that would cause him further embarrassment.

Rocky's opponent was to be Pete Fuller, a good-looking heavyweight prospect and the son of former Massachusetts governor Alvan T. Fuller. But when Rocky arrived in Lewiston for the first exhibition, he learned that Fuller wasn't available and asked his brother Sonny to substitute. Sonny was a senior at Brockton High School and weighed only 165 pounds, but he punched as hard as a heavyweight, and Rocky believed he could have become a middleweight contender. He had sparred with his brother and wouldn't be intimidated. But Sonny was also an outstanding baseball player who had his eye on a professional baseball career. Moreover, their mother never would have stood for two boxers in the family.

Still, Sonny looked nothing like Fuller; in fact, he looked like a younger, slimmer version of Rocky. On the first night of the tour, Rocky told Sonny to look a little taller when he entered the ring. "How am I supposed to do that?" asked Sonny. "Stand on my toes?" When Sonny was introduced and climbed into the ring, the crowd cheered, mistaking him for his older brother. When the real Rocky came out, the fans were momentarily confused. "Let's give 'em a show," Rocky told Sonny.

In the first round Rocky threw a left jab, a left uppercut, then a right cross—and stepped into a hard right to the chin from Sonny that sent his mouthpiece flying out of the ring. "I saw the look come into his eyes and his tongue stuck out of his mouth and I said to myself, 'Oh, I'm in trouble,'" recalled Sonny. Fortunately, he was able to defuse the situation by saying, "Rocky, I'm going to tell Ma."

In Lewiston that night and then in Rumford, Bangor, and Portland on successive evenings, Sonny battled his brother, who would pose as Fuller or another fighter. When the charade got out, Sonny admitted it to the *Boston Post*. "The people liked it. We gave them a show," he said.

Last-minute substitutions weren't unusual for exhibitions, especially since Rocky was the featured attraction. But the Maine Boxing Commission didn't appreciate being duped; it summoned Rocky and the local promoters to a disciplinary hearing.

On April 21, four days before the hearing, Rocky returned to the ring in Providence, in a rematch of his fight two years earlier in Boston against the former Italian champ Gino Buonvino. Rocky had struggled to put Buonvino away the first time, at rainy Braves Field, finally stopping him in the tenth. This time, Buonvino nailed Rocky with a strong right cross in the first round. But Rocky, his punches sharper and crisper than in the Savold debacle, knocked out Buonvino in the second with a vicious looping right.

Four days later, Rocky appeared before the Maine Boxing Commission and admitted that it had been his idea to have Sonny fill in. They didn't publicize Sonny's true identity, he said, "because my mother doesn't appreciate his fighting and I didn't want any press account of it." But Rocky didn't feel the fans were cheated. "I punched [Sonny] as hard as I punched Joe Louis."

The commissioners suspended Rocky for thirty days. Since the suspension would be honored by other states, they didn't make it effective until May 13, the day after his next scheduled fight, in Providence. The promoters were also suspended, for six months. They later appealed and had their suspensions overturned. Rocky never did. Years later, he called it the only regret of his career, "a stupid thing to do." But it was Sonny who paid the highest price for the stunt. He faced suspension from playing his senior high school baseball season, but after missing a few games, he was reinstated and allowed to play the rest of his senior year; one of the promoters had made a special appeal to the school authorities. The Maine incident cost Sonny a possible college scholarship for baseball, though he did go on to play in the minor leagues. The irony, said Sonny, was that he never got paid for the fights. Rocky had given Lena all the money he had made in Maine.

On May 12, Rocky dazzled 4,528 fans at the Rhode Island Auditorium as he and the former New England heavyweight champ Bernie Reynolds staged a spirited battle. Reynolds outslugged Rocky in the first round, stood toe to toe with him in a second-round slugfest, and came out for the third still swinging strong when Rocky connected with a terrific right to the jaw. The punch lifted Reynolds into the air, where he floated horizontally before crashing to the canvas, his shoulder blades and heels striking at the same time. The *Providence Journal*'s Mike Thomas called it "as hard a punch as ever was landed in a Providence ring."

It was also the last punch Rocky would throw in Providence. After twenty-eight fights there, and an overall record of 41-0, he had nothing left to prove in the minors.

◻ ◻ ◻

HE ROARED OUT of the west like a tornado, a wind howling over the Rockies and whistling across the prairies to wreak havoc with the eastern boxing establishment and Rocky's carefully plotted path to the title.

His name was Jack Hurley, a lean, angular, bespectacled man known as the Professor. Hurley was an old-school fight manager. The last of a dying breed, Hurley was irritable, egotistical, and domineering, but also a peerless teacher who got the most out of his fighters. Moreover, he knew how to stir up the public, grab headlines, and pick fights. In 1951, he picked a very public fight with the Octopus, one that threatened its grip on boxing.

In 1949, Hurley discovered a down-on-his-luck middleweight from Seattle named Harry "Kid" Matthews. Within three years, Hurley had brashly maneuvered Matthews into a heavyweight bout against Rocky, with the winner getting a shot at Jersey Joe Walcott for the title. Despite Matthews's nickname, earned when he turned pro at the age of fourteen, he was no kid. The son of an Idaho blacksmith, he was twenty-six when he met Hurley and, despite a gaudy record, was an also-ran fighting in front of small crowds in places like Salt Lake City, Boise, and Spokane. He wanted to quit after he broke his hand in a bout in Seattle, but his wife encouraged him to seek out a new manager instead. So he drove to Chicago to meet Hurley.

Hurley was a frustrated boxer from Fargo, North Dakota, who found his calling as a manager and promoter. His greatest success had been Billy "the Fargo Express" Petrolle, who had fought for the lightweight title at Madison Square Garden in 1932. Few of Hurley's fighters were of championship caliber, though. Still, that didn't deter him from demanding half the Kid's earnings instead of the standard one-third. When Matthews protested, Hurley asked how much he was earning now. Nothing, replied Matthews. "If I get half of that," said Hurley, "I won't get fat, will I?"

Matthews agreed, and became Eliza Doolittle to Hurley's Henry Higgins. Hurley taught him to be more aggressive and molded him into a light heavyweight contender. From 1949 to the middle of 1952, Matthews won thirty-five straight fights, including a nationally televised bout at Madison Square Garden that won over the skeptical New York press. Hurley also waged a relentless public-relations campaign that landed Matthews on the cover of *Ring* magazine.

Besides building up Matthews, Hurley went after the International Boxing Club as a corrupt monopoly that had denied "my athlete" a shot at the light heavyweight title. "We will never get the chance, because Jim Norris and those people run a nice little store and monopolize everything." Hurley criticized the IBC for hiring Al Weill as its matchmaker and accused Weill of breaking the law by continuing to secretly manage Rocky. His complaints caught the attention of Congress. Senator Harry P. Cain, a Republican from Washington, Matthews's home state, gave a speech on the Senate floor demanding a congressional investigation of the IBC. Senator Herman Welker of Idaho, Matthews's birthplace, accused the IBC of monopolizing boxing. "The boxing profession has reached a new low, to a point where it is ruined in the eyes of most of the American people," Welker thundered.

In the fall of 1951, the U.S. attorney general launched an antitrust investigation of the IBC, and the New York State Athletic Commission launched its own probe into the influence of gangsters in boxing, led by a new chairman, Robert Christenberry, who had been appointed by Governor Thomas E. Dewey to clean up the sport.

With the pressure ratcheting up, Norris persuaded light heavyweight champion Joey Maxim's manager to offer Matthews a title fight. The manager, who was secretly under the thumb of Frankie Carbo, sent a telegram to Senator Cain, conveying his offer of a title fight for Matthews.

But Hurley rejected the offer. He was holding out for boxing's biggest prize. He announced that Matthews was now a heavyweight and wanted a title fight against Jersey Joe Walcott. When it became apparent that Rocky was first in line, Hurley shifted his focus. He demanded a fight with Rocky, with the winner to face Walcott. "How about Marciano, this great star they're keeping in cellophane?" said Hurley. "Did he or did he not stink out the joint with Lee Savold?"

Hurley charged that Rocky was being given a clear path to the title because of Weill's connections. It didn't help when Christenberry criticized the arrangement as well. In a May *Life* magazine story on gangsters in boxing that prominently featured mug shots of Frankie Carbo, Christenberry questioned Weill's "true connection" to Rocky—and Weill's long and close association with Carbo. "Intensive scrutiny of their relationship is required, to see where one leaves off and the other begins," he wrote.

Sportswriters doubted that Weill would risk Rocky, his prized asset, in a fight against Matthews, not with the heavyweight title so close. But Norris had the Justice Department, the public, and his television advertisers breathing down his neck. The advertisers didn't like the negative publicity focused on a sport that had become a primary vehicle for them to sell beer and razor blades. Hurley taunted Norris, saying, "Jim, you've got to use this guy of mine, because otherwise I'm going to keep him in your hair every day. You get him licked and you can get rid of me."

Norris went to Weill and asked him to arrange a fight between Matthews and Rocky. Weill refused. Norris pleaded, saying the IBC needed the fight to silence Hurley and take the pressure off in the federal investigation. Norris argued that Rocky would beat Matthews easily, that he was overrated, a creation of Hurley's public-relations campaign. Still, Weill refused. So Norris turned to an ally to whom Weill couldn't say no: Frankie Carbo.

"Talk to Al and see what you can do," Norris asked Carbo.

A few days later, Weill slouched into Norris's office and agreed to the match. "If I hadn't talked to certain people, I would never have taken that match for you," he told Norris.

The Marciano-Matthews fight was announced on June 7, two days after Walcott retained his title with a dull fifteen-round decision over Charles. Rocky, expectant of a title fight against Walcott, was angry. Once again, he would have to wait for his title shot because of the machinations of the Octopus.

The fight with Matthews was scheduled for Yankee Stadium on July 28. Hurley, who predicted a million-dollar gate, dominated the prefight hype. His photograph, leaning over Matthews, even appeared on posters advertising the fight; no one could remember a manager's picture appearing on a prefight poster. When a writer wondered how Matthews felt about the fight, Hurley snapped, "Why? What's he got to do with it? I'm the manager." When Matthews was allowed to speak, he said of Hurley: "He talks, I fight. He worries, I box. He frets, I relax. It's the perfect partnership."

"Who are we fighting?" Charley Goldman groused. "Matthews or Hurley?"

Hurley trashed Rocky as someone who "never has learned how to fight" and would get hit long before Matthews did. "Let's see if he can take it," he taunted. The saloonkeeper Toots Shor quipped, "If I listened to Hurley for a week, I'd take off thirty pounds and fight Marciano myself." Rex Layne, who had lost to Matthews in his last fight, in May, predicted that the Kid would "counterpunch Rocky silly."

The *New York Times* summed up the prefight mood: "Nobody knows if [Matthews] can really fight, but Hurley made the boxing world think that he can." Adding to the mystery was Matthews's bizarre training schedule. When he showed up at the CYO gym in lower Manhattan—eschewing the traditional woodsy training camp—he sparred very little.

Rocky, meanwhile, trained with his usual intensity at Greenwood Lake. He embraced a summer heat wave, saying it reminded him of his days stoking furnaces for the Brockton Gas Company. During one fierce sparring session, Rocky missed with a left and was caught off balance by his sparring partner, who knocked him down with an overhand right. Embarrassed, Rocky claimed that he had slipped and insisted on going an extra round.

Some questioned whether the Kid belonged in the same ring with Rocky. Although he had eighty-one victories in eighty-nine fights and hadn't lost in his last fifty-two, he wasn't a true heavyweight and hadn't faced anyone who punched as hard. Rocky was a 2-to-1 favorite. The sportswriter Bill Heinz warned Hurley that he was "sending an armored Jeep against a tank." Hurley shrugged and said the Kid would outbox Marciano. Echoing Joe Louis's famous line about Billy Conn ("He can run but he can't hide"), Rocky said he wasn't worried if Hurley tried to outrun him. "I can catch up with Matthews no matter how much he backpedals." Still, the danger was that Matthews would outbox Rocky the way Conn had outboxed Louis in their classic first fight, building a lead before losing his head and trying to outslug the Brown Bomber. Unlike Conn, Hurley vowed that Matthews would not lose his head.

At the weigh-in the day of the fight, Matthews was just 179 pounds, four pounds over the minimum for a heavyweight and eight pounds lighter than Rocky. It turned out that the real reason Hurley had limited Matthews's workouts was because he was secretly fattening his fighter on mashed potatoes and custard pies. For insurance, he slipped lead weights into Matthews's shoes for the weigh-in.

The big controversy at the weigh-in involved Al Weill. While he and Rocky appeared on time at the Garden, Matthews was late. When someone asked Weill where Matthews was, he shrugged and said, "How should

I know? All I know is my fighter's here." With that slip of the tongue, Weill had publicly confirmed one of boxing's worst-kept secrets. New York boxing commissioner Christenberry was furious. Later that afternoon, he ordered the IBC to fire Weill as its matchmaker.

Thunder rumbled over Manhattan the morning of the fight, and afternoon rain showers did little to cool the muggy heat. When Rocky walked to the ring at Yankee Stadium that night, he wore galoshes over his ring shoes. Though the big gate that Hurley had envisioned didn't materialize, interest was high. Writers from across the country joined a crowd of 31,800 fans, who had paid $220,000 to witness the match. The fans in the cheaper bleacher seats were fenced off so they couldn't rush the ring, though several ran into the grandstand and had to be repelled by the police as the crowd jeered.

With rain threatening, the preliminary fight was stopped early and the combatants for the main event rushed into the ring shortly before 10:00 p.m. When the bell rang, to the surprise of everyone in Yankee Stadium except Jack Hurley, Matthews did not run away from the charging Rocky. Instead, he went right at him, crowding him inside and countering Rocky's wild rights with sharp jabs and combinations. Incredibly, Matthews was outboxing Rocky at close range. Hurley had determined that Matthews would be safer "being close to danger than out in the open." Staying in the middle of the ring and away from the ropes, Matthews moved in close and leaned in, so that Rocky's wild punches whistled harmlessly around his neck, then scored with effective counterpunching. Tying up Rocky frequently, Matthews also followed Hurley's instructions not to grab Rocky in their clinches. "He's too strong," Hurley warned. "Let him grab you, put your hands beside your chest, and as he reaches around punch up, *up*." Midway through the first, Matthews tattooed Rocky with three quick jabs, then, as Rocky lunged forward, tagged him with a straight right to the jaw. Matthews also opened a cut over Rocky's left eye. But Rocky, blinking his injured eye and licking blood from his lips, never slowed his furious assault. Just before the round ended, he caught Matthews with two stiff rights that seemed to hurt him.

Matthews won the first round on all three judges' cards, and the fans were amazed that Matthews had matched Rocky punch for punch. "Harry, this guy's a soft touch," Hurley yelled at his fighter. "Now you know the way to fight him, Harry, you've proved it already, now just get out there and stay close."

Over in Rocky's corner, it was Charley Goldman's turn to counter Hurley. "Hey, this guy's not running," he told his fighter. "He's standing right in front of you. Go out there and stand still. Just get right up in front of him and stand still." In training camp, Goldman had spent hours on Rocky's left hand, telling him that with a good boxer like Matthews, it was important to jab first, then follow with a left hook. "Jab before you hook," Goldman reminded him. Goldman was drawing on the ancient knowledge of his own legendary ring battles with Georgie Kitson, whom Goldman had befuddled with the left jab–left hook combination.

The second round began like the first, with Matthews moving inside and outboxing Rocky. But halfway through, Matthews did what Hurley had warned him not to—he pulled back. Maybe, as his trainer George Chemeres later said, Rocky had "hypnotized" the Kid by walking out slowly, as Goldman advised. Maybe Matthews got too cocky, like Billy Conn against Joe Louis. Or maybe, as Hurley theorized, the Pride of the Northwest suddenly realized he wasn't in Seattle anymore. Midway through the round, as the fighters broke from a clinch, Hurley later recalled, "he realizes he's fighting in Yankee Stadium in front of all those people, and he just gets frozen with fear."

When Rocky slowly approached and threw a right, Matthews lurched back, startled. Chasing Matthews across the ring, Rocky hit him with a left jab, then two left hooks that "damn near took his head off," Chemeres recalled. The first hook buckled his knees and sent him stumbling backward toward his corner. The second, flush on the jaw, knocked him down "like a limp rag doll," one writer said. Matthews's head struck the lower ring rope and then he slid to the canvas in a reclining position, nearly in Hurley's lap. He was counted out just over two minutes into the second round.

In the dressing room, Hurley, who had bet $10,000 on Matthews, didn't hide his disgust. "He went amateur on me," he complained. "He pulled back three times and each time he got nailed. He coulda stayed close all night. . . . The Kid would've won the fight. . . . Let me tell you, it's a long way from that ring to the dressing room at Yankee Stadium, and all the way back people are saying, 'Where's your great fighter now, Hurley?' and there I am bleeding in my shoes." Matthews, sitting nearby, nodded and murmured, "It was bad."

Rocky, on his way back to his dressing room, lost his police escort and had to fight his way through the crowd as fans pounded him on the back. Safely inside, he posed for a picture with the mayor of Brockton and held court with the writers crowded around him. Nearby, Goldman crowed, "I knew he'd fool him with that left jab. I knew he'd fool him!" Rocky was exultant. The last barrier to a heavyweight title fight had been swept away, and he looked ahead to Walcott. The two would meet in September in Philadelphia in the most anticipated heavyweight title fight in years.

Later, Weill boasted, in his fractured syntax, "Hurley wanted to be a Swengali but the strings broke."

◻ ◻ ◻

THE BALLAD OF Jersey Joe Walcott could have been a blues song.

Even measured against the hard lives of many boxers, Walcott had endured more hardships and bad breaks than most. A God-fearing, Bible-reading father of six from southern New Jersey, Walcott had toiled for years in boxing's backwaters. He wasn't exaggerating when he said, "I once went an entire decade being hungry." Even after he belatedly found success, he ate just two meals a day, conditioned to be "a naturally light eater," he said. When Walcott improbably won the heavyweight crown on July 18, 1951—on his fifth try—the press called him boxing's new "Cinderella Man." (James Braddock, who had come off Depression bread lines to win the title in 1935, had been the original.) *Life* magazine called Walcott "the oldest and most implausible heavyweight champion of the world." He had been around boxing so long that he had knocked out a father *and* his son—Phil Johnson in the third round in 1936 and Harold Johnson in the third round in 1950. As he prepared to face Rocky, Walcott was thirty-eight, going on forty-eight. His true age, like that of the ageless Satchel Paige, was a matter of mystery and speculation. "I'm not old," Walcott told a sportswriter. "I'm just ugly."

According to his birth certificate, Walcott was born on January 31, 1914. The actual year may have been 1911, based on what he told a sportswriter in 1949, which would have made him forty when he won the title.

Walcott, who preached at his church in Camden and had met the pope, said that he got no satisfaction from hurting an opponent. "I know it isn't right," he said, "but from the moment I step into the ring I forget I might hurt a fellow man. I become a creature threatened by destruction."

Walcott was born Arnold Raymond Cream, the fourth of twelve children, in Pennsauken, one of the oldest black communities in southern New Jersey. His father, a laborer and mason from the Caribbean island of Saint Thomas, struggled to support the family, who often went hungry. Arnold and his siblings developed rickets, a common bone disease among poor children suffering from a lack of vitamin D.

Boxing was the most popular sport in the neighborhood. Kids sparred in makeshift outdoor rings, encouraged by grown-ups who handed out candy. Arnold's father taught him to fight and gave him his first pair of boxing gloves. One night, when Arnold was taking out the trash, he overheard his father exclaim to his mother, "Let me tell you one thing, if this boy gets the right trainer and manager, he could become a champion." As a boy, Arnold stood in the rain to catch a glimpse of the first black heavyweight champion, Jack Johnson, when he swung through town. In the wake of Johnson's downfall and fast living, which scandalized white America, blacks were barred from title fights and treated shabbily by promoters, who often expected them to throw fights in return for bookings. Even after Joe Louis broke this color barrier, things were still hard for black fighters, especially during the Depression. But when Arnold's father died of heart disease in 1929, Arnold dropped out of school to help support the family, who couldn't afford to buy coal to heat their drafty house and had to huddle around a wood stove in winter. Arnold began boxing professionally in 1930 under a new name: Jersey Joe Walcott. It was an homage to his father's favorite fighter, the West Indian boxer Joe Walcott, also known as the Barbados Demon, who had become the first black welterweight champion in 1901.

Walcott married a minister's daughter and lived with his growing family in a shack with burlap over the windows. To supplement his meager income from boxing, he collected garbage, dug trenches, hauled ice and coal, packed cans at a soup factory, and was a stevedore on the Philadelphia docks. And yet ring opportunities kept passing him by. A trainer invited him to move to Chicago, where he was going to work with another young heavyweight, but Walcott came down with typhoid fever and couldn't go. The other fighter in Chicago was Joe Louis. Later, Walcott was hired to be Louis's sparring partner at his training camp at

Lakewood, New Jersey, but lost that job after he knocked Louis down during a workout. Walcott quit the ring several times, only to return to pick up some extra cash. He was often hungry and lost one fight after collapsing to the canvas in exhaustion. In another fight he broke his hand, couldn't work, and had to go on public assistance, collecting $9.50 a week.

But there were triumphant moments as well. In 1935 in Camden, Walcott knocked out a good heavyweight, Roxie Allen, with a vicious left hook. Two people of note were at the Camden Convention Hall that night. One was the original Joe Walcott, curious to see if his namesake was worthy. The old Barbados Demon was broke, but Walcott got his father's hero a ringside seat and took up a collection to help the old fighter. After the fight, his namesake told him, "You'll make it, boy. You're a great left hooker."

The second person of note at the fight in Camden that night was Felix Bocchicchio, who would resurrect Walcott's career a decade later.

During World War II, Walcott gave up boxing and settled into a steady job at a navy shipyard in Camden, chipping paint and caulking ships. He wasn't thinking about a return to the ring until he was introduced to Bocchicchio, a local sportsman who had just started promoting boxing in Camden. He remembered seeing Walcott knock out Allen years before, and promised to support Walcott and his family so that he could train properly without worrying about money.

Finally, Walcott had gotten the break in his thirties that future champions usually get in their early twenties. He started getting better fights, and within three years, on December 5, 1947, he was fighting Joe Louis for the title in Madison Square Garden. Walcott dominated the fight, knocking Louis down twice and showing surprisingly agile legs for an older fighter. The crowd was convinced he had won. So was Louis, who started to climb through the ropes. But the judges awarded Louis a split decision. Over the next four years, Walcott fought three more times for the title and lost—first in a rematch to Louis, then twice to Ezzard Charles.

After Charles's second uninspiring win over Walcott in March 1951, the clamor began to give someone else, like Rocky, a shot. Instead, Charles inexplicably agreed to fight Walcott again four months later in Pittsburgh. This time, Walcott's left hook flashed out of a humid night at Forbes Field to knock out Charles in the seventh round. The new heavyweight champion returned to a hero's welcome in Camden. After twenty-one years, his faith had been rewarded. Walcott bought his family a spacious ten-room house and enjoyed the perks of being champion, getting paid for personal appearances. He was in no hurry to defend his title. And when he did, he wanted a big box-office draw—he wanted Rocky, particularly after witnessing his sorry performance against Lee Savold. After the IBC forced him to defend his title against Charles, in a disappointing and dull fight that Walcott won by unanimous decision on June 5, 1952, there was nothing standing between him and Rocky—except the small matter of Felix Bocchicchio and his criminal record.

New York was the logical place to stage a heavyweight title bout of the magnitude of Marciano-Walcott. But Bocchicchio couldn't get a manager's license there. That spring, in his *Life* magazine exposé on gangsters in boxing, New York boxing commissioner Christenberry had singled out Bocchicchio as one of the tentacles in Frankie Carbo's Octopus. Bocchicchio's mug shot appeared in the article, along with a summary of his past arrests for pandering, jailbreaking, white slavery, bootlegging, and other serious crimes. In 1930, Bocchicchio had been arrested in Pennsylvania for felonious assault and robbery but broke out of jail while awaiting trial. Two years later, Bocchicchio was arrested after being shot in the knee during a robbery at a house of prostitution near Baltimore. The head of the fledgling Bureau of Investigation, J. Edgar Hoover, said that Bocchicchio was part of a vice ring that ran prostitutes in Maryland, Pennsylvania, and New Jersey. Bocchicchio was also wanted for questioning in the murder of a Pennsylvania gas station attendant.

Bocchicchio was sentenced to two years in prison for the jailbreak but escaped convictions on the more serious charges. By the time he met Walcott, he was aligned with Carbo's top lieutenant, Philadelphia numbers king Blinky Palermo, who also had a stable of fighters. Thanks to his friends on the Pennsylvania boxing commission, Bocchicchio was able to secure a pardon from the governor and obtain a boxing manager's license there. But New York would not follow suit, and Bocchicchio refused to take his fighter anywhere he could not be in his corner.

Instead, the fight was set for September 23, 1952, in the Philadelphia Municipal Stadium. Philadelphia: the City of Brotherly Love. Walcott's—and Bocchicchio's—home turf.

◻ ◻ ◻

AL WEILL WAS back. And Rocky wasn't happy.

As the IBC's matchmaker, Weill had had to keep his distance from his prized heavyweight. But three days after Rocky beat Kid Matthews—and Weill publicly called Rocky "my fighter"—the New York boxing commissioner summoned him and Jim Norris to a meeting and told them it was time to cut the charade. Weill immediately announced that he was resigning from the IBC to "resume" managing Rocky. He said that he wanted to give Rocky the full benefit of his years of experience as a manager. That didn't set well with Rocky. It meant that Weill was more visible and vocal, a grating presence as Rocky trained for his biggest fight.

Rocky's training camp had been moved from Greenwood Lake to Grossinger's, the famed Jewish resort in the Catskills. Big-name entertainers and tourists would drift up the mountain to watch Rocky spar in a ring set up in a corrugated tin airplane hangar next to the resort's private air strip. But Rocky stayed far from the hotel and its glittering nightlife, living in a Spartan, secluded cabin high up on the mountain. Like earlier writers and painters, Rocky shut himself off from the outside world and embraced the wilderness solitude of the Catskills. His opponent's name was never mentioned in his presence, unless by an inquisitive sportswriter. In the weeks before the fight, he read no mail and took no phone calls, not even from his wife. The final week, he wouldn't even shake hands, ride in a car, or eat any new foods. He wasn't allowed to read anything about the fight, lest he see something that might upset him. When he wasn't training, he talked about other things, like baseball, took walks in the mountains, played Ping-Pong, lazed in the sun, or plowed through the stack of Reader's Digests he kept by his bed. Rocky kept his thoughts focused on the task at hand. He didn't allow himself to think ahead to the morning after the fight, when he would be freed from this hermetic existence. "In my own mind," he said, "I'm boxing him all the time."

Weill burst into this tranquil scene like a thunderstorm on a lazy summer afternoon.

Weill was nervous and irritable, discouraging Barbara's presence as a distraction until finally she went home to Brockton. Weill quibbled with Rocky's friends and, in one particularly upsetting incident, ordered the chef who prepared Rocky's meals not to let anyone in the kitchen. When Rocky's father, Pierino, tried to go into the kitchen one night for a snack, the chef brusquely ordered him out. Rocky hadn't minded Weill driving Barbara away, since he accepted the sacrifices necessary to winning the championship. But in a rare outburst, he told Weill that he wouldn't stand for his father being treated that way. Weill backed down and told Rocky he didn't want to see him getting so excited.

Rocky also fumed over the terms of the deal with Walcott. As the challenger, he would only get 20 percent of the gate, versus 40 percent for Walcott. That was not unusual, but what really upset Rocky was that the contract called for a return match that guaranteed the same percentages, even if Rocky won.

Rocky and Allie also fretted about Weill's plan to be in his corner for the fight. Weill had put everyone on edge when he was there during Rocky's earlier fights against Gilley Ferron and Johnny Pretzie. But when Rocky told Weill that he'd prefer to have just Allie and Goldman in his corner against Walcott, an indignant Weill flatly rejected the idea. There was no way Al Weill wasn't going to be front and center with the whole world watching.

The *New Yorker*'s A. J. Liebling was impressed when he watched Rocky spar at Grossinger's. He saw that Rocky wasn't throwing as many long, looping punches. He could get away with that against Kid Matthews, Rex Layne, or even an aging Joe Louis, but wild misses would leave Rocky off balance and exposed to the more dangerous Walcott. But if Rocky couldn't unleash his Suzie Q, how would he be able to knock out the champ? Liebling remembered Goldman telling him how ineffective Rocky's short punches were, and he didn't think Rocky could outpoint Walcott. "His boxing had improved vastly—from terrible to mediocre," Liebling observed.

Rocky's sparring partners did a good job emulating Walcott's shuffling style, which made him hard to hit. Walcott was a cagey veteran—"a cutie pie," Rocky said—who had developed a dizzying array of tricks; he would punch an opponent, turn, and start to walk away, then whirl around and hit him with an explosive right or left hook. That's how he knocked down Joe Louis and knocked out Ezzard Charles. One sportswriter called it Walcott's "disconcerting flat-foot floogle dance." His style had enabled him to build a record of 51-16, with thirty-two knockouts.

Jack Dempsey dropped into Rocky's camp and proclaimed him a

changed fighter from the raw, wild kid he had first seen in Goldman's CYO gym three years earlier. He refused to pick a winner but predicted it "could be another Dempsey-Firpo fight," referring to the 1923 brawl featuring eleven knockdowns, when Luis Firpo knocked Dempsey out of the ring, only to be knocked out himself later on. It was considered one of the greatest heavyweight title bouts of all time.

Walcott, training in Atlantic City, was dismissive of Rocky. "He can't fight," said the champ. "If I don't whip him, take my name out of the record books." Walcott said he wouldn't shuffle away from Rocky but come right at him. Rocky dared him to. He spoke of a recurring dream he had, in which Walcott stood toe to toe with him, slugging it out. Sometimes the dream ended with Rocky catching him; other times Walcott got away.

Charley Goldman had no doubt that Rocky would knock out Walcott. "Rocky hits too hard, with either hand, to lose to a fighter of Walcott's age," he said. "Sure, Jersey Joe is a wise boxer. He packs a punch, too. But he will not stand up to Marciano." Goldman felt that criticism of Rocky for being crude was exaggerated. Sure, his footwork wasn't pretty, but he had learned to feint, to counter, to feel an opponent out and protect himself. "The boy may look like a sucker to some of the writers in the press rows," he said, "but take it from me, he isn't a sucker."

▫ ▫ ▫

THICK FOG BLANKETED the Catskills on the Monday morning that Rocky and his entourage broke camp, the day before the fight. A convoy of cars led by Steve Melchiore, a Philadelphia police detective in charge of Rocky's security, made the five-hour trek from the mountains to the City of Brotherly Love.

Within five minutes of his arrival at the downtown Warwick Hotel, Rocky's room was swarming with camp followers, reporters, photographers, and fans who had slipped in looking for a word or a picture or just a glimpse of the first unbeaten heavyweight challenger since James Jeffries in 1899. The room was bright with popping flashbulbs and the blinding lights of newsreel film crews. Goldman hustled Rocky through the crowd and off to a quieter room where he could have some lunch. "Rock's got to eat," explained Goldman. "He had breakfast at 9 o'clock. This is the first time since I knew him he's been without food six hours. He's dying." Surprisingly, later that evening a calm, confident, and relaxed Rocky invited reporters into his hotel suite to chat. It was the first time the writers could remember a fighter being so accessible on the eve of a big fight. The press conference ended when Rocky's chef summoned him to dinner, a large steak smothered in garlic sauce.

Philadelphia hummed with the anticipation of a championship fight. The fight crowd had descended on the city—old champions and managers, sportsmen, gamblers, bookies, hustlers, sportswriters, mobsters, celebrities, the rich and the famous. Trainloads of fans had come from Brockton. The Providence promoter Manny Almeida led a delegation of about fifty Rhode Islanders. Fight fans gathered in knots on sidewalks and thronged hotel lobbies and restaurants. They spilled out of the former lightweight boxer Lew Tendler's saloon and chophouse on Broad Street, the city's traditional gathering spot for the fight mob. It was at Tendler's that Blinky Palermo once asked Sugar Ray Robinson to throw a fight, and where Rocky's uncle Mike that week managed to place $40,000 in bets on his nephew for himself and other Brocktonians. Allie Colombo and Nick Sylvester walked into Tendler's the night before the fight and found it jammed with boys from Brockton. "They went berserk, berserk, berserk," recalled Sylvester. "They wanted to know how much to bet. I says, 'Bet everything.' . . . Allie was just, 'Shut up, shut up.'"

◻ ◻ ◻

THE DAY OF the fight, September 23, 1952, dawned gray and damp.

Rocky rose early, slightly stiff, and went for a jog with Allie and his police bodyguard, Steve Melchiore. They went to the park across the street from Municipal Stadium. Melchiore gestured at the silent stadium, where Gene Tunney had taken the title from Jack Dempsey twenty-six years ago on that date. The policeman told Rocky, "This is where you're going to become the world champion." Rocky dropped to his knees and mouthed a silent prayer, tears in his eyes.

After they returned to the hotel, Allie walked over to the office of the local promoter, Herman Taylor, to pick up some complimentary tickets. The office was busy with last-minute requests, and the secretaries didn't know anything about the tickets, so Allie walked into Taylor's private office without knocking. Stunned, he saw Taylor huddled with Felix Bocchicchio and Pennsylvania boxing commissioner Ox DaGrosa. The men seemed as surprised to see Allie as he was to see them, and they froze in mid-conversation. Allie got the tickets and left, suspicious that Bocchicchio had been trying to find out in advance the name of that night's referee, which was normally kept secret to guard against tampering.

Back at the hotel, Allie and Melchiore began hearing chatter that the odds were shifting on the fight. Rocky had opened as a strong favorite, but in the final hours the odds shifted toward Walcott until Rocky was favored only by a modest 8-to-5. They were hearing that a lot of Walcott money was coming in from Camden and Philadelphia. The only thing that may have prevented Walcott from becoming the favorite, Rocky said, was all the money bet on him by his Brockton supporters. People had mortgaged their homes, sold cars, borrowed money, and pawned possessions to place bets on Rocky. "My gang from Brockton came into Philly ready to mortgage everything they owned to back me," Rocky said later. "I didn't intend to let them down."

As he went about his prefight routine, Rocky didn't know about the suddenly shifting odds or the meeting Allie had witnessed in the promoter's office. Allie didn't mention it, not wanting to distract him. Rocky thought that Allie seemed more agitated than usual, but he knew that his friend was naturally nervous and figured this was a big night for him, too. Before they left the hotel for the stadium, though, Allie said cryptically, "You got to get this one over with quick. It don't look good to me from what I seen. I don't think you're going to get the best of it if it goes to a decision."

When they arrived at the stadium, Melchiore thought it strange to see DaGrosa sitting in the ring, in Rocky's corner. "I don't like the smell of this whole thing, Rock," he confided. "The price has been coming down fast all week. Be ready for anything."

□ □ □

IT WAS A fine September evening, crisp with the hint of autumn, a freshening breeze parting the clouds as the stars winked overhead. Forty thousand people filled the horseshoe-shaped Municipal Stadium, a football field in the industrial wasteland of south Philadelphia that hosted the annual Army-Navy game. They sat in the grandstands and on folding chairs set on the grass around the ring, which shone with a silvery light surrounded by the darkness.

Barbara, seven months pregnant, sat ringside near Frank Sinatra. Rocky's eleven-year-old brother Peter sat four rows from the ring with a cousin and a local priest who was a family friend. Sonny sat with his cousin Mike "Duna" Cappiello. Pierino sat nearby, holding a shoe box with an extra pair of boxing shoes, a habit he had gotten into in case his son forgot his shoes. Rocky's sisters, Alice, Concetta, and Betty, were also in Philadelphia. Lena, who had never seen her son fight, was in her usual pew at St. Patrick's Church in Brockton, with her friend Jennie Giantomaso. She always lit a candle for Rocky, but on this night she had a premonition and lit thirteen, then hugged her friend and thought back over her son's life, beginning with his near death as a baby. The two women and a priest were the only ones in the silent church.

Rocky, refreshed from his customary prefight nap, made his way through the crowd and into the ring, led by a phalanx of eight police officers. His robe was red and black, the colors of Brockton High School. Walcott waited in the ring, his chiseled features, broad chest, and sinewy thighs belying his age. He weighed 196 pounds to Rocky's 184 and had a seven-inch reach advantage.

The referee, Charley Daggert, called the two combatants and their handlers to the center of the ring to review the instructions. "I ask both youse boys give me no kidney or rabbit punches. I'm gonna call 'em if you do," he said. "I want both of youse to give me an honest, clean fight."

When the fight began, Walcott surprised everybody. He didn't dance and shuffle away from Rocky but came right at him, stinging him with hard rights and lefts. Midway through the first round, he staggered Rocky with a right to the side of the head, then popped him with a short left hook to the chin that knocked him on the seat of his pants. It was the first time in his career that Rocky had ever been knocked down. As the flashbulbs exploded at ringside and the crowd leaped to its feet, Rocky quickly rolled onto his side, unhurt but embarrassed and enraged. "You son of a bitch," he said to himself. "I'll get you."

Goldman felt that Rocky was fighting in a trance, just as Goldman had in 1912 when he lost to the bantamweight champion Johnny Coulon. Rocky was "daydreaming," said Goldman. "He wasn't overconfident, careless or anything like that, but he just couldn't believe that he, a kid from Brockton, Massachusetts, was really fighting for the heavyweight championship of the world. If he hadn't been wearing boxing gloves he'd probably have pinched himself to see if he was awake." Rocky agreed that his "subconscious seemed to take over. Here I was, face to face with my biggest crowd, my biggest purse and my biggest moment."

Goldman and Weill screamed at him to take an eight count to clear his head, but he ignored them and was up at the count of four. Walcott, who expected Rocky to stay down longer, had turned to walk to a neutral corner. He still had his back turned when Rocky rose shakily to his feet. Three precious seconds passed before Walcott could close on him, enough time for Rocky to raise his gloves in defense. "I should have finished it then but he got away from me," Walcott said. Rocky, who had always wondered how it would feel to get knocked down, later said, "It sure was nice to discover that I could get up with vision clear."

Walcott kept attacking, hooking another short left to the head, and Rocky's mouth started bleeding. Rocky fought back, trying to crowd Walcott but missing with several of his punches. The crowd roared in appreciation of the fast pace. Walcott kept the pressure on, tagging Rocky with hard rights and lefts to his jaw and pinning Rocky's hands so high in clinches that he couldn't swing back. Rocky stayed close, swinging wildly with both hands. Toward the end of the first round, Rocky hooked a left to Walcott's body, then a right and left to his head. And in the second round, he smashed a left hook to Walcott's jaw just before the bell. But Walcott was in command, slipping most of Rocky's hardest punches and punching with authority. By the end of the round, he had raised a bruise over Rocky's left eye.

A. J. Liebling, watching the fight from a concrete seat in the grandstand, noticed a black man seated to his right, entirely surrounded by whites, screaming, "Don't get mad, Joe! *Please* don't get mad!" But Walcott came out for the third round continuing to act mad, walking out to meet Rocky once more. Rocky began to assert himself, driving Walcott back toward the ropes. Walcott yielded grudgingly, hitting back all the time and making Rocky pay. He didn't break off and circle away as he had in other fights. Toward the end of the third, Walcott hit Rocky with a tremendous right to the head, but Rocky merely blinked and kept advancing, ripping a right to Walcott's head, then another left and right to the head that hurt Walcott. For several rounds, they continued to slug each other after the bell, with Rocky usually getting in the last punch. The fifth ended with Rocky battering Walcott against the ropes and the two exchanging heavy rights and lefts to the jaw. Liebling wondered how Walcott was able to remain standing. "The match now seemed to be following the script more closely," he noted. "Rocky was slowing him down. The old man would go in a couple of rounds. If he started running, he might last a little longer." Rocky, too, thought that he would be able to finish Walcott in another round or two.

But the fight took an unexpected turn late in the sixth round, as Rocky was battering Walcott again. During a furious exchange against the ropes, Rocky came out of a crouch and the top of his head collided with Walcott's forehead over the champ's left eye. Blood and gore began to pour from both men's wounds. Rocky wanted to make the cut over Walcott's eye a target, but suddenly blood started streaming down his own forehead and into his eyes and he couldn't see. He was cut but didn't know where. Both of his eyes began to burn. The bell rang, and Rocky retreated to his corner to regroup.

His corner was chaos. Everyone was shouting and talking at once. Weill, who had been agitated ever since Rocky's knockdown in the first round, was more excited than Rocky had ever seen him. Between the third and fourth rounds, Weill and Allie had gotten into a shouting match after Rocky wordlessly tried to push Weill away with his glove and Allie tried to get him to get to leave the corner. There was also a new face in the corner, the veteran trainer and cut man Freddie Brown, whom Weill had hired that morning for $50. With Goldman and Allie, that made four people trying to work on Rocky in the sixty seconds between rounds. Rocky, who usually didn't talk in his corner, shouted at Allie: "I can't see. My eyes are burning. Do something." Panicked, Weill grabbed a wet sponge and squeezed it on Rocky's head, sending blood and liquid streaming into his eyes and making it worse. Goldman and Brown finally found the cut, on the crown of his forehead, and applied medication and a salve to stop the bleeding.

When the seventh round started, Rocky advanced from his corner tentatively, blinking his burning eyes. The referee warned him about head butting. He was having such a hard time seeing that he backed away from Walcott. "I was just trying to fake it, anything to kill time until my eyes cleared," he said later. "I was throwing a left jab as quick as I could, just trying to keep Walcott away from me."

The next two rounds were dangerous for Rocky. Liebling, unaware of what was happening, was struck that Rocky unaccountably "began to flounder. He wavered and almost pawed the air, although he had not been hit by any one particular big punch. He seemed to be coming unstuck." Whenever Rocky rested his head against Walcott's shoulder in a clinch, his eyes started burning again. It seemed that Walcott had some substance between his neck and shoulder, where Rocky rested his head when he came in close.

But what? The medicine that Rocky's handlers had put on his head, or that Walcott's handlers had used for the cut over his eye? The liniment that had been rubbed on Walcott's body, to create friction and lessen the impact of punches? But those substances were typical in boxing matches and didn't cause fighters' eyes to burn. Rocky would later come to believe that it was something more sinister. Through the detective work of his bodyguard Melchiore, Rocky learned well after the fight that Blinky Palermo had provided some capsicum Vaseline to Bocchicchio, who had rubbed it on Walcott's gloves. Rocky's suspicions were confirmed when he watched a film of the fight from a different angle and saw Bocchicchio appear to rub something on Walcott's left glove between rounds. Marty Weill, Al's stepson, who was monitoring Walcott's corner, told Rocky after the fight that Bocchicchio had seemed to be "fooling around" with Walcott's gloves between those early rounds. Bocchicchio disputed that; he blamed the confusion in Rocky's corner and the medicine his own handlers had used to close his head wound. But Rocky would put those clues together with the suspicious meeting Allie had walked in on that morning with Bocchicchio and Ox DaGrosa, and become convinced of a plot to steal his shot at the title.

Rocky, of course, wasn't aware of any of this during the fight. He was just trying to survive. The first time he came into contact with Walcott in the eighth round, his eyes began burning anew. "I don't know how long this thing will go on," he said. "I'm still trying to keep him off balance and keep myself from being tagged, and at the same time maybe get in a lucky punch. I'm praying while I'm doing it. *Please, God, let me get my eyes clear. This is important for me. Please do that for me, and I can handle the rest.*"

Nor was Rocky fully aware of the drama unfolding in his corner. During the seventh and eighth rounds, Weill kept screaming at the referee, Charley Daggert, about Rocky's eyes. Ox DaGrosa threatened to have him removed by a police officer if he didn't sit down and shut up. So Weill quieted down but started telling Melchiore what to shout. When DaGrosa tried to silence him, Melchiore snapped, "I'm rooting for the guy, and nobody can stop me from rooting for him." Before the ninth round, Weill strode across the ring apron and pleaded with Daggert to check Walcott's gloves. But Daggert sent him back to his corner.

Finally, Freddie Brown, the fifty-dollar cut man, took charge. After both the seventh and eighth rounds, Brown had three big sponges soaking in ice water. Crouching in front of Rocky as he sat on his stool, Brown took a sponge from Allie, held Rocky's head back, and squeezed the water into one eye. Then he took another sponge and washed out the other eye, and kept alternating until the bell. All the while, as Weill was screaming at Rocky to knock Walcott out and Goldman fretted nervously, Brown spoke to Rocky calmly and quietly. "Now, listen, you don't have to see," he said. "Don't worry about it. Just get your hands on the guy's body so you know where he is and then fucking pound."

In the ninth round, Rocky's eyes began to clear. Walcott won that round, as he had the previous two, but he had slowed enough that Rocky had been able to make it through by sheer force of will. Now, Rocky began to reassert himself. He regained the momentum in the tenth, the fiercest round of what Liebling called "one of the stubbornest matches ever fought by heavyweights." Although Rocky could feel Walcott tiring, the champion was still hurting him with powerful body blows. Ringside observers marveled at Walcott's stamina as the fight moved into the later rounds, deeper than Rocky had ever fought, a true test of his mighty endurance. Walcott's legs were fresher than Rocky's, which were getting rubbery. At the bell ending the tenth, Rocky smashed Walcott with a terrific left to the jaw and started to wheel around to return to his corner. But then he turned to look at Walcott, "a strange flicker of emotion on his impassive face for the first time," observed the *New York Times*' Arthur Daley. "The look he gave Walcott was a strange, quizzical one. His lips didn't move but his eyes spoke very plainly. 'What holds you up old man?' they asked."

Rocky was hoping that Walcott would slug it out with him in the eleventh. Instead, the old man outboxed him, slipping his punches and winning the eleventh and twelfth rounds. In the eleventh, Walcott caught Rocky with a ferocious right to the heart that staggered him, then pummeled him with a volley of lefts and rights that opened a gash between his eyebrows and might have knocked him out if not for the bell. Walcott continued to punish Rocky in the twelfth. When Rocky returned to his corner after the bell, he asked his handlers how he was doing. All four shouted, "You've got to knock him out!"

In his ringside seat, Rocky's brother Peter was sobbing. He had been stunned to see his invincible big brother knocked down at the beginning of the fight. After the twelfth, Peter cried openly and begged the priest sitting with him to leave. Blood soaked Rocky's face and chest and stained Walcott's white trunks. The priest, Father Malone, told Peter to have faith and quiet down. Nearby, Sonny had bitten his fingernails bloody and kept pounding his cousin Duna on the back. By the late rounds, the cousin's jacket was bloody, too.

Nicky Sylvester was pale at ringside. He had bet a lot of money on the fight, and if Rocky lost he wouldn't be able to afford to go through with his planned wedding in three weeks. When a reporter asked what would happen if Rocky lost, Sylvester snapped: "I'll tell you what's going to happen. Fifty thousand Italians are going to commit suicide."

Later, Rocky confessed to the sports editor of the *Brockton Enterprise*: "It was a terrible feeling sitting there between the twelfth and thirteenth rounds. I was hurt and confused and everything around me was in bedlam."

The bell for the thirteenth round rang. Rocky rose from his stool and walked out to meet Walcott. Both men were clearly tired, probing, circling, not landing any punches. Rocky backed Walcott into the ropes, hooked a left. Walcott moved backward to evade it. Like a pair of gunslingers, Walcott cocked his right elbow to fire a punch at Rocky's unguarded jaw as Rocky pulled back his left and prepared to fire a straight right at Walcott's head. Rocky was a split second faster. His fist connected with Walcott's jaw with a frightful, bone-rattling crack audible at ringside. Walcott's head swiveled grotesquely, his face distorted like a gruesome rubber mask folded in on itself. The punch was economical, traveling no more than twelve inches. It was so quick that many in the crowd missed it. Frank Sinatra had turned to say something to Barbara Marciano. Liebling called it "a model of pugilistic concision" and, "according to old-timers, about as hard as anybody ever hit anybody." For good measure,

Rocky brushed the top of Walcott's head with a left hook, but it wasn't necessary. Walcott "flowed down like flour out of a chute. He didn't seem to have a bone in his body."

Walcott said later that he had tried a left jab a second earlier that jiggled the blood from his cut into his left eye, temporarily blinding him. If he had thrown the right first, if he had been able to see Rocky's right and stepped back, the exhausted Rocky might have fallen down from the force of the punch. Instead, Walcott sank slowly to the bottom rope and sat there, stunned, then fell forward onto his knees, his forehead pressed into the canvas. Daggert counted him out, forty-three seconds into the thirteenth round. Rocky raced exuberantly across the ring, kissed his glove, then did a little dance, his arms thrust skyward. Allie raced into the ring, jumped on his back, and wrapped him in a hug.

A sustained roar washed over the stadium like a tidal wave. Delirious Brocktonians stormed the ring, kicking over the press table and trampling typewriters. The police formed a flying wedge in front of the new champion, and his corner men locked arms behind him as they raced through the crowd to his dressing room. Joe Louis helped Rocky's brother Peter make his way through the crowd to see Rocky. Rocky's sisters Alice and Concetta also pushed their way through the crowd to his dressing room, which was overflowing with friends, relatives, writers, old fighters, and celebrities. Later, his youngest sister, Betty, made it in, too. Humphrey Bogart pumped Rocky's hand and told him he had fought "a helluva fight." Pierino stood over in a corner, weeping and saying over and over, "I'm proud." Later, after a doctor had put fourteen stitches in the cut on his scalp and adhesive tape over the cut between his eyes, Rocky smiled for a newspaper photo with Betty and Concetta kissing him on each cheek. There was a large purplish lump under his left eye.

It was well past midnight when Rocky finally called his mother in Brockton. Lena had not seen the fight, but she certainly knew the results from the pandemonium outside—the sound of firecrackers, honking horns, delirious cheers in the streets. She was stunned when she learned that he had won in the thirteenth round—that's how many candles she had lit at the church. She asked her son how he felt. Fortunately, she couldn't see his bloodied and bruised face. He told her he felt like a champion.

Rocky had lost his trousers in the confusion of his dressing room and had to wear his robe back to the hotel. He didn't want to take a chance at losing his most prized possession that night. So he entrusted his sisters with the right glove, the one still slick with blood that had knocked out Walcott, the one he had kissed and said a silent prayer over at his moment of triumph, thanking God for letting him see and, after his long improbable journey, making him the heavyweight champion of the world.

10

The Lion and the Lamb

O N A COOL SEPTEMBER NIGHT IN 1952, A CAR MADE ITS WAY NORTH ON a highway in Connecticut. It was well past midnight, but the police were out, searching for escapees from the women's prison in Danbury.

A police cruiser pulled the car over. Two female passengers claimed to be the sisters of Rocky Marciano, who had fought for the world heavyweight title in Philadelphia earlier that night.

The policemen, who like most people in America knew about the fight, and perhaps had stolen a few minutes during their shift to follow the updates on the radio, were skeptical. Yeah, yeah, they said, sure you are. The two women insisted. They were headed back to Brockton from Philadelphia, they explained, because they had young children at home. If the police wanted proof, the women said, they had proof in the trunk: We've got the glove. Curious now, the troopers watched as they opened the trunk. There was no prison escapee hiding inside—just a boxing glove, sheathed in a plastic garment bag, still bright with blood. The glove that had thrown the punch that delivered the crown to the son of a Brockton shoemaker in a savage fight that would go down as one of the greatest heavyweight championship bouts in history.

Excited, the officers asked the women if they would mind going to the police station with them, so they could show the other officers on the night shift. Rocky's sisters Alice and Concetta agreed. At the police station, they showed off the glove, which had hairs stuck in the matted blood around the laces. The sisters even signed autographs for the awestruck policemen. Then, cheered by the police, they continued home to a city in celebration of its improbable champion.

◻ ◻ ◻

ROCKY MARCIANO WAS the heavyweight champion of the world.

Pacing in his hotel room in Philadelphia after the fight, unable to sleep, he reminisced with Allie Colombo about how, just a few years ago, they had hitched rides to New York on a produce truck, rolling out at dawn looking like a couple of cauliflowers, as Charley Goldman used to say. Rocky marveled at everything that had happened since, "like the best movie I ever saw," he said later.

He had gotten a taste of what it would be like to be champion a few months before the Walcott fight, when he went to Lawrence, Massachusetts, to speak at a local dinner. Lawrence was an old factory town like Brockton, and Rocky received a hero's welcome befitting the man viewed as the next champ. When he asked to borrow a razor to freshen up, his hosts instead paraded him through the streets of the city, accompanied by a police escort, to a barbershop. It was Sunday afternoon, but the barber opened and proceeded to lather and shave Rocky while spectators crowded around and more people pressed up against the window outside. Afterward, they took him next door to a local haberdasher, who fitted him with a new suit.

In Philadelphia's Warwick Hotel, the celebration stretched late into the night. High rollers who had bet heavily on Rocky hosted the festivities. One of the hosts was Jimmy Cerniglia, known as Jimmy Tomatoes or the Tomato King, a wealthy tomato packer from Atlanta who had attached himself to Rocky after winning a big bet on him against Rex Layne. Guys were pouring out of the elevators onto Rocky's floor. Three men who weren't reporters or merrymakers detached themselves from the crowd and went into another suite. One of the men carried a satchel, which he opened and emptied onto the bed, revealing $250,000 in cash. The money represented winnings for some of the gamblers who had bet on Rocky, including one who later described the scene to the champ.

This was Rocky's world now, one of unimaginable wealth, fame, and power. No wonder he couldn't sleep. He felt like he was dreaming. After the party, he prowled restlessly in his suite. Allie had gone to bed. Nicky Sylvester had also fallen asleep, but a restless Rocky woke him up.

"Nitch," he said.

"What, champ?" Years later, Sylvester would still marvel at how naturally "champ" had slipped out of his mouth instead of "Rocky." They were overcome with emotion.

"Let's go for a walk," said Rocky.

The two men threw on their clothes and headed out into the early morning streets of Philadelphia.

As they were walking, Rocky's face battered, bruised, and bandaged, his eyes still red and puffy, though now with tears, a police officer carrying a billy club saw them. He was an Italian American, and he grabbed Rocky in a hug and told him how beautiful his triumph had been, and he started crying, too. He signaled another policeman, also Italian American, who also hugged Rocky and kissed him. Eventually, five of Philly's finest gathered around the champ. Rocky and Nicky wound up at Lew Tendler's bar. Even though it was morning, the bar was crowded with people reliving the fight. They went wild when they saw Rocky.

"They just loved him," recalled Sylvester.

Finally, Rocky went back to his hotel and slept for a few hours. "When I woke, I didn't know where I was or nothing, but I had a feeling something nice had happened. Then I remembered, 'Last night, I won the heavyweight championship of the world.'"

When he came home to Brockton on October 2, the parade was even bigger than the ones marking his victories over Rex Layne and Joe Louis the year before. As Rocky's plane from New York circled over Boston, delayed by foggy weather, he fretted that he'd be late and that the people of Brockton would think he was acting like a big shot. "Don't worry," said Goldman. "You're the champ. Everybody waits for the champ." They waited, more than a hundred thousand people—nearly twice Brockton's population and more than had turned out when Franklin Roosevelt and Harry Truman had campaigned in Brockton. Cheering people stood ten deep along the streets, waving welcome-home signs and throwing a blizzard of confetti and torn paper on Main Street. Schoolchildren, who had been let out of class for the afternoon, cheered and ran toward Rocky's open Cadillac convertible with a large golden crown on the hood. More than two hundred police officers, including Rocky's father-in-law, controlled the throng. The parade started at Edgar Playground and, after winding through downtown and past Brockton High School, ended at Keith Field, where Rocky was presented with the key to the city. One man who marched as a marshal in the parade, the fifty-four-year-old manager of Brockton's state unemployment office, was so excited that he collapsed on Main Street of a heart attack and died. Another celebrant, a fourteen-year-old boy, had his right hand bandaged after he lost parts of two fingers punching a ventilator fan during the raucous celebration in the Ward Two club the night of Rocky's victory.

Rocky's mother, Lena, rode in another open car. When the parade passed Edgar Playground, she began to cry. "I can't help it," she said. "This is the street where he grow up—where he was sick and almost die— where he play—where he wait on the corner for his poppa to come home from work—and now look—look!" That night, forty of Rocky's friends, who had reportedly won nearly $50,000 betting on the fight, feted him at a dinner and presented him with a new $5,000 green Cadillac with the license plate "KO." Rocky also visited the Ward Two Memorial Club, which he and his friends had built with a $7,000 bank loan. A raffle for a trip to New York to see Rocky fight Roland LaStarza two years earlier had raised $5,000 toward the mortgage, and now the champ brought a $2,000 check to pay off the rest. They celebrated by burning the mortgage papers.

It was at his hometown celebration, Rocky said later, that he began to see how much winning the championship meant. But it wasn't until he started traveling around the country, and even the world, that he recognized the power of the throne. America had numerous entertainment celebrities, like Frank Sinatra, Gregory Peck, and Milton Berle. There were ninety-six U.S. senators and forty-eight governors. Baseball, the only sport that surpassed boxing in popularity, had a roster of stars, and superstars like Ted Williams and the just-retired Joe DiMaggio. But there was only one heavyweight champion of the world. "Being the heavyweight champion is like being the President," wrote sports columnist Jimmy Cannon in the spring of 1953. "There's only one at a time. You and Ike, and that's all. Come right down to it, Rocky Marciano's bigger than any of them."

In the spring of 1953, President Eisenhower invited forty-three notable American sports figures to a White House luncheon. The guest list included Olympic gold medalist Jesse Owens, baseball Hall of Famers Tris Speaker and Lefty Grove, and golf great Gene Sarazen. (Al Weill also managed an invitation.)

When Eisenhower greeted Rocky, he sized him up thoughtfully and said, "So you're the heavyweight champion of the world?"

"Yes, sir."

"You know, somehow I thought you'd be bigger."

"No, sir."

After lunch, Eisenhower posed for photos, flanked by Rocky and DiMaggio as he playfully felt Rocky's balled-up right fist and said, "That's quite a hand!" Later, Rocky liked to joke that people in Brockton would watch him walk by and say, "Look at old Rocky. Stuck up ever since he got his picture taken with DiMaggio."

Rocky had never lacked for confidence as a fighter, but now he found a new reserve as the champ—like you were the strongest man in the world, and you could walk down the street knowing you could lick anyone. Celebrities who performed at Grossinger's would visit when he was train-ing, like Eddie Fisher and his future wife, Debbie Reynolds. One night Rocky went for a walk with the comedian Jerry Lewis, and Lewis told him, "Do you realize what you are, Rock? You are the boss of the world— the whole world."

While he wouldn't defend his title for several months, there was still plenty of money to be made outside of the ring. Weill booked Rocky on a whirlwind tour of public appearances: dinners, testimonials, television spots, refereeing gigs, sparring exhibitions. His initial fee was $3,000, and, at first, he felt funny taking it. What, after all, had he done to earn it? Three days after his Brockton parade, Rocky was in Havana. He wouldn't make it home for Nicky Sylvester's wedding that fall, and he was in Cali-fornia when Barbara gave birth to a daughter, Mary Anne, on Decem-ber 6, 1952. Early in 1953, Rocky toured the Pacific, fighting exhibitions in Hawaii, the Philippines, Japan, and Okinawa. In Manila, he was mobbed by admirers wherever he went. Instead of autographs, all they wanted was to feel his muscles. He was walking along the street one day when a man stopped his car in heavy traffic, jumped out, ran up to Rocky, felt his muscles and then returned to his car. When Rocky refused to box an exhibition on Sunday because he was Catholic, his decision was front-page news. (The Philippines is a heavily Catholic country.) He also visited a leper colony and freely mingled with the inhabitants. The lepers parted silently to make a path for him, calling out, "God bless you, Rocky." It was, he said, "one of the saddest things I ever saw."

Weill, who took his manager's cut of the appearance money, kept him on a grueling schedule. Rocky wanted to spend some extra time in Japan to sightsee, but Weill cut the trip short so he could get back to the States for an appearance in Kentucky.

Rocky's purse for the Walcott fight was $94,000, the biggest of his career. After Weill took his cut and deducted expenses, including for Charley Goldman and training camp, and after Rocky gave $9,400 to Allie Colombo, he got $38,000. Rocky bought a $35,000 brick fieldstone ranch house on the fashionable west side of Brockton, with a black metal silhouette of a boxer over the mailbox. Hundreds of curious residents drove by to see it, clogging the street. On Christmas morning, when Rocky was still asleep, the paperboy and a friend rang the doorbell and asked Barbara for the champ's autograph, for which he woke up and happily signed, remembering his own youth delivering the *Brockton Enterprise*. Rocky also delighted in sending his parents on a belated honeymoon to Italy. Accompanied by his sister Betty, Lena and Pierino were treated as celebrities wherever they went. At a restaurant in Naples one afternoon, they heard a commotion and saw people snapping up copies of the local newspaper, which carried a front-page story about the birth of Rocky's daughter. Rocky wanted his parents to stay for three months and visit their hometowns, but Lena insisted on cutting the trip short and going home to see her new granddaughter.

Rocky vowed to be a role model for children and to be a popular champion like Jack Dempsey, always happy to sign autographs. He appreciated his humble roots and didn't want to do anything to tarnish his crown. America was eager to embrace him. Although it was not often discussed overtly, people took note of the fact that Rocky was the first white heavyweight champion in fifteen years. After he'd beaten Joe Louis, the *Washington Post*'s Shirley Povich wrote that his being a white heavyweight "in a class dominated by colored fighters since 1936 makes him a stand-out box-office draw." A columnist for the black *New York Amsterdam News*, Jackie Reames, worried that boxing's "white-hope plan" to boost public interest in boxing would hurt worthy black fighters.

In January 1953, Rocky was honored at the annual Boxing Writers' Dinner at the Waldorf-Astoria in New York. The speaker of the House of Representatives, Joseph W. Martin Jr. of Massachusetts, praised Rocky as a role model for American youth and a symbol of the American way of life. "In these days of super-states, dictatorships and regimented societies," said Martin, "it is a wondrous thing that in America every kid, whether he is an Italian boy of humble parents, the son of a Negro sharecropper, or the boy from the mansion on the hill, has the same opportunity to be champion in whatever field of human endeavor he undertakes."

Pointedly absent from Martin's speech was any criticism of boxing, which Congress had investigated and which was the target of the Justice Department's ongoing antitrust case. Thanks to men like Rocky, said Martin, boxing had come of age, propelled to new heights by the power of television. The champion was "symbolic of the American spirit" and embodied American sportsmanship: fierce but fair competitors who want to win "clean but honest victories. They want to get to the top of the heap but they don't want to kick anyone down on the way." Sportswriters joined the chorus. Rocky, wrote Jimmy Cannon, "stood out in boxing like a rose in a garbage dump."

Rocky was also hailed as a great family man. The National Father's Day Committee honored him in the spring of 1953 as the sports father of the year. He appeared at the ceremony with another honoree, Henry Cabot Lodge Jr., the former Massachusetts senator and current ambassador to the United Nations, whose patrician background contrasted sharply with Rocky's blue-collar immigrant roots. Still, writers noticed the similarity in his speech to Lodge's—the soft, high-pitched, modulated voice; the southern New England accent that flattened a's and r's—and they said he sounded more like a cultivated Brahmin than a pugilist.

Rocky was conscious of the intellectual company he was now keeping and worked as hard to develop his fork work as he had his footwork. Invited to a fancy luncheon at Cardinal Spellman's impressive residence on Madison Avenue in New York, Rocky didn't dive into his food, as usual. Instead, he held back, confused by all the silverware, and watched the other guests to see which fork or spoon they picked up first. Later, he confided his embarrassment to George Stone, a Brockton friend who owned a local factory. Stone's wife began teaching Rocky the etiquette that a champion should know. He and Allie Colombo also started quizzing each other on vocabulary during downtime in training camp. Once, Rocky read a newspaper story that predicted he would lose to Ezzard Charles because Charles had more flexibility. He asked Allie what "flexibility" meant. Allie didn't know. So they got a dictionary and looked it up.

Now that he was in the public eye, the new champ told *Ring* magazine's Daniel M. Daniel, he had to wear the right clothes—but nothing fancy like a zoot suit. "I like blue serge best of all," he said. "Quiet ties—in fact, I am a quiet man."

Rocky was conscious of his image. He hadn't smoked since the army, and now he also avoided alcohol. If he was offered liquor at a party, he declined, asking for an apple instead. "I lived clean. I felt I had to look clean and dress right," he said. "I didn't belong to myself anymore. In a way, I belonged to everybody who had an interest in me." Learning how to be the champion, out of the ring as well as in it—"this was all part of my education in boxing."

◻ ◻ ◻

ROCKY RETURNED TO Grossinger's in January 1953 to begin training for his first title defense, a rematch with Walcott. His cabin was snowed in, so he stayed near the resort, which was quieter in winter. Rocky embraced running in the icy wind, believing that it would toughen his skin and make his face harder to cut, a continuing concern.

There was no complacency in the champion's camp. Pride and fear drove Rocky to train as hard as ever. He was embarrassed by his first career knockdown in the first Walcott fight and was determined not to surrender his title and hard-earned financial security.

The promoters bungled the second fight from the start. After the thrilling first fight, which had been billed as the greatest heavyweight title bout since Dempsey-Firpo, there should have been tremendous interest in the rematch. Instead, confusion reigned.

Felix Bocchicchio, Walcott's manager, was at the center of the controversy. After the first fight, Bocchicchio said that Walcott should retire. Then Walcott talked him out of it. Then Bocchicchio argued with Weill and Norris over where to hold the fight. He wanted it in Miami or Atlantic City, but the IBC balked. Weill wanted Yankee Stadium. Since Bocchicchio continued to be banned in New York, Norris settled on Chicago Stadium, which he conveniently owned. In the midst of talks, Bocchicchio was hospitalized after a heart attack.

There was also lingering bitterness between the two camps over dirty tactics. Rocky continued to believe that Walcott's handlers had intentionally blinded him in the first fight. Bocchicchio denied it and accused Rocky of being a dirty fighter whose head butt had cost Walcott the title. To emphasize his point—and perhaps hype the gate—he held a press conference with a billy goat.

The fight was originally scheduled for April 10, but two weeks before, Rocky's sparring partner punched him in the nose, rupturing several blood vessels in his right nostril and forcing a five-week postponement, to May 15. Cynical sportswriters said that the delay was due to flagging ticket sales; the IBC had greedily priced ringside seats at $50, versus $40 for the Philadelphia fight. Others said that Rocky's injury was real and that the delay would only further depress interest in the fight. The most likely scenario was that the ever-cautious Weill was protecting his investment. Rocky said later that it was just an ordinary nosebleed. "If they'd have given me my way, I'd have stayed in training," he said. "But they said why take a chance? So I did what they told me." In retrospect, the delay helped Rocky and hurt Walcott. Before the postponement, Rocky had looked slow and sluggish, perhaps stale from overtraining and not having fought in so long. Walcott, meanwhile, had looked strong and sharp, on schedule to peak by the night of the fight. But when both fighters resumed training in mid-April, after a two-week break, the roles had reversed. Rocky looked fresher and more energetic. Walcott struggled to get his aging body back into top form. At the official weigh-in, Walcott looked drawn, in marked contrast to his first fight against Rocky.

By now, Rocky had moved his training camp to Holland, Michigan, a picturesque town known for its annual tulip festival. The townspeople were excited to host a champion and named a black-and-red tulip—the colors of Brockton High School—after him. They also invited Barbara and him back after the fight to attend the tulip festival, which they did.

Ted Cheff, another wealthy benefactor who owned the Holland Furnace Company, had invited him to train there. When Barbara brought Mary Anne to visit early in camp (she was banished for the final six weeks), Cheff hosted her and other family members at his estate and took them for cruises on his yacht on Lake Michigan. When it was time for Rocky to go to Chicago for the fight, he made the 150-mile trip in Cheff's luxurious land cruiser, which was equipped with beds and a telephone.

At the weigh-in on the day of the fight, Rocky wore a pair of baggy sweatpants to conceal another injury. Six days earlier, he and Allie had been out for their usual walk after supper in Holland when Rocky felt something bump into his leg in the dark. He heard a growl and saw a large dog—a boxer—lunge at him. He jumped away in fright as the dog sank its teeth into the muscle behind his right knee. The dog ran away and Rocky inspected his bleeding leg. Allie was upset, wishing that the dog had bitten him instead. He worried that Rocky might get rabies. Rocky tried to make a joke of it, saying, "Rabies? Don't that mean you go mad? Is that bad for a fighter?" After Rocky got to Chicago, the wife of a Chicago police captain serving as Rocky's bodyguard told him, "I'm worried about that dog bite. You'd better end it in one round."

Rocky had studied film of Walcott's deceptive style and devised a strategy with Charley Goldman to attack Walcott immediately and try to put him on the canvas. To encourage a fast start, Goldman decided to have Rocky shadowbox for three rounds in his dressing room just before the fight. Typically, Rocky was a slow starter—"because he is absolutely without tension before a fight," Goldman explained. Rocky didn't shadowbox before the first Walcott fight and had been caught off guard by the left hook and wound up on the canvas.

A disappointing crowd of 13,266 paid to watch the Marciano-Walcott rematch at Chicago Stadium, generating $331,000 in ticket sales. Norris had also sold the radio and television rights for another $300,000.

The fight began dully and ended abruptly. Rocky chased Walcott, who retreated and clinched. Walcott fired a few jabs at Rocky's vulnerable nose that landed on his forehead instead. Rocky missed with a left hook, then threw a right with less than a minute to go in the first round. Walcott seemed to deflect the blow with his left arm, but referee Frank Sikora said later that it landed under Walcott's heart and made him wince. Rocky followed with another left hook. Walcott blocked it and ducked his head— directly into a short right uppercut from Rocky that cracked into his chin and dumped him backward onto the canvas. Walcott landed flat on his back and his feet flew up into the air. The referee started counting. At the count of two, Walcott pulled himself into a sitting position, his knees splayed in front of him like a man sitting on the grass in a park on a Sunday afternoon, his right arm resting on the rope. It seemed that he was being prudent and using the count to regroup before rising.

Rocky stood listening to the count and watching Walcott. He had hit him with better punches in their first fight that had not put him down, and fully expected him to get up. But as Sikora continued the count, something seemed off. Walcott wasn't looking at the referee but staring straight ahead, glassy-eyed. When the count reached eight, a stunned Rocky said to himself, "This guy's not getting up." When Sikora's hand came down at the count of ten, Walcott finally pushed himself up. But it was too late. The fight was over. Walcott made only a feeble protest, spreading his arms in surprise. Bocchicchio rushed into the ring to argue with Sikora. Rocky stared in amazement. Walcott was counted out at two minutes and twenty-five seconds of the first round—the second-fastest knockout in a heavyweight title fight, behind Joe Louis's KO of Max Schmeling at 2:04. Twenty-six years after the famous Long Count controversy in the Tunney-Dempsey championship fight in Chicago, the Windy City was now engulfed in a disputed Short Count.

The crowd was confused, then angry. The punch had come so quickly, and was such a short, inside blow—a mark of Rocky's refinement—that many hadn't seen it. Bob Hope had turned to shake hands with Tony Zale and missed it. If the spectators had seen the punch, they hadn't appreciated its true power. Despite his surprise, Rocky said he knew it was a good punch when he threw it. "I got good beef behind it," he said. But to many fans, it looked like Walcott had quit or taken a dive. They felt cheated and showered the ring with jeers and catcalls. As the booing intensified, Walcott became more animated and argued with Sikora. He gestured at Rocky to resume fighting. He banged his gloves together, then threw them down in disgust. When Rocky approached Walcott to shake hands, Walcott turned his back on him, still upset. "Joe, you wouldn't want to try it again, would you?" asked Rocky. Walcott turned and shook hands.

In his locker room, Walcott insisted that he had only gotten a count of nine and that he could have risen at two. But his protests came across as a face-saving gesture in the embarrassing end to a distinguished career. Most writers and observers agreed that Sikora had given a full and fair count. Films of the fight later backed them up.

So what happened? Some point to confusion in Walcott's corner and speculate that the fighter and his manager couldn't hear each other over the roar of the crowd and misjudged the count. But that would have been a rookie mistake for Walcott, and the referee was also signaling with his fingers. If Walcott did, indeed, misjudge the count, it's because Rocky's punch had packed more of a wallop than people realized. Sikora said that Walcott's eyes were glazed throughout the count. "It's silly to say Walcott could have gotten up before ten," said Sikora. "He didn't know what he was doing or what was going on while he was down. . . . Don't let anybody tell you that Walcott didn't get hit. . . . It may not have shown on television, but believe me I was the closest man seeing that punch and it was a knockout punch."

A more likely explanation is that Walcott suddenly became an old man, hastened by memories of his first fight with Rocky and that jolting uppercut. His trainer, Dan Florio, said later that Walcott had frozen up in the last twenty-four hours before the fight. "I tried all day to get him to talk fight, tactics, punches, anything. But Joe wouldn't talk. The guy was through before he went into the ring." The night before the fight, Jimmy Cannon ran into one of Walcott's business managers, Vic Marsillo, at a Chicago restaurant and asked how Walcott was. "I just left him," Marsillo replied. "He's reading the Bible. He's thinking about the last fight and he's dying."

Walcott continued his protests the next day, as he picked up his check for the $250,000 that Norris had guaranteed him for the fight. That eclipsed Rocky's purse of $166,000, his percentage of the disappointing gate and television revenue. Rocky was furious. Not only had he been shortchanged on the money, but his first successful title defense had been tarnished by controversy. Some writers praised Rocky's ruthless efficiency; his knockout punch demonstrated his evolution as a craftsman. But the overwhelming impression was that everyone had been a loser. Annoyed, Rocky said, "I would have gotten up and fought."

"This should have been the Rock's supreme moment of triumph," wrote Arthur Daley in the *New York Times*. "But circumstances over which he had no control have robbed him of the glory he so richly deserved . . . the Rock is an exciting and thunderous champion. It's the only important fact to emerge from the wreckage."

□ □ □

ROCKY HAD A new score to settle.

In the wake of the disastrous Walcott rematch, which critics said had set back boxing ten years and justified a congressional investigation of the entire boxing industry, Norris and Weill were eager to get Rocky back into the ring. With the heavyweight division in flux, there were only two logical opponents: Ezzard Charles and Roland LaStarza. Charles, the former champion, was less appealing from a box-office perspective and also because he was the more cunning and dangerous fighter. Prodded by Norris, Weill decided to let LaStarza back in from the cold. But Weill dictated onerous terms for LaStarza's title shot, with Rocky taking 42.5 percent of the gate and LaStarza getting just 17.5 percent.

Rocky had, of course, beaten LaStarza three years earlier at the Garden in his first big New York fight, in a highly anticipated pairing of two unbeaten rising young heavyweights. But it was the only split decision of his career, one that many observers felt he had lost and which LaStarza blamed on Weill's influence. Afterward, LaStarza's manager had slammed the locker room door in Weill's face, and LaStarza had been exiled to boxing Siberia while Rocky's trajectory continued to rise. Since his loss to Rocky, LaStarza had lost twice more in eighteen fights, avenging both losses by winning rematches against the mediocre heavyweights Dan Bucceroni and Rocky Jones. In February, he revived his career by beating Rex Layne, who was fading but still a big name, at the Garden.

LaStarza came into his rematch with Rocky with a 53-3 record, but he was the heavy underdog. He was still derided as the "college fighter"—too nice, too cautious, too mechanical. Lee Oma, a clever postwar heavyweight who sparred with LaStarza for three months at Stillman's, recalled what happened when Oma ended their lessons: "So then he says, 'Thank you very much, Lee.' What sort of guy is that? If he gets over that 'thank you' stuff he can be world's champion."

Rocky was also considered a nice guy, but one with a killer instinct when he climbed inside the ropes. A *New York Times Magazine* profile before the LaStarza rematch described the champ as "a lamb in lion's clothing. Dress him in slacks and polo shirt and he's the mildest of men. Put him in shorts and boxing gloves and he's a murderer." Even in the ring, Rocky's aggression was all business. He rarely lost his temper.

But this LaStarza fight would be an exception. LaStarza stoked Rocky's anger with some prefight comments to Bill Heinz for a profile in the *Saturday Evening Post*. "Oma said to me, 'No matter what anybody says, you have to live with your own brains. Don't take any punch you don't have to,'" said LaStarza, defending his cautious nature. "How long do you think Marciano is going to last, getting slugged the way he does?" LaStarza questioned why the experts who thought he'd beaten Rocky the first time were so convinced he'd lose this time. "They say he's improved. I ask you, how can a crude fighter like Marciano improve? Furthermore, where does everyone get the impression that he's a superman? Just because he's champion? He's a good puncher, sure, but I was still around and licking him at the end of ten rounds the last time. This business of building him up like he's superhuman—it would give me a laugh if it didn't make me so mad."

It was just prefight talk, and LaStarza had a right to be angry. But he had struck a nerve. Rocky could generally shrug off the "crude" label—he heard it often enough—but the suggestion that he was punchy enraged him. He was highly sensitive to the label, having seen broken-down fighters with their minds addled, and he did not want to wind up like them. Publicly, he admitted that LaStarza's remarks "have got under my skin more than any other prefight statements. He has the advantage of a college education and for an educated guy what he says just doesn't make any sense. But I still won't be mad at him when we meet in the ring."

Privately, Rocky vowed to punish LaStarza. He laughed when his friend Smokey Cerrone from Providence joked about "Rollover LaStagger." And he complained about the public perception that he had lost the first fight. "That SOB didn't come near me," fumed Rocky. "He didn't want to fight."

The fight drew a healthy crowd of 44,562 to the Polo Grounds on September 24, 1953, the attendance boosted by the IBC's decision not to carry it on free television.

The fight fell into a predictable groove in the first round. Rocky came out swinging awkwardly and missing wildly, and LaStarza made him pay with crisp counterpunching, winning the round easily. Rocky kept flailing away in the early rounds, trying and failing to land one big knockout punch. Lowering his head as he lunged clumsily in the second round, Rocky butted LaStarza near the right eye, opening a gash and drawing the first of several warnings from referee Ruby Goldstein. Just as the bell sounded ending the third, LaStarza landed a right to Rocky's head, and Rocky retaliated with a right that he was unable to restrain, drawing boos from the crowd. Rocky lost the sixth round after throwing a low blow and received another warning for hitting low in the seventh. There was nothing deliberate in Rocky's attack; it was a product of his clumsiness.

Though LaStarza was scoring points in the early rounds, he wasn't really hurting Rocky and was instead being steadily chopped up. In the second, he raised his left arm to block a vicious right and his arm went numb, neutralizing his left for the remainder of the fight. X-rays later revealed that the blow had broken blood vessels in LaStarza's forearm.

In the seventh round, Rocky adjusted his strategy and stopped trying to land the big knockout punch to the head. Instead, afraid of falling behind on points, he shifted to left hooks and inside combinations to the body. Late in the seventh, he buckled LaStarza with a left hook to the body. After that, Arthur Daley noted, "only a sadist could have enjoyed" the fight. Rocky punished LaStarza in the eighth, ninth, and tenth rounds, but the challenger refused to go down. Instead, it was Rocky who slipped and fell, losing his balance after trying to catch LaStarza in the corner with a wild right to the body.

At the start of the eleventh, the lion moved in for the kill. Springing at the retreating LaStarza, Rocky staggered him with a right to the jaw, then hit him with a left and a right that drove him through the ropes and onto the apron. LaStarza clambered to his feet at the count of nine, but he was defenseless as Rocky continued to pummel him until Goldstein mercifully moved in and stopped the fight, at 1:31 of the eleventh round.

"It was a butcher job," summed up Daley. "Rocky Marciano never even bothered to administer the anesthetic."

The fight tarnished Rocky's reputation, revived the old talk of his ring shortcomings, and won new respect for LaStarza.

"He was a lot tougher than I expected," said Rocky. LaStarza, gracious in defeat, called Rocky "a great fighter. He's definitely better than when I fought him before—5,000 percent better."

LaStarza talked amiably to sportswriters as his trainer held an ice bag against his head and the doctor examined his wounds—cuts over his right eye, under his left eye, on the bridge of his nose, behind his right ear, and inside his mouth, plus the left arm that had suffered a muscle hemorrhage. "He really busted me up, didn't he, Doc?" said LaStarza.

In the ring after the fight, LaStarza apologized to Rocky for some of his prefight comments about being punchy. Rocky tapped him on the shoulder in a gesture of forgiveness. Later, Rocky told Nicky Sylvester that he was sorry for what he had done. That night, Rocky went to a victory party at a New York nightclub where the guests included the actresses

Elizabeth Taylor and Gina Lollobrigida. In his limousine on the way to the party, a satisfied Rocky told the sportswriter Murray Olderman, "I learned the sonuvabitch a few things he didn't get in college."

LaStarza walked away with a purse of $77,000—more than double all of his prior earnings from boxing, and substantially more than the $13,500 he collected from his first fight with Rocky. Rocky's purse was $186,000, the largest of his career. Still, because of the severe tax bite on his earnings to date in 1953, it wouldn't pay for him to fight again until 1954.

"I want to be more than just a champion," he said after the fight. "I want to be a great champion."

Given his late start in boxing, time was already beginning to run out. Rocky was 45-0, and the long delays between fights limited his opportunities. It also meant that he couldn't fight as often as he needed to remain sharp.

At age thirty, observed Daley, "he's spread-eagled the field, outdistancing them all. He has only a few years left. Rocky hits too hard to build up business."

□ □ □

ROCKY'S FAME CAST a championship glow over Brockton. Suddenly, the city was more famous as the home of the world heavyweight champion than for the twelve million pairs of shoes a year it produced.

"Why, Rocky Marciano has done more to make this city famous than all the shoes ever made here," said Perley Flint, president of the shoe manufacturer Field and Flint. "Now they've heard of Brockton in places they don't even wear shoes."

Brocktonians were treated like minor celebrities wherever they went: as delegates to the national Democratic and Republican conventions in Chicago in 1952, as boys attending a national Boy Scout jamboree in California in 1953, as audience members at the taping of television shows in New York. When Charlie Ball, who had grown up with Rocky, checked into the historic U. S. Grant Hotel in San Diego with his wife, the manager eyed the register and said, "Brockton, eh? Do you know Rocky Marciano?" When Ball said that he did, the manager upgraded him and his wife to a suite.

When Rocky came home, boys seeking autographs would swarm

around his car, and he would ask his friend Alan Stone, who sometimes drove him, to stop at every corner to sign. Once when Rocky returned to his old neighborhood, eighty-five-year-old Dominic Alfieri, who had been friends with Rocky's grandfather Luigi, hurried through the bushes from his house next door and, tears in his eyes, clasped Rocky's hand in both of his, exclaiming, "*Rocco, Rocco, è bello vederti.*" (It's wonderful to see you.) Rocky, too, was overcome with emotion. Another time, an elderly widow, Laura DeAngelis, asked Rocky to visit her. Not long after Rocky had begun fighting in Providence, she had given one of Rocky's friends a few dollars and asked him to bet it on Rocky. She didn't know anything about boxing but knew Rocky as a boy growing up in the neighborhood. After he won, she took her winnings and bet on his next fight, and his next, and his next, and so on, and eventually parlayed it into enough money to buy her own house. "You are my life, champ," she said, embracing him.

The streets of Brockton were deserted when Rocky's fights were televised. Local appliance stores sold out of TV sets. When the fights weren't broadcast, as with Rocky's title fight against Jersey Joe Walcott in Philadelphia, thousands gathered outside the *Brockton Enterprise* office for updates posted in the window after each round. At police headquarters, officers on the night shift picked up a Canadian broadcast of the Walcott fight on a short-wave radio, but the broadcast was in French, so they moved the radio to the cell block so that a prisoner of French Canadian heritage could translate.

Red Gormley, who had tried out for the Cubs with Rocky and then turned down a chance to manage him as a boxer after they were cut in North Carolina, now worked as a mailman, delivering sacks of fan mail from all over the world. Before and after a big fight, hundreds of letters a day poured into Lena and Pierino's house. Overwhelmed, they turned to a neighborhood couple who owned a typewriter; the husband and wife worked early mornings and late evenings answering the letters.

After Rocky beat Joe Louis in 1951, friends advised him not to return to Brockton right away to avoid becoming entangled in a heated mayor's race. In 1952, shortly after he became champion, Adlai Stevenson's presidential campaign asked Rocky to ride with the candidate on a train between Providence and Boston, but he declined, wishing to remain neutral. A year later, a man challenging the Brockton mayor stopped by Rocky's house and told the champ, 'I just want to meet you because people ask me if I know Rocky Marciano and I want to tell the truth." So Rocky shook his hand, and he left.

Before each of Rocky's fights, a taxi driver drove an elderly Italian couple to a loan office so they could borrow money to bet on Rocky. Before Rocky's rematch with LaStarza, the couple borrowed $3,000 on their house.

"God help this town if he ever gets licked," said the cabbie.

◻ ◻ ◻

CULTURED AND REFINED, literate and musical, the former champion Ezzard Charles was another heavyweight considered too genteel to achieve true greatness. He had fluid footwork, strong defensive reflexes, and a lightning-quick repertoire of punches that earned him the nickname the Cincinnati Cobra, for the city where he grew up. Charles had climbed impressively through the ranks, from amateur to professional, from middleweight to light heavyweight to heavyweight, and had beaten many of the finest fighters of his generation: Joe Louis, Joey Maxim (three times), Archie Moore (twice), Jersey Joe Walcott (twice), Jimmy Bivins (twice), Gus Lesnevich, Lee Oma, and Bob Satterfield.

But Charles, who held the heavyweight title from 1949 to 1951, suffered from two shortcomings. First, he succeeded Louis, a national hero, and then demolished him in 1950 when Louis tried to reclaim the throne. Second, Charles was too timid in the ring. He admitted that he should have been more aggressive when he lost his second title fight to Walcott, in 1952, after retreating into a defensive shell. "Some day, maybe, the public is going to abandon comparisons with Joe Louis and accept Ezzard for what he is," Red Smith wrote in 1951, "the best fist-fighter of his particular time."

His timidity could be understood in light of one of his early fights, in 1948, when he pummeled the light heavyweight Sam Baroudi into a coma in Chicago. Baroudi died the next morning, and Charles wanted to quit boxing. He returned to the ring three months later but remained haunted by Baroudi. Despite continuing to win, he was never as aggressive. In the words of one of his former trainers, the legendary Ray Arcel, "He is like a good horse which won't run for you."

The criticism didn't seem to bother him. Asked if he ever got mad in the ring, Charles answered, "No, I can't say that I do. There's nothing to get mad about." He could be eccentric and enigmatic. After he beat Walcott for the title in 1949 in Chicago, Charles slipped out of his own victory party in dark glasses and went to a local jazz club; when the patrons recognized him, he tried to pass himself off as "Bob Harris," a bass player from Ohio. When that failed, he left the club.

Charles played the bass fiddle in training camp and entertained camp followers and reporters with card tricks and even hypnosis. When Charles got married, he kept it a secret and continued to live with his grandmother while his wife lived with her mother, an arrangement that he thought would be better for his training. He agreed to go public only after his wife had a baby in 1951. He emulated the style of his boyhood hero, the boxer Kid Chocolate, who had breezed into Cincinnati in an impressive car and an impressive suit and stopped at a candy store, where he boasted about his extensive wardrobe. Charles vowed, "I'm gonna be a fighter, and have clothes like that."

As heavyweight champion, Charles successfully defended his title eight times, including a lopsided decision over Joe Louis at Yankee Stadium. But then, with Rocky emerging as a title contender in 1951, Charles inexplicably fought Walcott for a third time and was knocked out in the eighth round. His career nose-dived, with another loss to Walcott followed by a loss to Rex Layne. Charles tried to come back, winning his next nine fights, but then lost twice in a two-month span in 1953.

After that humiliation, Charles "remade" himself by vowing to be more aggressive. He knocked out Coley Wallace, Rocky's former Golden Gloves nemesis, and then outslugged Bob Satterfield in January 1954. That was enough to earn Charles a date with Rocky at Yankee Stadium on June 17, 1954. He was thirty-two years old, with a record of 85-10-1.

This would be Rocky's first fight since beating LaStarza nine months earlier. Unlike his first two title defenses, Charles would be a fresh opponent, and an unknown quantity—though not one the oddsmakers were taking seriously.

□ □ □

ROCKY WAS ON edge as the fight approached. He was still getting accustomed to fighting less often as the champ and had been in training forever, it seemed, going to Grossinger's in the winter for the second straight year and essentially staying there for six months.

"It is this bleak life which is his talent," observed Jimmy Cannon. "The body protects him, and he lives in it like a hermit."

Adding to his irritation were the threatening letters he received as the fight approached; the price of fame, it seemed, included being targeted by crackpots. Rocky didn't take it too seriously; Barbara said he'd received threats before, but this was the first time threats were directed at her and the baby, "and it's scared us to death." The FBI opened an investigation into one letter, composed of words and letters cut out of the newspaper and mailed to Pierino in Brockton in March. "Listen, Mr. Marchegiano," the letter said, "either your son, Rocky, lets Ezzard Charles beat him in the June seventeen title fight or we'll bump off his wife and small child. We have a tremendous amount of money wagered on Charles and we're desperate. We know that a washed up bum like Charles has no chance against Rocky without a little cooperation from Rocky." The FBI was told that Al Weill was capable of having a letter like this sent to drum up publicity for the fight. But its investigation traced the letter to a twenty-three-year-old Pennsylvania man who lived with his parents and confessed to writing it "because he was for the underdog," according to FBI records.

Rocky's training routine was hard on his family life. While Rocky was preparing to fight Charles, Barbara suffered a miscarriage while on a trip to Acapulco. Rocky was unaware.

Two weeks before the fight, chatting with writers over dinner at his mountainside cottage above Grossinger's, Rocky grew wistful; Barbara and Mary Anne, now eighteen months old, had visited in April, but he hadn't seen them since. "I talked to her on the phone last night," said Rocky. "She can't quite manage a 'Hello, Daddy,' but she can give me that da-da stuff. As I said to my wife later on, a year ago at this time Mary Anne didn't even know me. I was a complete stranger to her, so busy was I with training. But I got to know her real good this winter. Gee, but I miss my wife and daughter." He paused and shrugged. "But I have a job to do . . . that's the price I have to pay. And, I might add, I have no regrets."

Charley Goldman walked in and urged Rocky to go down to the hotel, four miles away, and see a show; it would relax him.

"Naw," said Rocky, "I like just staying here."

"I've been in this boxing business fifty years, and I've never seen anyone like you yet," said Goldman. "Work. Work. Work. Train. Train. Train. Sometimes I suspect you're not even human."

The only thing Goldman had to worry about with Rocky was his appetite. Goldman limited him to two big meals a day but would catch him sneaking food. The trainer would slip into Rocky's room and find a loaf of bread and hunk of salami under his pillow, or a cut-up steak wrapped in a napkin in the bureau. One time when they went into town, Goldman caught Rocky hiding a grapefruit and bananas behind his back. One night, when Rocky said he was going to bed, Goldman eyed him suspiciously and asked, "What'd you stash up there tonight?" Rocky acted pained, but he had a large salami hidden in his bed. Still, he avoided sweets, and instead of sugar carried a jar of honey in his pocket to sweeten his coffee.

Rocky, meanwhile, stayed on Goldman's case about his smoking. Every time they formally opened a training camp before a fight, Goldman swore off his cigars and made a formal bet with Rocky that he could hold out. Each man put up a one-dollar bill. Goldman always won. "Then Rocky and I autograph the two bills and give them to a priest."

Rocky had also sworn off sex before a fight, believing, as many fighters did, that it would affect his performance. Still, that didn't stop many athletes from breaking their training and fooling around. Friends noticed the beautiful women among the crowds of spectators who visited Rocky's camp and watched him work out. "We had to push them away," said Marty Weill. Not that the fighter was interested. One day, according to family and friends, the Hollywood actress and bombshell Jayne Mansfield was at Grossinger's. Someone put her up to paying Rocky a visit in his cabin. She did, but stormed out not long after, rejected.

As Rocky always said, he had a job to do.

◘ ◘ ◘

THE STARS TURNED out on a clear, cool night at Yankee Stadium. The crowd of 47,585 included General Douglas MacArthur, New York governor Thomas Dewey, Manhattan district attorney Frank Hogan, New York Giants manager Leo Durocher, and the entertainers Humphrey Bogart, Bob Hope, Perry Como, and Jimmy Durante. With two hundred thousand watching on closed-circuit television in theaters in forty-five cities, and millions more listening on the ABC radio network, Ezzard Charles quickly silenced his doubters in what would be his most heroic fight.

Boxing brilliantly, Charles came out more aggressively than he had in ages. He wasn't going to stick and run as everyone expected, given his style and temperament. Instead, the Cincinnati Cobra pounded away at Rocky's midsection with quick and powerful rights and left hooks, then countered with right crosses and lightning combinations. The goal was to drain the strength from Rocky's mighty tree-trunk legs, the source of his power. Charles also scored with shots to the head, bloodying Rocky's nose and smashing a right against the side of the head that momentarily stunned the champ. But Charles would later voice regret that he couldn't cash in: "That first round chance never came again," he said.

Charles also showed he wasn't afraid of Rocky's power. In the first round, Rocky nailed him with a hard right to the side of his head. Charles shook it off. "That punch was one of Marciano's best," Charles reflected later, "and I said to myself, 'If that's all he's got, I can stay with him for fifteen rounds and maybe knock him out.'"

Rocky wasn't able to do much in the early rounds, falling into his bad habit of starting slowly. Charles controlled the first four rounds, and the crowd yelled with excitement at witnessing a true heavyweight clash. In the fourth round, his best, Charles opened the old cut above Rocky's left eye that he had suffered against Johnny Shkor in Providence three and a half years earlier. It began to bleed and would for the rest of the fight, hampering Rocky's vision. "I had to keep circling around Charles to see him," he later said. Freddie Brown, the cut man who had saved Rocky when he was blinded against Walcott in Philadelphia, went to work patching the deep cut, which was two inches long. "With a cut like that, you got to be nervous," said Brown. "A quarter of an inch further in, and it would have run like a faucet."

Charles began to attack the cut, sending blood flowing into Rocky's eyes and hampering his sight. The cut was "a deep and promising little gold mine," noted A. J. Liebling, who sat near Charles's corner. "There is a difference of a couple of hundred thousand dollars between the champion's and the challenger's share of a million-dollar gate. If Charles could work his vein properly, the return match would be sure to draw that."

Problem was, it turned out to be fool's gold. The cut distracted Charles from his original strategy of attacking Rocky's body to weaken his legs. Instead, the fight became the type of bloody brawl that Rocky excelled at. The champ began to assert himself from the fifth through eighth rounds, even as Charles continued to box well. Rocky was booed when he hit Charles after the bell ending the fifth. Rocky started to turn the tide in the sixth. A short left hook to the jaw shook Charles. A few rounds later—nobody was sure exactly when—Rocky hit Charles with a punch to the Adam's apple that took his breath away for several rounds and made it difficult to swallow. After the fight, Charles could speak in only a hoarse whisper. This was the turning point. The challenger had fought courageously in the seventh and eighth rounds—"the Indian summer of Charles' fight," observed Liebling—but now his knockout seemed inevitable.

With the rust shaken off, Rocky went to work punishing Charles with vicious rights. His relentless assault transformed Charles's handsome features and narrow face into "a squatty rectangle as we watched," recalled Liebling. "It was as though he had run into a nest of wild bees or fallen victim to instantaneous mumps." An egg-shaped lump erupted on the left side of Charles's jaw, a blood clot; his right eye gradually closed; his bottom lip was split and swollen. From the ninth round on, the crowd, and Rocky, waited for Charles to go down.

But he didn't. His endurance was a marvel. By now, Charles lacked the strength to win, though he did fight back well enough to take a few of the later rounds on some scorecards. Rocky was firmly in control, but as the fight edged past the tenth round and into the eleventh and twelfth, the champion still couldn't muster the strength for a knockout punch. Although Rocky was comfortably ahead going into the fifteenth and final round, his corner men were nervous and told him he'd better win the round. He did, finally trapping Charles against the ropes for the first time all night and pummeling him with a fusillade of punches. "I thought I almost had him at the end," said Rocky. Teetering, Charles held on until the final bell as the crowd thundered its approval. One writer hailed Charles for "a closing stand [that] will go down in ring annals as one of the greatest of all time."

Unfortunately, you don't win points for staying on your feet and taking a beating. The decision was unanimous. Referee Ruby Goldstein, who marveled that he didn't have to break the fighters from a single clinch all night, awarded the decision to Rocky, eight rounds to five, with two even. The two judges scored it 9-5-1 and 8-6-1.

Exhausted but pleased, Rocky called it "my toughest fight . . . much harder than my first fight with Walcott." It was the first time he had ever gone fifteen rounds, since nontitle bouts are only ten rounds, and just the sixth time in forty-six victories that he had failed to knock his opponent out. Consequently, Rocky also called it one of his worst fights. But that wasn't fair. As Al Weill put it, "He was great when he had to be great."

11

The Mongoose and the Mob

RATHER THAN WAIT ANOTHER YEAR TO FIGHT, ROCKY AGREED TO return to Yankee Stadium for a rematch with Ezzard Charles in September 1954, just three months after their first fight.

Rocky went back to the Catskills and trained as hard as ever, determined to redeem himself for failing to knock out Charles in June. But he was also grappling with the demands of life as the champion and the strain it put on his family life. For the first time, Barbara and Mary Anne were not banished from camp but living in a separate cottage at Grossinger's. They didn't see one another every day, but when Rocky had a day off he enjoyed spending time with them and going for family hikes in the mountains. Two weeks before the fight, he talked about how wonderful it was to get to know his twenty-month-old daughter. Before training camp, he and his family, including his parents and brothers and sisters, had spent time together at the beach at Cape Cod, Rocky's first real vacation in more than a year.

Rocky was also allowed to read his mail in training camp, as well as some of the newspaper stories previewing the fight. If he was more relaxed as the champion, he also, at times, felt caged. To protect his privacy, Grossinger's erected a wire fence around his cottage. Rocky apologized to a visitor one day, joking that he felt like a lion in the zoo. Looking out his window at the fence, he wondered, "Is that to keep the people out or is it to keep me in?"

There was a relaxed, businesslike atmosphere in camp as the fight approached. Two of Rocky's favorite movies were screened for the entire camp: *High Noon* and *On the Waterfront*. One day, the sportswriter Budd Schulberg, who had written the script for *On the Waterfront*, and the ex-boxer Roger Donoghue, Marlon Brando's boxing instructor for the film, stopped by for a visit. (Donoghue had quit boxing after killing Georgie Flores in the ring, and Carmine Vingo, after his own near death at Rocky's hands, had sought to comfort him at Flores's funeral.) As Rocky sat eating orange slices following a workout, they laughed and swapped stories about boxers who had appeared in the movie, including "Two Ton" Tony Galento and Lee Oma. Rocky praised the movie and said that Brando looked like a real fighter. "He would have been a good fighter," Donoghue agreed. "It took him only two days to learn to throw a left hook—and it took me three years."

Another time, Sonny Marciano recalled, Schulberg brought the Hollywood filmmaker Elia Kazan, who had directed *On the Waterfront*, to Grossinger's. They wanted to talk to Rocky about making a movie of his life. Al Weill had strict rules about who could see Rocky, so Sonny went upstairs to Rocky's bedroom, where his brother had been taking a nap. Rocky told Sonny to bring the visitors up, and they discussed the movie. Kazan talked about having Brando play Rocky, noting that they both had that same soft-spoken yet tough persona. Rocky liked the idea but said he was too busy with his career and would be interested in talking more after he retired.

All kinds of characters were likely to show up. One day, a man who called himself Tiger Louis called person-to-person from Memphis, Tennessee, to tell Rocky that his one ambition was to box him. "You're my idol," he said. Rocky politely put him off, but a few days later his cottage door was flung open and a paunchy, middle-aged man walked in, saying, "Hiya, champ. I'm Tiger Louis. I'm ready to box." He used to be a fighter, he said, but now he sold real estate. Tiger wound up living with the sparring partners and trying to pose for pictures with Rocky whenever the Grossinger's photographer came around. One day, Goldman put Tiger in the ring with one of the heavyweights who worked with Rocky; he was game, throwing a lot of punches, but his opponent rattled combinations off his chin. He wasn't allowed in the ring with the champ.

"Rocky is liable to kill you," a sportswriter told him.

"It would be a pleasure to be killed by him," Tiger replied.

There were two schools of thought about the upcoming fight. One was that if Charles could last fifteen rounds the first time, he could correct his mistakes and win. If not for the punch to his Adam's apple, Charles would have won. His best hope was cutting Rocky so badly that the referee would have to stop the fight. "Marciano didn't knock me out. He didn't knock me down," said Charles. "I think I hurt him as much as he hurt me." The other theory was that if Charles couldn't beat Rocky the first time, nothing was going to change. As Jersey Joe Walcott had shown in his second fight against Rocky, there was a psychological toll that came with climbing back into the ring with him after receiving one of his savage beatings. "A second chance," Schulberg wrote in *Sports Illustrated* about the fight, quoting Henry James, "that's the delusion, there never was but one." An assistant book editor for the *New York Times* viewed the fight in literary terms. Comparing Ezzard Charles to F. Scott Fitzgerald and Rocky to Ernest Hemingway, he quoted Fitzgerald's line that Fitzgerald spoke with the authority of failure while Hemingway spoke with the authority of success.

Charley Goldman's chief concern was the law of averages. "It's the psychological side of this fight that bothers me. How long can this go on, I mean Rocky winning? Any man who has won forty-six straight and never been beat has got to begin worrying about them mathematical odds."

Rain delayed the fight for two days, pushing it back to September 17 and depressing the already disappointing ticket sales. The public didn't share Charles's confidence that he would put up a good fight; only twenty-five thousand came out to see it.

The fight was a dull affair until Rocky's blood lent some color to a frantic finish. Charles once again outboxed Rocky in the first round, but he fought much more cautiously. He had put on seven pounds, weighing in at 192 pounds to Rocky's 187, hoping to increase his punching power, but the added weight made him more sluggish. When he did hit Rocky, the blows didn't bother the champ. Rocky wasn't rusty this time and fought back more effectively than he had in the opening rounds of their first fight—though he still got into trouble for hitting below the belt and after the bell. In the second round, Rocky surprised Charles with a left jab and a textbook right cross, then hit him with a tremendous punch under the heart that forced him a half-step backward. A pained expression crossed

Charles's face. Then Rocky drove two hard rights into his head that sent Charles sprawling to the canvas. He was up quickly, at the count of two, and even hit Rocky with two impressive left hooks. But the round ended with Rocky hooking a left to Charles's head. From there, Charles reverted to his earlier self, the cautious fighter in retreat, no longer looking to win the fight.

Then, coming out of a clinch in the sixth round, Charles's elbow slashed an inch-long cut straight up the tip of Rocky's nose. The freak blow sliced his left nostril in two, leaving the skin hanging in flaps. Blood spurted from the wound. The cut didn't hurt, Rocky said later, but "I knew something was wrong because the blood was running like from a faucet." When Rocky's thirteen-year-old brother Peter saw it, he got sick. After the round, cut man Freddie Brown went to work in the corner. As Dr. Alexander Schiff, the ring doctor, inspected the wound and Allie Colombo paced frantically, convinced the fight would be stopped, Brown applied thromboplastin, a quick-setting plastic, then smeared Vaseline over it. When the doctor tried to get a closer look, Weill pushed him back, saying that everything was all right.

Rocky looked like he was wearing a clown nose when he went out for the seventh. Charles quickly flicked away the swab that had been left in and tried to work on the nose, where blood oozed into the Vaseline. Rocky fought like a wild man. He chased Charles around the ring, shaking him with a left hook. He drew a warning from the referee for striking Charles with the heel of his right hand. The round ended with a furious volley. In Rocky's corner, Brown worked in vain to stanch the bleeding from his nose. When the bell ran for the eighth, Rocky charged out of his corner like a man living on borrowed time—and directly into a right from Charles that reopened the scar tissue over his left eye.

Dr. Schiff had just about seen enough; never in his twenty-nine years as a doctor for the New York State Athletic Commission had he seen such a bad cut. He planned to confer with Rocky's corner men after the eighth round and later said, "I doubt whether I would have let him come out for the ninth." If this had not been a championship fight, Schiff would already have stopped it and the decision would have gone to Charles. "In a championship bout," he explained, "you have to be more hesitant and give the handlers more time to patch up the wound."

With blood trickling from the new cut over his eye, Rocky rocked

Charles with a left hook to the face, a long right to the chest, and another long right to the head that knocked Charles down. He was back on his feet at the count of four, but half-dazed. He tried to tie Rocky up in a clinch, but Rocky wrenched free and chased him, staggering, across the ring. He hit Charles with two hard left-right combinations that knocked him down again. This time, reminiscent of the second Walcott fight, Charles stayed on the canvas, on his hands and knees, as if in prayer, as referee Al Berl stood over him, shouting the count. Charles rose a split second after Berl intoned "ten." Later, Charles said that he thought he had gotten up in time. But clearly he hadn't, and there was no protest from his corner. Charles stood facing Rocky, a slight smile on his face, and offered his congratulations. He was counted out at 2:36 of the eighth round. "You'll have to tell me what hit me in the eighth," he said. "I just didn't see 'em coming."

Knotting his tie in his dressing room, Charles said that he thought he had Rocky beaten, that the fight was on the verge of being stopped. Observers agreed. Weill said afterward that he would have stopped it after the eighth, to avoid risking a more serious, career-threatening injury. As it was, Rocky would require plastic surgery and would face worries about how the nose would stand up in future fights.

The fight underscored Rocky's indomitable will to win. Purists could pick at his flaws, but he had shown time and again his incredible determination in the face of adversity. Despite Goldman's fears, he continued to defy the law of averages and remained unbeaten, at 47-0.

"After Charles cut me a second time, all that blood made me nervous," an animated Rocky told the reporters who gathered around him in the Yankees' locker room. The scene was later captured in a painting for *Sports Illustrated*, a gauze bandage over Rocky's nose, his fists raised in midair as he reenacted the fight. "Didn't you see where I started to fight harder?"

Rocky looked across the room and saw the sportswriter Murray Olderman. The two had become friendly, and during a game of Ping-Pong at Grossinger's prior to the fight, Olderman had cut his forehead retrieving a ball under the stairs. Now, the bloodied Rocky interrupted the questions from other writers and called out in his high-pitched voice, "How's your cut, Murray?"

◻ ◻ ◻

THE THRILL WAS gone. In the fall of 1954, after beating Charles for the second time, Rocky started talking privately of retiring. He didn't enjoy boxing as much anymore, and the monastic training routine—sacrificing food, fun, and family—had become a grind. The fighter who had excelled because of his Spartan training regimen, pushing his body to the peak of conditioning and endurance, even started to hate the smell of leather and the gym.

Besides, being the world's heavyweight champ had opened new vistas. Two nights after the Charles fight, Rocky flew to Los Angeles to appear on the nationally televised *Colgate Comedy Hour*, broadcast live from the Hollywood Bowl. The host was the singer Eddie Fisher, Rocky's pal from Grossinger's, and the champ shared the stage with Louis Armstrong, the singer Peggy Lee, the violinist Mischa Elman, and the ballerina Maria Tallchief. Resplendent in a white suit, a bandage covering his busted nose, Rocky was poised and articulate as he reviewed the fight and teased Fisher about his romance with Debbie Reynolds, who sat in the front row. Weill also managed to push his way onto the stage, saying that he had "brought him here," then holding the smiling Rocky's and Fisher's arms up in the air triumphantly and declaring them both "real champions."

But beneath the surface, Rocky was simmering. The reasons for his discontent involved family, burnout, and his abrasive, controlling manager.

For the first ten months of his daughter Mary Anne's life, Rocky had barely seen her because he'd been in training. Once, when he came home and tried to pick her up, she ran away. "She didn't even know me," he lamented. His mother complained that he didn't come home much anymore, and when he did, he usually had an entourage and didn't spend much time with his family.

There was also the toll on his body to consider. Rocky had started his career late, fighting his first fight in Providence at the age of twenty-four, and consequently didn't have as much mileage on his body as other fighters his age. Still, he had been at it for six and a half years, and he was now thirty-one years old, past peak for many fighters. The back pain that had bothered him early in his career sometimes flared up, and he worried about that.

Then there was the question of what mountains were left to conquer.

In each of his first four title defenses, he had had motivation: proving himself after the rugged first fight against Walcott, avenging his split decision against LaStarza, showing he could beat a talented ex-champ in Charles, and then proving he could knock Charles out. Now, what? There were no great young challengers. There was talk of matching Rocky with Nino Valdes, a hard-hitting young Cuban, or Archie Moore, another old warhorse who was the light heavyweight champion and still packed danger in his fists. But Weill was taking no chances. Worried how Rocky's surgically repaired nose would stand up, Weill booked him instead to fight Don Cockell, the British heavyweight champion who had recently beaten Roland LaStarza and Kid Matthews but was a slow, pudgy, stand-up fighter and had recently been knocked out by a middleweight.

From Weill's perspective, the match made sense. Why couldn't Rocky defend his title and test his nose against an easy opponent? Joe Louis had had his Bum of the Month club when he was champ. Problem was, given the infrequency of Rocky's title fights, Cockell was more like the Bum of the Year. The fight was scheduled for the following May at Kezar Stadium in San Francisco. The IBC boldly predicted a million-dollar gate, with enthusiastic fans coming down from Seattle and Canadians loyal to the British Empire flocking down from Vancouver. The fight was so unappealing that it wouldn't have drawn back east. Nor did it generate much excitement on the West Coast, despite the novelty of the first title fight west of the Mississippi since Jack Dempsey defeated Tommy Gibbons in Shelby, Montana, in 1923.

The American press had a field day mocking the match. They called Cockell—a pleasant, cherubic pig farmer and apprentice blacksmith from Battersea, five foot ten and 217 pounds—the Battersea Butterball. There was no reason for the fight, sniffed Jimmy Cannon; England hadn't produced a good big man since Henry VIII. Cannon ripped Weill for not having more faith in Rocky and hurting his image with such a weak opponent, "giving him an obscurity that few heavyweights have known."

Rocky wasn't enthusiastic about fighting Cockell and wondered what was the point. His frustration with Weill was growing. Before his title fight against LaStarza the previous year, Rocky was passing the time with some friends at Grossinger's and mentioned that he was glad that he had gotten the match. Weill, who was in the room, turned on him angrily and said,

"You're glad *who* got this match? You think *you* got it? *I* got it. I made this match for you. You ought to pay me for making this match. What are you? You're just the fighter. Without me, you're nothing."

When they traveled, Weill always stayed in the hotel suite while Rocky got the single room. One time when they were in Dayton, Ohio, and the mayor presented Rocky with the key to the city, Weill asked grumpily, "Where's mine?" Weill was often irritated at Rocky's friends and relatives. One night he yelled at Rocky's cousin Duna when he returned to Rocky's cabin at Grossinger's late after a night of merrymaking at the resort. Another time, after Weill came up short on his private supply of choice tickets to one of Rocky's fights, he accused Nicky Sylvester of taking them. Before the Joe Louis fight, Sonny had found his ringside seat sold out from under him by Weill. "My family was nothing," said Rocky.

But Rocky liked being champion, and he liked the recognition it brought.

He was also eager to cash in. As the thrill of boxing began to fade and it started to feel more like a job, Rocky continued to be driven by his hunger for financial security. Sonny once found him reading a book called *How Fighters Lost Their Fortunes*. "He used to see guys who ended up broke," recalled his brother Peter. "He feared, literally feared, this happening to him." Sonny said that Rocky was bothered by the public perception that "if a champion spends his money foolishly, they ridicule him for that, and if he doesn't spend it, they call him cheap." Rocky was so frugal that, after he won the title, he was paid $2,200 to referee a wrestling match but went back to the arena because he had left behind a pair of socks. "I came from poor people. I know the value of a dollar," he said. "There were enough bad examples to remind me not to blow my dough." Rocky was generous with family, old friends, broken-down fighters, and charities, particularly churches and youth groups; before the second Walcott fight, Rocky donated a thirty-inch television set to St. Colman's Church in Brockton, where he'd been married. But he was more guarded with the new group of hangers-on, the wealthy businessmen eager to be around him and pay for things. "Someday this ship's gonna reach port, gang," he would say, "and that's as far as we go together."

Rocky was also secretive about money. He didn't trust banks and preferred cash. He also didn't trust Weill, who took half his earnings, even

from personal appearances outside the ring, or the IBC. His anger grew
after Weill and Norris shortchanged him for the second Walcott fight,
when he had to accept a smaller share of the purse, even though he was
the defending champion. When rain delayed the second Charles fight,
Rocky fretted about the money the bad weather cost him in lost ticket
sales. And when the gate for Cockell was disappointing, Rocky lamented
the absence of a big-money opponent in the heavyweight ranks. "I should
have come along during the Tunney-Dempsey period," he said. "Whenever I think of the $1 million Tunney got for the second Dempsey fight,
my palms itch. And to think he paid hardly any income tax."

Rocky opened his training in the winter at Grossinger's. On a snowy,
icy afternoon in February 1955, Weill staged a photo op to unveil the
champ's surgically repaired nose, which had been straightened as well
and bore only the trace of a scar. *Life* magazine ran a photo spread headlined, "The Most Famous Nose in Sport." Rocky was deeply tanned after
two months vacationing in Florida. Under the watchful eye of the press
and his handlers, he sparred three easy rounds with Keene Simmons, his
former opponent, wearing a leather helmet with a special face protector
to shield his nose. Afterward, Weill pronounced him ready to face Cockell
in May.

In the spring, Rocky moved his training camp west to the dusty town
of Calistoga, in the heart of California's picturesque Napa Valley wine
region north of San Francisco. But Rocky didn't feel comfortable there
and was out of sorts. One day he looked so ragged that he nearly slipped
to his knees after missing his sparring partner with a wild right. Weill
immediately ended the workout. The following week, another sparring
partner knocked him down with a left hook. Weill made a show of "con-
fiscating" photographs of the knockdown, which seemed like a ploy to
boost flagging ticket sales by making Rocky seem vulnerable. Still, the
knockdown was real and Rocky's father, Pierino, wept. Then he gave
Rocky a tongue-lashing for his carelessness.

Pierino had become the training camp's elder statesman, his son's biggest cheerleader and critic, watching over him, preparing special dishes
like his Italian salad and even checking on Rocky at night after he had
gone to sleep, slipping an extra blanket over him if it was chilly.

Pierino loved the Napa Valley. It was a slice of his native Italy. The valley's old Italian wine growers, with their long mustaches and boisterous

ways, reminded Rocky of his grandfather Luigi, Lena's father, who had made wine in the basement of the family home in Brockton and hosted raucous parties with the other Italian men of Ward Two. The Napa wine-makers plied Pierino with cases of wine that piled up in his room. Every day, Pierino held court as a small Italian orchestra—three accordions and a violin—serenaded Rocky with old Italian songs when he made his entrance to the gym and when he left.

Meanwhile, the fight was shaping up as a war of words between the American and the British press. The Brits bristled at the ridicule that Cockell received from the Americans. Arthur Daley compared him to the Fat Boy in Charles Dickens's *The Pickwick Papers*. Red Smith, describing a sparring session, observed that Cockell "moves in little jiggling steps like a fat man whose wife has insisted that he dance." Cockell was unfazed. "I have boxed against a hostile press before. I am in this for Britain," he declared.

Cockell had been studying with an eminent London psychologist and natural healer who had taught him to use positive thoughts to build his confidence. The healer had also taught him to use telepathic communication; if Cockell was punched in the jaw, for instance, his healer could supposedly send him a telepathic message that the blow hadn't hurt and to punch back.

To the British press, the brawling Rocky, with his penchant for low blows, embodied the dirty, hoodlum American style of boxing. The journalist Desmond Hackett described one of the champ's sparring sessions: "He looks to be an evil, ruthless man . . . he just throws crippling punches and keeps on throwing them, with his tiny eyes glinting, his tongue licking his lips like a tiger bending over his new-killed prey." The British writers were even more worried when the California State Athletic Commission ruled that the fight would be fought in a smaller, sixteen-and-a-half-foot-square ring, not the twenty-foot-square ring that Cockell's manager wanted. If Weill had his way, observed Daley, the fighters would battle "ankle deep in sand inside a telephone booth."

The British press also attacked American boxing as rife with corruption and dodgy characters. Cockell's camp refused to drink tea that had been sent as a gift, in case it was poisoned. Hackett wrote about an American boxer who had lost a fight ten days before the Cockell-Marciano fight, after possibly being drugged by a gambling ring; he had collapsed after eating an orange that a stranger had given him, and traces of barbiturates were found in his system. One writer profiled the rough, tough, gun-toting San Francisco cop assigned as Cockell's bodyguard, Inspector George "Paddy" Wafer. Precautions were necessary, Wafer said, because there was a lot of out-of-town money being bet on the fight, "and some pretty rugged characters have drifted in here from Las Vegas, Reno and the East Coast. We just don't take any chances."

There was some truth behind the hyperbole. Shortly before the fight, Rocky was with a California friend, Ed Napoli, when they received a visit from a gangster who offered Rocky money to throw the fight. According to Napoli years later, the mobster said, "Rocky, you can be set the rest of your life if you throw this fight." Rocky's daughter Mary Anne told his biographer Everett Skehan that she heard a similar story from a Mafia figure after her father died, that he was offered $2 million to lose. Cockell was a 5-to-1 underdog, and Rocky was told that after the gamblers cleaned up and paid him off, he could easily beat Cockell in a rematch and reclaim his championship. Rocky grew angry and ordered the mobster to leave. "You disgust me," he said. "I'm ashamed that you're Italian. Get outta here and don't come back."

The day of the fight, Eddie Fisher sent Rocky a good-luck telegram from Miami Beach: YOU KNOW THE BEST ACTS ARE THE SHORTEST ONES AND YOU ARE THE BEST. But this would not be one of Rocky's best fights.

Only eighteen thousand fans showed up for the fight at Kezar Stadium on the crisp late afternoon of May 16, 1955. And much to everyone's surprise, the British challenger put up a plucky fight. Despite the flab around his waist and his stumpy legs, Cockell had trained hard and gotten his weight down to 205 pounds. Rocky, who weighed in at 190 pounds, slightly heavier than usual, appeared his usual sluggish self in the early rounds after an eight-month layoff.

For three rounds, Cockell traded punches with the champion as they pushed and shoved each other around the ring. Rocky was missing overhand rights, but Cockell couldn't hurt him and failed to cut the champion's reconstructed nose. At the end of the third round, Rocky finally connected with a left hook to the jaw that buckled Cockell's knees. He bloodied the Brit's nose in the fourth and staggered him again in the fifth and sixth, but Cockell fought back gamely. The crowd cheered him, which seemed to anger Rocky. At the end of the eighth, Rocky battered Cockell against the ropes and left him hanging over them like a sheet over a clothes-line. The challenger then crashed through the ropes onto the apron, only to be saved by the bell.

Rocky was living down to his reputation as the ugly American. Twice he hit Cockell after the bell. He head-butted him several times, elbowed him, and struck a couple of low blows. At the beginning of the ninth round, Rocky knocked Cockell down, then hit him in the head when he was still kneeling on the canvas. Cockell rose, only to be knocked down again. Again, he staggered to his feet and waded in for more punishment. Finally, fifty-four seconds into the round, the referee jumped in and grabbed Cockell in his arms to end the fight.

Rocky was widely criticized on both sides of the Atlantic for his crude performance. The British press vilified him as a dirty fighter. Rocky apologized, saying that the fouls were not deliberate. He said that he had started to swing when Cockell had fallen to his knee in the ninth, and he couldn't stop the punch in time. "On my wife and baby, I don't do one of those things knowing I do it," he said. Still, the British writers, and even some Americans, felt that the referee should have called Rocky for fouls, or at least warned him. Jimmy Cannon called the fight "an act of vandalism," one that descended into "an atmosphere of wickedness." Rocky was a man of good character outside the ring, said Cannon, "but his deportment during business hours is alien to the honor he cherishes in his private life."

The British press hailed Cockell for having won a moral victory. The *London Daily Mirror*'s Pete Wilson praised "the kind of courage which refuses to bandage in front of the firing squad. The driving urge which made men die rather than surrender to Everest, or perish in the white wastes of the Antarctic while trying to bend the very Pole to their driving will."

The criticism made the win bittersweet for Rocky. "I want to have a good reputation all over the world," he said. "Something goes out of being the undefeated champion when you read and hear these things." Rocky planned to defend his title again in the fall. But after that, he said, he might call it quits. He had heard the critics say he'd lost his knockout punch after failing to put Cockell away sooner. He felt that he had not been progressing since his first fight with Ezzard Charles. "If I don't look the way I feel I should in the fall fight, I'll think about stepping out as a fighter," he said. "It's better to stop one fight too soon than too late."

□ □ □

ROCKY HAD OTHER reasons to be sick of the fight game—the Mafia.

As he confided to Mario Lanza, the opera singer and movie star, you had to play the game. After the Cockell fight, Rocky spent several days visiting Lanza in Los Angeles. The two men had become good friends. Both were the sons of Italian immigrants, born two years apart. Both had fathers who had been seriously injured in World War I. Both had changed their names as they become American icons; Lanza, whose golden voice popularized opera for a new generation of Americans, was born Alfredo Cocozza in Philadelphia. His breakthrough role had come in 1951, when he played Enrico Caruso in Metro-Goldwyn-Mayer's hit movie *The Great Caruso*. Lanza enjoyed boxing and liked to reminisce about his childhood getting into street fights in south Philly, where he said he had seen an uncle killed by a local mobster. When Rocky visited, the two would spar and work out together at the full-size ring Lanza had at his palatial Beverly Hills home. Lanza was a big eater and drinker and was frequently trying to lose weight for his movie roles. After one visit, Lanza's mother called Rocky to thank him for helping her son shape up, saying he felt terrific. Once, Lanza got into an argument with the former heavyweight champ Max Baer over Rocky's ring abilities. When Baer boasted that he would have beaten Rocky, Lanza leaped up and assumed Rocky's crouching style and dared Baer to show how he would've knocked him out. The two men began sparring in Lanza's living room, and Lanza knocked Baer onto the sofa with a left hook.

Lanza could be temperamental. He had walked off the set of the film *The Student Prince* after a clash with the director, and his profligate lifestyle led to financial problems and a feud with his studio, MGM. When Rocky visited him in the spring of 1955, he was in debt and worried about money. He was trying to get Rocky a small role in his new movie, *Serenade*, about a vineyard worker who becomes an opera star, which would be filmed partially in Mexico.

One day during this trip, Rocky came by the house with Irving Berman, a hanger-on in the Los Angeles boxing scene who liked to ingratiate himself with movie stars and other celebrities. A few days later, Lanza and Rocky were sitting in the living room when Berman brought two other men by. One was introduced as Tom Brown. The other man, whose name Lanza couldn't recall, was "a tough-looking Jew from New York" who did most of the talking. They were familiar with Lanza's financial situation and told him that if he were willing to work for Brown, all of his financial problems would go away. The man pointed out that Frank Sinatra had been in a similar situation a few years ago, and "look what we done for him."

Rocky would later tell Lanza that Mr. Brown was actually Thomas Lucchese, also known as "Three Finger" Brown because two of his fingers had been amputated in a childhood accident. Lucchese was one of the most powerful Mafia bosses in America, a former hit man and the leader of one of New York's Five Families. Frankie Carbo was a close associate of Lucchese. Eddie Coco, one of Lucchese's capos, was Rocky Graziano's manager and had helped fix fights; he had recently been sentenced to life in prison for murdering a Miami Beach parking-lot attendant. Over the past year, Lucchese had been active in Los Angeles, trying to obtain interests in movie stars and film productions.

Lanza told his visitors that he wasn't interested in their proposition. Lucchese sat quietly as the other man persisted. He said that they had an interest in a Hollywood film company and could produce profitable movies starring Lanza. He also told Lanza that they could arrange for him to make personal appearances and get paid under the table, to avoid income taxes. When Lanza continued to refuse, the Jewish racketeer got mad and called Lanza a "damn Dago." Lanza punched the man in the stomach. The man apologized, and the visitors left.

Rocky appeared apprehensive about Lucchese. He told Lanza that he shouldn't have punched the associate because that was a good way to get himself killed. Rocky said that he hated the mobsters he had to deal with back east and that he had to turn over half of his earnings to them through a go-between—Al Weill—to avoid having any contact with them.

One night Rocky was at a restaurant with Weill, Allie Colombo, and a few other men. Frankie Carbo was at another table, Rocky would recall. "Weill pointed out Carbo and said to me, 'Go ahead over there and say hello to Frankie and all his friends. Make him feel good.' So I did."

As the Justice Department's antitrust case against the International

Boxing Club gathered steam, other states began investigating the Mafia's infiltration of boxing. Four days after Rocky defeated Cockell, Jim Norris was called before the New York State Athletic Commission, which was looking into charges that the IBC had blacklisted a welterweight, Vince Martinez, after Martinez complained that his manager had withheld money from a purse and used some of the cash to pay off the referee and judges in the fight. Norris danced around his relationship with Carbo, admitting that he had known Carbo for twenty years but had no idea what he did for a living.

In California, the governor ordered a special committee to investigate boxing there. The probe revealed that a Los Angeles matchmaker close to Carbo controlled boxing on the West Coast and had fixed at least seven fights. A former lightweight contender testified that he had followed orders to "go down" in the fourth round of a fight in Los Angeles. When the investigation shifted to San Francisco, the committee uncovered some funny business involving Weill and Rocky's purse from the Cockell fight. On May 17, 1955—the day after the fight—someone cashed a $10,000 check to Weill from the fight's Bay Area promoter, Jimmy Murray. The money was handed out in ten one-thousand-dollar bills and promptly disappeared. The committee also dug up a letter to Murray a week before the fight from the IBC's Truman Gibson, Norris's right-hand man, on IBC stationery, confirming Murray's "arrangement" with Norris for "$10,000 off the top." Murray testified that he couldn't explain what the money was for. One thing was clear, though: the $10,000 had been skimmed off the top of the fight's revenues before Rocky's $120,000 purse was calculated.

For years, Rocky had put up with Weill's abuse and Norris's manipulations because they had steered him to the title. Now, there was proof of what he had long suspected—they were stealing from him.

□ □ □

WANTED, THE POSTER said. REWARD FOR CAPTURE AND DELIVERY OF ROCKY MARCIANO TO ANY RING IN THE WORLD . . . ADVISE (SHERIFF) ARCHIE MOORE.

The posters, with Rocky's mug shot, began circulating to sportswriters across America in the winter of 1954–55. It was part of an audacious public-relations campaign by Archie Moore, the flamboyant light heavy-weight champion of the world, to force a heavyweight title fight with Rocky.

Moore was an overnight boxing sensation twenty years in the making. "Good things come to those who wait," he liked to say. "Providing you have the ability to wait long enough."

A black fighter born in Mississippi in 1913, Moore had labored for years in dusty rings from Poplar Bluff, Missouri, to Keokuk, Iowa, and from Australia to Argentina, where he had become a favorite of the dictator Juan Perón. He burst into the limelight in 1949 and then beat Joey Maxim for the light heavyweight title in December 1952. The Mongoose, as he was nicknamed, was a wily craftsman and ring magician who had piled up more knockouts than any boxer in history—eighty-two—while building a 119-25 record. He looked like a bebop musician with his wispy Vandyke beard and pencil-thin mustache, and in fact wrote lyrics for his friend Eli "Lucky" Thompson, one of America's leading tenor sax players. One song he wrote, "Stay in There," was the story of his life:

> You've got to stay in there
> Tomorrow is that day
> You've got to stay in there
> Then all your cares will go away
> You've got to stay in there
> Now don't you ever stop
> You've got to stay in there
> If you want to get to the top

Moore entered the ring wearing stunning robes that he personally designed and had custom-made by a Harlem dressmaker. The night he knocked out the middleweight champion Bobo Olson, he wore a robe of white baby flannel imported from England, lined with gold satin and trimmed with ten-carat-gold braid and gold epaulets. "High style," he explained, "goes with fighting and showmanship."

Moore cultivated an air of mystery, from his true age (he said he was thirty-eight in 1954, but when confronted with evidence of his actual age, he quipped that he was three years old at birth) to his unusual training methods and ring tactics. He claimed to have learned a secret weight-loss trick from an Australian aborigine he had discovered in the bush throwing a boomerang. He drank a secret Argentine "strength extract" potion he called "goose juice," which was actually beef broth. He attributed much of his success in the ring to his personal theories of relaxism and escapology. "With each punch I try to build a bridge so I can escape over it if something goes wrong," he explained. Once, while trying to describe relaxism to a sportswriter, Moore fell asleep. He had a secret numbering system to catalog his punches; for instance, when he knocked out Bobo Olson with two rights to the head followed by a left hook that turned into an uppercut at the last instant, he called it his 4-6-9. Moore's swashbuckling style, including his rope-a-dope maneuver, would be adopted a decade later by a young protégé, Cassius Clay.

For all his showmanship, Moore was a legitimately skilled boxer who combined speed and power with a generation's worth of experience. Writers called him a throwback, the last of the great ring generals, boxing's Methuselah. As Moore's publicity campaign to fight Rocky captured the public's imagination, he became something that Rocky and the International Boxing Club desperately needed after the Cockell embarrassment: a worthy opponent. Moore's playfulness with the press helped him win the attention he had missed as a young black fighter starting out in the Great Depression, fighting for peanuts in tank towns.

"Remember that Archie is a professional guide," said the New York boxing writer Lester Bromberg. "He'll take you exactly where he wants you to go."

Moore wound up living in Toledo, Ohio, where a group of local business leaders and politicians, including the former mayor, backed his public relations campaign to force Rocky into the ring. The campaign, launched late in 1954, was "the like of which had never before been carried on in behalf of one athlete," wrote W. C. Heinz. The *Toledo Blade*'s cartoonist contributed caricatures of Rocky. Another supporter was Nicholas Dallis, the creator of two nationally syndicated comic strips, *Rex Morgan, M.D.* and *Judge Parker*. He created a character inspired by Moore—Archer Moran, a boxer who finally gets a chance at the title and wins. The campaign kicked off on November 17, with 427 letters mailed to sports editors and writers across the country. Over the ensuing months, the circulation list grew to nearly five hundred newspapers and magazines, and included every newspaper in a city with fifty thousand or more people.

Archie helped stuff envelopes, ran to the post office, and wrote most of the letters himself, up to 150 a day. He signed them "Archie Moore, the old guy who's chasing our Heavyweight Champion" or "The Father Time that Marciano and Weill want no part of." They got creative, devising the WANTED poster from "Sheriff Archie Moore" and buying classified ads that said, "Information Wanted on How to Make Rocky Marciano Defend His Heavyweight Title." Over the holidays, Moore sent Rocky a card wishing him a Happy New Year and asking him to make a resolution to fight him in 1955.

"My business is not prize fighting but merchandising," said Bob Reese, a Toledo car dealer and Moore's leading booster. "And I was out to merchandise Archie."

Archie traveled around the country, speaking at banquets and appearing on television and radio to challenge Rocky. When the Toledo group learned that Rocky was refereeing a boxing match in Washington, they put Moore on a plane that afternoon and he was at the arena that night, challenging Rocky from the crowd. They also played the IBC monopoly card. Michael DiSalle, a former mayor of Toledo who had served in President Truman's administration, met in Washington with the racket-busting senator Estes Kefauver about a possible investigation of boxing; DiSalle and Moore also appeared before the executive committee of the National Boxing Association in New York.

The campaign proved successful, first in the small towns that identified with the underdog Moore, and then in the bigger cities. As part of the PR offensive, Moore's group conducted a nationwide poll showing that 992 sportswriters desired a Moore-Marciano match, though 787 picked Rocky to win.

"What those who pick Marciano don't understand is the principle of offensive and defensive distance," said Moore. "I can be out of range of a man's punchin', but still within strikin' distance. I'll demonstrate that when I fight Marciano. I'll stop him in ten."

At first, Weill and Norris were not enthusiastic—to Rocky's frustration. In the fall of 1954, shortly after Moore had launched his PR campaign, Rocky met his friend Tim Cohane, the sports editor of *Look* magazine, at the Beverly Hills Hotel. Rocky was there for the plastic surgery on his nose following the second Ezzard Charles fight. Rocky told Cohane that he wanted to fight Moore but that the decision wasn't up to him. He asked Cohane what he thought. Cohane replied that Moore would draw a big gate and deserved a shot. "If you don't fight him, it will be a stain on your record that won't rub off," said Cohane. "He'll give you a tough fight, but I believe you will ultimately knock him out. If you do beat him, retire. You're at your peak now. Soon it will be all downhill."

Rocky certainly wasn't afraid of Moore. Nor was he bothered by the campaign. He had always been willing to fight anyone. Weill, who called the shots, also had no fears about the matchup. The fight just hadn't made financial sense until Moore's campaign generated such tremendous public excitement. In June 1955, the month after he beat Nino Valdes in Las Vegas, with Carmen Miranda and a pink-clad Liberace watching from ringside, Moore destroyed the hard-hitting middleweight champion Bobo Olson at the Polo Grounds. Valdes and Olson had both been potential candidates for Rocky's next title defense, which he had privately hinted might be his last. Moore, who had offered to fight both Valdes and Olson on the same night to earn a shot at Rocky, had now vanquished both.

Yes, Moore was old—thirty-eight by his count, forty-one by his mother's—but he was in peak condition and showed no signs of slowing down. "It's not the length of a career that wears a man out. It's the amount of punches he takes," observed Moore. "I didn't take too many."

The fight was set for September 1955 at Yankee Stadium. It was the most anticipated heavyweight title bout in years.

□ □ □

ROCKY'S TRAINING CAMP at Grossinger's was more relaxed leading into the Moore fight. After sparring 200 rounds before each of his previous title fights, he cut back to 135. One reason was a feeling that overtraining had caused him to start sluggishly in his previous two fights. But he was also burning out, and his back bothered him until he stretched it out. The fretful Charley Goldman worried that Rocky was losing his edge.

One day Rocky didn't train at all and invited a group of visiting New York Yankees players to breakfast. Afterward, the ballplayers, including Hank Bauer, Don Larsen, and Elston Howard, joined members of Rocky's camp in a softball game on the lawn outside his cottage. They asked Rocky to umpire, but he declined. When Bauer hit a ball over the fence and the umpire called it foul, he flew into a rage and Rocky laughed. "See what I mean?" he said. "No umpire's job for me."

Rocky still looked sharp and confident, banging around his sparring partners. But he was more reflective, projecting an inner peace that came with a new focus on a life beyond boxing. He turned thirty-two on September 1 and was thinking about his evolution and place in boxing history.

Early one morning, he was jogging with the sportswriter Murray Olderman when he stopped suddenly and asked, "Tell me, Murray—am I a good boxer?" Diplomatically, Olderman pointed out that Rocky had never lost a fight. Rocky pondered his words, then said, "I guess I am a lousy boxer."

Another time, Rocky asked his friend Smokey Cerrone from Providence, "How do you see me fighting now, versus the older days?" When Smokey told him that it seemed he had more of a plan now, Rocky's face lit up. "You're right," he said. "I'm looking for openings, weaknesses." Rocky took pride in the refinements he had made under Goldman's tutelage—shortening his stance and his punches, developing his left hook, tightening his defense. Goldman confessed that he had been reluctant to tighten Rocky's stance, for fear of taking away his vaunted looping right, the Suzie Q. But in several of Rocky's recent fights, most notably the first title match with Jersey Joe Walcott, he had won with shorter punches, so Goldman relented. Rocky joked that Suzie Q was retired. The last time he had used it to flatten an opponent was against Rex Layne. "I hit Layne with it in ring center," Rocky said. "End of fight. Maybe it also was the end of Suzie Q."

Two days after Rocky's birthday, Jack Dempsey visited his camp. That prompted Rocky to muse about how his style had been compared to Dempsey's, and how Dempsey had worked to develop his left hand at the end of his career. He also talked about Dempsey's rival Gene Tunney and said that he wanted to "retire on top" like Tunney—and as history's first unbeaten champion.

Sitting on the mountainside one evening after dinner, watching the setting sun paint the sky purple, Rocky talked about enjoying the life that his success had made possible. He and Allie Colombo wanted to start a summer camp for boys. He wanted to travel with Barbara, spend more time at home, have more children.

About ten days before the fight, he sat in the living room of his cottage with Weill, Goldman, and the *Chicago Tribune*'s David Condon.

"You know," he said, "this may be my last fight."

"He's gonna fight lots more," Weill interjected. Rocky ignored him.

"Yeah, maybe my last fight. It's getting too hard to train and keep in shape. I've been slipping and suddenly it has dawned on me. I worked like a horse getting ready for the Walcott fight. I worked almost as hard for the rematch. Since then I've had three more defenses, and I've been doing less work and training for each one. I was counting the other day and it scares me. For this match with Moore, I've boxed only about half the rounds I did in preparing for the first one with Walcott. You know what that means? I've lost the hunger or something. It means that someday I'll go into a fight in less than perfect condition and I'll get whipped. I think I'll quit before that happens to Rocky. I'm too proud to let Marciano beat Rocky Marciano. Yeah. I guess sometimes you lose the hunger."

Goldman gestured toward the kitchen, where the refrigerator was padlocked against Rocky's midnight raids, and whispered, "He ain't lost no hunger physically. If I slipped out of the room a minute, he'd chew the lock off the icebox."

In contrast to the contemplative nature of Rocky's camp in the Catskills, Moore's training camp 150 miles to the northeast, in the Berkshires of western Massachusetts, was a circus.

In early August, Moore descended on the town of North Adams in a chartered plane and was greeted at the airport by two thousand people, including a delegation of local officials. He had fought there six years earlier, when he was a nobody, and been captivated by the mountain scenery. The chamber of commerce installed him at a summer camp for children and renovated an ancient arena where he could spar. When he wasn't training or going for runs up Mount Greylock with the camp director's fourteen-year-old son, Moore drove around town in a red Thunderbird, sporting a jaunty blue yachting cap that he waved at local police officers with the greeting, "How's North Adams' finest?" To Jim Norris's horror, Moore also started taking flying lessons. Norris sent a desperate telegram from New York: I REQUEST MOST URGENTLY THAT YOU ABANDON SOLO FLYING FOR NOW. Moore also appeared at local Rotary and Kiwanis meetings to speak about juvenile delinquency, a favorite topic that he had addressed with President Eisenhower at a White House conference; as a boy, he had done time in reform school for stealing money from a trolley. He even found time to lecture on music, "From Bach to Pop to Bop," at nearby Williams College.

Lucky Thompson had brought his five-piece jazz band from Harlem, and they played as Moore warmed up for his workouts. Later, he hit the heavy bag to the rhythm of Lucky's saxophone, the pair looking, a *New York Times* writer observed, "like an Indian fakir and a cobra being piped into a basket." Moore's trainers were a pair of large men weighing nearly three hundred pounds each; the principal trainer, James "Cheerful" Norman, also ran a Toledo poolroom. But they deferred to Moore, who taped his own hands and dictated his own pace.

Moore also engaged in a good-natured war of words with IBC publicist Harry Mendel, who had been dispatched to North Adams to ensure a steady stream of anti-Rocky invective to hype the fight. When Mendel put out a statement from Moore that Rocky had lost his punch, Moore told reporters that those were Mendel's words, not his. When Mendel said he was a philosopher, Moore corrected the forty-one-year-old press agent: "You're too young. *I'm* a philosopher."

Rocky was a prohibitive 18-to-5 betting favorite. But there was much intrigue around the question of whether Moore could outthink him, using his superior defense to evade Rocky's wild punches and his speed to hammer away at the champion and open up cuts. Nor was power a problem. Moore weighed in at 188 pounds to Rocky's 188¼ and in fact looked bigger. The skeptics, like A. J. Liebling, believed that Moore was underestimating Rocky's strength. But Moore wasn't looking to simply outbox Rocky. He had studied films of Rocky's first fights against Walcott and Charles and had spotted moments where they had hurt Rocky but failed to press their advantage. Moore vowed not to make that mistake. "I believe I can get to Rocky, and if I hit him, I'll floor him," said Moore. Liebling had no doubt as to Moore's strategy: he was Captain Ahab, looking to harpoon the great white whale. "Would Ahab have been content merely to go the distance with the White Whale?" asked Liebling, who doubted that Moore could pull it off but wanted to see him try. "What would *Moby Dick* be if Ahab had succeeded?" observed Liebling. "Just another fish story."

Rocky was confident that his superior conditioning and strength would carry him to victory. His biggest concern was Moore's defense. "I got to figure how I'll be able to get a clean shot at him," said Rocky. "The guy's all arms and shoulders and elbows." Rocky was mostly bemused by the comments from Moore's camp. Some reporters wrote that he was livid. Allie Colombo played along, saying that Rocky never said anything when he read a negative story, just grunted. "But every time he grunts, I know somebody is in real trouble," observed Allie. "And the last time Moore's name was mentioned, Rocky grunted. So figure it out for yourself." In truth, Rocky understood prefight hyperbole and appreciated that Moore's flamboyance was selling tickets. "How can I dislike a fellow who's going to help me make that kind of money?" he asked.

The fight was shaping up as the most exciting heavyweight title clash in New York since the second fight between Joe Louis and Billy Conn in 1946. Television had transformed boxing since then, but for one night, Moore-Marciano rekindled the glamour of a faded era. Despite the large closed-circuit television audience, this was a fight that people wanted to see in person. Ticket orders flowed in from overseas and around the country. The New York Convention and Visitors Bureau reported an upswing in hotel, theater, plane, and train reservations. The festive atmosphere only increased as the fight was delayed a day by the threat of Hurricane Ione sweeping up the East Coast. The hurricane veered off into the Atlantic, giving the fight crowd that had descended upon the city another night of exquisite anticipation as they diverted themselves on Broadway and in the city's restaurants and nightclubs.

The night of the fight, September 21, was cool and clear, a crisp autumn evening more suited to a football game. Outside Yankee Stadium, the roads were bumper-to-bumper with taxicabs, the subway cars were jammed, and the concourses were packed with last-minute ticket buyers who snapped up all the $5 bleacher seats. Inside, on the field where the Yankees were preparing to face the Brooklyn Dodgers the next week in the World Series, an elevated ring had been pitched just beyond second base, to give fans in the stadium's far reaches a better view.

More than one thousand press credentials had been issued, including to reporters from Europe and South America. Western Union had more than seventy-five direct wires operating from ringside, unprecedented since Joe Louis's big fights. Reporters were packed so tightly together that Liebling complained he could only fit sideways—"the extra compression having been caused by the injection of a prewar number of movie stars and politicos." Among the faces in the crowd was Don Newcombe, the Dodgers' ace pitcher, who was asked if he was trying to get a feel for Yankee Stadium before his Game 1 start. "Not me," he said. "I just want to see the fight." The celebrity-studded crowd included Humphrey Bogart, who brought Lauren Bacall and sat on press row, as he was studying for the role of a press agent in the boxing film *The Harder They Fall*. Jackie Gleason, a regular at Toots Shor's saloon who had roasted Rocky at a boxing dinner, wore a pink suit. Gregory Peck, who was getting ready to play Captain Ahab in the Hollywood version of *Moby Dick*, was also there. Hollywood's hottest couple, Eddie Fisher and Debbie Reynolds, came down from Grossinger's, where they had attended Rocky's final workout and confided their plans to marry the following week. General Douglas MacArthur came, as did Secretary of State John Foster Dulles, taking a break from mediating a dispute between Greece and Turkey. Alice Roosevelt Longworth, Theodore Roosevelt's daughter and an avid boxing fan, insisted on coming despite a fractured hip. Surveying the crowd, Jimmy Cannon observed: "The hoods came out of the sewers of the underworld. There were big men present and pool room grifters and [the jockey] Eddie Arcaro was small and debonair in that vast multitude."

It was not a million-dollar gate but close—$948,000. Closed-circuit television brought in another $1.2 million.

At 10:30 p.m., the crowd of sixty-one thousand—the largest ever to see Rocky fight—cheered as the champion, clad in a royal blue robe with a blue monk's cowl pulled over his head, made his way to the ring. Rocky moved at a run, led by a flying wedge of three policemen and pushed by a phalanx of about forty more. He climbed the steps to the ring, observed Liebling, "with the cumbrous agility of a medieval executioner ascending the scaffold." Moore followed, resplendent in a robe of black brocade trimmed in gold, with a gold lining and wide Louis XIV cuffs that drew a roar of appreciation from the crowd. "No Othello was ever more lavishly costumed," noted *Sports Illustrated*'s Budd Schulberg.

The introductions of former champions took longer than usual, prolonging the suspense, as Jack Dempsey, Gene Tunney, Joe Louis, Max Baer, and Jim Braddock took a bow. Someone lifted a dwarf into the ring, advertising something; he dashed across and out the other side before anyone could react.

From his corner, Moore glared across the ring at Rocky, eyebrows arched and arms folded across his chest. Moore continued to stare him down when referee Harry Kessler summoned the two fighters to the center of the ring for their prefight instructions. Rocky looked impassively back. "Good evening, Rocky and Archie," Kessler greeted them. He reminded them that the mandatory eight-second rule was not in effect after a knockdown since this was a championship fight, and he told them to keep their punches high. "Now, Rocky and Archie, I want a nice, clean fight," he told them, prompting laughter on press row.

Finally, with the crowd on its feet, the floodlights illuminating the crowd went dark and the ring glowed white, surrounded by darkness. The bell rang and the fight began. Moore, as he had vowed, did not retreat from Rocky but moved in close, feinting and jabbing. Rocky started slowly but was more deliberate than rusty, throwing a series of probing left hooks that missed or lightly trimmed Moore's beard as the challenger adroitly ducked away.

The fight's key moment came in the second round. With both fighters picking up the pace in the first minute, Rocky missed with a right; then, as he threw a left, Moore stepped neatly inside the punch and hit him with a short, hard right square on the chin that knocked the champ down. Rocky dropped on all fours, his head nearly pressed to the canvas. It was only the second time in his career that he had been knocked down. And unlike his first-round knockdown at the hands of Jersey Joe Walcott, when his head had remained clear, this punch dazed him. Rocky didn't hear Kessler counting over his own confusion and the roar of the crowd, but he quickly clambered to his feet at the count of two. Moore stood nearby, in the closest neutral corner, ready to pounce. But inexplicably, Kessler kept counting and stepped between them as Rocky walked over to the side of the ring and rested his right hand on the rope, a confused smile on his face. At the count of four, Kessler stepped away and the fight resumed; Rocky immediately tied Moore up in a clinch.

But under the New York rules that Kessler himself had gone over before the fight, the mandatory eight-count rule was not in effect. Kessler, a veteran referee working his first championship fight, should have stepped aside as soon as Rocky regained his feet. Those precious seconds could have allowed Moore to finish Rocky when he was most vulnerable. Some writers noted the mistake, but it was not treated as a major controversy. Moore didn't mention it afterward, saying instead that he had erred by not attacking Rocky more quickly—ironic since he had criticized Walcott and Charles for making the same mistake. "When he got up," said Moore, "I let him get away."

Rocky thought so, too. "I couldn't understand why Archie didn't come at me then," he said. "I wasn't groggy, but I was dazed, and I couldn't see out of my left eye for a while. But I was ready for him."

Years later, though, Moore would blame Kessler for costing him the fight.

"I thought, 'I got him now, I got him,'" Moore told the *Washington Post* in 1985. "And he's standing up against those ropes, looking at the people as if he wants to apologize for going down. . . . All I have to do is swing out and hit him again, but Kessler swings his butt between me and Rocky." Moore said that Kessler counted six more seconds; all the while his corner men were shouting that there was no eight-count, and that he should hit Rocky. Moore said that Kessler wiped Rocky's gloves, then pulled them and snapped his head back, "and that gets him going again. . . . I'm standing there looking (Kessler) right in the eyes and he's looking in my eyes. And he sees the hate in my eyes, he sees it all right. And he knows I hate him. I hate him to this day."

But Moore was rewriting history. Kessler didn't count six more seconds, wipe Rocky's gloves, or snap his head back. The film shows Kessler stepping between the fighters, but, apparently realizing his mistake, he stops at the count of four and steps away quickly, his right hand briefly touching Rocky's left glove as he does.

When the fight resumed, a rubbery-legged Rocky still had to survive more than two minutes to make it to the end of the round. He stopped throwing the right-left combinations that Moore had countered so effectively and pulled back into his crouching shell to recuperate. Moore was still able to sting Rocky with a series of left jabs, straight rights, and a left uppercut, bloodying his nose and opening a puffy cut under his left eye. Rocky circled warily, watching carefully then advancing. In the final ten seconds, he exploded with a thunderous right to Moore's chin. At the bell, Moore seemed weary returning to his corner, perhaps realizing that he had missed his best chance.

In the third round, Rocky took control of the fight. Moore continued to box skillfully and courageously, making Rocky miss often and smiling as he slipped his punches and countered with quick combinations. But

Rocky began scoring with hard left hooks to the head, pounding Moore's body and hitting him with a right uppercut to the jaw. He even impressed Goldman with some feints of his own. Even when Moore blocked a punch, it still did damage. Moore would bring up his right arm, and it would absorb the blow of one of Rocky's clubbing left hooks. In the fourth round, Rocky hit Moore square on the forehead with a vicious right that dazed him; for the first time that night, referee Kessler said later, Moore "must have realized that he was in there with a devastating puncher." Later, Rocky trapped Moore against the ropes and pounded away at him for nearly a minute. Moore blocked most of his punches but was worn down by the effort. "It's like fighting an airplane propeller," he observed. "The blades keep whirring past your ear and over your head." As the bell sounded ending the furious round, Rocky hit Moore with a right to the face and Moore hit him back in his face with a hard right.

Moore fought back in the fifth, his best round since the second, but it was clear he was tiring. At one point, he leaned back against the ropes, daring Rocky to swing at him, hoping to tire out the champ. The fight was still close entering the sixth. Then Rocky, his tongue sticking out, knocked Moore down for a count of four at the beginning of the round and again near the end. The second knockdown came after a furious exchange between the two, as Moore met Rocky punch for punch. Moore climbed to his feet at the count of eight, just before the bell, and then both men wobbled back to their corners, Rocky hanging on to the rope for support. The *New York Times*' Joseph Nichols described it as "comparable to any single round in heavyweight title history." The ring doctor checked Moore but allowed him to continue.

Moore made his last stand in the seventh. Drifting away from Rocky, fighting as he moved, Moore drilled him with four left hooks and a right and started beating the wild-swinging champ to the punch. But a confident Rocky landed a crushing blow to the body that, though overlooked, was one of the hardest of the night. After Rocky hit him in the ear with an overhand right, Moore fell to one knee, but Kessler ruled it a slip.

Moore's trainer, Cheerful Norman, was massaging his fighter's tired legs between rounds. Rocky swarmed all over him in the eighth, dropping him to his knees with a right to the jaw near the end. The bell sounded at the count of six, granting Moore a temporary reprieve. Rocky didn't seem to realize the round had ended until Al Weill pounded up the steps with his stool. In Moore's corner, the ring doctor asked again if he wished to continue. As Moore recalled, "I told him that I, too, was a champion and I'd go down fighting."

In the ninth, he did. Rocky came out and landed a series of rights and lefts to Moore's head. Moore tried to fight back, but it was too much. Moore started to sink, pulled himself back up, then slumped to the canvas. He rose to his haunches at the count of eight, then collapsed in exhaustion as Kessler counted him out at 1:19. As Kessler intoned "ten and out," a bloody Rocky shouldered his way past the referee and crouched over the blinking, dazed Moore, who was trying to sit up. "Are you all right, Archie? You all right?" asked Rocky. Unable to speak, Moore tried to nod. Then his handlers lifted his limp form to his stool.

Joseph Nichols called it "one of the most savagely fought, thrilling duels in modern prize ring history." The crowd was dazzled by Moore's boxing and ability to withstand so much punishment, and by Rocky's power and tenacity. The boxing public was beginning to recognize Rocky as a great champion, his indomitable will and strength compensating for his lack of style. He had to be at his best to defeat Moore, and he had displayed some skillful boxing along with his devastating power. "The old-timers talk of Sullivan and Jeffries and Dempsey," wrote Budd Schulberg. "We may have another such immortal slugger in our midst. Are we too close to his shortcomings to recognize his incomparable virtues?"

Moore had to be helped out of the ring. Back in his dressing room, his right eye swollen completely shut, he regained his flair.

"If you fellows think I put up a good fight, then I'm extremely happy. I think Rocky enjoyed it. I hope the public enjoyed it, too," he said. Moore gave no excuses. "His consistency just overpowered me. Marciano is far and away the strongest man I've ever encountered in almost twenty years of fighting."

Afterward, Moore headed into the night to the Café Bohemia in Greenwich Village, where he tapped his toes to Lucky Thompson's saxophone.

◻ ◻ ◻

AFTER THE MOORE fight, reporters peppered Rocky with questions about retirement.

"My wife and my mother want me to retire, and I've thought about it," he said.

The ever-vigilant Al Weill, standing nearby, barked, "He's not retiring."

Later, Weill pulled Rocky into the shower room and demanded, "What's this about retirement?"

"Al, I've been thinking about it," Rocky replied.

"I can't make you fight if you don't want to," said Weill evenly. "But don't tell these guys. Let them think you're going to fight some more. There's plenty of dough can be made while you're still the champ. Once you retire, there's no money for you."

Later that night, in his suite at the Concourse Plaza Hotel near Yankee Stadium, the champion was more subdued. He hadn't called his mother yet, as he always did after he fought. He sat in the kitchen, resting his head in his hand, when his father walked in. Pierino was always great at making Rocky feel good after his wins, but tonight he was restless. His face was pale and he looked tired.

"Pop, what's the matter with you?" Rocky asked. "You look worried."

"I'm all right," he said. "I'm all right now."

Rocky pulled out a kitchen chair and told his father to sit down. But Pierino didn't. He walked out into the living room. Rocky could see him pacing back and forth. Someone else urged him to rest and he snapped, "This is my son. He fight a toughest man. Toughest like Walcott. This is not an easy life my boy has."

Just then, Weill came into the kitchen and shut the glass door. He implored Rocky not to announce his retirement. "You can retire if you want to, but don't say it. You don't have to say it for a year. We'll say we'll fight the best man."

"Yeah, Al," replied Rocky wearily, watching his father pace. "I'll tell them it's just talk." Rocky had been gratified to see the positive effects of his career on his father, who had been able to quit the shoe factory and loved the attention of being at camp and the father of a champion. But now, for the first time, Rocky also realized how tough it was on his father, seeing him in the ring, and how it might affect his fragile health.

The next day, at a postfight press conference, Rocky said that he'd like to make it an even fifty wins before he quit. But the idea of retirement didn't fade. A month or so after the fight, Rocky saw Charley Goldman. Goldman said he looked bloated. Rocky agreed. "And you know something? I haven't even been taking walks." Goldman said it was then that he knew.

After the fight, Rocky went to see Weill with Allie and a priest who was a friend, Father Paul McKenzie. Weill told Rocky that he'd lined up an exhibition tour in Italy. Rocky was skeptical and later talked it over with the priest. "You just got through with a big fight," Father McKenzie said. "I think you should spend more time with your family. It's all right for you to make money while you're fighting, but your family's more important. As a matter of fact, I think you should give some thought to retirement."

Rocky went to see Weill the next day and said he wouldn't go to Italy. Weill urged him to take a few weeks and think it over; in the meantime, he would line up some television appearances. Rocky said no. He just wanted to go home. Over the next few weeks, Weill kept calling him in Brockton. Rocky and Barbara decided to plan a trip to South America. Weill said he could arrange some appearances there, but again Rocky refused.

That winter, Rocky and Barbara went to Trinidad and then Venezuela, where big receptions greeted them at the airport in both countries. From there, they traveled to Brazil and visited São Paolo and Rio de Janeiro, where they stayed at the Excelsior Hotel on Copacabana Beach. Rocky was enjoying himself. Nightclubbing in São Paolo, they became friendly with other couples who shared stories of where they had traveled together. "All of a sudden I realized I never really had any kind of family life," said Rocky. Their new friends couldn't understand the life they led. One wife pulled Barbara aside and said that Rocky owed it to her and their daughter to spend more time with them. When they were alone, Rocky asked her if it was really that bad. "Really, it's no fun, you know, Rock. I get that from a lot of people."

One night, they were asleep in their Rio hotel when Barbara began thrashing around, her breathing hoarse. She gasped that she couldn't breathe and told Rocky to open a window. She said that this had happened before and pressed his hand to a lump on her throat. She had a thyroid problem, and the doctors had told her that she needed an operation. She hadn't told him before because he had been busy training. After she drifted back to sleep, Rocky lay awake, feeling guilty. He thought of Barbara's miscarriage while he was training for the first Charles fight. He remembered coming home after a fight, and his daughter running away from him in fright. He thought of his mother, complaining that he never seemed to have enough time for his family and friends in Brockton.

He also thought about boxing. He was burned out. His back ached and he also had an arthritic right elbow. There were no mountains left to climb. The International Boxing Club was rotten to the core. And then there was Al Weill. Early in April 1956, the stories hit the newspapers about the California boxing investigation and the $10,000 that Weill had gotten from the Cockell fight. Publicly, Rocky said that Weill would never cheat him. Privately, he felt that it wasn't the only time. According to his brother Peter, Rocky learned that Weill had held back several choice seats from the Moore fight and sold them under the table, pocketing a substantial amount of money for himself. And there was more. Rocky discovered that Weill had routinely created phantom training expenses for his fights— money that would be taken off the top of his purse before Rocky received his share. "I do all the hard work, but he gets fifty percent," complained Rocky. He vowed that Weill would never get another nickel from him.

A few weeks later, on April 27, 1956, nine years after his first professional fight as Rocky Mack in Holyoke, Rocky Marciano announced his retirement. He was a free man.

12

America's Guest

THE EX-CHAMP SITS ON A PLATFORM BEHIND AN OUTDOOR STAGE IN THE parking lot of the harness-racing grounds in Maywood Park, Illinois. It's a warm Monday night at the end of July 1957. Rocky wears a white short-sleeved sport shirt, open at the collar, and brown trousers. He is preparing to emcee an outdoor Italian festival to benefit the Villa Scalabrini, a home for the aged. But for now, the ex-champ is focused on the heir to his throne.

The new heavyweight champion, Floyd Patterson, is fighting Hurricane Jackson at the Polo Grounds in New York. Someone has carried a small black-and-white television set onto Rocky's platform. He hunches forward in his folding chair, his face a foot or so from the screen. When the opening bell rings, he clenches his fists and stares at the screen. Patterson knocks Jackson down, and the twenty or so onlookers surrounding Rocky shout. He remains silent, until someone asks him what he thinks. "Patterson landed some good punches," he replies softly, his eyes fixed on the screen. "To me, it's very interesting. It's very interesting to me." Rocky watches the second round with his right index finger on his chin, like Rodin's The Thinker, then gets up and shifts his chair to give a photographer a better angle. In the third round, the screen flickers and people scream for someone to fix it. Someone does. An earlier rainstorm has brought out mosquitoes that buzz around the stage and bite, drawing blood, but Rocky doesn't slap once. He watches intently as Patterson stalks his prey across the ring.

The photographer asks Rocky to make a motion with his fist. He does. "Rock, close your eyes tight," the photographer commands. He refuses.

"I wanna watch the fight!" he protests.

After the round, Rocky closes his eyes for the photographer. Later, the photographer asks him to throw a left. He does. "See," the photographer whispers to a companion. "Just tell him what to do."

A fan pats Rocky on the back and says, "Nobody hits as hard as you do."

"Thanks, pal," says Rocky.

Just before the sixth round, the three singing Di Mara sisters go onstage to start the show. A twelve-piece band begins to play. At the end of the sixth, Patterson hits Jackson hard and Rocky exclaims, "Wow!" After the seventh, Rocky hurries to his trailer to sign autographs, then returns for the start of the eighth. He turns his head to answer a question and misses Patterson knocking Jackson down again. When the referee stops the fight in the tenth and Patterson wins, the people watching with Rocky complain. Rocky shrugs. "I don't know," he says. "You gotta be there. In person. Television fools you." The band strikes up "Dime a Dance." Rocky heads back to his trailer to get dressed for his act. He is quiet. A fan presses him about the state of the heavyweight division, asking who else is out there to challenge Patterson.

"There is no one else," says Rocky.

"How about you, Rock?"

"Retired permanently, thank you."

□ □ □

THE DAY AFTER Rocky announced his retirement at a teary Manhattan press conference, he rode up to the Catskills, up the winding dirt road to his training camp at Grossinger's, and symbolically nailed boards across the doorway to his old white cottage.

Earlier, he had sat alone in his old bungalow, now christened "Rocky Marciano." He was excited but wistful. "What are they saying?" he asked a reporter who came by.

"They all think you did the right thing."

"Good, good," he said happily. "I think so, too."

Rocky fretted that his popularity would fade now that he had relinquished his crown, that his fans would think less of him for walking away. Did he still want people asking him for his autograph?

"You bet I do."

He spoke of pursuing business opportunities, working with children, and serving as a goodwill ambassador to help clean up boxing. The week before, the Justice Department's antitrust case against the International Boxing Club had finally gone to trial. Despite his regrets, Rocky was emphatic that he would never box again. He would not repeat the mistakes of Joe Louis and others who had attempted comebacks, or risk his record as history's only unbeaten heavyweight champion.

"Barring poverty, the ring has seen the last of me," he said. Barbara's days as a boxing widow were over. He joked that she might become a golf widow, but said seriously that he would be home more. He wanted more children.

Rocky's elated mother, Lena, in New York with Pierino for a family wedding, celebrated by going to St. Patrick's Cathedral and lighting a candle. Then she embarked on a whirlwind tour of Manhattan that showed where her son had gotten his stamina—lunch at Toots Shor's, where she told Joe DiMaggio he looked very handsome; a television interview at CBS, where the host put her on the phone with Perry Como; and a visit to Cardinal Spellman, who gave her rosaries and said, "I think Rocky made the right decision." A few nights later, Lena was back at Toots Shor's for dinner, where she was joined by Jackie Gleason and discussed a possible match between her teenage son Peter and Gleason's teenage daughter. "Look, Jackie, we're both fat but we're both happy people," she told him. When Lena started talking about her big Sunday family dinners, Gleason sighed and said, "Sundays are the best."

One week after Rocky announced his retirement, Brockton welcomed him home with one last tumultuous parade, complete with the Brockton High School marching band. "I never dreamed we would have another parade," Rocky told the crowd, moved to tears. "I thought I had to fight for one of them."

But if Rocky looked forward to more family time, he also worried about the future; his fears about money always lurked in the background. A skeptical Archie Moore predicted that Rocky would fight again "because he loves the jingle of the American dollar too much."

With liberation came restlessness. Without the long months of Spartan training and the championship as his goal, he needed a new sense of purpose. Without the fierce battles in the ring, he needed action. He was thirty-two years old. "I'm not thinking that retirement means sitting around and getting fat," he said. But what would he do with the rest of his life?

◻ ◻ ◻

Rocky's network of wealthy boosters was eager to help the ex-champ take his first steps in the business world.

Russ Murray, who had let Rocky train at his estate outside Brockton when he was just beginning, paid him $10,000 to do public relations for his Raynham Park dog track. Charles O. Finley, a wealthy Chicago insurance man who owned the Kansas City Athletics baseball team, advised him on investments. Rocky had met Finley when he was fighting and had given Finley's nine-year-old son his gloves from his first title defense against Jersey Joe Walcott. The furniture magnate Bernie Castro, the inventor of the Castro convertible couch, became partners with Rocky in Florida real estate.

Jimmy Cerniglia, the Tomato King, who had cohosted the postfight celebration party in Rocky's hotel after he won the title in Philadelphia and had become a close friend, helped him launch his first big venture—a nationwide farming, food processing, and investment business. Cerniglia had made a fortune after the war in tomatoes and had sold his business around the time Rocky quit boxing. He had been helping Rocky plan for his life after boxing, and came out of retirement to be his partner. Their signature product was potatoes, sold in supermarkets in a sack bearing Rocky's likeness and ring record. They had a quarter of a million dollars' worth of potatoes in the ground in Florida and New York, with plans to expand into Virginia, where they bought a warehouse. Their plan was to sell other fruits, vegetables, and salad mixes under the brand name "Rocky." Other investors included Jack Werst, the Diamond King and owner of the Vanderbilt Diamond, whom Rocky had met on his honeymoon, and another friend, Ernest Clivio, a Massachusetts dairy owner who had been a regular at his Grossinger's training camps.

In 1957, Rocky left Brockton and moved to Florida. On Christmas Eve, he, Barbara, and Mary Anne settled into a low, rambling ranch house on a canal in Fort Lauderdale, near the new offices of Rocky Marciano Enterprises. He decorated the office with more than one hundred boxing trophies. His new home had eight rooms, an indoor swimming pool, and a three-car garage; as a gift, Barbara converted part of the garage into a gym. He renovated his basement into a den and trophy room, including a glass coffee table containing one of his boxing belts, an idea he'd gotten from the New York Yankees shortstop Phil Rizzuto. Rocky gushed about coming home to blooming flowers in his backyard while it was snowing back in Brockton. "My little girl is splashing in our swimming pool and the mockingbirds are singing all night long. They tell me it's their mating season." He liked to get up early in the morning to play with Mary Anne in her bedroom, which was filled with stuffed animals he had brought her from his travels. After breakfast, he would drive her to school.

Rocky liked to fly his nieces Donna and Debbie, Conge's daughters, to Florida, or take them on trips to keep Mary Anne company. One time he took Donna to Atlantic City to a lavish party marking the release of a record by Bernie Castro's daughter. While Donna was thrilled to meet Dick Clark and Little Eva and do the twist with Chubby Checker, the entertainers were equally excited to meet Rocky.

Rocky took up golf, which he had started playing late in his career. Jackie Gleason was a frequent companion. Rocky golfed the way he had boxed, hitting the ball with power but not always certain where it would land. He spoke of opening a health club, with Gleason and Toots Shor as investors. He invested in a bowling emporium in West Hollywood, Florida; Frank Sinatra and the television actress Dagmar came to the opening. Rocky had never regarded bowling as a sport, he said. Now, he saw it as a pursuit that "keeps the stomach in good shape—mine needs it right now." No longer in constant training, Rocky became a glutton for food— spaghetti, steak, cake, ice cream, beer—instead of punishment. Charley Goldman wasn't around anymore to padlock the icebox. In his first year away from the ring, Rocky gained forty pounds, ballooning to 230 pounds. He would go on diets and work out, but his fluctuating weight was a frequent topic of conversation. He joked that Barbara said he looked like a retired brewer. But he was enjoying himself. One night he was in Boston visiting Ted Williams, and the Red Sox slugger invited him to his apartment after a game at Fenway Park. Williams pulled two cartons of ice cream out of the freezer and handed one to Rocky with a spoon, explaining that he liked to eat ice cream after a game.

Around the time he moved to Florida, Rocky received an invitation to visit Jim Norris at his home in Coral Gables. But this was no social call. Norris's International Boxing Club was struggling without Rocky. Two days before his retirement, the Justice Department had filed its long-awaited antitrust suit against the IBC for monopolizing boxing. Norris had been trying desperately to lure Rocky back to the ring and had prepared an offer that he believed the champ couldn't refuse. But Rocky had his own plans.

Rocky came to the meeting with his brother Sonny, who had recently finished his minor-league baseball season in the Florida State League. Sonny knew how much Rocky hated Norris, a rich, showy playboy whom he blamed for screwing him out of money on the second Walcott fight, among others. Sonny told Rocky that it wasn't like him to give in to Norris and wondered why they were wasting their time on a visit. "Don't worry," Rocky said. "I'll handle it."

Norris's opulent mansion reeked of luxury and privilege. He ushered Rocky and Sonny into an immense book-lined study, where he served them drinks and made small talk about Rocky's retirement and his golf games with Jackie Gleason. Then Norris got to the point. "The sport of boxing desperately needs Rocky Marciano back in the ring," he said. "How would you feel about a comeback with some serious money?"

Rocky asked what he meant by serious money. Norris said he would guarantee him $2 million—worth $18 million today. "I don't think that's enough," Rocky said in his soft voice. Norris looked stunned. Rocky said that maybe $3 million would interest him. Or $4 million. Or $5 million. Norris said that was ridiculous, that no fight would draw that kind of money. Finally, Rocky told Norris that no amount of money could entice him to return. Norris, who knew of Rocky's love of money, was dumbfounded and asked why. Was it because of Al Weill? Norris said that they could cut Weill out of the deal. Rocky said that it wasn't just Weill—he hadn't appreciated how Norris had treated him, either. "I've been your biggest fan, Rocky," Norris protested. They shook hands and bid each other a cordial farewell. Back in the car, Rocky smiled. He had enjoyed seeing Norris squirm. "I got more satisfaction out of that," he told Sonny. "The dirty mother."

◻ ◻ ◻

DESPITE HIS VOW to spend more time at home, Rocky traveled frequently for speaking engagements and as an ambassador for boxing, attending big fights and offering his commentary. He endorsed products, ranging from Breakstone yogurt to STP, a popular gasoline additive. A classified ad in the *Wall Street Journal*, headlined "Rocky Marciano," said, "Ret. World Champ, will permit use of name and endorse your product or business. Available for personal appearances, meetings, conventions, etc." Because he still had a contract with Al Weill, Rocky insisted on cash for paid appearances, so he wouldn't have to give half to his former manager. "I'm not gonna pay that bastard," he told his friend Smokey Cerrone. "I've shed enough blood for him."

Like many athletes before him, Rocky also was interested in show business. In the fall of 1956, he studied with Marilyn Monroe's acting coach in preparation for a guest stint on Red Skelton's television comedy show. He was no Laurence Olivier, but he had worked hard on his public speaking and did a creditable job. He was soon invited to appear on other television programs.

Rocky's first screen role came in *The Delicate Delinquent*, a 1957 film starring his friend Jerry Lewis. Watching Lewis grapple with a Japanese wrestler, Rocky says, "Hey, them guys is going to kill themselves out there." He also appeared in an episode of *Combat!*, the World War II television series, as a soldier greeting a Red Cross truck.

"Fighting has given me all the confidence I need," he said after filming the scene. "It has given me the confidence to face people, talk before large groups and now I have the confidence to go before a camera as well as under the ring lights. I still have lots of energy . . . that's why I think acting will be good for me. I can channel all this energy into it."

Rocky conferred with Hollywood producers, who thought there might be a place for a famous ex-champ to play an affable blue-collar character or a tough guy. One idea was a situation comedy starring Rocky as a small-town sheriff dealing with the problems of friends and children. Nothing ever came of it, but not long after, a similar program debuted starring an established actor, *The Andy Griffith Show*. Rocky did get to play a deputy sheriff in *College Confidential*, a movie starring Steve Allen. He had a small role as a lawman cracking down on a college professor for teaching sex education. When Rocky flubbed a line, he beat the director to the punch and yelled, "Cut," to the amusement of the experienced hands on the set.

On a visit to Cuba in 1957, Rocky landed a part on an episode of *Captain David Grief*, a television action series based on Jack London's short stories about a South Seas adventurer. He played the bad guy—the leader of a band of smugglers who was supposed to be punched out by the hero. But Rocky balked at being knocked out on-screen. He was shot instead. He also managed to get a bit part for his brother Sonny, who was playing baseball in Havana. Sonny laughed so hard at Rocky in his white-and-black-striped pirate shirt that he couldn't utter his line. They had to shoot the scene again. Annoyed, Rocky told his brother not to look at him.

When he was in Havana, Rocky met with his pal Jimmy Durante at the Hotel Nacional to finalize plans for a nightclub act. Durante was a stage version of Rocky, a rough-around-the-edges, raspy-voiced performer and comedian who had grown up the poor son of Italian immigrants, in his case in New York. He was a former vaudeville star who had found new life in his sixties as a television star. His most famous feature was his big nose, earning him the nickname Schnozzola. Durante had performed at Grossinger's when Rocky trained there and had met Rocky's parents in the dining room.

"I'll make an actor out of you," Durante said.

Quipped Rocky, "I'll probably make a fighter out of him."

Rocky was looking forward to their act, which was scheduled to open in March for a three-week run at the Chez Paree in Chicago, then go on the road if successful. He'd always been so busy with sports that he'd never even acted in a school play, he said. He approached it like a boxing match, saying that he needed three weeks to train and do roadwork to get in shape. Instead of Charley Goldman, Durante helped him with his footwork. "Jimmy is going to teach me some dance steps," he told reporters.

The act would open with Rocky coming onstage in white tie and tails and punching a heavy bag to music. Then Durante would join him in a duet about how they were going to transform Rocky into an actor, followed by a soft-shoe dance together with top hats and canes. Later, they would change into zoot suits and dance to rock-and-roll music. The finale had Rocky jitterbugging with an overage, three-hundred-pound chorus girl.

But Al Weill objected. He still had Rocky under contract through the end of 1958, and he vetoed the act. The old dance champion said that he was still looking out for Rocky and didn't want him "making a monkey out of himself . . . he's no actor. If I let Rocky stay in the act, I collect my end. By taking him out, there's no end to collect." But Weill was making a point as well about who was in charge.

According to Rocky, Weill had another motive. Weill told him that Durante would have to use a dance team that Weill represented as their opening act—or the show was off. Rocky was furious at being forced to renege on Durante. He threatened to fight Weill in court. But he didn't. The act had to be canceled. A Chicago gossip columnist joked that if Rocky did break into show business, his first song would be, "Al Weill, Who Needs You?"

This was not their only clash. Elia Kazan and Budd Schulberg, the director and screenwriter for *On the Waterfront*, picked up their conversation with Rocky about making a movie about his life. But then Weill inserted himself into the conversation, demanding a prominent place for himself in the movie. The talks fizzled. When the *Saturday Evening Post* bid $75,000 for his life story, Rocky told Weill that he wasn't going to let him take half his earnings anymore. Until their contract expired, Weill could have 20 percent or nothing. Weill tried to bargain, but Rocky refused. The *Post*'s editors convinced Weill that 20 percent of $75,000 was better than nothing, and he accepted. Finally, Rocky had gained the upper hand on his manager.

◻ ◻ ◻

THE RUMORS WERE persistent: Rocky was going to come back. Sometimes he fanned the flames; it was good for his ego, and the attention was good for business. And his pride was insulted when people said that he *couldn't* come back. But was he serious?

The comeback rumors had never gone away since his retirement in 1956. That fall, after he watched Floyd Patterson knock out Archie Moore to claim his vacant crown, Rocky was bombarded with questions about whether he would challenge the new champion. It was too soon, though. He was enjoying his new life. "I'm the most relaxed man in the world," he said. Privately, he vowed not to fight as long as he was under contract to Weill.

The rumors persisted. Doc Kearns, Jack Dempsey's former manager, offered Rocky $1 million to fight Patterson in Tijuana, Mexico, as part of a weeklong sports festival that would include the world's top bullfighters. Sportswriters and fans implored him not to come back. Jimmy Cerniglia, Rocky's friend and business partner, joked that if he tried, he would run Rocky over with his car. Gene Tunney, the only other heavyweight champion to retire on top, sent Rocky a telegram, urging him to stay retired. The *New York Post* sports columnist Milton Gross, who had collaborated with Rocky on his life story for the *Saturday Evening Post*, bet Rocky $1,000 that he would come back but told him, "You'd be crazy if you tried." Rocky's biggest fight was against his waistline. A friend cracked that a derrick would be needed to hoist Rocky into the ring again. "You got to be hungry to be any good," said Rocky. "And I just ain't hungry."

After years of holding his tongue, Rocky now publicly blasted Al Weill. "I was the unhappiest champion in the history of fighting," he said. Weill, who professed to being hurt and said he had always looked out for Rocky's best interests, was struggling since losing control of the heavyweight title. He had a small, unimpressive stable of fighters (including one with the dubious name Jim Crow), and he had dumped Charley Goldman, which upset Rocky. Weill was also feuding with Jim Norris, which delighted Rocky. Meanwhile, a federal judge had ruled that the International Boxing Club was a monopoly and ordered it disbanded. With the uncharismatic, light-hitting Patterson as champ, boxing needed Rocky more than Rocky needed boxing.

In 1959, though, Rocky seriously considered returning to the ring. In June, Ingemar Johansson surprised Patterson by knocking him out at Yankee Stadium, becoming the first Swede to hold the heavyweight title. Rocky was there, covering it for the Hearst newspaper chain. He had predicted that Johansson might knock out Patterson who, for all his positive attributes, "still travels middleweight style in the heavyweight class."

Rocky was friendly with Johansson, giving him an award at a black-tie benefit that Rocky cohosted for the Fort Lauderdale Symphony Orchestra and golfing with him in Florida. But when a photographer asked them to put their heads close together for a photo on the golf course, Rocky joked, "Hell, we're not that friendly."

Rocky's produce business with Cerniglia had fizzled, after a frost killed most of their potatoes, heightening speculation that Rocky might be tempted back into the ring for the money. Rocky remained outwardly upbeat, saying he didn't have to worry about money and had several other business ventures, which was true. But the fear of poverty still haunted him. He reminisced about his childhood in Brockton, playing an American Legion baseball game in Chelsea, Massachusetts, and watching the former great black heavyweight Sam Langford led onto the field. Langford had lost to Jack Johnson in Chelsea in 1906 and, because of boxing's subsequent color line, was regarded as the best boxer never to hold the title. By the time Rocky saw Langford, he was blind and the baseball fans were passing the hat to help him out. Rocky asked after the game and learned that they had collected $18. "I might have wound up blind and broke, too," he said.

In November, Rocky wrote a column in the *Boston Globe* that began, "I won 49 fights in a row and that makes a guy feel pretty cocky and there's no real reason I shouldn't come back and use Johansson to make my score an even 50." Johansson was the only potential opponent who excited him, and Rocky predicted it would be the "fight of the century," with "the biggest gate the world has ever seen." At the age of thirty-six, Rocky noted that he was one year older than Bob Fitzsimmons when he took the title from Jim Corbett, two years older than Jess Willard when he became champion, and younger than Jersey Joe Walcott when he won the title. "I'm doing fine now, but show me a guy who can't use an extra three or four hundred thousand bucks." Rocky confessed that he had started working out and eating healthier in June, after Johansson beat Patterson, and had dropped fifteen pounds. He would need eight months to get into fighting shape and wanted Charley Goldman to train him. His contract with Weill had expired, so "I'm a free agent now."

Lou Duva, the boxing manager who had apprenticed under Goldman and had become Rocky's friend, said that Rocky was serious about wanting to fight Johansson. He recalled attending a meeting with him at a New York hotel with a prospective promoter and Rocky saying, "Let me fight this guy."

Rocky went to Bernie Castro's horse farm in Ocala, Florida, and started training. But he kept getting distracted by business; among other things, he and Castro were involved in developing land in the area. He also had lingering concerns about his bad back, which had plagued him since 1949. After surviving the pain to become champion and defend his title six times, he was in Brockton one day soon after his retirement when he playfully tossed his daughter Mary Anne in the air and caught her and felt like he'd been stabbed. He spent more than a week in the hospital as a result of the back pain. Now, after about a month of training at Castro's farm, Rocky abandoned his comeback bid. He hadn't rekindled the old spark and realized it would be foolhardy to try. "Pretty stupid thinking, wasn't it?" he said sheepishly to the *New York Times*' Arthur Daley. "Right now I am the only heavyweight champion in the entire history of boxing who ever was undefeated when he retired. No one ever can beat that record. Never."

Rocky looked tanned, fit, and energetic. He had gotten his weight down to 210 pounds. "I'm in good shape, but not for fighting," he said. "I'm in good shape for living." He would never consider fighting again. "This is the way to live," he said. "Why should I fight again? Peace, it's wonderful."

◻ ◻ ◻

PEACE BECAME A relative term as a new decade dawned. As more years separated Rocky from his boxing career, he often felt restless and rootless.

On September 1, 1961, far from his monastic training camp days in the Catskills, Rocky celebrated his thirty-eighth birthday on the Strip in Las Vegas. He threw a 2:00 a.m. cocktail party at the Dunes Hotel to celebrate his new television talk show, *Main Event*, which fused boxing and celebrity. Rocky showed films of famous fights and talked to celebrity guests ranging from Milton Berle to Zsa Zsa Gabor. In one episode, he arm-wrestled with Jerry Lewis, who said, "You're still an ox. You could take care of Russia alone." In another, Rocky talked baseball with Joe DiMaggio. He visited Marilyn Monroe to recruit her for the show, but their schedules didn't work out. He came away thinking that she seemed lonely. His brother Sonny said that Rocky became friendly with Monroe and that she confided in him about her turbulent relationship with DiMaggio.

Rocky was keeping different company now, moving with a faster crowd. When he was in Los Angeles, he stayed with Vic Damone, the Italian American heartthrob singer. He went to Billy Gray's Band Box, a popular venue for racy stand-up comics, movie stars, and mobsters like Mickey Cohen, who used it as his headquarters. Rocky was roasted at the nightclub at one of its weekly stag dinners for Saints 'n Sinners, a celebrity-studded men's charity club.

The former middleweight champ Mickey Walker saw a different side to Rocky one night when they had dinner at a Los Angeles nightclub. Watching a scantily clad troupe of women dance to Strauss's Vienna

Waltz, Rocky said that they reminded him of boxers. "Watch their movements. They step away from one another like fighters moving out of punching range." Then he surprised Walker by talking about Strauss. Rocky praised the dancers' "interpretation [of] the changing moods in Strauss's music," Walker remembered Rocky saying. "He was always fighting with himself, his desire for contentment in old age conflicting with his nostalgic yearning for youth."

When Jackie Gleason wanted to lose weight for an upcoming movie role, he asked Rocky to train him for a few weeks. They met at Rocky's old friend Russ Murray's estate outside Brockton, where Rocky had trained as a young fighter. Rocky told Gleason that they would begin the next morning at seven with Jackie running and walking as far as he could, and gradually increase the distance every day. Afterward, they would go to the gym and do calisthenics. Rocky also planned to watch what Jackie ate, much as Charley Goldman had once guarded Rocky's appetite. But on the eve of his fast, Gleason wanted one more feast. So they ordered a stack of pizzas and gorged themselves, washed down with copious amounts of alcohol.

The next morning, Gleason called Rocky and said, "I can't do this." He headed back to New York to begin filming *The Hustler*. Perhaps he was scared away by Rocky's grueling training regimen. Or perhaps he reconsidered the requirements of the role: the pool shark Minnesota Fats.

Rocky fell into a nomadic lifestyle. He traveled around the country and around the world in an endless loop of speaking engagements, business meetings, charity dinners, television appearances, and boxing events. He might be in Chicago one day, Minneapolis the next, then on to Denver, with a stopover in Omaha. People paid for his plane tickets, hotels, meals, and any other expenses. Often, he would show up in rumpled khakis and a T-shirt and his hosts would outfit him with a new suit.

"Everybody wanted to be around Rocky," said his childhood pal Izzy Gold. "When you're a hero, that's how it is in this country."

Jimmy Durante teased that Rocky was "America's guest," which annoyed him.

"We'd go to breakfast in Florida," recalled Smokey Cerrone, his old friend from Providence, "and he'd say, 'Don't even think about putting your hand in your pocket. I'm on the cuff.' He was always looking for the green stuff. I never seen him take five dollars out of his own pocket."

Rocky was generous with his family, bringing his mother bags full of cash, often $5,000 or $6,000. She would count it out on the kitchen table, stacking the hundred-dollar bills in neat piles, and ask, "What do you want me to do with it, Rocky?" "Keep it, Ma, for spending money," he'd reply. He paid for his brother Peter to attend the University of Miami and flew his parents, sisters, and their families to Florida for family vacations. He was always willing to support a church or a charity, especially those that benefited children, and eager to help out destitute old fighters.

Even though he no longer needed to hide money from Al Weill, Rocky still insisted on being paid in cash, which he hoarded like a Depression housewife. He carried it around in paper bags, as much as $50,000, and stashed it in bizarre places—pipes, curtain rods, drop ceilings, toilet bowl tanks—because he didn't trust banks. His pockets jangled with keys to safety deposit boxes where he also stashed cash, but he kept no records of their whereabouts. He hid a lot of cash in a bomb shelter on Bernie Castro's horse farm in Florida.

His peripatetic lifestyle was partially due to strains in his marriage. Although he idolized Mary Anne, he and Barbara had grown apart. Barbara, dealing with her glandular condition, had put on weight, and smoked and drank, which Rocky disliked. After years of sacrifice, Rocky gave in to his sexual appetites and slept with women he met on the road. There was no shortage of women eager to go to bed with the former heavyweight champ, even as his waistline expanded and his hairline receded, prompting him to start wearing a hairpiece. His brother Sonny recalled Rocky going into Toots Shor's and seeing women who were with Frank Sinatra or Dean Martin flock to him.

Richie Paterniti, who became a close friend and frequent companion, described his efforts to feed Rocky's sexual appetite. "Rocky was the heavyweight champion of girls," said Paterniti. "Forget about the fights. He was crazy about the girls; that's all he wanted to do. Rocky constantly had orgies and parties, night and day." Paterniti said that he carried a suitcase containing vibrators, creams, and oils for Rocky's pleasure. "We went to Pennsylvania and we were with these mob guys and they were bringing us girls and Rocky said, 'Don't let 'em know we got all that stuff. They'll think that we're weird or somethin'.'"

Driven by his lusts, for women, money, and attention, Rocky was searching for his place in a changing world. He was a man of contradictions. A

Massachusetts priest, Bernie Sullivan, recalled Rocky attending charity functions at his church and taking him on trips. On a visit to Chicago, the priest found himself splashing with Rocky in the pool at Hugh Hefner's Playboy Mansion, surrounded by beautiful young women.

"I believe he truly was restless because he still had fights left in him," said Sonny. "I don't honestly know what it was that drove him. He certainly showed that he was very restless, and to this day I have my doubts as to exactly what he was looking and searching for."

Rocky had a network of people he could count on to pick him up at the airport, arrange for his hotel, and take care of his needs. He was a terrible driver and preferred to have others chauffeur him around. When Mary Anne was thirteen, Rocky gave her a gold Firebird 400 that he had received from a local car dealer for doing a commercial—then asked his daughter to pick him up at the airport. Another time, Mary Anne was driving alone in Fort Lauderdale when she was pulled over by a motorcycle cop. When he discovered that she not only didn't have a license but was only thirteen, he sped away to fetch her father. The policeman returned with Rocky, shirtless and wearing Bermuda shorts, on the back of the motorcycle, his arms around the officer's waist. The cop asked Rocky for his autograph, then sped off. "The world's worst driver then drove me home," recalled Mary Anne. "My dad did not even have a license."

Another time, Rocky's fifteen-year-old nephew and godson Vincent Pereira, the son of Rocky's sister Alice, was home in Brockton when Uncle Rocky called from Boston's Logan Airport, saying he needed a ride. When Vincent said that his parents weren't home, Rocky asked if their car was in the driveway and if Vincent knew where the keys were. His nephew protested that he only had a learner's permit and wasn't allowed to drive on the highway. "Get the keys," Rocky commanded. Obeying, the teenager drove white-knuckled through Boston traffic to fetch Rocky. When he met his uncle at the airport, Rocky said he had an appointment in the city and told his nephew to drive the wrong way on a busy section of Commonwealth Avenue that was one-way. Then Rocky directed his nephew to park on the sidewalk in front of the building. As Rocky got out, a Boston police officer on a horse rode up, screaming at them.

"Then he sees my uncle and says, 'Hey Rocky, how ya doin'?' " recalled

Vincent. "Rocky tells him he has an appointment inside and the cop says, 'No problem, champ' and he directs traffic around the car for a half hour while Rocky's inside." When Rocky returned and saw his stressed-out nephew, he asked what was wrong. Vincent explained that he wasn't even supposed to be here, that angry motorists had been giving him the finger, and then pointed at the one-way sign they had parked in front of.

"Let that be a lesson to you," Rocky told him. "Signs are for people with no direction."

Rocky traveled with a messy pile of papers bound with a rubber band—scraps of paper with the names of people who owed him money, coded references to where he had stashed money, people he needed to see, a woman's phone number, sayings that he would use in speeches and philosophical musings. His sportswriter friend Murray Olderman remembered him writing down the phone number of a barmaid named Sally under "Saul."

"His whole life was in his pocket," said Vincent. "Those were the things that were important to him. It ran the gamut from prostitutes to playboys to gangsters. They all wanted to be near him, to touch him."

◻ ◻ ◻

FRANK SACCONE BECAME an unlikely companion on Rocky's travels. Saccone was a young accountant in Abington, Massachusetts, the town next to Brockton. At 10:00 p.m. on Christmas Eve 1959, he was home with his family when he received an unexpected telephone call.

"The phone rang, and we were celebrating, and I answered and I asked who it was and he said, 'Rocky.' And I said, 'Rocky who?' He says, 'Rocky Marciano,'" recalled Saccone. "And, my God, it suddenly dawned on me that it was Rocky Marciano."

Rocky told Saccone that he was interested in buying a nearby restaurant. Saccone was the owner's accountant, and Rocky asked if he could go over the numbers right away. Saccone rushed over to Lena and Pierino's house, which was crowded with family celebrating the holiday, and spoke with Rocky in the upstairs hallway. Rocky didn't buy the restaurant, but that night marked the beginning of a close business association and friendship. Over the next decade, Saccone traveled the world with Rocky. No matter where they went, Rocky was "the king of the world."

"He had enough friends in the world where, if he needed something, he could get it," recalled Saccone. "He was a powerful man in his day. People from all over the world would just do anything to be with Rocky."

As a result, Rocky never worried about the consequences of his poor business decisions. He didn't keep any records, didn't like written contracts, and avoided checks. Saccone would find crumpled-up checks that Rocky had never cashed—$25,000, $50,000, $100,000—but to Rocky they were just scraps of paper.

Conversely, Rocky was obsessed with cash. Once, after a speech in Montreal, his host handed him a check for $5,000. Rocky looked at the check and asked the man if he could cash it for him. But it was Sunday night; the banks were closed. Rocky insisted. "Look, you've got to do this. I'm leaving tonight and I'll take half. I'll take $2,500 and I'll give you the check." The host was puzzled but returned an hour later with $2,500 in cash. Now, Saccone protested. "Rock, this is crazy. You've got a perfectly good cashier's check for $5,000 and you're accepting $2,500." Saccone told Rocky he would personally guarantee the $5,000 and cash the check the next morning. No, Rocky said, he wanted the cash now.

Another time, Rocky showed up at a banquet where he was to speak and found a punching bag hanging in a large banquet room that was full of people. "What's this for?" he demanded. One of his hosts said that they thought it would be great if he would hit the bag. Annoyed, Rocky said he wasn't a trained monkey and that, sure, he'd hit the bag, but only if they gave him a thousand bucks for each punch. In cash. When the hosts asked where they could come up with the money, Rocky looked over the crowd and told them to collect it. They did, and he hit the bag a few times in addition to his speech.

When Rocky was in Cuba with Sonny, he asked his brother to bring a bag full of cash back to Florida with him. Before he did, Sonny ran short of cash and took a few hundred dollars from the bag. When he delivered the bag to Rocky, his brother counted the money and confronted him about the missing amount. Rocky didn't mind that Sonny had taken the money but told his brother to tell him next time. "I know how much money I have at all times," he told Sonny. "Nobody can fool me when it comes to money."

Lou Duva was having lunch with Rocky in New York one day when Rocky asked him to hold a brown paper bag for him. Duva left the bag in the coatroom and forgot about it until they were in a cab later and Rocky asked for it. Rocky was upset, and they hurried back to the restaurant and retrieved the bag. Inside was $50,000 in cash.

"I loved Rocky, but he was a terrible businessman," said Saccone. "I told him right to his face, 'Rocky, you're terrible when it comes to business. . . . You're a hell of a guy, but you're going to lose your shirt if you don't pay attention.'"

But for Rocky, a handshake was good enough. "And if they reneged on this handshake," said Saccone, "he had his own way of taking care of it."

Saccone witnessed Rocky's way one day in Brockton. They were walking down the street when Rocky suddenly said he had some business to attend to and popped into a poolroom run by a local character named Brockton Eddie. He had borrowed $5,000 from Rocky but hadn't made a payment in months and was ducking him. Standing on the sidewalk, Saccone heard a commotion and looked up to see Brockton Eddie hanging out a third-floor window, Rocky's hands around his throat.

"I've waited long enough," shouted Rocky. "No more stalling. I want my money. Now . . . Now!"

Rocky emerged from the building soon after, counting several twenty-dollar bills. He assigned Saccone to make future monthly collections from Brockton Eddie.

In the early 1960s, when Smokey Cerrone, Rocky's friend from Providence, was living in Florida, he received an urgent call from Rocky to meet at a favorite breakfast place. When they met, Cerrone recalls, Rocky said to him, "You gotta do me a favor, Smokey. You gotta punch the shit out of this guy." The guy in question had borrowed $7,000 from Rocky to start a scaffolding business, but the company had folded and Rocky hadn't been repaid. Cerrone demurred, but the two of them drove to the man's office in Hollywood. They walked in and announced themselves to the secretary. When she called back to tell him who was there, the man jumped out his second-floor window, shimmied down a drainpipe, and sped away.

"Rocky, let's get out of here before the cops come," said Cerrone.

"That SOB," said Rocky. "I'd like to kill him."

Rocky may have recruited Cerrone because he was being sued for assault in another dispute. In 1960, Gene Schoor, the author of popular children's biographies of athletes, got into an argument with Rocky in a Manhattan steakhouse over payment for a magazine article Schoor was ghost-writing for him. Schoor charged that Rocky punched him in the head and permanently damaged his hearing. "I passed out," he said in his complaint. "Bells have been ringing in my head ever since and I had a fuzzy feeling for weeks." Rocky acknowledged having a discussion with Schoor but denied hitting him, or even making a fist. A judge disagreed and awarded Schoor $5,000. "The stronger the man, the more important the man, the more restraint he must exercise," the judge said.

More often, though, Rocky practiced the restraint of a former champ accustomed to barroom challengers seeking to prove their manhood. Once, approached by a large man in a bar who said he thought he could take him, Rocky smiled calmly and told the man that he had just been thinking the same thing—that of all the people in the bar, he was the last guy Rocky would want to tangle with. Satisfied, the man walked away. Barbara said that some drunk who wanted to brag about fighting the world champion would often take a swing at Rocky when the couple went out. Rocky would "just move away," she said. "But I wanted to smash them."

The actor Burt Reynolds became friendly with Rocky, and the two used to drink together at a bar in Hollywood, Florida. "Every time I went with Rocky, some guy would come over and challenge him," said Reynolds. One night, he was at the bar with Rocky, eyeing the champ's short arms and thinking that he could throw a little hook and knock him down. "Then Rocky looked at me and he said in that high-pitched voice, 'Don't even think about it.' I said, 'How'd you know what I was thinking?' He said, 'I always know. Don't even think about it.'"

Rocky was a one-man bank and collection agency, lending money to people all over the country, charging them interest, and collecting on his travels. "Whenever he went to Baltimore or Cleveland or San Francisco, he'd meet up with some of these people that owed him money and he always got it in cash," said Saccone. "Ten thousand, twenty thousand, he'd always get cash. And he'd put it in paper bags or put them in a suitcase. . . . And he'd come to the airport and he'd throw the bag at you, [and say,] 'Hold this for me.'" He loved coming home to Brockton, handing his mother a bag of money and then sitting in the kitchen while she cooked him a hearty Italian meal.

His relatives would stumble across cash that he had stashed at his parents' house in Brockton. One day, his sister Conge and her husband were cleaning Lena and Pierino's house when they found a suitcase stuffed with cash that Rocky had left behind. Another time, his sister Alice, who lived in the house, found a bag holding $25,000 in the back of her closet. When she told Rocky, he replied, "Oh, that's where that is."

"Money meant everything and nothing to him," recalled Rocky's nephew Vincent Pereira. "I said to him once, 'What do you do with all your money?' He said, 'I don't think you understand—money is just a way of keeping score.'"

When he was in his early teens, Vincent said, his uncle taught him a lesson about money. Vincent had lost a black onyx ring his parents had given him and didn't want them to know. So he asked his uncle Rocky for the money to buy a new one. Rocky handed the boy a hundred-dollar bill, then said, "You've gotta pay me back—with interest." Vincent was stunned and asked his uncle if he was joking. He wasn't. "I'll see you in a month, and I want $110 back," Rocky said. Over the next month, Vincent shoveled snow and earned the money. When his uncle returned and Vincent repaid him, Rocky reached into his pocket and handed his nephew five hundred-dollar bills, a gift for doing the right thing. "You've learned a lesson," said Rocky. "Nothing is free."

Rocky accumulated large sums of cash in suitcases and took them to Bernie Castro's bomb shelter in Florida. The shelter, which Vincent visited once with Lena, was like a huge underground vault, but well-appointed with rugs on the floor and paintings on the walls. Vincent and Rocky's daughter, Mary Anne, recalled Rocky mentioning storing money there. According to Saccone, Castro kept his cash there and gave Rocky a room in the vault. Izzy Gold recalled traveling to the bomb shelter and Rocky telling him that a suitcase belonging to Castro was filled with hundred-dollar bills. "They put the money in the vault . . . and Rocky took his own bags in there, too. I said to Rock, 'What's the story?' He said, 'I think it's money he just wants to bury.' So I never said nothing. It was none of my business."

One of Saccone's jobs was to pay Rocky's bills, an exercise in frustration. If Rocky got an electric bill for $20, he'd ask Saccone if he could talk them down to ten. "I said, 'Rock, it's an electric bill, pay it' . . . no, no, no. Let's see if we can get it down." He would also give Saccone his mother's bills, then fly into a rage when he discovered that the accountant had paid them in full instead of bargaining them down. His gardener in Florida took him to court over an unpaid bill of $706; the judge ordered Rocky to pay up or face thirty days in jail. Saying it was an oversight, Rocky paid.

Saccone never had a salary arrangement with Rocky and only presented him with a bill once in ten years—"and he almost threw me out the window." Saccone tore up the bill and never regretted it. "Rocky had his own way of taking care of people that worked for him, helped him. For instance, a CPA, his attorneys, he never paid them, but he made sure that they were taken care of in his own way. He would open the doors for many, many people that assisted him, and they would be paid off tenfold through that door opening." Another friend referred to Rocky as "the golden key."

As tight as he was with his cash, Rocky was too trusting when it came to bigger deals. He lost money on several investments, including swampland in Florida and a nightclub in Maryland. "He'd get conned in deals he knew nothing about," said Gold.

Rocky's pathological hatred of the phone company led him to one of his worst business partners. All of Rocky's mistrust seemed to be wrapped up in the telephone system. He felt that the phone company cheated people, and he used slugs, wires, and other tricks to cheat pay phones. One time, Saccone watched in horror as Rocky went berserk after he lost a dime in a pay phone at New York's LaGuardia Airport. He screamed at the operator, then ripped the receiver out of the phone and threw it on the floor. Then he walked along the bank of pay phones on the wall, pressing the coin-return buttons, poking his finger in the slot, and tearing those receivers out, too.

One day, Rocky and Saccone were riding in an elevator to the fortieth floor of a New York skyscraper when they met George DiMatteo, a slick, handsome businessman. DiMatteo was seeking financing for a company that had invented a device for which the American Telephone & Telegraph Company was paying him royalties. Rocky was dazzled by DiMatteo's talk of can't-miss deals and liked the idea of an investment that would make the telephone company pay *him* money. By the time they were going back down in the elevator, Rocky had given DiMatteo a check for $25,000, despite Saccone's protests to let him check him out first. "Go to it, George," said Rocky. "I hate the telephone company. If you can beat them, I'll back you up 100 percent."

DiMatteo turned out to be a con man, taking Rocky for several hundred thousand dollars on various ill-fated ventures, according to Saccone. Rocky lost more than $100,000 on one DiMatteo project alone, the development of the Belgian Village at the 1964 New York World's Fair. "He took Rocky for a lot of money," said Saccone. "And in spite of all that, Rocky continued to be friendly. He just didn't care about the money. It was always a check, never cash."

◻ ◻ ◻

THE UNDERWORLD COMMISSIONER of boxing was in trouble. In the early 1960s, the law knocked Frankie Carbo out for good.

Carbo's long slide had begun in the years following Rocky's retirement, as criminal and congressional investigators encircled the Octopus. In 1957, a federal judge in New York ruled for the Justice Department and declared that the International Boxing Club had violated the Sherman Antitrust Act. The judge found that the IBC had used its power to promote more than 90 percent of all championship fights from its creation through the mid-1950s, during Rocky's reign. The judge ordered the IBC to disband and Jim Norris and Arthur Wirtz to sell their ownership stake in Madison Square Garden. In January 1959, the U.S. Supreme Court affirmed the decision. Desperate to salvage his credibility and save the Octopus, Norris offered the top job at the IBC to FBI director J. Edgar Hoover, but he wasn't interested. Norris hung on for a few years, then quit in disgust.

Meanwhile, the Manhattan district attorney charged Carbo with the unlicensed management of fighters. He pleaded guilty. Carbo's hair had turned almost all white when he appeared for sentencing on November 30, 1959. He was still dapper but was battling kidney disease and diabetes.

"The name of Frankie Carbo today symbolizes the degeneration of professional boxing into a racket," said the prosecutor. "This man is beyond redemption." The judge told Carbo, "You had a long and merry dance in pursuit of power in the boxing game, but the time has now come when the piper must be paid." Given Carbo's poor health, the judge sentenced him to two years at the Riker's Island penitentiary.

In 1960, Carbo's name was prominent in U.S. Senate hearings into boxing led by Senator Estes Kefauver of Tennessee. The first witness,

Jake LaMotta, admitted that he had taken a dive in 1947. Carbo had made a $35,000 "killing" by placing bets on the fight. The IBC's Truman Gibson testified that Carbo had controlled every important manager, including Al Weill. Norris admitted that Carbo had used his influence to force Weill to match Rocky against Kid Matthews in 1952 and to persuade Jersey Joe Walcott's reluctant manager, Felix Bocchicchio, to accept the return match with Rocky in return for the $250,000 guarantee that so angered Rocky.

Carbo was hauled before the committee and asked whether he and the Philadelphia numbers king Blinky Palermo secretly controlled Sonny Liston, a rising young heavyweight contender. Liston had denied it, but he was in fact being supported by Palermo, the man Rocky suspected of plotting to blind him during his title fight in Philadelphia against Jersey Joe Walcott. Carbo didn't answer, instead invoking his Fifth Amendment right against self-incrimination.

A few months later, Carbo and Palermo went on trial in Los Angeles on charges of extortion and threat of violence. The jury convicted the two men of threatening a West Coast boxing manager who refused to cede control of one of his fighters, the welterweight champ Don Jordan. According to police wiretaps, Carbo snarled, "I have had that title twenty-five years and no punks like you are going to take it away from me.... You are going to be dead." The tapes also captured a Carbo associate describing how he had beaten another defiant manager, Ray Arcel, with a lead pipe in Boston years earlier.

Palermo was sentenced to fifteen years in prison and was paroled in 1971. Carbo was sentenced to twenty-five years in prison, shipped to Alcatraz, and died behind bars in 1976, at the age of seventy-two.

Shortly after Carbo's sentencing, on May 31, 1961, Rocky was the leadoff witness before another round of Senate hearings in Washington. Kefauver kicked off the hearing by asking if Rocky was considering a comeback to round his record up to 50-0. Rocky said no.

Rocky urged Congress to pass a law empowering the federal government to regulate boxing. A boxing czar backed by a team of investigators—a "little FBI"—could clean up boxing, he said, "like a policeman on a corner with a big stick." Rocky testified that the underworld had never tried to cut in on him because he had been very lucky to have a good manager in Al Weill to protect him. Asked what he thought of Carbo's recent conviction, Rocky said that he had learned an awful lot recently about things that boxers had been kept in the dark about.

Rocky didn't reveal that for many years he had been friendly with Carbo. Lou Duva, the boxing trainer and Rocky's friend, recalls having dinner with Rocky in New York one night when Rocky excused himself to go see Carbo about a fighter who was fighting that night. Another time, Rocky brought Carbo home to Brockton for one of Lena's big Sunday dinners. "Please, Ma," Rocky implored his mother beforehand. "Don't ask him a lot of questions about what he does." Lena couldn't resist quizzing Carbo, who was very gracious. The nieces and nephews whispered in the kitchen about the bulge under Carbo's jacket, which he didn't remove for dinner. Later, Rocky's sister Conge pulled him aside and asked him what he was doing bringing Carbo to their home. "When Frank Carbo wants to meet your family for Sunday dinner," Rocky replied, "you don't say no."

◻ ◻ ◻

WHILE ROCKY PUBLICLY lamented the influence of the Mafia in boxing and the negative image it gave honest, hardworking Italian Americans, he also had a fascination with wiseguys, hung out with them, and even did business with some.

They shared a mutual admiration. The wiseguys adored him and protected his all-American-boy image. One Buffalo mobster praised him as "a countryman." His brother Peter said that the mobsters were proud of him—he was their "knight in shining armor, and they treated him like an absolute flower." And Rocky respected them "for what they did for their people. He felt that they kind of went against the odds, very much like Rocky did." Growing up, his brother Sonny said, their father always told them: "Hold your head up high and do the right thing and don't be like the mob. We are a decent, respectful family." Rocky was careful to keep his image clean and avoided being seen in public with Mafia figures. Nevertheless, said Sonny, he had an "infatuation" with the mob and the power it wielded.

Wherever he went, Frank Saccone said, Rocky received the red-carpet treatment from the mob. When he was in New York, the wiseguys would treat him to lunch or dinner, get him a chauffeur, arrange for him to stay at the Waldorf-Astoria. Saccone said they would sit around a huge table with fifteen, twenty underworld characters, but he didn't realize it. He was a naive accountant from Brockton. He thought they were just friends of Rocky's, until he told them who they were. They'd tell Rocky they had a beautiful tailor, and take him there and buy him six suits, three dozen shirts. "He loved it and *they* loved it," said Saccone. Rocky was also drawn to the danger and excitement of their lives, a vicarious substitute for the danger he had faced in the ring.

Rocky flirted with danger when he considered investing in a casino in Havana. His friend Steve Melchiore, the Philadelphia policeman who had served as his bodyguard for the first Walcott fight, was also close to Philadelphia mob boss Angelo Bruno, who had casino interests in Cuba. According to FBI records, Melchiore checked with Bruno, who advised that Rocky shouldn't invest.

Cuba was tense, with the guerrilla leader Fidel Castro's strength growing. The Boston promoter Sam Silverman traveled to Havana in October 1958 with Rocky and Kid Gavilan to discuss the two fighters working for a casino run by close associates of Cuban dictator Fulgencio Batista. Silverman said that they left Cuba enthusiastic about the deal. But before they could return later that fall to finalize it, guerrillas had shot up the casino. A few months later, on New Year's Day 1959, Castro overthrew Batista, putting the Mafia's tropical paradise out of business.

Closer to home, Rocky was friendly with the head of the New England mob. In December 1962, a hidden FBI listening device in the Providence headquarters of Raymond Patriarca caught the Mafia boss trying to catch a thief—in order to help Rocky. A mobster reported to Patriarca that Rocky had some fur pieces that had been stolen from a car and wanted to come see "his friend Raymond" for help in retrieving them. The gangster advised Rocky not to come to Patriarca's office personally but promised to ask the mob boss himself. Patriarca tried to determine who the thief was; he questioned two criminals about it but was apparently unsuccessful.

In May 1963, Rocky went to Buffalo to do public relations for Leisureland USA, a new family recreation center outside the city. FBI agents conducting surveillance of Buffalo mobsters saw Rocky having lunch with a man who worked for the local mob boss Steve Magaddino, a member of the Mafia's national ruling commission. Rocky was out with the man until 4:00 a.m. The mobster tried to arrange for Rocky to meet with the leaders of a mobbed-up union about a vending-machine contract for Leisureland. The reason for the meeting: Leisureland's owners "didn't want to step on anyone's toes." Later, when Buffalo's mob leaders discussed the deal among themselves, "Magaddino commented that Marciano was a countryman of his and is a smart man. He commented that naturally the development would be a profitable place," according to a confidential FBI memo. "He then added that they would not bother anybody and nobody was going to bother them."

Two FBI agents interviewed Rocky in Brockton in July. He said that a Rhode Island lawyer had contacted him about lending his name to Leisureland, and that Rocky would serve as its "physical director" and have the option to buy stock in the company. Rocky said they were looking for vending machines but that the lawyer handled most of the negotiations. The development did not succeed and later burned to the ground.

Rocky's involvement in a Pennsylvania insurance company illustrates how his worlds converged. In December 1964, the FBI reported, Rocky attended the Pennsylvania Society dinner at the Waldorf-Astoria in New York. He came with Peter Rugani, his partner in the Coal Operators Casualty Company, a workers-compensation firm near Pittsburgh. The two men were very friendly with Russell Bufalino, the Scranton/Wilkes-Barre boss, and Billy Medico, one of his top lieutenants. Rocky and Rugani were pushing their insurance in the Wilkes-Barre and Hazleton areas, and Medico introduced Rocky to many businessmen at the dinner. In January, Rocky was the guest speaker at a YMCA dinner in Hazleton. Bufalino boasted that he was friends with Rocky and had gotten him to come to both dinners.

That June, Rocky visited Saint Paul, Minnesota, with Rugani as they sought to buy an insolvent Saint Paul insurer that was under federal and state investigation. "Insurance is all high class," Rocky told a local reporter, as he did push-ups in his hotel room in Bermuda shorts. But the deal fell through, and Rugani was later indicted for federal insurance fraud.

In September 1965, an FBI informant reported that Rocky had met at the Friars Club of Beverly Hills with Las Vegas promoter Maurice Friedman and notorious mobster Johnny Roselli, a major player in Hollywood and Vegas. (Roselli had been involved in the Mafia's purported plot to assassinate Castro, and shared a mistress, Judith Exner, with President

John F. Kennedy.) Friedman and Roselli were interested in taking control of the New Frontier, one of Las Vegas's first casinos, and building a new high-rise hotel and golf course. They discussed giving Rocky one point in the casino, worth $40,000 (about $310,000 in today's dollars), to use his name to publicize the hotel. The hotel was beset with licensing problems, however, as the FBI aggressively investigated the Mafia for hidden ownership. Eventually, the reclusive billionaire Howard Hughes bought it.

The closest Rocky came to getting in trouble concerned his involvement with Peter DiGravio, a Cleveland loan shark. Rocky also dabbled in managing fighters, and in his travels he took on a young heavyweight from Cleveland named Tony Hughes. Through Hughes, he met DiGravio, a stylish, urbane loan shark who drove a Cadillac and was known as the mayor of Cleveland's Little Italy. DiGravio ran what he called a legitimate loan business, but the Cleveland police suspected him of illegal transactions as well, and he operated on the fringe of local organized crime. He had an arrest record dating back to 1944 and had operated a notorious after-hours club with the head of the Cleveland mob.

DiGravio liked to run and spar to stay in shape, and Rocky took a liking to him. According to Saccone, DiGravio told Rocky, "If you've got some cash and want to make some money on it, I've got the outlet. Guaranteed. No bad debts in my place." Rocky invested more than $100,000 in the business, Saccone said. Rocky justified it by saying that he was just lending him money; he wasn't involved in "the dirty end of the business."

Rocky and DiGravio became good friends. Rocky stayed with him when he was in Cleveland, and the two also spent time together in New York. Rocky even invited him to join Frank Sinatra's famed Rat Pack in Las Vegas. Rocky remained friendly with Sinatra, who was a big fan; one night, Saccone recalled, they stayed up most of the night in Sinatra's suite at the Sands Hotel, reminiscing about Rocky's old fights.

Another time, when he was in college in New York, Rocky's nephew Vincent Pereira received a spur-of-the-moment invitation from his uncle to fly to Las Vegas and see Sinatra in concert. They had front-row seats, and before the show Sinatra knelt on the edge of the stage in front of them and invited Rocky to his hotel suite later. After the show, Rocky and Vincent arrived at Sinatra's suite to find that the singer had ordered steaks for them and their companions but not for the man who served as Rocky's driver. When Rocky complained, Sinatra pulled out a twenty-dollar bill and said, "Tell your gopher to go buy a hamburger." Angrily, Rocky grabbed Sinatra's steak and gave it to his driver, saying, "Fuck you, Frank—*you* go out for a hamburger." Sinatra just shrugged and called room service for another steak, and the evening continued pleasantly. "That's the first time," said Vincent, "I realized that my uncle was bigger than life."

In the fall of 1967, an official in President Lyndon Johnson's White House asked the FBI if it had ever investigated Rocky. It was not clear why, but the request came from one of Johnson's closest aides, Mildred Stegall, who was the White House's liaison to the FBI. (A few years earlier, Johnson's press secretary had laughed off reports that Johnson was going to appoint Rocky as director of the president's physical fitness program, which never happened.) The FBI responded that it had not investigated Rocky but passed along information it had received in 1965 and 1966 that he was a "close associate" of Pete DiGravio, "a Cleveland hoodlum and longtime shylock."

On May 29, 1968, Congress passed a law limiting the interest rates that loan companies could charge. DiGravio told the *Cleveland Press* that the new law would kill his business; he denied that he was tied to the Mafia. "We need the Mafia like we need cancer," he said. "We bend over backwards to avoid those people." The Cleveland police were watching, and DiGravio confided to a friend that the Mafia was trying to muscle in on his business. Meanwhile, the Internal Revenue Service was investigating his loan business. According to Saccone, the IRS had asked DiGravio about an unexplained influx of cash into his business, and DiGravio said that Rocky had lent it to him. There was nothing on paper, of course, so agents in the IRS's Cleveland office invited Rocky in to explain. Saccone said that Rocky's loose business practices and love of cash had attracted questions from the IRS before, but the accountant had always been able to deflect them by having Rocky schmooze with local agents in Massachusetts about his boxing career. But Cleveland was more worrisome.

On June 21, 1968, as Rocky and Saccone were headed to Cleveland to meet with the IRS, DiGravio golfed at the suburban Orchard Hills Country Club, where he went several times a week. At the sixteenth hole, as DiGravio was about to tee off, his companions heard a loud crack. DiGravio fell, screaming, "I'm shot!" Three more shots rang out; one pierced his skull, killing him.

The IRS dropped its investigation. Rocky hurried out of town, successfully avoiding any negative publicity. The money he had lent DiGravio was gone, one more bad investment.

13

The Fiftieth Fight

IN THE WINTER OF 1964, ROCKY WAS RIDING IN A CAR IN MIAMI WITH Joe Louis and his friend Lou Duva, the boxing manager and trainer. The men were in town to see the heavyweight champion Sonny Liston defend his title against a brash young challenger named Cassius Clay.

Duva was driving and the car radio was on. The announcer mentioned that Clay was getting $315,000 while Liston's share was more than $1 million. Rocky and Joe looked at each other in amazement, then ordered Duva to stop the car.

"They jumped out of the car, Rocky first, and started jogging," recalled Duva. "They joked that they were going back into training and wanted to do some roadwork."

The charismatic Clay represented the exciting new face of boxing, but the old guard was wary of him. He was a heavy underdog to Liston, a glowering throwback and Mafia-controlled fighter who had learned to box while serving time in the Missouri State Penitentiary for armed robbery. The now-imprisoned Frankie Carbo and Blinky Palermo had helped launch his career. Liston was menacing, scowling, brooding, a thickly muscled puncher with bludgeoning force. Arthur Daley in the *New York Times* called him "the last man anyone would want to meet in a dark alley." The black poet LeRoi Jones (later Amiri Baraka) said that Liston was "the big black Negro in every white man's hallway." Other heavyweights avoided him. President John F. Kennedy had tried to dissuade Floyd Patterson from fighting Liston, for the same reasons civil rights leaders had—they feared the "wrong" type of black man winning the title. But the gentlemanly Patterson thought it only fair to give Liston a shot, and Liston demolished him in the first round to take the title in September 1962. Ten months later, Liston knocked him out again in the first. Ali went into the ring against Liston as a 7-1 underdog.

Before the fight, Rocky stopped by the Miami gym where Liston was training. The two started talking.

"Hey, Rocky, what do you think you would've done with me?" asked Liston. "I know what I would have done with you. You wouldn't have hit me at all, and if I hit you, I'd knock you out."

The affable Rocky usually walked away from confrontations outside the ring; asked if he could beat one of the top modern fighters, he'd deflect it with a joke: "If I said I could beat him, I'd be bragging. If I said I couldn't, I'd be lying." Now, in the face of Liston's belligerent needling, Rocky got mad.

"They started to get into it," said Duva. "They were yelling at each other. Rocky wanted to fight him right there in the gym. All the mob guys were there, and they took Liston right out of the gym."

Still, like most of the sportswriters and oddsmakers, Rocky picked Liston to win. Instead, sitting ringside at the Miami Beach Convention Center on February 25, he bore witness to the birth of an outrageous new champion.

"Unbelievable! Utterly unbelievable!" were the first words of Rocky's account for the *Brockton Enterprise*. "Cassius yelled. He screamed. He hurled insult after insult at Sonny. It not only was wild. It was downright weird."

When Liston failed to answer the bell for the seventh round, the twenty-two-year-old Clay thrust his arms up triumphantly and screamed, "I'm king of the world! I'm king of the world!" As confusion reigned, Rocky climbed onto the apron of the ring and touched his left shoulder, signaling to the crowd that Liston had quit because he had injured the shoulder.

Rocky and the rest of the world had never seen anything like Clay. He had won an Olympic gold medal in Rome in 1960, and this was just his twentieth professional fight. He combined grace and power, speed and strength—he floated like a butterfly and stung like a bee. And there was his mouth. The words poured out in torrents: boastful, loud, poetic, unapologetic. Like many of the aging white sportswriters from the 1940s and 1950s, Arthur Daley had trouble accepting this "loudmouth braggart." He wrote that Clay "is light-hearted and breezy and has just enough twinkle in his eyes to take most of the obnoxiousness from the wild words he utters. When they are imprisoned in print, however, the twinkle is never captured and Cassius just becomes nauseous."

Before the fight, Clay had taunted Liston as "the Bear" and called him out at his house in the middle of the night. At the weigh-in on the day of the fight, Clay started shouting, "I am the greatest!" and became so hysterical that his friend Sugar Ray Robinson backed him against the wall and tried to calm him down. "I am a great *performer*," Clay shouted in Robinson's face. Clay carried a cane given him by Malcolm X, and was a Black Muslim, something that much of America didn't understand.

The day after the fight, Clay announced that he was dropping his "slave name" in favor of a new name—Muhammad Ali. Before long, Rocky was denying reports that he would come out of retirement, in his early forties, to fight Ali; one rich Texan supposedly offered Rocky $4 million to silence the loudmouthed young champ.

If Ali sometimes went too far, as when he criticized Joe Louis as the white man's champion, Rocky saw something else in him. He was exciting, and he had breathed new life into a sport that was struggling. Five years later, in 1969, thanks to the controversy swirling around Ali, Rocky finally got his fiftieth fight. At the age of forty-five, he signed a contract to fight Ali, who was twenty-seven.

Except it wasn't real. It was a gimmick. The two champions would spar in front of television cameras, then their vital statistics and tendencies would be fed into a super computer that would predict how the fight would unfold and who would win. The film would be edited accordingly, and shown in movie theaters across the country and overseas, the outcome a closely guarded secret. Not even Rocky or Ali would know.

Ali desperately needed the money because he had been stripped of his title for refusing to be inducted into the U.S. Army and fight in Vietnam. During his five-year legal battle to win conscientious objector status as a member of the Nation of Islam, Ali was barred from fighting and had to live off of speaking fees and odd engagements, like his starring role in a Broadway musical that lasted just five days.

For Rocky, it was another payday. While Ali opted for a smaller initial payment and a percentage of the box office, Rocky characteristically wanted his money up front. But this was about more than the money. Rocky was a proud man, determined not to embarrass himself in his sparring sessions with Ali. He had been embarrassed when he saw himself on *The Red Skelton Hour*. "Look at me, the fat man!" he said. "That's not Rocky Marciano, the champ. I'm ashamed of the way I look." Training for the Ali fight, even though it wasn't real, gave him a new sense of purpose. He cut back on his rich diet and started running and working out at the gym. He dropped fifty-three pounds.

The Ali fight also came at a time in his life when Rocky was feeling increasingly restless and adrift. The feelings were more acute whenever he came home to Brockton, where he was the prodigal son, his visits a cause for celebration. Often he would show up to Sunday dinner with a guest— Frankie Carbo, Jerry Lewis, an Italian opera singer, or some other famous, interesting person. His nephew Robert Langway, Conge's son, remembers his uncle as fun and playful. He and the other children would pepper Rocky with questions about their heroes he knew, like Ted Williams. Sometimes, Bob and his friends would sneak into his mother's closet and pull out the plastic bag containing the glove that Rocky had used to knock out Jersey Joe Walcott, still crusty with dried blood, take it out, and put it on. The kids thought that Uncle Rocky was the strongest man in the world. They asked if he could lift up their house. Rocky went outside to a corner of the house, crouched down, placed his hands on the foundation, and pretended to lift it a tiny bit.

Homecomings could be bittersweet. Lena worried about Rocky and pleaded with him not to travel so much; he should be home with his wife and daughter. "I like to know that you're home at night. I never know where you are. If the phone rings, I never know . . ."

"Oh, Ma," Rocky answered. "Do you think if I was home sleeping every night that you and Conge and Bob [her husband] and the kids would go to Florida? You want me to go home at night? I'll go home at night and you'll have nothing, if that's what you want."

Lena laughed and said, "Oh, you're gonna drive me crazy. Good thing I have Sonny and Peter."

In an effort to stabilize their own shaky family life, Rocky and Barbara had adopted a baby boy, whom they named Rocco Kevin, early in 1968. The boy resembled Rocky, and Mary Anne came to suspect that her new brother was the biological child of Rocky and a Florida woman with whom he had had a relationship. Barbara had suffered multiple miscarriages after having Mary Anne and had become desperate to adopt, according to her daughter, when a lawyer close to Rocky suddenly said he knew of a mother willing to give up her child for adoption. Rocky's brother Peter visited him in Florida in the summer of 1969, and he remembers Rocky picking up the boy from his crib and proudly showing him off, saying, "Isn't he something?" Rocky told Peter that the boy was his biological child. He didn't offer any details, and Peter didn't ask.

At times there was a sadness about Rocky as he watched his sisters go about their daily lives and family routines. Once when he was leaving Brockton, his nephew Bob heard Rocky tell Conge, "You don't know how lucky you are. You've got it all. This is so nice. I don't have any of that. I'm on the road, I'm doing this and that all the time. Everyone wants something." He would say similar things to his sister Alice. "The life he had in his mind as perfection was what we had—a roof over our head, three square meals a day, a job, two and a half kids, a dog, and nobody stops you on the street for your autograph," recalled Alice's son Vincent Pereira. It was as if he was a prisoner of his own fame. "The problem was that he had a wife, he had a daughter, he had a dog. But it was not for him," said Pereira. "He wasn't satisfied. There's a saying that once you've seen Paree, it's tough to go back to the domestic life. But some part of him was ashamed for not having it. What was it Joe Louis said, 'You can run, but you can't hide.'"

When Vito Genovese, the Mafia's boss of bosses and the man responsible for countless murders, lay dying in a federal prison in Leavenworth, Kansas, early in 1969, he sent word through the Baltimore fight promoter Benny Trotta that he wanted to see Rocky. The former champ went and showed Genovese films of his fights. "A lot of us have done some bad things in our lives," the frail mob boss whispered. "You, Rocky, have made us all proud." He died a month later.

Rocky was also losing people close to him. A few months earlier, on November 11, 1968, Charley Goldman died of a heart attack. He was eighty years old. At a 1966 boxing dinner in New York, Rocky and his trainer had paid what turned out to be a final tribute to each other.

Introducing his little trainer, Rocky said, "He is considered the greatest teacher of boxing in the entire world. I have to say that he had to be because he brought a raw-boned, awkward, clumsy 210-pounder to the title. This man has been a father to me, a trainer, a brother, adviser—everything."

When Goldman spoke, his voice was soft and still pure Brooklyn, "a sweet-sounding, solicitous elderly man not used to addressing formal gatherings," observed the writer Ronald K. Fried.

"If you were there looking at Rocky's training and the way he lived, it was hard to believe that a man could sacrifice so much of life and his family life and keep fightin'," Goldman said.

As Goldman went on, Rocky tried to stop him. "That's good, Charley," he whispered gently. When Goldman was through, Rocky spoke again. "You wouldn't believe that this little man could be so rough in the gymnasium. He certainly demanded discipline. He certainly had the patience of a saint. And I just can't tell you what he did for me."

Rocky sent forty-nine red roses to Goldman's funeral—one for each of his fights—and one white rose—"for Charley." But he couldn't be there in person, because that same day he was a headliner at a testimonial dinner in Chicago to raise money for Ezzard Charles, who had been stricken with Lou Gehrig's disease. Charles was confined to a wheelchair, but when he was introduced he insisted on standing. Archie Moore grabbed him by one side, and Rocky by the other, and together the three former champions made their way to the podium, tears streaming down Rocky's cheeks.

Rocky had a soft spot for ex-fighters, and he did what he could to help them out. When Willie Pep went broke, Rocky persuaded one of his wealthy friends to put Pep on his company's payroll. Rocky helped Joe Louis land a job as a greeter at a Las Vegas casino. And when he found the former lightweight champion Beau Jack shining shoes at the Fontainebleau Hotel in Miami Beach, Rocky told his rich friends to give him a large tip. When the grateful Jack offered to shine Rocky's shoes, Rocky said no, that Jack had been too great a champion to ever shine Rocky's shoes.

Allie Colombo had climbed off the carousel when Rocky retired. Now he was married, with two daughters he adored and a small stable of fighters he worked with on Saturday mornings at the Brockton VA Hospital recreation center. He taught his daughters to jab on an inflatable Bozo the Clown punching bag. He went to Red Sox games with his brother and sat in the front row of the bleachers at Fenway Park so they could yell at the players. He saw his old friend Rocky occasionally when he came to town, bringing his girls along to sit with the champ at a coffee shop or a relative's house.

On a cold, snowy night in January 1969, Allie went to work at the Stop & Shop warehouse outside of Brockton, where he drove a forklift. He fretted about going to work that night because his wife Lilly had the flu. A few hours later, he was walking in the warehouse, reading the newspaper sports page. He didn't see the truck backing up until it had pinned him against the loading dock and crushed his chest. He was rushed to Boston City Hospital, where he died a few hours later. He was forty-nine years old.

Rocky was in Las Vegas when he got the call from his brother Peter. He was speechless. Allie, the dreamer, the organizer, the worrier, was gone. It was Allie who had organized all their childhood baseball games at Edgar Playground, Allie who thought Rocky could be heavyweight champion when everyone else had laughed, Allie who had run with him all those mornings in Brockton, rain or shine. It was Allie who had arranged his first professional fight in Holyoke and written the letter to Al Weill, Allie who had hitched to New York with him and shared the dollar room at the Y. It was Allie who had been by his side at every training camp and in his corner for every fight.

Peter broke the long silence on the telephone by telling Rocky to let him know when he was flying home. Rocky paused, then said he didn't know if he could make it—he had some things going on. Peter was incredulous and grew angry with his brother. Rocky cut him off, saying, "I knew Allie better than anybody. I want to remember him the way I do. I don't think I can come." Then he hung up.

An hour later, Rocky called back and told Peter he had arranged a flight home. When Peter picked him up at the airport, an awkward silence filled the car. Finally, Rocky said, "Peter, the things Allie and I went through—it's too much to explain." Then he apologized for his behavior. They timed their arrival at the funeral home to be after the wake had ended. Then Rocky asked the funeral director for some time alone with his old friend. Afterward, when Rocky walked into Allie's house, where the mourners had gathered, Peter recalled, "everybody started crying."

Rocky served as a pallbearer at Allie's funeral the next day.

"He kept my interest in boxing alive through all the difficult moments," said Rocky. "I wouldn't be where I am without him."

■ ■ ■

ROCKY MARCIANO AND Muhammad Ali met at a film studio in North Miami for three days that winter and again for two days in the summer of 1969.

They seemed like polar opposites—the Great White Hope from the fifties and the Angry Black Man from the sixties, a hero from boxing's Golden Age versus an antihero from the sport's New Age. Rocky had been a quiet conformist during his career, holding back his anger at Al Weill and the system. Ali held back nothing. The day after he refused the army draft in 1967, he famously said, "I ain't got no quarrel with them Viet Cong." After he changed his name to Muhammad Ali, he tormented fighters like Floyd Patterson who insisted on calling him Cassius Clay. "What's my name?" he screamed over and over, as he pummeled Patterson before knocking him out in 1965.

But he and Rocky shared a bond that was stronger than their differences. As a scrawny boy of twelve in Louisville, Kentucky, Ali went to the gym to learn to box so he could "whup" the person who had stolen his bicycle. His boxing dreams were inspired by Don Dunphy's voice in his transistor radio, announcing Rocky's fights from glamorous, far-off arenas. The florid voice intoned, "heavyweight champ-i-on of the world." Ali wanted to *be* Rocky. In 1967, on the morning of his fight against Ernie Terrell, Ali watched the film of Rocky's epic first title fight against Jersey Joe Walcott. "He'd be hell to fight," he said. "It wouldn't be no fight—it would be a war."

On July 24, 1969, a judge rejected Ali's plea for a reduced sentence for refusing his army induction and resentenced him to the maximum five years in prison and a $10,000 fine. Ali immediately appealed, which meant it would be a year or more before a resolution. "I was in the deep freeze part of my exile, and there was no thaw in sight," he wrote in his autobiography. Days later, Ali met Rocky in Miami to complete filming of their "super fight."

The fight was the inspiration of Murray Woroner, a short, pudgy disc jockey and promoter from Miami. That summer, computers had helped put a man on the moon. Woroner wondered why they couldn't also compare and rank the best athletes of all time. So he asked 250 boxing writers and other experts to rank famous fighters on fifty-eight different variables, from speed and punching power to killer instinct and ring generalship. He developed a list of the top sixteen heavyweights of all time, from bare-knuckler John L. Sullivan to the dancing Ali. Then he fed all his information into a National Cash Register 315 computer the size of two refrigerators. The NCR 315, as it was known, spit out a blow-by-blow account of how the hypothetical matchups would unfold. Woroner developed a sixteen-week radio series in 1967, using real ring announcers to provide the commentary, and dubbed it the All-Time Heavyweight Tournament and Championship Fight.

Veteran radiomen panned the idea, but it was wildly popular, taking barroom arguments into a brave new world of computer algorithms. But it didn't erase human passions or disagreements; Woroner received weekly letters from angry fans who accused the computer of taking a dive. Newspapers covered the fights, and Las Vegas posted weekly odds. Rocky advanced to the finals against Jack Dempsey. The two old champions sat together in a Los Angeles restaurant and listened to the final, which was broadcast to 16.5 million listeners on 380 stations. Rocky was amused when the announcer described him unleashing "a brutal shot to the heart, a slamming left and right to the jaw" to drop Dempsey late in the thirteenth round. He was even happier when Woroner presented him with a jeweled championship belt worth $10,000.

The next year, Woroner staged an all-time middleweight tournament and planned a tournament of history's greatest college football teams. The possibilities were endless, he said, letting his brain run wild. Hitler against Napoleon. Abraham Lincoln versus George Washington. Socrates takes on Karl Marx. Why not?

Ali was not so pleased. After knocking out Max Schmeling in the first round of Woroner's tournament, he lost to Jim Jeffries. He had been stripped of his title by then for his draft resistance and sued Woroner for $1 million, claiming his reputation had been damaged and he had been held up to public ridicule. Woroner shrewdly settled the suit for $1 and Ali's agreement to appear in the filmed computer fight with Rocky. In addition, he paid him $9,999 up front, plus a percentage of any profits. Rocky got between $15,000 and $25,000 but no cut of the "gate."

The two ex-champions sparred in a tightly guarded studio with blacked-out walls and windows. It felt like a movie set, with cameramen and production people bustling about and Woroner barking directions for Rocky to throw a right cross or Ali to use a left hook. Rocky sported a new toupee that made him look younger. His stomach was flat, his body trim. But Ali dwarfed him. He was six foot three, 211 pounds, his arms ten inches longer. Because Ali hadn't fought in two years, he was flabby, in worse shape than Rocky. Over the course of the filming, they sparred more than seventy one-minute rounds, acting out a variety of scenarios that had been mapped out by the NCR 315 based on detailed questionnaires that had been filled out by more than two hundred writers and boxing experts.

Rocky and Ali acknowledged that they were just playacting. "This is bullshit," said Rocky. They threw mostly body punches, took few shots to the head, and didn't clinch. But sometimes they got carried away and forgot to pull their punches, leading them to wonder what would have happened if they could have met for real, when both were in their prime.

One day, Rocky deviated from the script and cut loose with a right cross, then shoved Ali into the ropes. Ali's eyes flared, and he fired a few jabs to Rocky's face. Later, Rocky hit Ali hard in the ribs, dropping him to one knee. Rocky apologized. Another time, Ali bloodied Rocky's nose, a cut that the makeup artists enhanced with fake blood. Ali flicked his lightning jabs within inches of Rocky's face, prompting Rocky to walk back to his corner muttering, "My God, the kid is *so* fast."

Ali kept flicking off Rocky's toupee, forcing additional takes. Rocky, self-conscious about his bald spot, got mad. He told Ali if he did it again he'd bang him on the arms. Another time, Rocky stalked Ali into a corner and beat him on the arms and biceps, raising angry welts, then smashed a right to his solar plexus. "Ooofh," Ali exhaled. The taping stopped. Ali returned to his corner and demanded that Woroner pay him another $2,000, in cash. He sat on his stool and refused to continue until Woroner sent a driver to the bank to cash a check and bring the money. Ali's arms were so sore, he couldn't lift them for a week.

Staging knockdowns was tricky. Rocky had only been knocked down twice in his career, Ali never. During one try, Ali shouted, "Drop the Wop" and hit Rocky, who fell to the canvas, took out his mouthpiece, and burst into hilarious laughter. When it was Rocky's turn to knock Ali down, Ali refused. Woroner cajoled him. Rocky joined in, parodying Ali's nonsensical patter—"It's the onliest way I can be beat by any man is to knock me out." Ali relented and let Rocky knock him down.

"You're too pretty to fight," Ali teased.

"I've been boxing a long time," Rocky replied.

"What do you box—oranges, grapes, or bananas?" Ali shot back.

Rocky laughed.

During a break one day, the two men grew serious. Their conversation turned to the racial divisions in America and the riots that had swept the country—Watts in 1964 and 1965, Detroit and Newark in 1967, cities all over the country in the wake of Martin Luther King Jr.'s assassination in 1968.

"Wouldn't it be great if there was something we could do, me and you together, a white guy and a black guy?" said Rocky.

Ali liked the idea. He and Rocky sat on the floor beside the ring, sharing a bag of grapefruits. Ali would peel a grapefruit, tear a section off with his large fingers, and hand it to Rocky. Rocky talked about the two of them doing a bus tour of inner-city neighborhoods. Ali grew enthusiastic. "Imagine, Muhammad Ali and Rocky Marciano, going into the worst areas," he said. "Watts, all these bad areas, saying, 'Hey, guys, c'mon, look at us two. We get along.'"

"We could shake up the world, me and you! Would you do it? Would you do it? Would you do it?"

"Yeah, I'll do it," said Rocky.

Ali's wife Belinda, who was there, said that Rocky was trying to "soothe Muhammad's soul, give him confidence that he would fight again. At that time, that's what he needed. It was a bad time." Rocky told Ali about his family migrating from Italy and the prejudice they had faced. He told him not to get discouraged, that he had stirred public wrath not just because he was black but for "going against the grain." "People fear change," said Rocky.

"I thought he was the sweetest man," recalled Belinda, now Khalilah, Ali. Her father had idolized Rocky when she was growing up, and she was thrilled to meet him. One day during another break in the filming, she pulled Rocky aside and asked his advice about whether she would be able to get Ali to walk away from the ring when it was time.

"Darling, he has an ego so big that if you tell him to stop he ain't gonna do it," he replied. "He has the fever, and he ain't gonna stop until someone takes it away from him in the ring."

One night, Rocky and Ali went to dinner at a fancy Miami restaurant. The comedian Henny Youngman was there and came over to their table and joked around.

Rocky's brother Peter, who was also in Miami for some of the filming, felt that Rocky and Ali were genuine in their talk about an inner-city tour. Had things worked out differently, they might have done it. The two champions came away from their encounter with new respect for each other. The film went into the can. Not even the fighters knew who would win. They would have to wait until the following winter, when it would be shown in theaters across America.

"He's as good or better than anybody I fought," Rocky said a few weeks later. "I really don't know if I could have beaten him. I would have liked to have fought him."

Ali wrote in his autobiography that he felt closer to Rocky during their sparring sessions than he ever did to any other white fighter. The month after they parted, Ali said, "He was the onliest one that would've given me some trouble."

"Our work was phony," said Ali. "But our friendship became real."

◻ ◻ ◻

NEW YORK WAS changing. White flight to the suburbs, rising crime, and drug use had stripped midtown Manhattan of much of its old savoir-faire. Trash piled up in the streets during a sanitation strike and peep shows proliferated in grimy Times Square. Toots Shor had to shutter his saloon. He tried reopening in a new location, but that didn't work out, either, despite help from friends like Rocky, who came to see him one day and handed him $5,000.

Then Madison Square Garden closed. The fabled arena at West 50th Street and Eighth Avenue, where Rocky had nearly killed Carmine Vingo and had ended Joe Louis's career, shut its doors in February 1968, more than four decades after it had opened. Rocky and Bob Hope christened the new Garden on West 33rd Street, above Penn Station ("You should see the crazy set of trains they have down in the basement," cracked Hope). After staging a mock boxing match, Rocky and Hope waltzed together in the ring. Then Jack Dempsey and Gene Tunney climbed through the ropes and cut in, Dempsey dancing with Rocky and Tunney with Hope. The cheers of more than nineteen thousand people rose to the shiny new rafters; missing was the haze of cigar smoke that had hung over the old Garden, sucked away by a sophisticated "air-control" system.

Rocky clung to the city's remaining institutions. One night toward the end of August 1969, outside the Copacabana, Leo Ball bumped into his old friend from Brockton. Leo was the Jewish boy who had grown up in Ward Two, the boy on whose bicycle young Rocco Marchegiano had once pedaled off. Now Leo was a renowned trumpet player and bandleader working for Paul Anka, who was performing at the Copa. Leo saw Rocky as he was leaving the club and at first hardly recognized him. They had run into each other occasionally over the years in New York. Rocky had introduced him to Al Weill at Delsomna's Italian restaurant. And Leo had, at Rocky's request, introduced him to Abbe Lane, the beautiful singer with the Xavier Cugat band. Although Rocky was champion at the time, he was nervous and tongue-tied. Now, as Leo studied him at the entrance to the Copacabana, Rocky seemed more sophisticated. His stomach was flat and his expensively tailored suit fit perfectly. They chatted awhile, two boys from Brockton.

"His feelings of self-assurance and class practically bubbled out of him, and the thought hit me that he'd finally understood who he had become, and what he had accomplished, and I felt good for him," Leo recalled.

Leo asked Rocky about the Ali fight, and if he thought he could have taken him in his prime. "He reverted to Brook Street behavior with a look and a wink we both understood," Leo recalled. The two men laughed and hugged. "As he left, I thought about how nice the rest of his life was going to be."

About a week later, Rocky postponed his plans to fly home to Florida and instead boarded a small private plane from Chicago to Des Moines. It was August 31. He promised Barbara that he'd be home a day late to celebrate his birthday on September 1, as well as hers, which was August 30. Barbara had a surprise waiting: their seventeen-month-old son, Rocco, had learned to walk.

For years, Rocky's friends and family had urged him to avoid small private planes and stick to commercial flights. They had heard the stories of the harrowing flights he had survived. Once he escaped injury when a small plane crash-landed. Another time, Frank Sinatra lent him his plane to fly from Los Angeles to Palm Springs. The pilot was hungover and at one point nodded off. Unfazed, Rocky slept, too. The pilot woke up and landed the plane without incident. It was not the first time Rocky had slept through turbulence, as calmly as he had napped before a big fight. Smokey Cerrone said Rocky often joked about bumpy flights, including one time when the engine failed.

Ben Bentley, an International Boxing Club employee assigned to Rocky's training camps, recalled flying back to Grossinger's in a four-seat airplane after a visit to New York during training for the Archie Moore fight. "Coming back, we hit weather. The pilot is sweatin' and has me lookin' for landmarks. Me. Up in those Catskill mountains. Allie Colombo is ready to jump out. Rock's reading a paper. Finally, I spot the Grossinger barn and we land, though we skid like hell on the wet grass." When Weill heard that, he screamed, "That's it! No more plane flights for my million-dollar property."

In 1965, Rocky took Mary Anne and one of her friends to Hawaii, hitching a ride on a cargo plane from Los Angeles and strapping the girls into jump seats while he and a friend sat on the luggage. "A window blew in and we went into a nosedive and a red light came on and I thought, 'I'm twelve and I'm going to die,'" Mary Anne later told *Sports Illustrated*'s William Nack. "My father kept saying, 'Don't worry, you're gonna be okay.'"

Lena asked Rocky if he was ever afraid of flying, given all the accidents involving small planes. "Don't worry," he told her. "When my time comes, it comes." Sometimes it seemed that Rocky courted the danger, as a substitute for the adrenaline rush of the ring. "He thought he was infallible," said Peter. Besides, there was always a private pilot, often a wealthy businessman with his own plane, eager to share his cockpit with history's only unbeaten heavyweight champ. Rocky would cash in his commercial plane ticket, which someone else had usually paid for, and add the money to the paper bag on his lap. It was no different from when he and Allie had hitched rides on overnight produce trucks from Brockton to New York.

When the Cessna lifted off from Chicago's Midway Airport that night, Rocky had a plane ticket from Chicago to Fort Lauderdale in his pocket. He also had the promise of a $500 speaking fee and a willing young woman for the night, according to his friend Dominic Santarelli, a Chicago mobster and real estate developer who saw him off at Midway, along with Benny Trotta. The fight promoter was in town to talk to Rocky about a promising young fighter he was thinking of signing. Rocky invited Trotta to join them, but the promoter said he had to get home. Rocky told Santarelli he would see him tomorrow.

Rocky was flying to Des Moines to celebrate the opening of a steakhouse owned by Frank Farrell, as a favor to Farrell's uncle, Frankie "One Ear" Fratto, a Chicago gangster. Fratto had a rap sheet dating back to 1941 that included more than ten arrests and suspicion in two murders, including that of a Chicago alderman in 1963. He was a member of the Chicago syndicate that had muscled its way into the North Side's aluminum siding and storm window business. Rocky and Fratto were good friends. They traveled and partied together, and whenever Rocky came to the Midwest, Fratto could be counted on to meet him at the airport and make the necessary arrangements for his stay. Fratto had entertained Rocky's parents during one of their visits to Florida, seeing to it that they got an excellent table at the celebrity-studded Diplomat Hotel.

Frank Farrell, who joined Rocky on the flight, had hired the pilot Glenn Belz to take them to Des Moines. That decision would prove fateful as their Cessna flew into the setting sun and into a giant storm whipping up in the gathering darkness over the prairie. With visibility deteriorating, the inexperienced Belz was not rated for instrument flying.

Back in Brockton, the Marchegianos were having a Sunday afternoon cookout at the home of Rocky's sister Betty and her husband, Armond, to bid farewell to Peter and his family. Peter was moving to San Jose, California, to work in one of Rocky's latest businesses, a chain of fast-food-style Italian spaghetti restaurants. Sonny was already living and working in the Bay Area.

Rocky had been in Brockton the week before, in good spirits. He was excited about the restaurant venture, and he also talked about how he was working on a new image. He had hired some comedy writers and wanted to make another stab at show business. He envisioned a nightclub act, with him telling jokes and doing tricks with a punching bag. Rocky Graziano was doing comedy, so why not him? He told his parents he wanted to take them to Italy in the fall. He walked over to James Edgar Playground and watched some neighborhood boys play baseball. From Brockton, he went to New York, then home to Florida and on to Chicago.

Late that Sunday afternoon, Pierino went home, feeling tired and restless. Lena stayed at Betty's. She was there when a hornet stung one of her grandsons, and the boy's eyes swelled up. Then her one-year-old grandson woke up from his nap, ran outside, and tripped on a rock, gashing his head. Armond took the two boys to the hospital and then drove Lena home, where Pierino was watching *The Ed Sullivan Show*. It was around this time that Rocky's pilot was radioing the control tower in Des Moines that he was lost in a maze of clouds and couldn't locate the airport.

Lena felt depressed and couldn't concentrate on the show, so she went to bed early.

It was past midnight when Hank Tartaglia, who always stayed up late in Brockton, heard the bulletin on the radio. He called Peter, who was still awake. "It was like a dream, a bad dream," said Peter.

Peter went to his parents' house to break the news. Lena became hysterical and cried out repeatedly, *Figlio mio, cuore della mia vita! Figlio mio, cuore della mia vita!* A doctor came and gave her a sedative.

In Fort Lauderdale, Barbara screamed when the local police chief came to her door to give her the news. She asked him if he was mistaken, if it was actually Rocky *Graziano*.

In California, Sonny was listening to the television news as he got ready for bed when he heard a bulletin that a former boxing champion from Massachusetts had been killed in a plane crash. They didn't say who, and promised more details after a commercial break. Sonny was wild with fear. He told himself that maybe it was Jack Sharkey, who was also from Massachusetts. They hadn't said undefeated champion, just champion. But he knew.

The next morning at Fort Benning, Georgia, Rocky's niece Donna Thoreson, Concetta's twenty-one-year-old daughter, was getting ready to drive with her army husband, Mike, to Florida to celebrate Rocky's and Barbara's birthdays. Her uncle had called her a few days earlier and urged her to come. "It's my birthday," he implored. On a chain around her neck, she wore a small gold boxing glove with a diamond in the palm, a gift from her uncle when she was a little girl and he had won the heavyweight title. Rocky had surprised her a few months earlier when he showed up at her wedding at West Point, causing a commotion when he walked into the chapel as the couple stood at the altar. When West Point officers vying for a glimpse of the champ crowded into the officers' club for the reception and ran up the bar tab, Rocky gave Donna's father $1,000 to cover it. It was the last time the Marchegiano family had all been together. Now, when Donna heard the news on the radio that something bad had happened to her uncle Rocky, she ran outside, not wanting to listen anymore.

Over the next week, the stunned and grief-stricken poured out in Brockton and Fort Lauderdale for Rocky's funeral services, and he was laid to rest in a mausoleum at Lauderdale Memorial Gardens. The world mourned the shoemaker's son from Brockton who had become one of the unlikeliest and greatest boxing champions. Perry Como sent a pair of boxing gloves with forty-six roses, the age Rocky would have been. Mario Lanza's mother sent a bouquet of forty-nine roses in the shape of a heart. Lena and Pierino were too frail and grief-stricken to attend Rocky's second funeral in Florida, where celebrities like Jackie Gleason and Henny Youngman paid their respects. Muhammad Ali, who had cried when he heard the news, ran red lights to make it to the service on time. When he saw people seeking autographs, he grew angry. He later said he hoped that Rocky was taking names so he could whup them at the pearly gates.

In the years before his death, Rocky had written his own ring obituary, one that reflected not only his debt to boxing but also his disillusionment.

"I've begun to worry what my children and later my grandchildren will think of me when they see films of my fights," he said. "I worry that they may think of me as a brutal ruffian."

Soon after Rocky retired in 1956, two Roman Catholic theologians in Italy had debated the morality of boxing. Alfredo Boschi, a Jesuit priest writing in the church newspaper *Palestra del Clero*, argued that boxing violated the Sixth Commandment: Thou shalt not kill. "Professional boxing can not be justified from a moral viewpoint but must be condemned as something gravely illicit in itself," he wrote. "It not only produces but aims to produce serious injuries which can become permanent and can lead to death."

The Vatican's official newspaper *L'Osservatore Romano* published a response by another priest, Filippo Robotti: "Boxing is not something to be exalted or encouraged by Catholics. . . . But it is not considered immoral and, in consequence, can at least be tolerated. Should boxing matches be gravely immoral, all promoters, boxers, managers and spectators would be in mortal sin." But, he continued, "Rocky Marciano is a fervent practicing Catholic."

Undaunted, Boschi responded with a long article citing authorities from Saint Thomas to Joe Louis. "Boxing makes a beast of man," he wrote.

Rocky, who had met the pope, was inclined to agree with Boschi. "Man is a competitive animal," he said. "And there is no place where this fact is more obvious than in the ring."

Two years before Rocky died, a British writer came across the ex-champ holding court in a London hotel room. Standing barefoot in a whorl of blue cigar and cigarette smoke, looking pudgy in battered trousers, Rocky was in his fighter's stance and swinging his arm to illustrate a story he was telling when the writer walked in.

". . . So I keep coming forward like this, left foot first, and I hit him a shot with the right, and I see his eyes roll up in his head and I give him the left to finish him . . ."

The conversation shifted to British efforts to ban boxing. Rocky turned philosophical.

"Well, it's got to come! It's *got* to—in fifty, twenty-five years' time—no, less than that—it's got to come," he said. "As people get more *civilized*, they're going to ban boxing."

"Rocco, my baby!" protested a stout American lying on a divan. "Whaddya *sayin'*?"

"They will outlaw boxing," continued Rocky, his eyes sad and gentle. "A hundred years from now we'll be like the gladiators, something out of history."

◻ ◻ ◻

ON JANUARY 20, 1970, the Super Fight between Rocky Marciano and Muhammad Ali aired in more than six hundred theaters across America and around the world. It was a huge success, taking in $2.5 million.

Murray Woroner had filmed seven different endings, and the winner was a closely guarded secret. Not even the fighters or their families knew. Bonded couriers delivered copies of the film to theaters thirty minutes before the 10:00 p.m. start.

Seven thousand people came to Boston Garden to see the film, which was preceded by a live preliminary boxing card. The crowd roared as the celluloid Rocky, bloodied and trailing on points to the bigger, quicker Ali, rallied in the thirteenth round. Then it happened. Rocky hit Ali with a left hook to the jaw, another left to the body, and a short right to the jaw. Ali toppled to the canvas. The referee counted him out and raised Rocky's arms in triumph.

Pierino, in the cheering Garden crowd, smiled for the first time in months. Then he cried. "Rocky won his fiftieth fight," he said. Lena, of course, had stayed home.

Peter and Sonny attended the Ali computer fight in California. When it was over, Peter turned to Sonny.

"We've got to call Ma and tell her Rocky won."

Epilogue: Ghosts

ON SEPTEMBER 21, 1985, THE HALL OF FAME BOXING ANNOUNCER DON Dunphy was at ringside at the Riviera Hotel in Las Vegas to witness possible history.

Heavyweight champion Larry Holmes, 48-0, was heavily favored against Michael Spinks to win his forty-ninth professional fight and tie Rocky Marciano's record. With his anticipated victory, fifty also seemed well within reach.

Dunphy had called more than two thousand prizefights in a career dating back to the Great Depression, including more than two hundred title fights. He was at ringside when Joe Louis beat Billy Conn in 1941, and he called many of Rocky's most famous fights: the 1951 knockout of Louis, the epic title-winning fight against Jersey Joe Walcott in Philadelphia in 1952, and the defenses against Ezzard Charles and Archie Moore. Dunphy's voice coming over the radio from New York was the sound track to boxing's golden age and had inspired young Cassius Clay in Louisville and his dreams of becoming the world heavyweight champion. Dunphy went on to announce more than two dozen of Muhammad Ali's fights, including his battles with Sonny Liston and Joe Frazier.

Caesars Palace had flown in Rocky's children, Mary Anne and Rocky Jr., and his brother Peter for the occasion, which fell on the thirtieth anniversary of Rocky's last fight, against Archie Moore. Dunphy said in his prefight broadcast that any list of the greatest heavyweights of all time should have Louis, Marciano, and Ali at the top, in no particular order. Holmes, who had held the title for seven years, also belonged in their company, he said—but he would drop should he lose to Spinks or a subsequent opponent.

Spinks was the light heavyweight champion, and no light heavyweight had ever won the heavyweight title. Consequently, much of the prefight talk focused on Holmes's bout with history and his assault on Rocky's record. Holmes had even brought in Archie Moore as an adviser. And once again, Moore expressed his bitterness toward the referee Harry Kessler for, in his view, unfairly keeping him away from Rocky after he had knocked him down in the second round of their 1955 fight at Yankee Stadium. There was so much talk about Rocky that Dunphy said he "began to wonder whether Larry was fighting Spinks or Rocky's ghost."

Perhaps Rocky's ghost was in Spinks's corner that night. Before the fight, Peter Marciano had spoken to Spinks, telling him, "You know that Rocky is going to be pulling for you." In an improbable fight, Spinks outran and outpunched the slower Holmes and won a close, but unanimous, decision. Afterward, an angry Holmes said he had been robbed and took out his frustration on Marciano.

"I'm thirty-five fighting young men and he was twenty-five, fighting old men," said Holmes, his swollen eyes hidden behind sunglasses. "To be technical, Rocky Marciano couldn't carry my jockstrap. They didn't want me to win because people want a white hope."

Then, Holmes turned on Peter Marciano, who was standing at the back of the room during the press conference. "He's out there, staying at Caesars Palace," Holmes said dismissively. "Freeloading off his brother.... What's your name? Sonny?"

Peter, standing with Mary Anne and Rocky Jr., stepped forward two paces. He looked and sounded like Rocky, as if he might want to fight. "My name is Peter, Larry," he replied. "And if you want to talk ..." But Holmes cut him off.

Holmes later tried to strike a conciliatory tone, offering to buy Peter a beer, telling him about the pictures of Rocky he had back home in Easton, Pennsylvania. But the damage had been done. Later, Holmes apologized to the Marciano family, saying that he was frustrated that night and hoped he could make peace. In 2012, when the city of Brockton dedicated a statue of Rocky, Holmes attended the ceremony.

"The man was the legend," said Holmes, who had talked to many former greats, including Jack Dempsey, Joe Louis, and Archie Moore, who had seen or faced Rocky. "The man was tough. Man, he was tough."

But that didn't mean Holmes's opinion had changed that he could have beaten Rocky.

So where does Rocky stand in the all-time heavyweight annals? His crudeness will never win him style points. Other fighters, from Louis to Ali, were flashier and reigned longer. Louis was at the end of his career when Rocky beat him. The Brown Bomber didn't have the right hand he had had in his prime to complement his lethal left jab, and his legs were gone. But as Ali discovered when he entered the ring against Rocky for their computer fight, Rocky's strength would have been a worthy match for Ali's speed. How would the smaller Rocky have stood up to a destroyer like Mike Tyson, or Holmes in his prime with his punishing left jab, or any of the new class of behemoths who have emerged in recent years?

Rocky remains in the conversation because of his punching power and his ability to absorb punishment and keep coming, thanks to his ferocity, endurance, and determination. Critics can question the caliber of his opponents, or point to his controversial wins over Roland LaStarza and Tiger Ted Lowry. But other champions faced similar criticisms, most notably Louis with his "Bum of the Month" club. The fact is, Rocky never lost. He fought the best fighters of his era, and he fought courageously against underrated boxers like Jersey Joe Walcott, Ezzard Charles, and Archie Moore, even though they were all older than he was when they met. Rocky may not have looked pretty, but as his trainer Charley Goldman pointed out, his opponents didn't look too good, either, when they were flat on their back.

Shortly after Rocky retired, *Look* magazine convened a panel of six boxing experts, who rated him as the sixth-best heavyweight of all time, tied with Jim Corbett. Ahead of him were Jack Johnson, Jim Jeffries, Jack Dempsey, Bob Fitzsimmons, and Gene Tunney. Trailing Rocky were Joe Louis, Sam Langford, and John L. Sullivan. One panelist, *Ring* magazine's Nat Fleischer, ranked Rocky tenth "because he lacked a number of essentials for greatness—too wide open, no cleverness—and he depended wholly on his terrific punching power." Johnson, Dempsey, and Louis, he said, would have knocked out Rocky or cut him so badly that it would have been necessary to stop the fight. Tunney and Corbett would have outboxed him for fifteen rounds while avoiding his Suzie Q.

Another panelist, the old featherweight champ Abe Attell, offered a dissenting view. Rocky, he said, surpassed his peers in "stamina to keep attacking no matter how much punishment he was taking . . . no matter how long the fight was going. He won on pace as well as punch. He would keep them moving backward and that sapped their speed. I can't see why some people can't get the real picture of him. They said Marciano didn't do anything right, yet what he did always turned out right."

Rocky also appears on many lists of the top ten heavyweights when more modern fighters like Larry Holmes, Lennox Lewis, Evander Holyfield, Joe Frazier, and George Foreman are included. The boxing historian and writer Bert Sugar rated him sixth. But drawing comparisons with recent fighters can be misleading because the heavyweights that followed were, well, heavier. The minimum weight for heavyweights has crept up from 175 pounds when Rocky fought to 200 pounds today. As fighters have gotten bigger, a new class of "super heavyweights" has emerged. Today, Rocky would be a cruiserweight. He faced just three opponents who weighed more than 200 pounds: the overstuffed Don Cockell, Lee Savold, and the aging Joe Louis. Only the recent heavyweight champion Wladimir Klitschko of Ukraine rivals Rocky for punching prowess, with a career knockout rate of 89 percent versus Rocky's 88 percent. But while Rocky usually fought at 185 pounds, Klitschko weighed 232 pounds and would have had a fourteen-inch reach advantage over Rocky.

"No man reached the championship with more physical handicaps," wrote Arthur Daley.

In 1955, engineers with the United States Testing Company scientifically studied Rocky's punch. They concluded that he hit with twice as much force as the impact of a bullet from a Colt .45 handgun. Using sound amplifiers that could calculate into millionths of a second, an engineer found that Rocky's hardest punch landed with a force of 925 foot-pounds. (A foot-pound is the energy required to lift one pound one foot off the ground.) The Colt .45 landed with a force of 420 foot-pounds.

Rocky's friend Lou Duva was driving home with his wife and children in New Jersey when he heard the news on the radio that Rocky had been killed. He nearly drove off the road and had to stop the car as he dissolved in tears.

"I always said after Rocky died that one day I'm going to get a fighter," Duva said years later. "And if I get that fighter it's going to be a heavyweight and that heavyweight is going to win the world title. And when I win that world title . . . I'm going to point up to Rocky in heaven and I'm going to say, 'Rocky, I'm dedicating this here to you. This is your fight. You're still champion of the world.'"

Duva's moment came in Las Vegas on October 25, 1990, when Evander Holyfield, whom he had helped train, knocked out Buster Douglas to win the heavyweight title. Duva went on to a Hall of Fame career as a trainer and promoter, handling nineteen world champions, including Pernell Whitaker, Mark Breland, and Vinny Pazienza.

◻ ◻ ◻

IN THE YEARS following his death, Rocky, like boxing and the era that produced him, faded from the public consciousness.

Seven weeks after Rocky's fatal plane crash, Al Weill died in a Miami Beach nursing home at the age of seventy-five. His fortunes had declined after his break with Rocky, as he lost money in investments and gambling. He had managed four world champions, but his attempts to come back failed. In eulogy, Arthur Daley wrote, "The boxing business has always been populated by connivers and Weill was a champion among them." Within the span of a year, the four men who had formed an essential partnership in Rocky's career had died: Charley Goldman, Allie Colombo, Rocky, and Weill.

In 1976, seven years after Rocky's death, an unknown actor and boxing enthusiast named Sylvester Stallone made a movie about a crude, underdog Italian American fighter who faces a fast-talking heavyweight champion modeled after Muhammad Ali—in Philadelphia. Stallone, who called himself a failed actor, was looking to write a story about "people who can't fulfill their desires." He watched a tape of the Ali-Marciano fight, and was intrigued by their contrasting styles. Then, in 1975, he saw the unheralded heavyweight Chuck Wepner knock down Ali and take him into the fifteenth round before Ali stopped him in the final seconds to retain his title. Inspired, Stallone wrote a script about a boxer named Rocky Balboa. *Rocky* went on to win the Oscar for Best Picture and become one of the most successful sports films of all time. Rocky's wizened old trainer with the cauliflower ears, played by Burgess Meredith, was reminiscent of Charley Goldman, as was his training technique of tying Rocky's shoelaces together to improve his footwork. Early in the film, when Rocky returns to his dilapidated apartment after a dreary club fight, the camera pans to a large poster of Rocky Marciano on the wall. Late in the film, on the eve of Rocky's climactic Christmastime fight against Apollo Creed, he ponders the Marciano poster again, now framed in garland and holiday lights, with a cotton Santa Claus beard and whiskers taped on Marciano's face.

In the years that followed, Brockton would remember its native son in an attempt to recapture its glory as the shoe factories closed and the city's fortunes declined. A monument to Rocky was dedicated in James Edgar Playground. In 1999 the city celebrated when the U.S. Postal Service issued a Rocky Marciano postage stamp. On September 23, 2012—the sixtieth anniversary of Rocky's title-winning fight against Jersey Joe Walcott—the World Boxing Council unveiled a two-ton, twenty-foot-tall statue of Rocky overlooking the football stadium at Brockton High School. The school had changed its nickname from the Shoe Men to the Boxers, and the football team played in Rocky Marciano Stadium. Rocky's brother-in-law Armond Colombo had become the winningest high school football coach in Massachusetts history, then retired and handed over the reins to his son Peter, who has continued his success.

More ghosts would haunt the ceremony at the football stadium. In 2011, as she prepared to travel from her home in Florida to Brockton for a planning meeting about the statue, Mary Anne Marciano died suddenly from respiratory problems. She was fifty-eight years old. Her mother, Barbara, had died from cancer on September 8, 1974, nearly five years to the day after her husband had been killed. She was forty-six. In her last days, Barbara lay in bed and hallucinated, seeing Rocky beckoning for her to join him. "Rocky, I'm not ready to go yet," she protested. "I have to take care of Mary Anne and Rocky." She was entombed beside Rocky in the family mausoleum at Lauderdale Memorial Gardens. "When he died, a piece of my mother died," said Mary Anne.

The family struggled following Rocky's death. The champ's mistrust of banks meant that his fortune remained lost. Barbara and the children had to leave their oceanfront home, and Barbara sold her diamonds to pay the bills. For years, they searched in vain for his money. Mary Anne even asked someone she knew at the CIA to check for Swiss bank accounts. Believing that her father had stashed money in safety deposit boxes, she tried to decipher his cryptic scribbled notes for clues and came to suspect that he may have used the aliases Mr. Rocco and Mr. March. The family asked Bernie Castro to search his bomb shelter, but he said that was ridiculous—there was no money there. They watched as other people from Rocky's entourage suddenly bought restaurants and other businesses.

Before his death, Rocky's sister Alice had asked him what his family would do if anything ever happened to him. He wrote down the name of a Rhode Island lawyer and said they should contact him. Unbeknownst to the family, it was the same lawyer who had brought Rocky into the negotiations with the Buffalo mob regarding the recreation center Leisureland in 1963. But when they tried to track down the lawyer, they discovered that he had committed suicide after being indicted in a racketeering case.

Following Barbara's death, her widowed mother, Betty Cousins, moved into the family's modest ranch house in Florida and took care of Mary Anne and Rocky Jr. It was a rough time in Mary Anne's life. She became addicted to drugs and was jailed after a series of arrests for using cocaine, delivering crack, violating her probation, and, in 1991, participating in an armed robbery of the Club Elvis in Fort Lauderdale. The police accused her, another woman, and two men of using a broken pool cue to beat up a man, then steal his keys, his wallet, and a cash register. Mary Anne admitted to taking several bottles of vodka. With her uncle Sonny pleading with the judge for leniency, Mary Anne received a twenty-two-month prison sentence and served eight months.

"I made a few mistakes. I just got mixed up with the wrong people," she said. "I never hurt anybody. The only people I ever hurt were myself and my family. I was brought up very well. I had a good family background."

Mary Anne said that her father's death had been devastating. "I tried to be strong and follow in his footsteps," she said. "I think being in his shadow maybe defeated me."

In 1993, the *Sports Illustrated* writer William Nack sat in the Marciano kitchen with Mary Anne and her grandmother Betty Cousins. Mary Anne laughed about the time her father had taken her and her friend on the cargo plane to Hawaii when she was twelve and the window blew out.

"You should *never* have got on that plane," said Betty. "God, he was tight!"

"But Nana, I could get anything I wanted out of him," said Mary Anne.

"And me?" said Betty. "I even bought my own ticket to see him fight Joe Louis. And he lived with us!"

Betty said that Barbara should have divorced Rocky.

"Maybe I'll be six feet under, but . . . when I get to the other side, I'll tell loverboy a thing or two."

Mary Anne turned her life around and worked for years at a market research company. She helped raise Rocky Jr., who was fifteen years younger, and she was "team mother" for his baseball teams. A longtime smoker, like her mother, Mary Anne was diagnosed with pulmonary disease. Following her death at age fifty-eight, her brother said that she possessed their father's qualities: strength and warmth. "I know she's looking down on us," Rocky Jr. said. "She's up there with my mom and dad. She's at peace now."

Rocky Jr., who studied electrical engineering at Florida Atlantic University, made his career in real estate and business. In 2017 he launched a new Italian red wine from his grandfather's birthplace, Ripa Teatina, called Rocky Marciano Montepulciano d'Abruzzo. He spoke of how his father built his strength as a boy by carrying the heavy crates of grapes into his grandfather Luigi's basement and then turning the winepress.

"My one regret in life," he said, "is that I didn't get to know my father."

◻ ◻ ◻

ROCKY ALWAYS SAID that he drew his strength from his mother and his restraint from his father.

Pierino Marchegiano, whose quiet life of toil in the shoe factory was transformed by his son's success in the ring, died on April 4, 1973, at the age of seventy-nine, from the respiratory problems that had plagued him since he had been gassed during World War I.

Pasqualena Marchegiano remained a vibrant presence for thirteen more years and worked to preserve the memory of her firstborn son, her *figlio mio, cuore della mia vita*. She helped found the Rocky Marciano Scholarship Foundation. In 1981 she was invited to a private reception at the White House with President Ronald Reagan to mark the opening of the Smithsonian Institution's Champions of American Sport exhibition, which featured Rocky.

Lena died on January 7, 1986, four days after her eighty-fourth birthday. Even three decades later, "she's with us in everything we do," said her grandson Robert Langway. He remembered sitting at her kitchen table as a boy, as she dictated letters to him in her broken English. "Dear Dolly," began one typical letter. "I am thinking of you and our beautiful sons, one Italian lady to another." It wasn't until she had him address the envelope that Bob realized she was writing to Frank Sinatra's mother.

Asked how she wanted her son to be remembered, she said, "Rocky was a great champion and he was a little rough fighting, but he was a kind, gentle, humble man who loved his family, loved children, and loved life."

◻ ◻ ◻

TWO DECADES AFTER Larry Holmes failed to tie Rocky's record, Peter Marciano was invited back to Las Vegas on August 26, 2017, to witness another challenge to it—Floyd Mayweather's bid to go 50-0 in a heavily hyped light-middleweight fight against the mixed-martial-arts star Conor McGregor, who had little boxing experience. This time Peter declined the invitation, echoing many critics when he called the match a "circus" that should have been staged as an exhibition. But if boxing had largely faded from the prominence of Rocky's time, this "Money Fight" attracted widespread interest and a purse that Rocky would have envied. Mayweather earned more than $300 million; McGregor more than $100 million. Mayweather toyed with McGregor before putting him away in the tenth round with a series of punches to the face that prompted the referee to stop the fight.

Afterward, Mayweather announced that he would retire from boxing with a 50-0 record, breaking Rocky's mark. He paid tribute to Rocky, calling him "a legend."

The legend of Rocky Marciano has endured longer than the man himself, even as the number of people who saw him fight grows ever smaller. Rocky's world seems far removed from ours, but in some ways he saw what was coming. In the final years of his life, this most brutish of fighters recognized the brutality of the sport that had given him everything, and he predicted its decline.

A man of his times, Rocky Marciano saw his time fading away and viewed himself as the last gladiator of his age. He reveled in the glory he had reaped, the improbable journey from Brockton and its shoe factories to the world stage. But he also worried about the cost—how he had strayed from his family and lost his way. He told his sisters that he envied their lives of tranquil domesticity, and yet it was too late for him to go back.

Rocky was no longer the pure and innocent kid from Ward Two. Yet, had he lived to see his forty-sixth birthday and beyond, some of his friends and relatives think he would have found his way back. Or perhaps he would have simply kept going. Among his scribblings on scraps of paper, he once wrote: "Live fast, die hard." His nephew and godson Vincent Pereira said he can't imagine his uncle growing old in a nursing home, weak and frail.

"He was a human being with flaws and greatness, only his flaws and greatness were larger, his highs were higher, his lows were lower," Pereira said. "His legend will live bigger and brighter because he died young."

Appendix
Rocky Marciano's
Professional Ring Record

Date	Opponent	Result/Round	Location
1947			
March 17*	Les Epperson	KO/3	Valley Arena, Holyoke, Mass.
1948			
July 12	Harry Bilazarian	TKO/1	Rhode Island Auditorium, Providence, R.I.
July 19	John Edwards	KO/1	Rhode Island Auditorium, Providence, R.I.
August 9	Bobby Quinn	KO/3	Rhode Island Auditorium, Providence, R.I.
August 23	Eddie Ross	KO/1	Rhode Island Auditorium, Providence, R.I.
August 30	Jimmy Meeks**	TKO/1	Rhode Island Auditorium, Providence, R.I.
September 13	Jerry Jackson	TKO/1	Rhode Island Auditorium, Providence, R.I.
September 20	Bill Hardeman	KO/1	Rhode Island Auditorium, Providence, R.I.
September 30	Gil Cardione	KO/1	Uline Arena, Washington, D.C.
October 4	Bob Jefferson	TKO/2	Rhode Island Auditorium, Providence, R.I.
November 29	Pat Connolly	TKO/1	Rhode Island Auditorium, Providence, R.I.
December 14	Gilley Ferron	TKO/2	Convention Hall, Philadelphia
1949			
March 21	Johnny Pretzie	TKO/5	Rhode Island Auditorium, Providence, R.I.
March 28	Artie Donato	KO/1	Rhode Island Auditorium, Providence, R.I.
April 11	James Walls	KO/3	Rhode Island Auditorium, Providence, R.I.
May 2	Jimmy Evans	TKO/3	Rhode Island Auditorium, Providence, R.I.
May 23	Don Mogard	W/10	Rhode Island Auditorium, Providence, R.I.
July 18	Harry Haft	KO/3	Rhode Island Auditorium, Providence, R.I.
August 16	Pete Louthis	KO/3	New Page Arena, New Bedford, Mass.
September 26	Tommy DiGiorgio	KO/4	Rhode Island Auditorium, Providence, R.I.
October 10	Tiger Ted Lowry	W/10	Rhode Island Auditorium, Providence, R.I.
November 7	Joe Dominic	KO/2	Rhode Island Auditorium, Providence, R.I.
December 2	Pat Richards	TKO/2	Madison Square Garden, New York
December 19	Phil Muscato	TKO/5	Rhode Island Auditorium, Providence, R.I.
December 30	Carmine Vingo	KO/6	Madison Square Garden, New York

1950			
March 24	Roland LaStarza	W/10	Madison Square Garden, New York
June 5	Eldridge Eatman	TKO/3	Rhode Island Auditorium, Providence, R.I.
July 10	Gino Buonvino	TKO/10	Braves Field, Boston
September 18	Johnny Shkor	KO/6	Rhode Island Auditorium, Providence, R.I.
November 13	Tiger Ted Lowry	W/10	Rhode Island Auditorium, Providence, R.I.
December 18	Bill Wilson	KO/1	Rhode Island Auditorium, Providence, R.I.
1951			
January 29	Keene Simmons	TKO/8	Rhode Island Auditorium, Providence, R.I.
March 20	Harold Mitchell	TKO/2	Hartford Auditorium, Hartford, Conn.
March 26	Art Henri	TKO/9	Rhode Island Auditorium, Providence, R.I.
April 30	Red Applegate	W/10	Rhode Island Auditorium, Providence, R.I.
July 12	Rex Layne	KO/6	Madison Square Garden, New York
August 27	Freddie Beshore	TKO/4	Boston Garden, Boston
October 26	Joe Louis	KO/8	Madison Square Garden, New York
1952			
February 13	Lee Savold	KO/6	Convention Hall, Philadelphia
April 21	Gino Buonvino	KO/2	Rhode Island Auditorium, Providence, R.I.
May 12	Bernie Reynolds	KO/3	Rhode Island Auditorium, Providence, R.I.
July 28	Harry Matthews	KO/2	Yankee Stadium, New York
September 23	Jersey Joe Walcott***	KO/13	Municipal Stadium, Philadelphia
1953			
May 15	Jersey Joe Walcott***	KO/1	Chicago Stadium, Chicago
September 24	Roland LaStarza***	TKO/11	Polo Grounds, New York
1954			
June 19	Ezzard Charles***	W/15	Yankee Stadium, New York
September 17	Ezzard Charles***	KO/8	Yankee Stadium, New York
1955			
May 16	Don Cockell***	TKO/9	Kezar Stadium, San Francisco
September 21	Archie Moore***	KO/9	Yankee Stadium, New York

*Fought under the name Rocky Mack
**Meeks was mistakenly identified as "Weeks" in contemporary accounts of the fight, and his name still appears incorrectly in many listings of Marciano's record.
***Title fight

A Note on Sources

I was eleven years old when Rocky Marciano died and so never had the opportunity to speak with him directly. But his words endure in numerous television appearances and newspaper and magazine interviews, as well as ghostwritten, first-person accounts of his life, most notably a six-part autobiographical series that ran in the *Saturday Evening Post* in 1956, after he retired.

I interviewed several of Rocky's relatives, including his three surviving siblings, Louis "Sonny" Marciano, Peter Marciano, and Betty Colombo, along with her husband, Armond Colombo; his son, Rocky Marciano Jr.; his nephews Robert Langway and Vincent Pereira; his niece Donna Thoreson; and his cousin Mike "Duna" Cappiello. Langway, the son of Rocky's sister Concetta, or Conge, also shared family scrapbooks, photographs, and letters. I interviewed John Sylvester, who grew up near Rocky and whose older brother, Eugene Sylvester, was one of Rocky's best friends. Charlie Ball, who also grew up in Rocky's neighborhood, shared his memories as well as an unpublished memoir by his older brother, Leo Ball, who grew up with Rocky and went on to see him in New York after Leo became a successful musician. I interviewed many others who knew Rocky, including Charlie Tartaglia and Ralph Galante in Brockton, Smokey Cerrone in Providence, Jimmy Breslin and Steve Acunto in New York, and Lou Duva and Al Certo in New Jersey. While Rocky's opponents are all dead, I spoke to the sons of Ted Lester, Jimmy Meeks, and Harry Haft, and friends of Les Epperson and Joe Dominic.

I went through old news clippings, letters, photos, and memorabilia at the Brockton Historical Society, and the photo archive at Stonehill College of Stanley Bauman, the former *Brockton Enterprise* photographer who chronicled Rocky's career from his schoolboy baseball days. The archives of the Supreme Judicial Court in Massachusetts yielded a transcript of the 1950 trial in boxing promoter Gene Caggiano's lawsuit against Rocky, referred to in the notes that follow as the Caggiano lawsuit. The transcript, including testimony from Rocky, his parents, his uncle, his trainer Charley Goldman, his friend and trainer Allie Colombo, and Providence promoter Manny Almeida, revealed many details of Rocky's early career.

In the archives of *Sports Illustrated*, I found lengthy summaries of unpublished interviews with Rocky and his family and friends by *Life* magazine reporters in 1952, for a profile shortly before he won the heavyweight title. Detailed notes from the reporters, including Kathleen Shortall's typewritten twenty-two-page report from Brockton and dispatches from other reporters in New York and at Rocky's training camp at Grossinger's, were in the files of *Sports Illustrated*, a Time-Life publication that started two years later. These will be referred to as the *Life* interview notes.

From the archives of ESPN, I obtained unedited transcripts of interviews conducted for the informative 2000 documentary *Rocky Marciano*, including interviews with Sonny and Peter Marciano, Rocky's childhood friends Izzy Gold and Nick Sylvester, and his friend and accountant Frank Saccone. Gold, Sylvester, and Saccone have all since died. These will be referred to as the ESPN transcripts.

Several books have been written about Rocky, but two stand out. One, by the sportswriter Everett Skehan, who grew up in Brockton, was originally published in 1977 as *Rocky Marciano: Biography of a First Son* and contained interviews with many of Rocky's contemporaries who were still alive in the years immediately following his death. An expanded version was published in 2005 as *Undefeated Rocky Marciano: The Fighter Who Refused to Lose*, featuring additional interviews and photos. The other notable biography is *Rocky Marciano: The Rock of His Times*, published in 2002, a thoughtful examination of his life and times by Russell Sullivan, now the executive director of the Sports Museum in Boston. In addition, Michael N. Varveris, an Ohio weekly newspaper editor who befriended Rocky's parents in the 1970s, interviewed Rocky's mother, Pasqualena, and wrote a memoir, *Rocky Marciano: The 13th Candle*. I also interviewed Varveris's wife, who remembers Rocky's parents staying at their house in Ohio for several weeks.

Old newspaper and magazine accounts bring to life Rocky's career and the colorful era in which he fought. I spent many fruitful hours in the company of such legendary New York sportswriters as Red Smith, A. J. Liebling, Budd Schulberg, W. C. Heinz, Jimmy Cannon, Lester Bromberg, Al Hirshberg, Milton Gross, and Arthur Daley, as well as long-forgotten publications like the *National Police Gazette*, archived at the New York Public Library, and the *Saturday Evening Post*. The archives of the *Brockton Enterprise* and the *Providence Journal* contain extensive coverage of Rocky's early life and career.

FBI files provided insights into Rocky's ties to Mafia figures, chronicled the extensive criminal career of Frankie Carbo, and documented organized crime's control of boxing. Transcripts of congressional hearings into the Mafia and boxing, including testimony from Rocky, tracked the rise and fall of the International Boxing Club, also known as the Octopus.

Many excellent books have been written about boxing history, but three were invaluable: Barney Nagler's *James Norris and the Decline of Boxing*, Jeffrey T. Sammons's *Beyond the Ring: The Role of Boxing in American Society*, and Ronald K. Fried's *Corner Men: The Great Boxing Trainer*.

Toots, a documentary about fabled New York saloonkeeper Toots Shor by his granddaughter Kristi Jacobson, is a great window into the Manhattan sporting scene. Nicholas Pileggi shared with me his memories of being a young newspaperman in New York and of the rich boxing scene there. Ric Burns's excellent *New York: A Documentary Film* captures the changing city and the working-class underpinnings that fueled boxing in that golden age. David Halberstam's *The Fifties* and two collections of *New Yorker* articles, *The 40s* and *The 50s*, also provided useful background for the era in which Rocky fought.

Prologue: Two Funerals

I relied on contemporary news accounts to describe Rocky's death in the plane crash in Iowa, his funerals in Brockton and Fort Lauderdale, and the world's reaction to his death. I also interviewed Sonny and Peter Marciano, Betty and Armond Colombo, Robert Langway, Charlie Tartaglia, and John Sylvester.

The *Chicago Tribune* published a short article, "How Rocky Keeps in Shape," about his jogging along Lake Michigan on August 30, 1969—the day before he died. On September 6, 1969, Neil Milbert wrote a more detailed story for the *Tribune* about Rocky's last days in Chicago, "Rocky's Last Hurrah Almost Went Unnoticed."

John Lennon and Paul McCartney talked about Rocky during a 1965 recording session for the Beatles' album *Rubber Soul*, while working on the song "Think for Yourself." Their conversation can be heard in the outtakes.

Chicago Tribune columnist David Condon described Toots Shor's conversation with Billy Conn about Rocky in a September 16, 1969, column.

Rocky's quote about handling fear in the ring was something he wrote for an ad for National Car Rental shortly before his death, which ran in newspapers following his death. His quote, "I was a nobody. In the ring, I became a somebody" was something he said many times. I took this from the final part of his six-part autobiographical series in the *Saturday Evening Post*, "It Was Worth It," which ran on October 20, 1956.

Chapter 1: The Terrific Three

The description of the shoes that Brockton manufacturers made for Rocky comes from "Brockton's Boy," a magazine story that W. C. Heinz wrote for *Cosmopolitan* in June 1954 and which is included in *The Top of His Game*, a collection of Heinz's work edited by Bill Littlefield.

The account of how Luigi Picciuto, Rocky's grandfather, came to America and his life in Brockton, including his winemaking and rowdy eating and drinking gatherings at his house, is related by Rocky in "They Said I'd Get Murdered," the second part of his autobiographical *Saturday Evening Post* series, published September 22, 1956. Sonny and Peter Marciano and Betty Colombo also talked to me about this. Robert Langway told me stories that he heard from his grandmother Pasqualena Marchegiano about her childhood in Italy, including her father Luigi's anger about her sneaking off to school.

Several friends and family members, including Lena, discussed the family's roots and Rocky's childhood in the *Life* interview notes. Lena told the *Life* researcher, for instance, that while her husband wanted only two children, she wanted six. I also drew on my own interviews with Rocky's friends and family, as well as several magazine and newspaper accounts, most notably Rocky's autobiographical *Saturday Evening Post* series and a September 20, 1952, *Saturday Evening Post* profile by Al Hirshberg, "Can Any Man Living Beat Him?"

Dr. Phaneuf's description of Rocky's birth, including his joke that he was the first one to hit Rocky, was contained in Heinz's magazine story "Brockton's Boy." Rocky's near death as an infant from pneumonia was a widely told story, described in detail in the *Life* magazine notes, *Rocky Marciano: The 13th Candle*, and Everett Skehan's biography, and also discussed in several newspaper and magazine interviews.

The exploits of the Terrific Three—Rocky and his childhood friends Izzy Gold and Eugene Sylvester—were described by Izzy Gold in the ESPN transcripts, and by Rocky in his *Saturday Evening Post* autobiography and in several other interviews with reporters through the years. I also interviewed Eugene Sylvester's brother John, who remembered many of the episodes. Leo Ball's unpublished memoir describes the time that Rocky and Eugene Sylvester "borrowed" his bicycle and Rocky's famous childhood fight with Julie Durham, which is also described in several newspaper accounts, in the *Life* interview notes, and in Nick Sylvester's ESPN transcripts. Rocky described Peg-Leg Pete's dice game in the woods in his *Saturday Evening Post* autobiography, and I also interviewed Ralph Galante, who grew up in the neighborhood and knew Rocky and remembered the Terrific Three's attempts to steal money from the dice game. Rocky reminisced about meeting the burlesque dancer Sally Rand at the Brockton Fair in a newspaper interview, and Skehan described it in his biography, *Rocky Marciano: Biography of a First Son*.

I learned about the history of Brockton, including its stature as the shoe capital, its pioneering role in Thomas Edison's development of electricity, and the birth of the first department store Santa, from the book *History of Brockton, 1645–1911* and an October 1987 *Yankee* magazine article, "After the Brockton Blockbuster." I also interviewed Carl Landerholm of the Brockton Historical Society. The story of Sacco and Vanzetti, including their arrest on a Brockton streetcar near Rocky's neighborhood, is told in Susan Tejada's comprehensive book *In Search of Sacco and*

Vanzetti. I interviewed Sonny Marciano about his grandfather Luigi's disgust at the prejudice that Italian immigrants faced. Michael Musmanno's 1965 book *The Story of the Italians in America*—a book that Rocky liked to read—chronicled the anti-immigration wave in Congress that targeted Italians in the 1920s. Jerre Mangione and Ben Morreale's *La Storia: Five Centuries of the Italian American Experience* provided context for the immigration of Rocky's grandparents and parents from Italy. I learned about Ripa Teatina, the Italian town where Rocky's father, Pierino, was born, from an online history, a video provided by Rocky's friend Steven Acunto, and my interviews with Sonny and Peter Marciano. They told me about the region's motto, *forte e gentile*, which means "strong and gentle," and how Pierino was guided by that philosophy in teaching his children how they should bring honor to the Marchegiano name.

Rocky remembered seeing Primo Carnera when he visited Brockton in his *Saturday Evening Post* autobiography and in the May 13, 1955, *Collier's* article, "How It Feels to Be Champion of the World." Izzy Gold, in the ESPN transcript, talked about the Terrific Three and described how he and Rocky met Joe Louis at the Brockton Arena when they were boys. Gold also talked about their days working and gambling after Rocky dropped out of high school and before he joined the army.

Chapter 2: Brawler in the Brig

I obtained Rocky's army service records from the National Archives in Saint Louis, including his medical records and his court-martial file, which includes his mug shot, witness statements, and the transcript of his military trial in England in 1944. The records allowed me to track his progress through the war and afterward to a military prison in Indiana, from which he was released in the spring of 1946.

For further details of Rocky's military service and what life was like in his company, I drew on an excellent 1946 history of Rocky's unit, *Pack Up and Move: A Pictorial History of the 348th Engineer Combat Battalion* by Keith Bryan, who served with the battalion. I also interviewed the author's son, Tom Bryan, who edits a newsletter about the 348th, and Basil Reed, who is believed to be the last surviving member of Rocky's company. Another helpful resource was the book *From Boston to Berlin: A Journey Through World War II in Images and Words,* by Christopher Mauriello and Roland J. Regan Jr., the son of Roland J. Regan, who served with Rocky. I interviewed Roland Jr., who shared his father's stories about Rocky boxing in Wales and his fight with an Australian soldier in a British pub. Rocky reminisced about being stationed in Wales and his army fights, including the pub encounter with the Aussie, in a *London Sunday Telegraph* column on November 7, 1965.

Rocky described his gambling success on the ship to Europe in Part 2 of his *Saturday Evening Post* autobiographical series, "They Said I'd Get Murdered," and in Ed Fitzgerald's January 1953 *Sport* magazine article "The Blockbuster from Brockton."

Robert Langway shared letters that Rocky wrote to his sister Concetta, or Conge (Langway's mother), during the war.

Rocky's amateur fight in Brockton against Ted Lester was covered by the *Brockton Enterprise*. I interviewed Rocky's cousin Duna Cappiello, who was at the fight, and Lester's son, Michael Van Leesten, and found 1950 court testimony in the Caggiano lawsuit from Lester's manager, John Powers, describing the fight. Peter Marciano described the fight in the ESPN transcripts and other relatives described it in the *Life* interview notes.

I found details of Rocky's boxing career at Fort Lewis in issues of the weekly base newspaper, the *Fort Lewis Flame*, which are preserved at the Washington State Library. The *Washington Post* published a story in 1953 about Rocky's sparring with Big Bill Little in Tacoma, and it's also described in John D. McCallum's 1974 book, *The World Heavyweight Boxing Championship: A History*. The *Portland Oregonian* covered Rocky's participation in the national junior AAU championships in August. An excellent account from Joe DeAngelis of his victory over Rocky in the finals was published in *Yankee* magazine in September 1984. Rocky talked about his injured hand and the Japanese American doctor who saved him with a "miracle operation" in Al Hirshberg's 1952 *Saturday Evening Post* profile and also in Part 2 of his *Saturday Evening Post* autobiography, "They Said I'd Get Murdered." I discovered more details, including reports on the surgery and the doctor's name (Tom Taketa), in Rocky's army medical records. I spoke to Taketa's son, Dr. John Taketa, who told me about his father's background and how his father's parents were sent to an internment camp during the war.

Chapter 3: Rocky Mack

The May 1950 trial in Gene Caggiano's lawsuit against Rocky provided a wealth of information about Rocky's boxing and baseball activities from his army discharge at the end of 1946 to his decision to turn pro in the summer of 1948. Among the witnesses who testified were Rocky, Caggiano, Allie Colombo, Charley Goldman, and Rocky's parents and uncle. They described his early training methods, his fight as Rocky Mack in Holyoke, his tryout with the Chicago Cubs, his triumph in the Lowell Golden Gloves, his controversial loss to Coley Wallace in New York, and the growing friction between Rocky and Caggiano.

Rocky gives a lengthy description of the Rocky Mack fight in his *Saturday Evening Post* autobiographical series. Hirshberg's 1952 *Saturday Evening Post* profile, "Can Any Man Living Beat Him?," also discusses the fight, and Russell Sullivan offers a good account in his biography *Rocky Marciano: The Rock of His Times.* The *Holyoke Transcript-Telegram* covered the fight, and the Holyoke Public Library has files on the history of the Valley Arena, including a remarkable scrapbook of its wrestling shows. I interviewed George Desgres, who attended fights at the Valley Arena, and Charles Della Penna, an ex-fighter who was friends with Rocky's opponent Les Epperson and recalled Epperson's account of the fight. I also interviewed retired *Springfield Republican* writer Michael J. Burke, who wrote about the Holyoke fight scene, and P. J. Moynihan, whose 2004 documentary *Fight Town* offers an absorbing look at Holyoke's sporting history.

Rocky often talked to writers about his love of baseball and his tryout with the Chicago Cubs. I also spoke to Sonny and Peter Marciano and John Sylvester, whose brother, Eugene, tried out with Rocky in North Carolina. Rocky's friend Red Gormley, who also tried out with him, talked to W. C. Heinz about it for his 1954 *Cosmopolitan* article "Brockton's Boy," and also to Rocky's biographer Skehan. The tryout is also described in the *Life* interview notes. An October 7, 2015, article by Dan Trigoboff, "Rocky Marciano's Fayetteville Ties," in the local magazine *CityView*, provides additional details about his tryout.

Sonny Marciano described Rocky's training regimen and sneaking out of the house to train so his mother wouldn't know he was fighting.

Rocky's courtship of Barbara Cousins is described by Rocky in Part 1 of his autobiographical *Saturday Evening Post* series, "Why I Retired," and by Barbara in a June 20, 1956, *New York Daily Mirror* story and a first-person story, "Every Time the Bell Rings . . . I Pray!," that Barbara wrote for the *Washington Post* on June 13, 1954.

The *Lowell Sun* and *Brockton Enterprise* covered the New England Golden Gloves tournament that Rocky won in 1947 and his controversial loss to Coley Wallace in New York. A January 16, 2006, *Lowell Sun* feature by Carnine Frongillo described the tournament's history and atmosphere, including Arthur Fiedler's ringside presence and Rocky's participation. Rocky talked about the Wallace fight in several interviews later in life, including a *Sports Illustrated* story, "Rocky Calls It Skulduggery" on January 25, 1965. Eddie Egan and Pete Mello are quoted that they believed Rocky beat Wallace in a September 30, 1952, *Chicago Tribune* story by Wilfrid Smith.

Testimony in the Caggiano lawsuit details Gene Caggiano's falling-out with Rocky and Rocky's decision to turn pro. Rocky told the story of getting fired by the gas company, and later offering his old boss ringside seats for doing him that favor, in a July 22, 1968, story by Robert Markus in the *Chicago Tribune*.

Chapter 4: Suzie Q's Broadway Debut

Rocky's trip to New York with Allie Colombo to meet Al Weill and Charley Goldman for the first time is a story that has been told by the participants in numerous interviews that I came across. The meeting is described in detail in testimony in the Caggiano lawsuit, the *Life* interview notes, Al Hirshberg's 1952 *Saturday Evening Post* profile, and Rocky's autobiographical *Saturday Evening Post* series. Another good account comes in the chapter on Charley Goldman in Ronald Fried's book *Corner Men: Great Boxing Trainers*. Sonny and Peter Marciano also were familiar with the story, having heard it from Rocky and their uncle Mike, who drove him to New York.

Weill and Goldman were two of the most colorful characters in boxing, and much has been written about them. Three good profiles of Weill were Dan Parker's "The Westkit King, Al Weill," in *Boxing Illustrated* in 1940, Meyer Ackerman's "Brains Behind the Brawn," in *Ring* magazine in March 1941, and Eddie Borden's "From the Manager of the Year 1952 . . . to the Forgotten Man of Boxing—Al Weill," in *Boxing & Wrestling*

Annual, 1953. His son Marty Weill wrote "Al Weill, My Father" in *Ring* in 1970. Four good profiles of Goldman were "Fight Trainer" in *Life* in 1951, Jersey Jones's "Big Little Guy" in *Ring* in 1953, Frank Graham's "The Man Behind the Champ" in *Sport* in 1953, and Mike Casey's "Charley and the Talent Factory," on Boxing.com in 2012. Robert Fried's *Corner Men* also provides excellent background on Goldman's own boxing career and his training methods. Goldman had a ghostwritten series, with Lester Bromberg, about training Rocky in the *New York World-Telegram & Sun* in September 1953. I obtained newspaper stories and photos documenting Goldman's boxing career in the early 1900s from the Boxing Hall of Fame. Two invaluable resources describing boxing's outlaw years in the early 1900s in New York were Jeffrey Sammons's book *Beyond the Ring* and "In the Ring and Out: Professional Boxing in New York, 1896–1920," by Steven A. Riess, which appears as a chapter in the 1985 book *Sport in America: New Historical Perspectives*. Another good book about boxing when Goldman and Weill came of age is Allen Bodner's *When Boxing Was a Jewish Sport*.

Chapter 5: Timmmberrr!

I worked for thirty years as a reporter for the *Providence Journal* and drew on my extensive knowledge of the city's history, sports tradition, and mob culture for this chapter. Among the people I interviewed with knowledge of Rocky's time in Providence were Richard Acetta, Bernie Buonanno, Sharkey Buonanno, Smokey Cerrone, Robert Craven, George Patrick Duffy, Ed Iannuccilli, Lou Marciano (no relation), Tom McDonough, and Clark Sammartino. I also read FBI files on New England mob boss Raymond Patriarca, who frequented the fights and controlled the bookies at the Rhode Island Auditorium. Sonny and Peter Marciano, Duna Cappiello, and Armond Colombo told me about Rocky's fights in Providence and the atmosphere there.

Numerous stories about Charley Goldman, including those cited in the previous chapter's notes, described how he worked to develop Rocky as a fighter without curbing his natural strengths. I interviewed Lou Duva, who was close to Goldman and met Rocky and observed how they trained. Rocky described their relationship in his autobiographical series in the *Saturday Evening Post* and talked about how he and Allie Colombo hitched rides on produce trucks to New York to train and about life in New York then. One story involved how he and Allie saw Willie Pep walking down Broadway and followed him. Nick Sylvester spoke in the ESPN transcripts about working out with Rocky in Brockton and being with him in New York during this time. Testimony from the Caggiano lawsuit also provides details of Rocky's life in New York.

I read the *Providence Journal*'s extensive coverage of Rocky, who fought twenty-eight times in Providence from July 1948 to May 1952, as well as stories in the *Brockton Enterprise*. I interviewed New York congressman Gregory Meeks, whose father Jimmy Meeks (incorrectly spelled "Weeks" on the program) fought Rocky. I also interviewed Joe Dominic's friend Charles Della Penna. Another resource was the work of *New Yorker* writer A. J. Liebling, who worked for the *Providence Journal* early in his career and wrote nostalgically about the local fight scene, most notably in his 1953 *New Yorker* story "The Boy from South Main Street," about Providence fighter George Araujo, which is contained in Liebling's book *The Sweet Science*.

Bernie and Vincent Buonanno told me about Rocky's fight with Bill Wirtz at their grandfather's Providence restaurant. Wirtz mentioned the fight in interviews he did in the years prior to his death in 2007. I interviewed his son Rocky Wirtz, the current owner of the Chicago Blackhawks, who told me the story as his parents had told it to him, including the fact that James Norris had to come to Providence to get Bill Wirtz out of jail.

Allie Colombo talked about Rocky's back pain and the Peter Louthis fight in a November 24, 1965, *Boston Globe* story by Will McDonough. Rocky also described it in Part 1 of his autobiographical *Saturday Evening Post* series, "Why I Retired."

Harry Haft, who died in 2007, told his story to his son, Alan Scott Haft, including the allegations that he had been threatened in his dressing room before his fight with Rocky. His son later wrote a book, *Harry Haft*, about his father's life and the fight. I interviewed Alan Haft.

Tiger Ted Lowry, who died in 2010, wrote a memoir, *God's in My Corner*, that chronicled his life and career, including the pressure he faced in other fights to deliberately lose. But he didn't address whether he took a dive against Rocky. I interviewed Robert Craven, a Rhode Island state legislator and former state prosecutor, who is the son of the late Providence firefighter Richard Craven. Richard Craven was working at the arena that night and described to his son his dressing-room encounter with Lowry after the fight, in which Craven asked in disgust why he threw the fight and Lowry replied that he had to feed his family. *Providence Journal* reporter Angelo Cataldi wrote a story on October 24, 1982, "The Night Tiger Ted Beat Rocky, the Night Rocky Beat Tiger Ted," that quoted an unnamed Rhode Island boxing official who said he witnessed a representative of Weill's telling Lowry that Rocky had to win the fight. I interviewed Cataldi, now a sports radio talk-show host in Philadelphia. Cataldi told me that the boxing official was Patsy Apice, who died in 1994. I spoke to Apice's daughter, Lorraine Luzier, who shared clippings of her father's involvement with boxing in Rhode Island but said that he never told her about the Lowry-Marciano fight. When Cataldi asked Lowry if he threw the fight, Lowry refused to say what happened and said he never would, because Rocky wasn't there to defend himself. "I can remember his face when I confronted him about the fix, and he never made eye contact," Cataldi wrote me in an e-mail. "He looked down the whole time, embarrassed. In his own way, he was confirming the story, as his on-the-record refusal to discuss what really happened also revealed. There's no doubt the fight was fixed, and Patsy was there to witness the order to Tiger Ted to stop fighting after the fourth round." Cataldi said that many readers were angry with him over the story, including his father; they felt that Cataldi had betrayed his Italian heritage.

Rocky's family disputes the notion that Lowry threw the fight. They blame Lowry for running away from Rocky and refusing to fight. Regardless of what happened, there's no evidence that Rocky knew.

Chapter 6: A Good Dream and a Hard Fall

Two *Saturday Evening Post* stories chronicle the brutal Vingo-Marciano fight and the tense vigil that followed as Vingo lay near death in the hospital: "The Worst Experience of My Life," Part 3 of Rocky's autobiographical series in 1956 and Vingo's first-person "I Was Slaughtered to Please a Crowd," on January 12, 1952. Jimmy Cannon wrote a column in the January 13, 1950, *New York Post* about his hospital visit with Vingo. I also read the extensive newspaper coverage of the fight. I interviewed

Peter Marciano about the fight. Sonny Marciano spoke about the fight in the ESPN transcripts.

Rocky and Charley Goldman described what it felt like when Vingo punched him and made him nearly black out in an interview with the *New York Post*'s Milton Gross for a September 12, 1952, column.

Blinky Palermo and "Poor Richards" are featured in a March 15, 1978, *New York Times* column by Red Smith, "Blinky Is More Sad Than Angry."

Ira Berkow's account of Vingo's life as a night watchman in January 1971, his troubled life, and his wife's bitterness toward Rocky is contained in a 1975 book of Berkow's newspaper stories, *Beyond the Dream*.

Chapter 7: The Octopus

Rocky describes his first meeting with Frankie Carbo in Part 5 of his autobiographical *Saturday Evening Post* series, "He Ran My Life." In the same story, he recounts being summoned to Al Weill's office to sign a new secret contract after Weill was named matchmaker for the International Boxing Club, and Weill scolding him about who should get credit for lining up his fights. Nick Sylvester and Izzy Gold spoke in the ESPN transcripts about Weill's mistreatment of Rocky.

I obtained Frank Carbo's extensive FBI file documenting his long criminal career and control of boxing. The files also detailed Weill's ties to Carbo and identified Rocky as one of the fighters controlled by Carbo. I read transcripts of congressional hearings into the Mafia's control of boxing. I also obtained the FBI file on the IBC chairman James Norris, which documented his ties to mobsters associated with Al Capone.

The history of boxing and the Mafia is treated in several books. The 1920s, the 1930s, and the rise of Mike Jacobs are well covered in Jeffrey T. Sammons's *Beyond the Ring*, David Margolick's *Beyond Glory*, Kevin Mitchell's *Jacobs Beach*, and Jimmy Breslin's *Damon Runyon: A Life*. The formation of the International Boxing Club was well covered by newspapers and magazines and dissected in criminal investigations and congressional hearings. Barney Nagler's *James Norris and the Decline of Boxing* is an excellent overview of the IBC's rise and fall. IBC official Truman Gibson discusses his role in creating the IBC in his memoir *Knocking Down Barriers*. The April 23, 1956, *Sports Illustrated* article "The Case Against the IBC," by Martin Kane, also provides an overview of how the

IBC operated and exemplifies the aggressive investigative reporting that *Sports Illustrated* did on corruption in boxing.

The exchange between Rocky and Weill about whether he should fight Roland LaStarza is contained in Part 5 of Rocky's autobiographical *Saturday Evening Post* series, "He Ran My Life." Starting with his first LaStarza fight, Rocky's New York fights began to attract widespread press coverage, which I drew on in telling the story of this pivotal fight. "He's Mad at the Champ," a W. C. Heinz profile of LaStarza in the September 19, 1953, *Saturday Evening Post*, provided good background on Rocky's early rival. Sam Silverman described his exchange with Weill over making the LaStarza-Marciano match in Skehan's biography, *Rocky Marciano: Biography of a First Son*.

Charley Goldman's comments that he was afraid Rocky would lose to LaStarza are in Al Hirshberg's September 20, 1952, *Saturday Evening Post* story "Can Any Man Living Beat Him?" Rocky's comments about being "keyed up" before the LaStarza fight after nearly killing Carmine Vingo appear in a June 15, 1954, Milton Gross column in the *New York Post*. Wilfrid Diamond describes LaStarza's angry manager slamming the dressing room door in Weill's face after the fight in his 1955 book *This Guy Marciano*. Norris's letter to Madison Square Garden saying that the LaStarza-Marciano fight had been a financial success is contained in Nagler's *James Norris and the Decline of Boxing*.

Look magazine sports editor Tim Cohane, who was friends with Rocky, wrote about Carbo owning 10 percent of the fighter in his book *Bypaths of Glory*.

Chapter 8: Requiem for a Heavyweight

Charley Goldman's comments about Rocky's performance in the LaStarza fight appeared in Al Hirshberg's September 20, 1952, *Saturday Evening Post* profile. Rocky's remarks about the win convincing him he could win the title were in a *New York Post* column by Milton Gross.

The account of the trial in the Caggiano lawsuit is based on the transcript of the testimony. The information that Allie Colombo was so nervous he developed a nosebleed was mentioned in the 1952 *Life* interview notes.

The descriptions of the Eatman, Buonvino, and Shkor fights are based on newspaper accounts. Sam Silverman told Skehan the story of Shkor's manager Johnny Buckley, including his false teeth flying out of his mouth. The description of the second Tiger Ted Lowry fight, including Lowry's quotes, comes from newspaper accounts in the *Providence Journal* and *Brockton Enterprise*.

Rocky recalled Weill finally giving him permission to get married in Part 5 of his autobiographical *Saturday Evening Post* series, "He Ran My Life." Nicky Sylvester recalled Rocky's wedding in the ESPN transcripts and in interviews with Skehan. Weill's controversial wedding toast is recounted in several places, including my interviews with Peter and Sonny Marciano, and Rocky's autobiographical *Saturday Evening Post* series, which also describes the honeymoon and how Weill summoned him back to New York early on boxing business.

The Keene Simmons fight description is based on newspaper accounts and is also referred to in a February 12, 1951, *Life* magazine photo essay on Goldman, "Fight Trainer." I also interviewed Sharkey Buonanno, son of the referee who chose not to stop the fight despite Rocky's severe bleeding. Silverman's comments were in Skehan's biography.

The account of the Rex Layne fight is based on numerous newspaper accounts, my own viewing of a videotape of the fight, Rocky's recollections to Hirshberg in the 1952 *Saturday Evening Post* profile, and his autobiographical series in the *Saturday Evening Post*. I also interviewed Sonny and Peter Marciano. The victory parade in Brockton was described in stories in the *New York World-Telegram & Sun*, the *Boston Globe*, and the *Brockton Enterprise*.

Izzy Gold, in the ESPN transcripts, recalled listening with Rocky to Joe Louis's victory over Max Schmeling on the radio at the Brockton Fair. Goldman, in a first-person series written with Lester Bromberg, "How a Champ Is Made," recalled the debate within Rocky's camp about whether it was the right time to fight Louis. Rocky talks in his autobiographical *Saturday Evening Post* series about wanting to fight Louis earlier in his career in an exhibition fight. Sonny Marciano told me about asking Rocky whether he could beat Louis, and Rocky admonishing his brother never to doubt him. Rocky confessed in his *Saturday Evening Post* autobiography that he was privately concerned about Louis.

Much has been written about Louis. I relied on contemporary newspaper and magazine accounts and books for Louis's background and the buildup to the fight, most notably Nagler's *James Norris and the Decline of Boxing*, Randy Roberts's *Joe Louis*, and David Margolick's *Beyond Glory*. Louis's animosity toward Al Weill is described in Tim Cohane's *Bypaths of Glory* and in Joe Bostic's October 27, 1951, *Amsterdam News* story "Hot Feud with Al Weill Spurs Louis vs. the Rock." *Washington Post* columnist Shirley Povich described the scene in which Weill and Goldman wake Rocky in his hotel before the Louis fight in a September 14, 1954, column.

Liebling wrote an article about the fight for the *New Yorker* on November 17, 1951, "Broken Fighter Arrives," contained in his book *The Sweet Science*, that included a visit to Rocky's training camp and the description of the former champ Abe Attell watching Rocky spar. I relied on extensive newspaper and magazine coverage of the fight, watched the film, and interviewed Sonny and Peter Marciano and Duna Cappiello, who attended. Rocky's recollection of fans being upset at him for beating Louis, including the woman throwing a bottle into the ring, was told to Joe Falls in 1966 and published in a *Sporting News* column, "Of Rocky and a Father-in-Law," on September 13, 1969. He also talked about the upset woman in a July 22, 1968, *Chicago Tribune* story by Robert Markus, "Life for Marciano Anything but Rocky."

Red Smith described Louis in his dressing room after the fight in his classic October 27, 1951, *New York Herald Tribune* column, "Night for Joe Louis."

Chapter 9: Twelve Inches to Glory

Rocky talked about having his father retire after the Louis fight in his autobiographical series in the *Saturday Evening Post* and also in several newspaper interviews. His family talked about it in interviews with me, and also in the *Life* interview notes.

Rob Sneddon's 2016 book *The Phantom Punch*, about the second Ali-Liston fight in Lewiston, Maine, contains a detailed account of Rocky's controversial exhibition tour in Maine. I also read several newspaper stories about it and interviewed Sonny Marciano, Rocky's "opponent" on the tour. Rocky talked about it in his autobiographical *Saturday Evening Post* series.

The Savold fight was documented in newspaper and magazine stories. Rocky also spoke often about it as one of his worst fights.

Jack Hurley's buildup of Kid Matthews is chronicled in many stories, including "Rocky Is Guy Hurley Wants for Matthews," by Red Smith in the February 26, 1952, *New York Herald Tribune*, and "Jack Hurley and His Tiger," by Arthur Daley in the July 14, 1952, *New York Times*. Also, *Sports Illustrated* published a two-part profile of Hurley by Jack Olsen, "Don't Call Me Honest" and "Fifty Percent of Harry," in the issues of May 15 and May 22, 1961. Two in-depth looks at Matthews and Hurley and the Marciano fight can be found in the August 2, 2011, *Sportspress Northwest* story "Wayback Machine: Jack Hurley and Kid Matthews," by David Eskenazi and Steve Rudman, and Charles Burgess's "Harry 'Kid' Matthews: A Sports Celebrity with Substance," in the summer 2013 issue of *Columbia: The Magazine of Northwest History*. Matthews's co-trainer George Chemeres told Burgess how he and Hurley put lead in the fighter's shoes at the prefight weigh-in.

The story of how James Norris enlisted Frankie Carbo to pressure Al Weill to match Rocky against Matthews is contained in Norris's testimony on December 8, 1960, to the U.S. Senate Subcommittee on Antitrust and Monopoly during its investigation of boxing. Barney Nagler also described it in his book *James Norris and the Decline of Boxing*. Contemporary news accounts exhaustively covered the Matthews fight and its buildup. I watched the film of the fight.

Numerous newspaper and magazine stories provided the story of Jersey Joe Walcott's life and career, and his relationship with Felix Bocchicchio. The *Chicago Tribune*'s Frank Mastro wrote a series on Walcott's life in December 1947, after his controversial loss to Joe Louis. The *New York Daily News*' Gene Ward and *Washington Post*'s Dave Brady each wrote a series about Walcott's life in the summer of 1951, after he won the title. There also is an excellent biography by James Curl, *Jersey Joe Walcott: A Boxing Biography*. News stories documented Bocchicchio's criminal record, as did a May 26, 1952, *Life* magazine story, "My Rugged Education in Boxing," by New York boxing commissioner Robert K. Christenberry.

Rocky described his prefight dreams of fighting Walcott to the *New York Herald Tribune*'s Red Smith in a September 12, 1952, column, "Rocky Would Like This."

I interviewed Sonny and Peter Marciano, Duna Cappiello, and Charlie Ball, who were all at the Walcott-Marciano fight. The Marciano brothers and Nick Sylvester described their experiences at the fight in the ESPN transcripts. I watched the tape of the fight, in which referee Charley Daggert's prefight instructions are audible, and read numerous newspaper and magazine accounts. Rocky devotes an article to the fight, "Dirty Work at Ringside," Part 4 in his autobiographical *Saturday Evening Post* series, including his suspicions that Bocchicchio tried to blind him. A. J. Liebling wrote a rich account of the fight, "New Champ," for the *New Yorker* that appears in his book *The Sweet Science*. Jimmy Breslin described Freddie Brown's advice to Rocky in his corner when he was blinded to Russell Sullivan in *Rocky Marciano: The Rock of His Times*. Sonny Marciano and Duna Cappiello told me about the postfight celebration, including getting Humphrey Bogart into Rocky's dressing room. Lena Marciano recalled her usual church vigil back in Brockton and her premonition to light thirteen candles before the fight in *Rocky Marciano: The 13th Candle*. Betty Colombo, Donna Thoreson, and Robert Langway told me about Rocky giving his sisters his bloody glove in his dressing room after the fight.

Chapter 10: The Lion and the Lamb

The account of Rocky's sisters taking the glove back to Brockton and being stopped by the police in Connecticut is based on my interviews with Betty Colombo and Concetta's children Robert Langway and Donna Thoreson.

The anecdote about Rocky's visit to Lawrence, Massachusetts, is related in "A Shave for Marciano," an editor's note in the September 20, 1952, *Saturday Evening Post* that accompanied Al Hirshberg's profile, "Can Any Man Beat Him?"

The scene when Rocky kneels outside the stadium in Philadelphia the morning of the fight is described in Skehan's biography, as is Allie Colombo's description of being with Rocky in their Philadelphia hotel after the fight. Rocky recalled the victory party, including the gamblers carrying the suitcase of money, in his autobiographical *Saturday Evening Post* series. Nick Sylvester described their early morning walk in Philadelphia in the ESPN transcripts.

Rocky spoke frequently in interviews about the impact of being the heavyweight champion. He described waking up in his Philadelphia hotel the morning after the fight in a May 13, 1955, *Collier's* article, "How It Feels to Be Champion of the World." In the same article, he also described his meeting with President Eisenhower. Rocky went into depth in his autobiographical *Saturday Evening Post* series, including recalling his conversation with Jerry Lewis, who called him "the boss of the world," and his visit to a leper colony in the Philippines. Rocky also talked about taking etiquette lessons after his luncheon with Cardinal Spellman and his efforts to expand his vocabulary. Lena described the trip to Italy that Rocky sent his parents on in *Rocky Marciano: The 13th Candle*, as did his sister Betty, who accompanied them, in an interview with me.

I read several newspaper stories about Rocky's training camp for his second fight against Jersey Joe Walcott, and about the fight itself, and I also watched the film. The coverage closely examined the controversial first-round knockout and whether Walcott had received a fair count before being ruled out. The story of Rocky getting bitten by a dog during training camp in Michigan is told in a September 2, 1969, column by the *Chicago Tribune*'s David Condon. Another Condon column, on September 4, 1969, quotes the former International Boxing Club representative Ben Bentley on how Bob Hope missed Rocky's knockout of Walcott.

Sonny and Peter Marciano told me about Rocky's sensitivity to Roland LaStarza's comments before their second fight about Rocky becoming "punchy" because of his wild fighting style. I also interviewed Rocky's friend Smokey Cerrone, who joked about it with Rocky before the fight, and the sportswriter Murray Olderman, who discussed it with him while sharing a cab after the fight. Besides reading the news coverage of the fight, I watched a film of the fight that aired on Rocky's 1960s television show *Main Event*, with Rocky providing commentary. Nick Sylvester spoke in the ESPN transcripts of Rocky's regrets about beating up on LaStarza, and Peter Marciano told me that Rocky felt bad about it. The LaStarza prefight comments that Rocky found upsetting appeared in W. C. Heinz's September 19, 1953, *Saturday Evening Post* profile of LaStarza, "He's Mad at the Champ." Rocky admitted that LaStarza's comments had irritated him in a September 13, 1953, *New York Times* column by Arthur Daley, "A Soft-Hearted Guy." LaStarza's postfight apology to Rocky is described in Arch Ward's *Chicago Tribune* column, "In the Wake of the News," on September 26, 1953. A good in-depth look at Rocky during this period is the September 20, 1953, *New York Times Magazine* profile, "A Lamb in Lion's Clothing," by Harvey Breit.

I consulted several good profiles of Ezzard Charles, including W. C. Heinz's "The Strange Case of Ezzard Charles" in the *Saturday Evening*

Post and "The Haunting of Ezzard Charles," by Clarence George, published by Boxing.com on February 20, 2013. In the training camp scene in which Rocky talks about missing his family, Charley Goldman talks about how hard Rocky trains, and Goldman's bet with Rocky over not smoking was captured in a June 6, 1954, column by Arthur Daley in the *New York Times*, "Visit with the Champion." I read the news coverage and watched the film of the fight itself.

Chapter 11: The Mongoose and the Mob

The *New York Post*'s Milton Gross wrote a September 9, 1954, column, "Speaking Out," describing the more relaxed atmosphere at Rocky's training camp prior to his rematch with Ezzard Charles, including Barbara and Mary Anne staying at Grossinger's. Jimmy Cannon's September 6, 1954, *New York Post* column told the story of Tiger Louis, the eccentric fan from Tennessee who came to camp and wanted to spar with Rocky. The *New York Journal-American*'s Frank Graham wrote a September 13, 1954, column, "Close-Up of a Champion," that described Rocky's visit with Budd Schulberg and Roger Donoghue from *On the Waterfront*. Sonny Marciano told me about Schulberg and Elia Kazan talking to Rocky about a movie of his life.

Among the many news accounts of the second Marciano-Charles fight I read, a particularly good one is Budd Schulberg's "Rematch Is No Match," from the September 27, 1954, issue of *Sports Illustrated*. I also watched the film of the fight. The description of Charles in his dressing room after the fight comes from another story in the same issue of *Sports Illustrated*. Ring doctor Alexander Schiff's comments about how close he came to stopping the fight appeared in a sidebar to Lester Bromberg's December 1954 *National Police Gazette* story, "There's Danger Ahead for Rocky Marciano."

Sonny and Peter Marciano and Duna Cappiello spoke to me about Rocky's growing interest in quitting and his conflicts with Al Weill, including his anger over Sonny and Duna coming into the cottage at Grossinger's late one night and how Weill would scalp their complimentary tickets to Rocky's fights. Rocky, in Part 5 of his autobiographical *Saturday Evening Post* series, "He Ran My Life," focused on his deteriorating relationship with Weill, including the time Weill scolded him over who had gotten him the second LaStarza fight and how Weill always took the best hotel room when they traveled together. Rocky also talked about his growing unhappiness at being away from his family and his recurring back pain, which he had concealed from Weill. Nick Sylvester, in the ESPN transcripts, talked about tensions with Weill, including how the manager accused Sylvester of stealing some fight tickets. Lena Marchegiano's conversations with Rocky about not spending enough time with his family appear in *Rocky Marciano: The 13th Candle*. Peter and Sonny Marciano talked to me about Rocky's worries about money and his frugality. The *Washington Post*'s Shirley Povich, in a September 7, 1969, column, recalled Rocky's frugality and returning to the arena to fetch a pair of socks he left behind.

An internal *Sports Illustrated* reporter's memo of February 17, 1955, described Rocky's photo-op winter workout at Grossinger's to test his new, surgically repaired nose. There were many entertaining news accounts of Rocky's fight with Don Cockell, the Battersea Butterball. Two notable examples are Jimmy Cannon's February 20, 1955, *New York Post* column, "Weill's Sure-Thing Craftiness Harms Rocky's Popularity," and Red Smith's May 13, 1955, *New York Herald Tribune* story, "Cockell's Training Camp Far Cry from Sussex Pub." Cockell's use of a London natural healer was reported in a March 24, 1955, Associated Press story. Desmond Hackett, sports editor of the *London Daily Express*, wrote a syndicated story for U.S. newspapers on May 16, 1955, that quoted the San Francisco police detective preparing for unsavory elements to attend the fight; Hackett also watched Rocky spar and described him as "an evil, ruthless man."

Rocky's friend Ed Napoli and Rocky's daughter Mary Anne told Skehan about the alleged attempt to bribe Rocky to throw the Cockell fight.

I found a confidential memo written on November 27, 1956, by Federal Bureau of Narcotics agent Howard W. Chappell to his supervisor describing the 1955 encounter that Lanza and Rocky had with mobster Thomas Lucchese and two henchmen at Lanza's house in Beverly Hills. Chappell, who was investigating Mafia infiltration of Hollywood, heard the story from an informant and then from Lanza's business manager. On November 21, 1956, Chappell and another agent visited Lanza at his home and interviewed him. Lanza was "very cooperative" and told them the story of

Lucchese's visit. Sonny Marciano told me that he was aware of the encounter. Terry Robinson, who was Lanza's friend and trainer, also talks about it in his 1980 book with Raymond Strait, *Lanza: His Tragic Life*.

A June 8, 1955, story by the syndicated Hollywood columnist Sheilah Graham said that Rocky was in town touring Los Angeles nightclubs but spending most of his time with his close friend Mario Lanza, who was trying to get him a small role in his movie *Serenade*. The Associated Press's Hollywood Scene columnist Bob Thomas toured Mario Lanza's mansion in October 1954, saw Lanza's boxing ring, and wrote a column, "Hollywood Scene," that mentioned the tenor's friendship and sparring sessions with Rocky. Rocky talked about their friendship in his autobiographical *Saturday Evening Post* series, and Lena Marchegiano described it in *Rocky Marciano: The 13th Candle*.

Rocky described his New York restaurant encounter with Frankie Carbo in his autobiographical *Saturday Evening Post* series. Newspaper stories about the California and New York boxing probes, and Barney Nagler's *James Norris and the Decline of Boxing*, chronicle the story of how Al Weill skimmed $10,000 from the box-office receipts of the Marciano-Cockell fight.

Archie Moore's colorful life is detailed in his autobiography *Any Boy Can*, in Mike Fitzgerald's *The Ageless Warrior*, and in W. C. Heinz's September 17, 1955, *Saturday Evening Post* profile, "The Mystery of Archie Moore." Herbert Brean's July 18, 1955, *Life* magazine story, "A Fighting Man Who Is a Writing Man Too," focused on Moore's public-relations campaign to get Rocky into the ring; it also includes the lyrics to the jazz song that Moore wrote. *Sports Illustrated* published Budd Schulberg's assessment of Moore's career on July 4, 1955, in "After Disposing of Most of the Heavyweight Contenders, Archie Moore Licks a Middleweight and Thus Earns a Shot at the Title," and a conversation with Archie Moore in which he analyzed his style and fight strategy, in Ezra Bowen and Martin Kane's "How's Marciano Gonna Hit Me?" on September 19, 1955. Moore looked back on his life, and his fight against Rocky, in "Up Against the Ghetto and the Freeway: Keep Fighting the Good Fight, Archie Moore," by Shirley Streshinsky in the February 20, 1972, *Los Angeles Times*. The colorful details of Moore's training camp in North Adams are captured in Gilbert Millstein's September 11, 1955, *New York Times Magazine* story, "In This Corner, at Long Last, Archie Moore!" Russell Sullivan mentioned Moore's Williams College music lecture in his biography *Rocky Marciano: The Rock of His Times.*

The *New York Times*' Joseph C. Nichols wrote a September 17, 1955, story, "Marciano Enjoys Day of Rest: Yankees' Players Perform at Camp," about the New York Yankees players who visited Rocky at Grossinger's. Rocky reflected on his possible retirement in a conversation at Grossinger's with *New York Daily News* columnist Gene Ward, who wrote about it on August 3, 1955, in his column, "Inside Sports." Rocky's conversation with the *Chicago Tribune*'s David Condon about possibly quitting, including the comments from Al Weill and Charley Goldman, was described in Condon's September 2, 1969, column, "In the Wake of the News." Murray Olderman and Smokey Cerrone told me about their conversations with Rocky about his evolution as a boxer. Rocky's quote, "Some day this ship's gonna reach port," about his entourage, was recalled by the International Boxing Club's Ben Bentley in David Condon's September 4, 1969, *Chicago Tribune* column, "In the Wake of the News."

A. J. Liebling's October 10, 1955, *New Yorker* story, "Ahab and Nemesis," contained in his book *The Sweet Science*, is an excellent account of the fight, as is Budd Schulberg's October 3, 1955, *Sports Illustrated* story, "A Champion Proves His Greatness." Of the many newspaper stories I read, none made a big deal of referee Harvey Kessler's mistake in starting a mandatory eight-count after Moore knocked Rocky down in the second round. The closest is a reference near the end of a story the day after the fight by the *New York Times*' Joseph Nichols, "Undefeated Marciano Wants 50th Victory Before He Retires from Boxing." Nichols wrote that Kessler, "for no ascertainable reason," continued counting to five even though Rocky had risen at the count of two. Moore, who seemed cheerful in his postfight remarks, doesn't complain about Kessler, either, saying only that he, Moore, may have erred in not taking advantage of Rocky's momentary fogginess to finish him off. Years later, a bitter Moore changed his story in a September 19, 1985, *Washington Post* article by John Ed Bradley, "For Moore, Close Didn't Count; 30 Years Haven't Lessened Pain for Marciano's Rival." Moore claims in the story that Kessler takes another six seconds, pulling Rocky's gloves and snapping his head back. But I reviewed the film of the fight, and that didn't happen. (Ironically, Kessler can be heard on the film, during his prefight instructions, reminding the fighters that there is no mandatory eight-count because it's a championship fight.) A shorter item in Schulberg's "A Champion Proves His Greatness," titled "After the Fight," describes Moore's post-fight trip to the Greenwich Village jazz club.

Peter Marciano told me that Rocky discovered that Al Weill had cheated him by billing phantom expenses to his fights and by selling tickets to the Moore fight and pocketing the money.

Rocky's conversation with Charley Goldman in which he says he's stopped taking walks and Goldman knew he wouldn't fight again is recounted in notes of an interview with *Sports Illustrated* stringer John Hanlon, which I found in the magazine's archives. Rocky described his postfight conversations with his father and Al Weill about retiring, as well his trip to South America with Barbara that winter, in his auto-biographical *Saturday Evening Post* series.

Chapter 12: America's Guest

Rocky did not fade from the public eye when he retired. I read scores of news stories from 1956 to his death in 1969 that chronicled his travels, business ventures, public appearances, boxing commentary, flirtation with a comeback, life in Florida, and fluctuating weight. I also was granted access to the archives of *Sports Illustrated*, which contained memos from stringers detailing what Rocky was up to.

The opening scene at the Illinois racetrack was drawn from a July 30, 1957, *Sports Illustrated* memo that was boiled down to a short item published on August 12, 1957. Rocky's interview at Grossinger's the day after he retired was given to *Sports Illustrated*'s Joan Flynn Dreyspool for a May 7, 1956, story, "Subject: Rocky Marciano." For the same story, Dreyspool spent a few days following Rocky's mother, Lena, around New York as she hobnobbed with celebrities like Jackie Gleason at Toots Shor's. The *Washington Post*'s Shirley Povich reported on May 6, 1956, that Charles Finley was a financial adviser to Rocky.

A *Sports Illustrated* stringer wrote a March 20, 1956, memo detailing Rocky's trip to South America. An untitled January 2, 1958, *Coral Gables Times* story by Don Cuddy, which was sent to *Sports Illustrated* and which I found in the magazine's files, talked about Rocky's move to Florida and the new food company he was opening with James Cerniglia. *Sports Illustrated* memos in May 1958 described the expansion of the food company, including its investment in $250,000 worth of potato crops.

Donna Thoreson told me about Rocky flying her to Atlantic City for the music concert with Chubby Checker and Little Eva.

The story of Rocky eating ice cream with Ted Williams is from David Condon's September 4, 1969, *Chicago Tribune* column. Sonny Marciano and Duna Cappiello told me about Rocky's friendship with Williams.

Sonny, who accompanied Rocky to his meeting with James Norris in Coral Gables, described the meeting to me.

New York Times reporter Gay Talese wrote a story on January 12, 1957, "Marciano Seeks Career as Actor," in which he interviewed Rocky about his Hollywood aspirations, including his talks with studios about a possible sitcom where he would play a small-town sheriff. Sonny Marciano, who also appeared in the episode, told me about Rocky's appearance in Cuba in the television show *Captain David Grief*. Rocky's nightclub act was described in a memo by a *Sports Illustrated* stringer on March 12, 1957; the act, and Rocky's dispute with Al Weill over killing it, was discussed in "Rock, Weill Near Saturation Point," a March 25, 1957, *New York Daily Mirror* column by Harold Weissman, and a March 16, 1957, *New York World-Telegram & Sun* column by Joe Williams, "Weill Says He Wanted to Save Rocky's Dignity." *New York Post* columnist Earl Wilson accompanied Rocky on the set when he filmed his scenes for the Steve Allen movie *College Confidential* for a column that ran on March 3, 1960, "An Actor with a Punch."

Cerniglia and Rocky talked about his possible comeback, including Cerniglia's joke that he would run him over with his car if Rocky tried, in an April 29, 1958, *New York Post* story by Jimmy Cannon, "No Kind of Money." I interviewed Lou Duva about how Rocky came close to returning against Ingemar Johansson. Rocky talked in greater detail to the *Boston Globe*'s Will McDonough in a June 30, 1966, story about that attempted comeback, "Marciano Bares Aborted '59 Comeback." Rocky told the *New York Journal-American*'s Frank Graham about seeing Langford as a boy in Brockton, in a March 5, 1957, column, "Visit with Marciano." Rocky wrote a first-person story saying he was considering a comeback in the November 15, 1959, *Boston Globe*, "Marciano Eager to Fight Johansson." I interviewed Lou Duva about Rocky's comeback deliberations.

Dan Parker wrote an October 21, 1956, *New York Daily Mirror* column, "Weill Recovering from Jolt," in which he interviewed Al Weill about his decline following Rocky's retirement, including his management of a fighter named Jim Crow.

A *Sports Illustrated* stringer wrote a memo on September 5, 1961, describing Rocky's Las Vegas cocktail party to celebrate his thirty-eighth birthday and his new talk show, *Main Event*. I watched several episodes of the show, which ESPN later aired and can be found online. Sonny Marciano told me about Rocky being friendly with Marilyn Monroe. Everett Skehan describes his meeting with Monroe in his biography.

Mickey Walker described his conversation with Rocky about music and Strauss in his July 1955 *National Police Gazette* article, "The Rocky Marciano I Know."

Peter Marciano told me about Jackie Gleason asking Rocky to train him prior to filming *The Hustler*.

Several people, including Peter and Sonny Marciano, Robert Langway, Vincent Pereira, Lou Duva, and Smokey Cerrone, told me about Rocky's eccentricities involving money. Izzy Gold, Nick Sylvester, and Rocky's longtime accountant Frank Saccone also gave examples in the ESPN transcripts. William Nack's *Sports Illustrated* story "The Rock," on August 23, 1993, describes Rocky's enigmatic lifestyle in his final years. Family members talked with me about his marital problems and infidelity, and Saccone did so in the ESPN transcripts. Richie Paterniti's comments about Rocky's sexual appetites appeared in Nack's article. I interviewed former Massachusetts priest Bernie Sullivan about Rocky's charity work for the church and their travels together, including their visit to the Playboy Mansion. I interviewed Vincent Pereira about his times with Rocky, including driving him in Boston, borrowing money from his uncle to replace his lost ring, and their trip to Las Vegas to see Frank Sinatra. Saccone, in interviews with ESPN and for Nack's *Sports Illustrated* article, talked about Rocky's haphazard business dealings and the episode in Montreal where he refused to take a check and his roughing up of Brockton Eddie to collect a debt. Sonny Marciano told me about carrying cash for Rocky and Rocky scolding him for borrowing some without asking. Duva told me about holding the bag with $50,000 in cash for Rocky in a New York restaurant. Cerrone described to me how Rocky enlisted him to help collect a debt from the Florida businessman. An April 24, 1963, *New York Times* story described the New York Supreme Court ruling against Rocky in the civil suit by the writer Gene Schoor, who had accused Rocky of punching him. I also reviewed the court judgment.

Burt Reynolds tells the story of drinking with Rocky in the April 16, 2004, episode of *Dinner for Five*, a television series in which the actor/filmmaker Jon Favreau has dinner with different celebrities.

Izzy Gold, in the ESPN transcripts, described carrying suitcases of cash to Bernie Castro's bomb shelter in Florida. Rocky's daughter Mary Anne told *Sports Illustrated*'s Nack that he kept money there; Saccone also told Nack that Rocky stashed money with Castro. Vincent Pereira told me of visiting the bomb shelter with Rocky's mother. Peter Marciano told me he believed Rocky put money there.

I reviewed congressional testimony before Senator Estes Kefauver's subcommittee in the spring of 1961, including Rocky's, and I also interviewed Steve Acunto, who supported Rocky's efforts. Lou Duva told me about Rocky's relationship with Frankie Carbo, including the encounter in the New York restaurant. Robert Langway and Anthony Pereira told me about Carbo coming to dinner in Brockton.

Peter and Sonny Marciano told me about Rocky's desire to protect his reputation but also his fascination with mobsters. Sam Silverman told Skehan about traveling to Cuba with Rocky and Kid Gavilan to discuss the casino deal. Sonny Marciano told me that Rocky considered a casino deal before Fidel Castro's revolution. I obtained FBI records describing how Rocky sought advice from Angelo Bruno, through Steve Melchiore, regarding whether to invest in the Havana casino.

FBI records detailed Rocky's ties to New England mob boss Raymond Patriarca and the incident involving the stolen furs. In addition, Peter Marciano told me that they were friendly and that he gave a copy of Skehan's biography of Rocky to Patriarca in Providence in the 1970s. FBI records described Rocky's dealings with the mob in the Leisureland deal in Buffalo, the Coal Operators Casualty Company in Pennsylvania, and the New Frontier casino in Las Vegas. A May 9, 1963, *Sports Illustrated* memo quoted Rocky on the state of boxing and said that he made his remarks while in Buffalo promoting Leisureland. Another *Sports Illustrated* memo, from June 19, 1965, reported on Rocky's visit to Minneapolis as the vice president of the Coal Operators Casualty Co. and quoted Rocky saying that insurance was "high class" as he did push-ups in his hotel room. A November 1, 1965, *Wall Street Journal* story reported on the indictment of Peter Rugani. Robert Langway said that Rocky and Rugani were friends.

A September 19, 1966, FBI memo said that Rocky was a "close associate" of Cleveland loan shark Peter DiGravio. James Neff's book *Mobbed Up* provided background about DiGravio and how he was shot to death on the golf course. Frank Saccone said in the ESPN transcripts that Rocky invested more than $100,000 with DiGravio, and also spoke about the IRS audit. Saccone also talked to *Sports Illustrated*'s Nack. Sonny Marciano told me that Rocky was going to Cleveland to visit DiGravio, then got out of town after his murder to avoid any negative publicity. I obtained the FBI memo about Rocky and DiGravio written in response to a request from Lyndon Johnson's aide Mildred Stegall. I checked with the Lyndon Baines Johnson Library and Museum for any documents related to Stegall's request. But many files of Stegall, who dealt with a number of confidential matters, remain classified.

Chapter 13: The Fiftieth Fight

Lou Duva told me about his trip to Miami with Rocky and Joe Louis for the first Ali-Liston fight, and about Rocky's confrontation with Liston in the gym. I read Rocky's first-person story analyzing the fight in the February 26, 1964, *Brockton Enterprise*, "Unbelievable!—Rocky."

I interviewed Robert Langway and Vincent Pereira about Rocky's visits to Brockton and conversations with his mother and sisters about his lifestyle and how he envied them. Lena Marchegiano also talked about this in *Rocky Marciano: The 13th Candle*. Rocky's daughter, Mary Anne, told *Sports Illustrated*'s William Nack about her brother's adoption, and the suspicion that he was Rocky's biological child with another woman. Peter Marciano told me about visiting Rocky in the summer of 1969 and Rocky telling him that his son was his biological son.

The boxing dinner at which Goldman and Rocky paid tribute to each other was described by Ronald K. Fried in *Corner Men*. I interviewed Allie Colombo's daughter Cindy Colombo and read Rich Bergeron's February 22, 2010, "A Tribute to a True Hometown Hero: Allie Colombo," which ran on Bleacherreport.com.

Peter Marciano told me about Rocky's prison visit to the dying mob boss Vito Genovese, which is also recounted in Everett Skehan's biography. Peter also told me about his argument with his brother when Rocky was reluctant to attend Allie Colombo's funeral.

I interviewed Peter Marciano and Muhammad Ali's then wife Belinda, now Khalilah Ali, about Rocky's computer fight with Ali. Both were present for the filming in Miami, and both heard Rocky and Ali talking about trying to go into America's inner cities to preach racial harmony. I also read a long report by *Time* magazine correspondent Joseph Kane, which I found in the files of *Sports Illustrated*, that described what went on in the top-secret film sessions, including the two fighters' reluctance to be knocked down and their kidding around with each other. I also read several *Sports Illustrated* stories about the promoter, Murray Woroner, including a September 16, 1968, feature by William Johnson about his computerized sports shows, "And in This Corner . . . NCR 315."

Rocky's appearance at the new Madison Square Garden with Bob Hope, Jack Dempsey, and Gene Tunney was described in Arthur Daley's February 13, 1968, *New York Times* column "The Old and the New" and Donal Henahan's February 12, 1968, *New York Times* story, "Hope Tops Card at Garden No. 4."

Leo Ball's encounter with Rocky at the Copacabana in New York is described in Ball's unpublished memoir.

Several family members and friends described Rocky's harrowing exploits on small planes and their urging him not to take the risks. His daughter Mary Anne's story of the flight to Hawaii was in Nack's *Sports Illustrated* story. Ben Bentley described their scary flight to Grossinger's in David Condon's September 4, 1969, *Chicago Tribune* column, "In the Wake of the News."

Betty and Armond Colombo told me about the cookout at their house the day of Rocky's plane crash. I interviewed Peter and Sonny Marciano and Charlie Tartaglia about the crash and the funeral. Donna Thoreson told me about her reaction to Rocky's death and about his attendance at her wedding at West Point earlier that summer.

Time magazine ran the unbylined article "Is Boxing Sinful?" on June 18, 1956. The scene of Rocky in the London hotel room comes from "Gentle as a Rock," an interview with John Summers published in the *London Sunday Telegraph* on November 7, 1965.

Pierino Marchegiano's viewing of the Ali-Marciano computer fight at Boston Garden was described in *Rocky Marciano: The 13th Candle*. Peter and Sonny Marciano told me about going to a theater in California, and saying afterward that they needed to call Lena to tell her who won.

Epilogue: Ghosts

Don Dunphy's recollections are from his autobiography, *Don Dunphy at Ringside*. The Holmes-Spinks fight and Holmes's postfight comments about Rocky are described in contemporary news accounts and in Gavin Evans's book *Kings of the Ring*. Holmes also talked about Rocky in Alex Bloom's September 20, 2012, *Brockton Enterprise* article, "Larry Holmes on Rocky: 'The Man Was Tough.'"

The *Look* magazine article "How Great Was Marciano?" ran on October 16, 1956. The scientific test of Rocky's punch is described in a February 10, 1955, story, "Marciano's Fists Hit Harder Than Bullet from a .45," by Andy O'Brien in *Week-End Magazine*.

Lou Duva talked to me about Rocky's death and legacy. He described his dedication of Evander Holyfield's title to Rocky in the ESPN transcripts.

Barbara Marchegiano's death, her daughter Mary Anne's struggles, and the family's search for Rocky's money are described in William Nack's August 23, 1993, *Sports Illustrated* article, "The Rock." Peter Marciano, Robert Langway, and Vincent Pereira also talked to me about these issues. Mary Anne's criminal troubles are recounted in contemporary Florida news accounts.

Robert Langway told me about writing a letter to Frank Sinatra's mother for his grandmother Pasqualena. Her comments on how she wanted people to remember Rocky appear in Michael Varveris's book *Rocky Marciano: The 13th Candle*.

Peter Marciano's reaction to the Mayweather-McGregor fight and Mayweather's comments about Rocky were described in contemporary news accounts. He also spoke to me about it.

Bibliography

Abramson, Jesse. "Marciano Set for Savold Bout on Wednesday." *New York Herald Tribune*, February 11, 1952.

Ackerman, Meyer. "Brains Behind the Brawn." *Ring*, March 1941.

Acunto, Steve. *Boxing's Champion: The Remarkable Life Story of Steve Acunto.* New York: V&G Publishing, 2013.

Ahern, John. "Brockton Mourns Its Hero, Rocky." *Boston Globe*, September 3, 1969.

Ali, Muhammad. *The Greatest: My Own Story.* New York: Random House, 1975.

Anderson, Dave. "Ex-Champ's Bitter Ego." *New York Times*, September 23, 1985.

Associated Press. "Marciano Says He Will Beat Louis but Refuses to Predict Knockout." *New York Times*, October 25, 1951.

———. "Cockell Uses 'Nature Healing, Psychology.'" *Washington Post*, March 24, 1955.

Beck, Sam. *Manny Almeida's Ringside Lounge: The Cape Verdeans Struggle for Their Neighborhood.* Providence, R.I.: Gavea-Brown, 1992.

Benson, James E. *Brockton.* Mount Pleasant, S.C.: Arcadia Publishing, 2010.

———. *Brockton Revisited.* Mount Pleasant, S.C.: Arcadia Publishing, 2012.

Bergeron, Richard. "A Tribute to a True Hometown Hero: Allie Colombo." *Bleacher Report*, February 22, 2010.

Berkow, Ira. *Beyond the Dream.* New York: Atheneum, 1975.

Bessette, Roland L. *Mario Lanza: Tenor in Exile.* Portland, Ore.: Amadeus Press, 1999.

Bingham, Kenneth E. *History of Brockton, 1645–1911.* Brockton, Mass.: Independent Press, 2014.

Bloom, Alex. "Larry Holmes on Rocky: 'The Man Was Tough.'" *Brockton Enterprise*, September 20, 2012.

Blunk, Frank M. "Marciano Shows a Nose for News." *New York Times*, February 16, 1955.

Bodner, Allen. *When Boxing Was a Jewish Sport*. Albany, N.Y.: State University of New York Press, 2011.

Borden, Eddie. "From the Manager of the Year 1952 . . . to the Forgotten Man of Boxing—Al Weill." *Boxing & Wrestling Annual*, 1953.

Bostic, Joe. "Hot Feud with Al Weill Spurs Louis vs. the Rock." *New York Amsterdam News*, October 27, 1951.

———. "Louis Center of Multiple Manipulations at IBC as Biggies Seek Marciano Bout for Sept. 26 Gala." *New York Amsterdam News*, August 11, 1951.

Bowen, Ezra, and Martin Kane. "How's Marciano Gonna Hit Me?" *Sports Illustrated*, September 19, 1955.

Bradley, John Ed. "A Champion and His Home." *Washington Post*, September 15, 1985.

———. "For Moore, Close Didn't Count." *Washington Post*, September 19, 1985.

Brady, Dave. "Ike Feels Marciano's Fist and Sees Stars." *Washington Post*, June 6, 1953.

———. "Joe Walcott's Life Story, 'A Punch and a Prayer.'" *Washington Post*, July 29–August 3, 1951.

Brean, Herbert. "A Fighting Man Who Is a Writing Man Too." *Life*, July 18, 1955.

Breit, Harvey. "A Lamb in Lion's Clothing." *New York Times Magazine*, September 20, 1953.

———. "The Rival Fight Camps Speak, One of Failure, One of Success." *New York Times*, September 14, 1954.

Breslin, Jimmy. *Damon Runyon: A Life*. New York: Dell, 1991.

Bromberg, Lester. "Archie Moore—Boxing's Black Dynamite." *National Police Gazette*, March 1953.

———. "From a Car to 4-Pound Steak Brockton's All Goes to Rocky." *New York World-Telegram & Sun*, November 21, 1951.

———. "Marciano KO's Charges He's Dirty Fighter." *New York World-Telegram & Sun*, May 18, 1955.

———. "Marciano Ward Two Idol Way Back When." *New York World-Telegram & Sun*, November 20, 1951.

———. "Rocky Can't Wait to Return to Baby Girl in Brockton." *New York World-Telegram & Sun*, May 13, 1953.

———. "Rocky Marciano: A New 'Manassa Mauler'?" *National Police Gazette*, February 1952.

———. "There's Danger Ahead for Rocky Marciano." *National Police Gazette*, December 1954.

Bryan, Keith. *Pack Up and Move: A Pictorial History of the 348th Engineer Combat Battalion*. Columbus, Neb.: The Art Printery, 1946.

Buck, Al. "Why Ezz Can Beat the Rock." *National Police Gazette*, April 1954.

Burgess, Charles. "Harry 'Kid' Matthews: A Sports Celebrity with Substance." *Columbia: The Magazine of Northwest History* 27, no. 2 (Summer 2013): 17–21.

Burick, Si. "Al Weill, Manager of Champs, Made Them Retire Gracefully." *Dayton Daily News*, October 22, 1969.

Burton, Lewis. "Marciano Lacks Plenty, but Packs the Punch." *New York Journal-American*, October 21, 1951.

Cahn, William. *Good Night, Mr. Calabash: The Secret Life of Jimmy Durante.* New York: Duell, Sloan and Pearce, 1963.

Callinicos, Constantine, and Ray Robinson. *The Mario Lanza Story.* New York: Coward-McCann, 1960.

Cannon, Jimmy. Column of the Week. *Sports Illustrated*, September 6, 1954.

———. Jimmy Cannon Says. *New York Post*, January 13, 1950.

———. Jimmy Cannon Says. *New York Post*, July 8, 1951.

———. "Lou Stillman." In *Writing New York: A Literary Anthology*, edited by Philip Lopate, 913–15. New York: Library of America, 1998.

———. "No Kind of Money." *New York Post*, April 29, 1958.

———. "Weill's Sure-Thing Craftiness Harms Rocky's Popularity." *New York Post*, February 20, 1955.

Casey, Mike. "Charley and the Talent Factory." Boxing.com, November 7, 2012.

Cataldi, Angelo. "The Night Tiger Ted Beat Rocky, the Night Rocky Beat Tiger Ted." *Providence Journal*, October 24, 1982.

Cesari, Armando. *Mario Lanza: An American Tragedy.* Fort Worth, Tex.: Baskerville Publishers, 2004.

Christenberry, Robert K. "My Rugged Education in Boxing." *Life*, May 26, 1952.

Cohane, Tim. *Bypaths of Glory.* New York: Harper & Row, 1963.

Collins, Bud. "Rocky Impressed Even Clay." *Boston Globe*, September 2, 1969.

Condon, David. "In the Wake of the News." *Chicago Tribune*, September 2, 1969.

———. "In the Wake of the News." *Chicago Tribune*, September 4, 1969.

Conklin, William. "Marciano Retires from Boxing; Heavyweight Ruler Undefeated." *New York Times*, April 28, 1956.

Considine, Bob. *Toots.* New York: Meredith Press, 1969.

Cope, Myron. "Rocky Calls It Skulduggery." *Sports Illustrated*, January 25, 1965.

Corum, Bill. "Al Gets More Rent Money." *New York Journal-American*, December 28, 1956.

———. "Kings Seldom Walk off a Throne." *New York Journal-American*, May 22, 1955.

———. "Rocky Wins It Big and Hits Real Hard." *New York Journal-American*, July 13, 1951.

———. "Watch Out for This Marciano!" *New York Journal-American*, July 25, 1952.

Curl, James. *Jersey Joe Walcott: A Boxing Biography.* Jefferson, N.C.: McFarland, 2012.

Daley, Arthur. "Abdicating as Prince of Caution, Jersey Joe Misses Early Chance." *New York Times*, September 24, 1952.

———. "Everyone Was Short-Changed." *New York Times*, May 17, 1953.

———. "Jack Hurley and His Tiger." *New York Times*, July 14, 1952.

———. "Mitt Machiavelli." *New York Times*, October 21, 1969.

———. "No More Dreaming." *New York Times*, June 7, 1954.

———. "The Old and the New." *New York Times*, February 13, 1968.

———. "A Soft-Hearted Guy." *New York Times*, September 13, 1953.

———. "Splitting the Atom." *New York Times*, February 15, 1952.

———. "The Supreme Test." *New York Times*, February 13, 1952.

———. "Visit with the Champion." *New York Times*, June 6, 1954.

———. "Wrong Education." *New York Times*, September 27, 1953.

Daniels, Daniel M. "Al Weill Sees Nine Major Attractions." *Ring*, August 1949.

———. "Marciano Has Problems." *Ring*, January 1953.

Davis, Miller. "Rocky Marciano in Retirement." *Boston Globe*, May 18, 1969.

Dawson, James P. "Bronx Boxer Placed on Critical List in Hospital After Knock-out at Garden." *New York Times*, December 31, 1949.

———. "Marciano Knocks Out Layne for His 36th Victory in Row." *New York Times*, July 13, 1951.

Demaris, Ovid. *Captive City: Chicago in Chains*. New York: Lyle Stuart, 1969.

Diamond, Wilfrid. *This Guy Marciano*. London: Sidney Press, 1955.

Dodson, James. "After the Brockton Blockbuster." *Yankee*, October 1987.

Doherty, A. Raymond. "All Brockton Hails Rocky as Next World Champion." *Boston Globe*, July 17, 1951.

Dreyspool, Joan Flynn. "Subject: Rocky Marciano." *Sports Illustrated*, January 23, 1956.

———. "Subject: Rocky Marciano." *Sports Illustrated*, May 7, 1956.

———. "Victorious Mama." *Sports Illustrated*, May 14, 1956.

Duckworth, Ed. "Man in Middle Enjoys Heavyweight Memories." *Providence Journal*, May 6, 1966.

Dunphy, Don. *Don Dunphy at Ringside*. New York: Henry Holt, 1988.

Durante, Francesco, ed. *Italoamericana: The Literature of the Great Migration, 1880–1943*. New York: Fordham University Press, 2014.

Eskenazi, David, and Steve Rudman. "Wayback Machine: Jack Hurley and Kid Matthews." *Sportspress Northwest*, August 2, 2011.

Evans, Gavin. *Kings of the Ring: The History of Heavyweight Boxing*. London: Weidenfeld & Nicolson, 2005.

Falls, Joe. "Of Rocky and a Father-in-Law." *Sporting News*, September 13, 1969.

Farley, Glen. "He Was Brockton." *Brockton Enterprise*, May 7, 1999.

———. "In the 13th Round, Brockton Became City of a Champion." *Brockton Enterprise*, August 29, 1993.

"Fight Trainer." *Life*, February 12, 1951.

Fitzgerald, Ed. "The Blockbuster from Brockton." *Sport*, January 1953.

Fitzgerald, Mike. *The Ageless Warrior: The Life of Boxing Legend Archie Moore*. Champaign, Ill.: Sports Publishing, 2004.

Fitzgerald, Ray. *Champions Remembered*. Brattleboro, Vt.: Stephen Greene Press, 1982.

Florio, Clem. "Death in the Ring: Think Fast, Here He Comes Again." *Washington Post*, December 9, 1979.

Florio, John, and Ouisie Shapiro. *One Punch from the Promised Land*. Guilford, Ct.: Lyons Press, 2013.

Fried, Ronald K. *Corner Men: Great Boxing Trainers*. New York: Four Walls Eight Windows, 1991.

Frongillo, Carmine. "In This Corner." *Lowell Sun*, January 16, 2006.

Gems, Gerald. "Sport and the Italian American Quest for Whiteness." *Sport in History* 32, no. 4 (2012): 479–503.

George, Clarence. "The Haunting of Ezzard Charles." Boxing.com, February 20, 2013.

Gibson, Truman K., Jr. *Knocking Down Barriers*. Evanston, Ill.: Northwestern University Press, 2005.

Goldman, Charley. "Everything Was Against Marciano at Start." *New York World-Telegram & Sun*, September 9, 1953.

———. "How Marciano Can Be Beaten." *Collier's*, January 17, 1953.

———. "Rocky Learned a Lot—and He'll Be Greater." *New York World-Telegram & Sun*, September 14, 1953.

———. "Rocky's Road to Title Mapped by Al Weill." *New York World-Telegram & Sun*, September 12, 1953.

———. "Weill 'Managed' Rocky to World's Title." *New York World-Telegram & Sun*, October 28, 1953.

Graham, Frank. "Close-Up of a Champion." *New York Journal-American*, September 13, 1954.

———. "The Man Behind the Champ." *Sport*, February 1953.

———. "Man Who Knows Marciano." *New York Journal-American*, July 19, 1952.

———. "Visit with Marciano." *New York Journal-American*, March 5, 1957.

Graham, Sheilah. "A Bit Part for Rocky?" *Boston Globe*, June 8, 1955.

Granger, Betty. "The Night of Tears." *New York Amsterdam News*, November 3, 1951.

Greenberg, Martin H., ed. *In the Ring: A Treasury of Boxing Stories*. New York: Bonanza Books, 1986.

Gross, Milton. "The Last Time for Rocky." *New York Post*, September 3, 1969.

———. "Speaking Out." *New York Post*, September 12, 1952.

———. "Speaking Out." *New York Post*, April 16, 1954.

———. "Speaking Out." *New York Post*, June 15, 1954.

———. "Speaking Out." *New York Post*, September 9, 1954.

Grossinger, Tania. "Growing Up at Grossinger's; or, Raised Without Reservation." *New York Times*, January 13, 1974.

Hackett, Desmond. "British Writer Discusses Rocky; Picks Him to Win; Hopes He Won't." *Boston Globe*, May 16, 1955.

Haft, Alan Scott. *Harry Haft: Survivor of Auschwitz, Challenger of Rocky Marciano*. Syracuse, N.Y.: Syracuse University Press, 2006.

Halberstam, David. *The Fifties*. New York: Villard Books, 1993.

Hanlon, John. "Marciano Crumples Haft." *Providence Journal*, July 19, 1949.

Hauser, Thomas. *The Black Lights: Inside the World of Professional Boxing*. New York: Simon & Schuster, 1991.

———. *Muhammad Ali: His Life and Times*. New York: Simon & Schuster, 1991.

Haygood, Wil. *Sweet Thunder: The Life and Times of Sugar Ray Robinson*. New York: Alfred A. Knopf, 2009.

Heinz, W. C. "He's Mad at the Champ." *Saturday Evening Post*, September 19, 1953.

———. "The Mystery of Archie Moore." *Saturday Evening Post*, September 17, 1955.

———. "The Strange Case of Ezzard Charles." *Saturday Evening Post*, June 7, 1952.

———. *The Top of His Game*. Edited by Bill Littlefield. New York: Library of America, 2015.

Heinz, W. C., and Nathan Ward, eds. *The Book of Boxing*. Kingston, N.Y.: Total/Sports Illustrated, 1999.

Heller, Peter. *In This Corner*. New York: Simon & Schuster, 1973.

Henahan, Donal. "Hope Tops Card at Garden No. 4." *New York Times*, February 12, 1968.

Hirshberg, Al. "Can Any Man Living Beat Him?" *Saturday Evening Post*, September 20, 1952.

"How Great Was Marciano?" *Look*, October 16, 1956.

Hurwitz, Hy. "Is Marciano New Dempsey? Or Will Louis Murder Him?" *Boston Globe*, October 23, 1951.

Iannuccilli, Ed. *Growing Up Italian*. Woonsocket, R.I.: Barking Cat Books, 2008.

Isenberg, Michael T. *John L. Sullivan and His America*. Urbana: University of Illinois Press, 1988.

Jacobson, Kristi. *Toots* (documentary). 2006.

Jones, Jersey. "Big Little Guy." *Ring*, January 1953.

Kaese, Harold. "Goldman Took Rocky to Title." *Boston Globe*, November 13, 1968.

———. "Rocky-Colombo Great Pairing." *Boston Globe*, January 10, 1969.

Kahn, Roger. *A Flame of Pure Fire: Jack Dempsey and the Roaring '20s*. New York: Harcourt Brace, 1999.

Kalinsky, George. *Garden of Dreams: Madison Square Garden 125 Years*. New York: Stewart, Tabori & Chang, 2004.

Kane, Martin. "The Case Against the IBC." *Sports Illustrated*, April 23, 1956.

Keaney, Bob. "He Beat Marciano." *Lynn Item*, November 18, 1986.

Keller, Larry. "Judge Defers Sentencing of Famed Boxer's Daughter." *Fort Lauderdale Sun-Sentinel*, March 26, 1992.

———. "Marciano's Daughter Hit in Losing Fights Drug Conviction." *Fort Lauderdale Sun-Sentinel*, February 15, 1992.

Kimball, George, and John Schulian, eds. *At the Fights: American Writers on Boxing*. New York: Library of America, 2011.

Klein, Frederick. "How Arthur M. Wirtz, Unrenowned Chicagoan, Has Built Sport Empire." *Wall Street Journal*, November 30, 1972.

Lee, Bill. "Rocky Marciano Puts Rex Layne to Sleep in Sixth at Garden." *Hartford Courant*, July 13, 1951.

Leonard, Pat. "Who's the Only Man Who Ever Beat Rocky Marciano . . . This Kid from Charlestown, Mass., Joe DeAngelis." *Yankee*, September 1984.

Liebling, A. J. *Just Enough Liebling*. New York: North Point Press, 2004.

———. *A Neutral Corner*. New York: North Point Press, 1990.

———. *The Sweet Science*. New York: North Point Press, 2004.

Lowry, Ted. *God's in My Corner: A Portrait of an American Boxer*. Baltimore: Publish America, 2006.

Mangione, Jerre, and Ben Morreale. *La Storia: Five Centuries of the Italian American Experience*. New York: HarperCollins, 1992.

Marciano, Barbara. "After Meeting the Future Champ, There Was Never Anyone Else," Part 4 of five-part series, "Why I Made Rocky Quit!" *New York Daily Mirror*, June 20, 1956.

———. "Champ, Who'll Never Fight Again, Must Now Decide on Future," Part 5 of five-part series, "Why I Made Rocky Quit!" *New York Daily Mirror*, June 21, 1956.

———. "Every Time the Bell Rings . . . I Pray!" *Washington Post*, June 13, 1954.

———. "First Walcott Bout the Worst Fight of All—and Torture for Barb," Part 2 of five-part series, "Why I Made Rocky Quit!" *New York Daily Mirror*, June 18, 1956.

———. "His Little Girl the Big Reason Champ Put Away His Gloves," Part 1 of five-part series, "Why I Made Rocky Quit!" *New York Daily Mirror*, June 17, 1956.

———. "No Truth to the Rumors of Barb's 'Feud' with Manager Al Weill," Part 3 of five-part series, "Why I Made Rocky Quit!" *New York Daily Mirror*, June 19, 1956.

Marciano, Rocky. "Marciano Eager to Fight Johansson." *Boston Globe*, November 15, 1959.

Marciano, Rocky, as told to Milton Gross and Al Hirshberg. "Dirty Work at Ringside," Part 4 of "I Fought All the Way." *Saturday Evening Post*, October 6, 1956.

———. "He Ran My Life," Part 5 of "I Fought All the Way." *Saturday Evening Post*, October 13, 1956.

———. "It Was Worth It," Part 6 of "I Fought All the Way." *Saturday Evening Post*, October 20, 1956.

———. "They Said I'd Get Murdered," Part 2 of "I Fought All the Way." *Saturday Evening Post*, September 22, 1956.

———. "Why I Retired," Part 1 of "I Fought All the Way." *Saturday Evening Post*, September 15, 1956.

———. "The Worst Experience of My Life," Part 3 of "I Fought All the Way." *Saturday Evening Post*, September 29, 1956.

———. "Unbelievable!—Rocky." *Brockton Enterprise*, February 26, 1964.

Marciano, Rocky, and W. C. Heinz. "How It Feels to Be Champion of the World." *Collier's*, May 13, 1955.

Margolick, David. *Beyond Glory: Joe Louis vs. Max Schmeling and a World on the Brink*. New York: Knopf, 2005.

Markus, Robert. "Life for Marciano Anything but Rocky." *Chicago Tribune*, July 22, 1968.

Martin, Whitney. "Bill Little's Bigness Delayed His Eclipse." *Washington Post*, February 9, 1953.

Mauriello, Christopher E., and Roland J. Regan Jr. *From Boston to Berlin*. West Lafayette, Ind.: Purdue University Press, 2001.

McCallum, John D. *The World Heavyweight Boxing Championship: A History*. Radnor, Pa.: Chilton, 1974.

McDonough, Will. "Marciano Bares Aborted '59 Comeback." *Boston Globe*, June 30, 1966.

———. "Marciano Learned How to Live, Fight with Pain." *Boston Globe*, November 24, 1965.

Milbert, Neil. "Rocky's Last Hurrah Almost Went Unnoticed." *Chicago Tribune*, September 6, 1969.

Millstein, Gilbert. "In This Corner, at Long Last, Archie Moore!" *New York Times Magazine*, September 11, 1955.

Mitchell, Kevin. *Jacobs Beach: The Mob, the Fights, the Fifties*. New York: Pegasus Books, 2010.

Montville, Leigh. "Holmes: Rocky Couldn't Have Carried My Jock." *Boston Globe*, September 23, 1985.

———. *Sting Like a Bee: Muhammad Ali vs. the United States of America*. New York: Doubleday, 2017.

Moore, Archie. *Any Boy Can*. Upper Saddle River, N.J.: Prentice Hall, 1961.

Moynihan, P. J. *Fight Town* (documentary). Holyoke, Mass.: Digital Eyes Film, 2011.

Murray, Jim. "Life Finally Caught Marciano with a Sucker Punch." *Los Angeles Times*, September 2, 1969.

———. "The Real Rocky." *Los Angeles Times*, July 12, 1977.

Musmanno, Michael. *The Story of the Italians in America*. New York: Doubleday, 1965.

Nack, William. "The Rock." *Sports Illustrated*, August 23, 1993.

Nagler, Barney. *James Norris and the Decline of Boxing*. Indianapolis: Bobbs-Merrill, 1964.

Neff, James. *Mobbed Up: Jackie Presser's High-Wire Life in the Teamsters, the Mafia, and the F.B.I.* New York: Atlantic Monthly Press, 1989.

New Yorker. The 40s: The Story of a Decade. New York: Random House, 2014.

New Yorker. The 50s: The Story of a Decade. New York: Random House, 2015.

New York Times. "Marciano Must Pay $5,000 For Assault." April 24, 1963.

Nichols, Joseph C. "Brockton Fighter Wins 27th in Row: Ends LaStarza's Streak." *New York Times*, March 25, 1950.

———. "Challenger Ready for Walcott, Boasting 'I Can Lick Anyone.'" *New York Times*, July 29, 1952.

———. "Marciano Enjoys Day of Rest: Yankees' Players Perform at Camp." *New York Times*, September 17, 1955.

———. "Marciano Wants 50th Victory Before He Retires from Boxing." *New York Times*, September 23, 1955.

———. "Marciano Knocks Out LaStarza in 11th Round and Retains Heavyweight Title." *New York Times*, September 25, 1953.

Oates, Joyce Carol, and Daniel Halpern, eds. *Reading the Fights*. New York: Henry Holt, 1988.

O'Brien, Andy. "Marciano's Fists Hit Harder Than Bullet from a .45." *Week-End Magazine*, February 19, 1955.

O'Brien, Tom. "Controversy After Title Bout Leaves Marciano Untouched." *Brockton Enterprise*, May 16, 1953.

Olderman, Murray. *The Draw of Sport*. Seattle: Fantagraphic Books, 2017.

Olsen, Jack. "Don't Call Me Honest." *Sports Illustrated*, May 15, 1961.

———. "Fifty Percent of Harry." *Sports Illustrated*, May 22, 1961.

Papadopoulos, Maria. "Always by the Champ's Side." *Brockton Enterprise*, December 26, 2013.

———. "Daughter of Brockton Boxer Marciano Dies at 58." *Brockton Enterprise*, June 11, 2011.

Parker, Dan. "Rover Boy in the Jungles of Boxing." *Sports Illustrated*, November 15, 1954.

———. "Weill Recovering from Jolt." *New York Daily Mirror*, October 21, 1956.

———. "The Weskit King, Al Weill." *Boxing Illustrated*, 1940.

Pincetich, John. "Nine 'Simons' Register KOs in AAU Fights." *Portland Oregonian*, August 22, 1946.

———. "PAL, Ft. Lewis Battlers Leading in AAU Tourney." *Portland Oregonian*, August 23, 1946.

Plimpton, George. *Shadow Box*. New York: G. P. Putnam's Sons, 1977.

Povich, Shirley. "Marciano Rallies to Decision Charles." *Washington Post*, June 18, 1954.

———. "This Morning . . ." *Washington Post*, September 14, 1954.

———. "This Morning . . ." *Washington Post*, May 6, 1956.

——— "To Whom It May Concern." *Washington Post*, September 7, 1969.

Reemes, Jackie. "A Setback in Boxing." *New York Amsterdam News*, April 8, 1950.

Rein, Joe. "Stillman's Gym: The Center of the Boxing Universe." *Mr. Beller's Neighborhood: New York City Stories*, June 1, 2003. https://mrbellersneighbor hood.com/2003/06/stillmans-gym-the-center-of-the-boxing-universe.

Relihan, Tom. "Brockton's Marciano Family: Mayweather Win Shouldn't Count Toward Rocky's Record." *Brockton Enterprise*, August 23, 2017.

———. "A Rocky and a Hard Place—Mayweather Record Bitter for Brockton." *Brockton Enterprise*, August 27, 2017.

Remnick, David. *King of the World*. New York: Random House, 1998.

Rice, Grantland. "Marciano Finally Brings Punch Back into Boxing." *Boston Globe*, October 31, 1951.

Riess, Steven. "In the Ring and Out: Professional Boxing in New York, 1896–1920." In *Sport in America: New Historical Perspectives*, edited by Donald Spivey, pp. 95–128. Santa Barbara, Calif.: Praeger, 1985.

Robbins, Jhan. *Inka Dinka Doo: The Life of Jimmy Durante*. New York: Paragon House, 1991.

Roberts, James B., and Alexander G. Skutt. *The Boxing Register*. 5th ed. Ithaca, N.Y.: McBooks Press, 2011.

Roberts, Randy. *Joe Louis*. New Haven, Conn.: Yale University Press, 2010.

Roberts, Randy, and Johnny Smith. *Blood Brothers: The Fatal Friendship Between Muhammad Ali and Malcolm X*. New York: Basic Books, 2016.

Rose, Murray. "Ezz Says, 'I'll Get Rocky Next Time.'" *National Police Gazette*, September 1954.

———. "Rocky Marciano's Secret Plans." *National Police Gazette*, January 1956.

Rutter, Jon David. "White Hopes: Heavyweight Boxing and the Repercussions of Race." PhD diss., University of Texas, August 2001.

Sammons, Jeffrey T. *Beyond the Ring: The Role of Boxing in American Society*. Urbana: University of Illinois Press, 1988.

Schulberg, Budd. "After Disposing of Most of the Heavyweight Contenders, Archie Moore Licks a Middleweight and Thus Earns a Shot at the Title." *Sports Illustrated*, July 4, 1955.

———. "A Champion Proves His Greatness." *Sports Illustrated*, October 3, 1955.

———. "Marciano's Battering of Don Cockell Was More—and Less—Than a Ring Battle." *Sports Illustrated*, May 30, 1955.

———. "Rematch Is No Match." *Sports Illustrated*, September 27, 1954.

———. *Ringside: A Treasury of Boxing Reportage*. Chicago: Ivan R. Dee, 2006.

Silverman, Stephen, and Raphael D. Silver. *The Catskills: Its History and How It Changed America*. New York: Alfred A. Knopf, 2015.

Skehan, Everett M. *Rocky Marciano: Biography of a First Son*. New York: Houghton Mifflin, 1977.

———. *Undefeated: Rocky Marciano, the Fighter Who Refused to Lose*. Cambridge, Mass.: Rounder Books, 2005.

Smith, Marshall. "And New Champion?" *Life*, September 22, 1952.

Smith, Red. "Blinky Is More Sad Than Angry." *New York Times*, March 15, 1978.

———. "Charlie's Iron Hat." In *To Absent Friends*, pp. 199–200. New York: Atheneum, 1982.

———. "Cockell Gives Fans Graphic Exhibition of British Pluck." *New York Herald Tribune*, May 17, 1955.

———. "Cockell's Training Camp Far Cry from Sussex Pub." *New York Herald Tribune*, May 13, 1955.

———. "The Day Rocky Took the Count." *New York Times*, September 2, 1969.

———. "The Fighter Was Hungry." *New York Herald Tribune*, September 23, 1952.

———. "Gentlemen, Be Seated." *New York Herald Tribune*, May 17, 1953.

———. "Night for Joe Louis." *New York Herald Tribune*, October 27, 1951.

———. *The Red Smith Reader*. New York: Skyhorse Publishing, 2014.

———. "Rocky Graceless but Great." *New York Times*, September 3, 1969.

———. "Rocky Is Guy Hurley Wants for Matthews." *New York Herald Tribune*, February 26, 1952.

———. "Rocky Would Like This." *New York Herald Tribune*, September 12, 1952.

Smith, Wilfrid. "Foe's Injury Shakes Rocky." *Chicago Tribune*, October 2, 1952.

———. "Rocky a Fighting Soldier." *Chicago Tribune*, September 30, 1952.

———. "Rocky Glover: Bored by Job, He Turns to Ring for Action." *Chicago Tribune*, October 1, 1952.

Smits, Ted. "Moore Lauds Rocky's Great Fight, Concedes Mistake After Knockdown." *Los Angeles Times*, September 2, 1955.

Sneddon, Rob. *The Phantom Punch*. Camden, Me.: Down East Books, 2016.

Strait, Raymond, and Terry Robinson. *Lanza: His Tragic Life*. Englewood Cliffs, N.J.: Prentice Hall, 1980.

Stratton, W. K. *Floyd Patterson*. New York: Houghton Mifflin Harcourt, 2012.

Streshinsky, Shirley. "Up Against the Ghetto and the Freeway: Keep Fighting the Good Fight, Archie Moore." *Los Angeles Times*, February 20, 1972.

Sugar, Bert. *100 Years of Boxing*. New York: Galley Press, 1982.

Sullivan, Jerome. "Rocky Returns, 100,000 Cheers Rock Brockton." *Boston Globe*, October 3, 1952.

Sullivan, Russell. *Rocky Marciano: The Rock of His Times*. Urbana: University of Illinois Press, 2002.

Summers, John. "Gentle as a Rock." *London Sunday Telegraph*, November 7, 1965.

Talese, Gay. "Fight Trainer Pines for Cauliflower Days of Old." *New York Times*, January 14, 1958.

———. "Marciano Seeks Career as Actor." *New York Times*, January 12, 1957.

Tejada, Susan. *In Search of Sacco and Vanzetti*. Boston: Northeastern University Press, 2012.

Thamel, Peter. "The Valley Arena." *Springfield Union-News*, July 11, 1996.

Thomas, Bob. "Hollywood Scene." *Associated Press*, October 28, 1954.

Thomas, Michael J. "Marchegiano Steals Show at Auditorium Blasting Weeks Down in Opening Round." *Providence Journal*, August 31, 1948.

———. "Marciano Flattens Connolly with One Punch in the First." *Providence Journal*, November 30, 1948.

———. "Marciano Gets Decision over Ted Lowry." *Providence Journal*, October 11, 1949.

———. "Marciano Wins but Knockout Streak Ends." *Providence Journal*, May 24, 1949.

Torres, Jose. *Sting Like a Bee: The Muhammad Ali Story*. New York: Abelard-Schuman, 1971.

Tosches, Nick. *The Devil and Sonny Liston*. New York: Little, Brown, 2000.

Trigoboff, Dan. "Rocky Marciano's Fayetteville Ties." *CityView*, October 7, 2015.

United Press. "Press Agent: Copperhead 'Just Misses' Marciano." *New York Times*, October 16, 1951.

United Press International. "Man Who Beat Rocky Recalls Amateur Bout." *Boston Globe*, September 2, 1969.

Varveris, Michael N. *Rocky Marciano: The 13th Candle*. Youngstown, Ohio: Ariana Publishing, 2000.

Vingo, Carmine. "I Was Slaughtered to Please a Crowd." *Saturday Evening Post*, January 12, 1952.

Walker, Mickey. "The Rocky Marciano I Know." *National Police Gazette*, July 1955.

Wall Street Journal. "Insurance Official Indicted for Fraud Refuses to Resign." November 1, 1965.

Ward, Arch. "In the Wake of the News." *Chicago Tribune*, September 26, 1953.

Ward, Gene. "Jersey Joe Walcott Tells Truth About That Louis Knockdown in Sparring Bout." *Chicago Tribune*, July 20, 1951.

———. "Inside Sports." *New York Daily News*, August 3, 1955.

———. "So Long, Rocky Marciano." *New York Daily News*, September 2, 1969.

Weill, Marty. "Al Weill, My Father." *Ring*, March 1970.

Weissman, Harold. "Rock, Weill Near Saturation Point." *New York Daily Mirror*, March 25, 1957.

Williams, Joe. "Weill Says He Wanted to Save Rocky's Dignity." *New York World-Telegram & Sun*, March 16, 1957.

———. "Weill Set for a Ring Comeback." *New York World-Telegram & Sun*, March 3, 1962.

Wilson, Earl. "An Actor with Punch." *New York Post*, March 3, 1960.

———. "The Champ's Wife Took the 6th Av. Subway Home." *New York Post*, September 22, 1955.

———. "Mrs. Heavyweight Champion." *New York Post*, September 26, 1954.

Wilson, Harvey. "Marciano—Fair or Foul?" *National Police Gazette*, September 1955.

Yassen, Ron. *Rocky Marciano* (ESPN SportsCentury documentary). 2000.

Acknowledgments

I would first like to thank Rocky's family for sharing their stories. His brothers Sonny and Peter Marciano, sister Betty Colombo, brother-in-law Armond Colombo, and nephew Vincent Pereira were generous with their time and memories. Robert Langway, Rocky's nephew, was a gracious host on my visits to Brockton, sharing stories from his mother, Concetta; wartime letters that Rocky wrote home illuminating his role as the caring big brother; and memories that helped bring to life Rocky's remarkable parents, Pasqualena and Pierino Marchegiano. Concetta's daughter Donna Thoreson and her husband, Mike, were generous with their memories. I'd also like to thank Rocky's son, Rocky Marciano Jr., who was only one year old when his father died but has been a keeper of the flame. Their love and admiration of him shines through, even as they acknowledge his flaws. It hasn't always been easy to have a loved one in the public eye and have his imperfections held up to public scrutiny. In rendering Rocky's complicated personality, I was guided by his brother Peter's words that if Rocky had been the Boy Scout everyone made him out to be, he never would have hit anyone or become heavyweight champion of the world.

Charlie Ball was a warm, thoughtful, and engaging tour guide of Brockton and helped bring to life Ward Two, where Rocky grew up. An ex-newspaperman with the *Brockton Enterprise*, *Boston Herald*, and *Boston Globe*, Charlie grew up in one of the neighborhood's only Jewish families and helped me understand the city's ethnic diversity and immigrant roots.

I'd also like to thank my old friend Jonathan Saltzman of the *Boston Globe* for introducing us.

George's Café, in business since 1937, is a Brockton institution. To step inside is to be transported back to Rocky's time as a young fighter, when he would sit in a corner booth late at night chewing over his latest victory in Providence with Allie Colombo and co-owner Snap Tartaglia, who was also his sparring partner. The walls are lined with dozens of old photographs of Rocky and celebrities who have visited, everyone from Frank Stallone, Sylvester's brother, to five former heavyweight champions: John Ruiz, Riddick Bowe, Leon Spinks, Larry Holmes, and Muhammad Ali. I was honored to join their ranks, listen to the stories of the proprietor, Charlie Tartaglia, who grew up with the Marchegianos, and replenish myself after a day of research with the stuffed shells with sausage and peppers. The enormous meatballs gave me a new appreciation for Rocky's prodigious appetite.

I am grateful to my old *Providence Journal* colleague Mary Beth Meehan, who grew up in Brockton, for introducing me to people there, including her lovely parents, Nancy and Edward Meehan. Thanks also to Mike "Duna" Cappiello, Rocky's cousin, and his sons Mike and Rich Cappiello, Allie Colombo's daughter Cindy Colombo, Eugene Sylvester's brother John Sylvester, Ralph Galante, Larry Sisskind, David Gemelli, and Stephen Damish of the *Brockton Enterprise*. Carl Landerholm, president of the Brockton Historical Society, not only shared his memories but opened his treasure trove of scrapbooks and memorabilia. Lucia Shannon and the staff of the Brockton Public Library were extremely helpful in sharing their files on Rocky and Brockton's history and assisting my review of old issues of the *Brockton Enterprise* on microfilm. And thanks to Jonathan Green, assistant director of archives at the Stonehill College Archives & Historical Collections, for his help in accessing the remarkable Stanley Bauman photo collection.

Jeff Brophy, the executive director of the Boxing Hall of Fame, provided valuable archival material on Charley Goldman, Al Weill, and the early history of boxing.

I'd like to thank Theresa Fitzgerald, supervisory archivist at the National Archives in Saint Louis, where military records are kept, and archivist Cara Moore Lebonick for helping me dig out Rocky's army record, including the voluminous file on his court-martial. Thanks also to

Tom Bryan, whose father served in the 348th Army Combat Engineers and who publishes a newsletter for surviving members and their families. And a special thank-you to Basil Reed, who served with Rocky and spoke to me. I'd also like to thank Roland Regan Jr. for sharing his father's stories of serving in the army with Rocky (including sparring with him) and his coauthor, Christopher E. Mauriello, for their memoir of their fathers' military service, *From Boston to Berlin*. Thanks also to Francois Lienher, webmaster for a website about the 348th, and Tim Gray, chairman of the World War II Foundation, whose award-winning documentaries preserve the history of the Greatest Generation. The British boxing historian Miles Templeton helped me reconstruct Rocky's amateur fights while serving in the army in England and Wales. And a special thanks to Washington State librarian Mary Shaff, who arranged for me to review microfilm of 1946 issues of the *Fort Lewis Flame* military newspaper, containing stories about base life and Rocky's army boxing career; she also provided me copies of the *Portland Oregonian*'s coverage of Rocky competing in the national junior AAU championships there.

Thanks to Michael Van Leesten for telling me about his father, Hendrick Van Leesten, who fought as Ted Lester and beat Rocky in an amateur fight in Brockton in 1946.

In Holyoke, where I went to reconstruct Rocky's first professional fight on St. Patrick's Day as "Rocky Mack," thanks to my old comrade Tommy Shea, the talented documentary filmmaker P. J. Moynihan, and the retired *Springfield Republican* sportswriter Michael Burke for sharing their memories and rounding up the old Valley Arena gang for a memorable sit-down at Pic's Pub, including Charles Della Penna and George Desgres. Thanks also to the incredibly helpful staff of the Holyoke Public Library.

Thanks to Elizabeth Bouvier, head of archives at the Massachusetts Supreme Judicial Court in Boston, for helping me locate the voluminous trial transcript in Gene Caggiano's 1948 lawsuit against Rocky.

Providence is a theme park for journalists, and I had a great ride there in my three decades at the *Providence Journal*. I am grateful to my former colleagues Tom Mooney and Michael Delaney for helping me round up old clips and photos. Thank you, M. Charles Bakst, for putting me onto the story of Rocky's barroom fight with Bill Wirtz and for sharing photos and boyhood memories of meeting Rocky at Grossinger's. (Of course, Charlie met Rocky; he's met *everyone*!) Thanks also to my former *Journal* editor and mentor Thomas Heslin, for keeping his eyes open and connecting me to some helpful Brockton sources. And thanks to the *Journal*'s human resources director Tom McDonough for introducing me to his father, Tom McDonough, who worked as a stick boy for the Providence Reds and got to sit close enough to the ring when Rocky fought to have an opponent's mouthpiece fly into his lap. Tom was a wealth of knowledge about the Rhode Island Auditorium, Rocky's time in Providence, and the mobsters, bookies, and gamblers who frequented the Auditorium. So were the dearly departed George Patrick Duffy, Sharkey Buonanno, the brothers Bernie and Vincent Buonanno (no relation to Sharkey), Clark Sammartino, Ed Iannuccilli, Louis Marciano (no relation), Richard Acetta, Lorraine Luzier, and the brothers Tony, Gerald, and Gino Simone. Thanks also to Jimmy Burchfield, president of Classic Entertainment & Sports, Rhode Island's leading boxing promoter, and his associate Michael Parente. And thanks to Providence Police Department deputy chief Thomas A. Verdi, retired Rhode Island State Police detective commander Brian Andrews, and former Rhode Island State Police superintendents Brendan Doherty and Steve O'Donnell. Thanks also to retired FBI special agent W. Dennis Aiken and to Patrick Conley. I owe a debt of gratitude to the staffs of the Rhode Island Historical Society and the Providence Public Library.

Thank you, Smokey Cerrone, who told me about his friendship with Rocky that began when he fought in Providence and continued after both had retired to Florida. And thanks to the late Bernie Sullivan, who befriended Rocky during his time as a priest and went on to a successful career as a journalist at the *Providence Journal* and the *Fall River Herald News*.

Thanks to Angelo Cataldi, former *Providence Journal* sportswriter and current host of *Angelo Cataldi & the Morning Team* on Sportsradio 94WIP in Philadelphia, for writing a courageous story about the controversial Tiger Ted Lowry fight and sharing further details with me. I also appreciate former Rhode Island state prosecutor and current state legislator Robert Craven telling me about his father's conversation with Lowry in his dressing room after the fight.

A special thanks to Rocky Wirtz, the owner of the Chicago Blackhawks, who shared his father Bill Wirtz's memories of getting into a barroom scrape with Rocky Marciano in Providence when Bill was a football player and student at Brown University. Their fight resulted in a friendly relationship that helped inspire Rocky Wirtz's first name.

I'd also like to thank New York congressman Gregory Meeks, son of the fighter Jimmy Meeks, who shared his father's memories of being knocked out by Rocky. Thanks also to Alan Scott Haft for talking to me and writing a moving memoir of his father Harry Haft's incredible journey from the Nazi concentration camps to a fight with Rocky in Providence.

In New York and New Jersey, I appreciate the time that Jimmy Breslin and Lou Duva spent with me before their deaths. Thanks also to Murray Olderman, Ira Berkow, Nicholas Pileggi, Al Certo, and Kristi Jacobson, granddaughter of Toots Shor and the filmmaker who made the documentary *Toots*. A special thanks to old ProJo colleague Dan Barry of the *New York Times* for connecting me with people who helped me re-create that golden age of New York sports. Thanks also to Kevin McCabe, Dan Klores, Ron Yassen, and Larry Schwartz. I'd also like to thank the helpful reference staff at the New York Public Library. Thanks to James P. Quigel Jr., the head of Historical Collections and Labor Archives at Penn State University, for his help in accessing the Harry J. Anslinger papers, and to Grace Schultz of the National Archives at Philadelphia. The author and investigative reporter James Neff offered helpful advice about searching FBI files and about the Cleveland loan shark Peter DiGravio. And thanks to George Anastasia for helping with background on the Philadelphia mob.

Thanks also to Rick Green, assistant managing editor of the *Hartford Courant*, for opening his newspaper files on Rocky, and to *Yankee* magazine editor Mel Allen, who shared stories from his archives. And thanks to retired British newspaper photographer Arthur Steel for sharing his remarkable photographs and memories of Rocky in London, and to his son Patrick Steel.

I am deeply indebted to two great institutions in sports journalism, *Sports Illustrated* and ESPN.

Former *SI* writer William Nack shared his experiences writing his explosive story "The Rock." Senior editor Richard Demak opened *SI*'s actual vault to share priceless files about Rocky dating back to the early 1950s, including memos from reporters and detailed interview notes. Thanks also to former *SI* writer Alexander Wolff for introducing me, and for his encouragement and support. And a special thank-you to Susan Szeliga for saving the files from deep storage during *SI*'s move to its new headquarters and for her gracious hospitality.

John Dahl, vice president and executive producer of ESPN Films & Original Content, generously shared the unedited transcripts of interviews conducted for the 2000 ESPN SportsCentury documentary *Rocky Marciano*. Thanks also to Steve Buckheit, feature producer at ESPN and a teaching colleague at the University of Connecticut, for his help and encouragement.

My second family at the University of Connecticut provided me with a supportive and invigorating environment. Thanks to Maureen Croteau, journalism department chair, for her strong support and enthusiasm for this project. And thanks to colleagues Marcel Dufresne, Kate Farrish, Steve Kalb, Michael Lemanski, Paul Lyzun, Gail MacDonald, Julie Serkosky, Marie Shanahan, Steve Smith, Scott Wallace, Wayne Worcester, and Robert Wyss. Thanks also to Becky Ortinez and Lisa Caruso. A special thanks to UConn librarian Steve Batt for helping me find old newspaper and magazine databases and other valuable material. Finally, I'd like to thank my terrific journalism students at UConn for providing me with inspiration and hope for the future.

Sadly, as this book was going to press, another valued UConn colleague, Terese Karmel, died, on December 26, 2017, after a battle with cancer. T.C., a graceful sports writer and beloved teacher, offered valuable feedback and support throughout my research and writing. She will be missed by everyone in Storrs and the many beyond whose lives she touched.

Thanks to the staff at Henry Holt, including Stephen Rubin, Maggie Richards, Patricia Eisemann, Gillian Blake, Fiona Lowenstein, Danique Robinson, and Caroline Wray.

An author needs great corner men, and I am blessed to have had Andrew Blauner and Paul Golob in mine. Andrew has been a trustworthy agent and reliable sounding board since we first worked together on *The Prince of Providence*. Thank you, Andrew, for your enthusiasm and counsel. Paul, executive editor at Henry Holt, has been my Charley Goldman, a sage tactician and judicious cut man whose encyclopedic knowledge encompasses everything from heavyweight title fights in Shelby, Montana, to the boundaries of Red Hook. Thank you, Paul, for your faith and guidance.

I am sorry that my good friend and investigative reporting partner Bill Malinowski from the *Providence Journal* could not be here to see this book. Bill helped put me in touch with sources in law enforcement familiar with organized crime during Rocky's time and with people who knew Rocky, and he also provided valuable feedback during my research. Bill, who died in August 2016 from Lou Gehrig's disease, would have loved this. I would also like to thank Bill's wife and another former ProJo colleague, photographer Mary Murphy, for her support and my book jacket photo.

I am grateful to my sister Ann Hughes and brother-in-law Kevin Hughes for their support, and to my wife's cousin Sarah Showfety for connecting me to Kristi Jacobson. Thanks also to Aura and Larry Showfety for their warm hospitality on my research trips to New Jersey, and to Richard Showfety for his constant questions about how the Rocky book was coming.

My sincerest love and appreciation go out to my mother- and father-in-law, Sue and Hugo Hodgin, the best mother- and father-in-law a guy could ever have. Sue passed away as this book was going to press and is deeply missed and warmly remembered.

I wrote this book in memory of my father, Earl T. Stanton, who grew up in Massachusetts and attended Bryant College in Providence when Rocky fought there. Dad was a fan of Rocky's, and when I was going through his things after he died, I found an autographed poster of Rocky. This one's for you, Dad. And thanks, also, to my late mother, Mary Stanton, who always encouraged my writing.

Finally, I would like to thank my wonderful family for having my back and putting up with the long days and nights and research trips away from home—my daughter, Emma, who asks perceptive questions; my son, Henry, who could one day be general manager of the Boston Red Sox or Boston Celtics; and, most of all, my loving wife and partner, Susan Hodgin. She is *my* rock.

Illustration Credits

Index